JOHN KNOX

JANE DAWSON is John Laing Professor of Reformation History, School of Divinity, University of Edinburgh. An expert on sixteenth-century Scotland and Calvinist politics and religion, she is the author of *The Politics of Religion in the Age of Mary, Queen of Scots* (2000) and *Scotland Re-formed, 1488–1587* (2007), and the editor of a number of collections of primary sources.

Further praise for *John Knox*:

'Superb ... The Knox that emerges from these pages is pleasingly multi-faceted ... Until now, we have usually had to make do with caricatures. Dawson has brought nuance and peerless scholarly rigour to a cautionary but also rather inspiring tale.' Jonathan Wright, *Glasgow Sunday Herald*

'The very model of what academic biography can achieve. It displays all the virtues of the academy in that it is judicious and even-handed without being hobbled by caution. It brings to bear new source and archive material on its subject and is suffused with deep reading on the period.' Stuart Kelly, *Scotsman*

'Knox emerges as a much more complicated and laudable person: a loving husband, a steadfast friend, a fervent believer who was still frequently troubled by doubts, a brave fighter in the service of his faith.' Lucy Wooding, *Times Higher Education*

'This is a biography of the entire man, not a facet of his life or thought ... Rather like the portrait on the cover of the book, gentle cleaning and restorative work has led us to look at the man afresh ... This biography will undoubtedly be the standard work on Knox for many years to come.' Calum S. Wright, *Reviews in History*

'A work of meticulous scholarship. In the tightly-packed but never heavy pages we have a minutely detailed biography.' Revd Dr John Harrod, *Methodist Recorder*

'A lively and popular account of the life of arguably the most influential churchman in the history of Presbyterianism in Scotland.' *Life and Work*

'This is an excellent biography ... highly recommended for both its scholarship and lively prose.' R. Ward Holder, *Expository Times*

'This is the best biography of Knox to have been written ... Dawson's work deserves a wide readership not only in Scotland but in England and beyond.' Paul Richardson, *Church of England Newspaper*

John Knox

JANE DAWSON

YALE UNIVERSITY PRESS
NEW HAVEN AND LONDON

Cover image: John Knox, sixteenth century. Edinburgh University Library, Scotland. With kind permission of the University of Edinburgh / Bridgeman Images.

Published with assistance from the foundation established in memory of Oliver Baty Cunningham of the Class of 1917, Yale College.

For information about this and other Yale University Press publications, please contact:
U.S. Office: sales.press@yale.edu   www.yalebooks.com
Europe Office: sales@yaleup.co.uk   www.yalebooks.co.uk

Typeset in Adobe Caslon Pro by IDSUK (DataConnection) Ltd

Library of Congress Cataloging-in-Publication Data

Dawson, Jane E. A.
    John Knox / Jane Dawson.
        pages cm
    Includes bibliographical references and index.
    ISBN 978-0-300-11473-7 (cl : alk. paper)
1. Knox, John, approximately 1514-1572. 2. Presbyterians—Scotland—Biography.
3. Theologians—Scotland—Biography. 4. Reformation—Scotland. 5. Scotland—Church history—16th century. I. Title.
    BX9223.D39 2015
    285'.2092—dc23
    [B]
                                                                            2014047022

A catalogue record for this book is available from the British Library.

ISBN 978-0-300-21970-8 (pbk)
Printed and bound by CPI Group (UK) Ltd, Croydon, CR0 4YY
10 9 8 7 6 5 4 3 2 1

Contents

Illustrations and maps

Maps   *pages*

Preface and acknowledgements

John Knox has been a brooding presence throughout my academic life, with his writings featuring in my PhD thesis and a number of early publications. When I moved into other areas of Scottish and British history, he remained lurking in the background. Since his statue dominates the courtyard at New College in the University of Edinburgh where I work, I frequently walk past 'the wee man in the quad'. Assuming that I possessed more than a nodding acquaintance with him, I finally decided to attempt a biography of Knox. He proved to have plenty of surprises up his sleeve, and I discovered that writing in this genre posed a greater challenge than I had anticipated. As well as sharing her deep knowledge of the period, Jenny Wormald has given great encouragement as I wrestled with that challenge. Not least by listening to frequent moans and groans, Linda Frost has kept me going to the end of this book.

Throughout its very long gestation I have benefited immensely from the generosity of a wide range of other people in different contexts. Fellow scholars at all levels have given their time, knowledge and expertise to discuss historical points and answer my questions. I have equally been sustained by the humour, companionship and neighbourliness of many people who probably did not realize how much help they gave. To all I extend my great thanks and, as the list is extremely long, I apologize for not being able to name each individual.

I have accumulated many scholarly debts over the years. Since much of the new material for this biography rests upon the papers of Christopher Goodman, particularly his Letter-book, I am very grateful to Jane Brunning and her colleagues at the Denbighshire Record Office for their help and especially to Dr Lionel Glassey, with whom I published an edition of most of the newly discovered Knox letters. Two friends came to my aid with excellent translations of the letters Knox wrote in Latin. Dr Jamie Reid-Baxter generously offered me his translation of the Tinoterius letter to Calvin. To Dr Paul Parvis I owe all the

Latin translations from the Goodman Letter-book and many interesting details and points he identified along the way. I have been ably assisted by the staff at the Chester Record Office, the Inner Temple Library, the Bodleian Library, University of Oxford, the British Library, the National Archives and the National Archives of Scotland, as well as by my Edinburgh friends and colleagues in New College Library, the University Library's Special Collections and the National Library of Scotland. I am grateful to a number of owners for permission to use illustrations, and full acknowledgements can be found in the List of Illustrations. In 2013 the Leverhulme Trust's generous funding extended my university research leave, enabling me to write this book, and earlier grants from the Arts and Humanities Research Council and the British Academy helped work on the Goodman Letters. From the biography's inception Heather McCallum at Yale University Press has been an exemplary editor and the inestimable Nancy Bailey readied the manuscript for submission with her accustomed cheerful efficiency. The suggestions made by the two readers for the Press were particularly helpful and I thank them warmly for having improved the book; all the errors and deficiencies that remain are my own.

For many years I have been privileged to be a member of the History of Christianity Subject Area and to enjoy a remarkable level of friendship and support from my colleagues. This book is dedicated to them, especially the late Professor David Wright and his wife Anne-Marie. Alongside his expertise in Patristics and on John Calvin, David was deeply knowledgeable about Knox and the Church of Scotland and willingly shared his insights. After his death Anne-Marie kindly gave me David's notes on his exciting discoveries about John Knox's Bible and they have enriched this biography. This book conveys my thanks and celebrates the survival, amid the current pressures upon academic life, of collegiality in the old-fashioned and best sense that his life exemplified. Knox and his fellow Scots also prized what they called 'kindness', and that quality is worth rediscovering from the past.

Jane E. A. Dawson,
New College, Edinburgh

1 Knox and the three kingdoms of Scotland, England and Ireland.

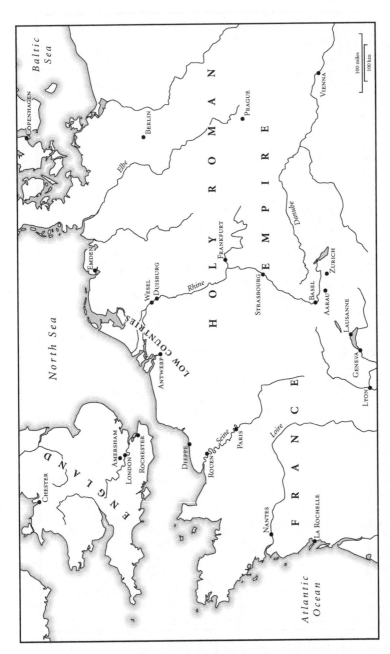

2 Knox's Europe.

CHAPTER ONE

Rare and wonderful gifts

23 MAY 1557, GENEVA

It was a Sunday, not like any other Sunday in John Knox's life. As the afternoon sermon came to an end, Knox was standing beneath the pulpit proudly cradling his newborn son in his arms.[1] Being a man to whom tears came easily, he was probably weeping with happiness. At his shoulder was his close friend William Whittingham, who had supported him through thick and thin in the recent troubles at Frankfurt, and was standing godfather, or gossip, to him and his son. The minister, Christopher Goodman, Whittingham's friend since childhood, came down from the pulpit after preaching the sermon. These three men of such different temperaments had forged a deep friendship at Frankfurt, and now in Geneva Knox and Goodman served as co-ministers to this church for English-speaking exiles, while Whittingham organized the congregation's great biblical translation project. They had all been involved in writing the service of baptism that was about to begin.

Before turning to the assembled congregation, Goodman addressed the ritual question to his two friends, 'Do you present this childe to be baptised, earnestly desiring that he may be ingrafted in the mysticall bodye of Jesus Christ?'[2] Knox had himself frequently spoken the Exhortation that followed, which explained to the congregation the purpose of the sacrament of baptism. As a father, the words became charged with new meaning because it was his son who was joining the Church. Knox heard for himself the reassurance, 'our infantes apperteyne to hym [God] by covenant . . . they be conteyned under the name of God's people'. On behalf of the baby boy, Whittingham and Knox repeated together the familiar words of the Apostles' Creed and the entire congregation joined in the Lord's Prayer. The communal repetition of the prayer Jesus taught his disciples expressed most deeply the experience Knox treasured of being part of one flock, following one Shepherd. Through obedience to the Shepherd's voice, Christians became members of the people of God united across all ages. From the basin, Goodman took the water and laid it on the boy's forehead, and baptized Nathaniel in the name of the Father, of the Son and of the Holy Ghost. Knox experienced a profound satisfaction from the stark simplicity of combining the Trinitarian formula with the simple application of water. In this congregation's worship the 'superstitious ceremonies' he believed had defaced the sacrament had been banished. Man-made inventions, even signing with the cross, transgressed the maxim for the worship of God that every part must rest upon the words of Scripture alone. Though it might appear spare and unadorned, Knox believed this new *Forme of Prayers* was the first liturgy in English to follow the Old Testament maxim of neither adding to nor subtracting from the Scriptural injunctions.

Knox had chosen his son's name with great care. In Hebrew Nathaniel meant 'gift of God' and enabled him to express his sense of gratitude and thanksgiving at the birth of his first child. That name fitted perfectly with the thanksgiving in the post-baptismal prayer for the 'rare and wonderfull gyftes' God had given those who had been marked 'wyth thys Sacrament as a singuler token and badge of thy love' and would be numbered among the saints.[3] Knox hoped his son would always wear and acknowledge the badge of his Christian faith, and he probably cherished the thought that his son might follow his father and become a preacher.

The final request was that God 'take this infant into thy tuition and defence'. For a Scot like Knox this phrase was full of strength, with tuition meaning far more than scholarly instruction and extending to guardianship and complete protection. Gone was the custom of naming children after saints and expecting that saint to act as their protector. Similarly, the exorcism of the Devil at the start of the baptism had been removed. Instead, Christ was to be the child's defender in the battle against sin and the Devil that, aided by divine power, 'he maye so prevayle against Satan, that in the end, obteyning the victorie, he may be exalted into the libertie of thy kingdome'. Knox was convinced that a triumphant gazing upon the kingdom of God was the right note to end the baptismal service celebrating a new addition to the congregation and reminding every existing member of their participation in God's covenant.

With the baptism complete, the familiar faces of friends and supporters would have crowded around Knox and his son in the intimate space of the Auditoire church in Geneva. Like most mothers of the time, Knox's wife Marjorie would have remained at home recovering from the birth and would hear all the details later from her friends. This particular congregation was a self-selected group of exiles from religious persecution, many of whom had settled in the city specifically to follow Knox and his views on Reformed worship. When they came together to form the English-speaking congregation they created a powerhouse of Protestant commitment. It generated an intense spiritual solidarity that Knox found exhilarating, and the Genevan congregation provided him with a close religious family bound together by the profound spiritual kinship of the 'mystical body of Jesus Christ'. He never forgot the security and religious strength this congregation had brought him and for the remainder of his life it was the model of what an ideal Reformed community should be.

Acutely conscious that he had received many rare and wonderful gifts, Knox might have chosen Sunday, 23 May 1557 as one of the happiest days of his life. He had a dear wife and son, and his family and household were safe in Geneva and far away from the heresy trials and executions in England. He enjoyed the best of working relationships with his fellow minister Goodman and with the other officials and members of the congregation, and they had created a model of a Reformed kirk. In addition, he lived in the most perfectly Reformed city in Europe, where he was able to learn from the great Master Calvin and from the other theologians and scholars who were resident there.

This particular day in his life has been reconstructed to challenge many of the traditional assumptions made about John Knox. He has been regarded, especially within Scotland, as the personification of the puritanical kill-joy who championed the strictest Presbyterian tenets on all issues and delighted in haranguing Mary, Queen of Scots. Having been claimed as the country's Protestant Reformer, Knox's activities in Scotland have taken centre stage, downgrading or even excluding other periods of his life. The concentration upon his famous tract with its eye-catching title, *The First Blast of the Trumpet against the Monstrous Regiment of Women*, has given rise to the view that Knox was a misogynist or a woman-hater and has distorted understandings of Knox's political thought and his other writings. The reconstruction of the happy day in 1557 when Nathaniel Knox was baptized in the English-speaking exile church in Geneva offers a sharp contrast to that conventional image. The relaxed and happy John Knox was not preaching or prophesying doom, but behaving as an ordinary father and family man. He was not expounding misogynist ideas but was surrounded by female friends and about to return to his dear wife. He was not in Scotland bringing in the Protestant Reformation, but was part of an English congregation located in a Swiss city. He was not behaving as a puritanical Calvinist, but was laughing, joking and looking forward to a celebration. This biography also acknowledges, and even emphasizes, the darker side to Knox with his 'holy hatred', increasing intransigence, bouts of depression and gloomy predictions about the future of Protestantism. By challenging the monochrome portrait of the dour Scottish Reformer that has dominated popular perceptions, it shows the many different shades within Knox's character that make this complex man such a fascinating subject. This fresh and more nuanced account of Knox's life reveals new aspects of the interconnected and many-layered story of Protestantism in the sixteenth century. The biography also provides a re-assessment of the worlds through which Knox moved as he lived during the age of Reformations in Scotland, Britain and Europe.

SOURCES

A recent 'rare and wonderful gift' has made this biography possible: the discovery of new evidence from the pen of Knox himself and about his life revealed aspects of his personality only glimpsed before. The first new Knox material unearthed since 1875 has been discovered in the manuscript papers of his best friend, Christopher Goodman.[4] They contain six previously unknown letters written by Knox – one holograph letter in Chester and five others in fine eighteenth-century transcripts in the surviving copy of Christopher Goodman's Letter-book at Ruthin in north Wales. One of the new Knox letters dates from 1555 and the others fall in the period 1566 to 1572. Equally significant, Goodman's papers contain many additional documents that have a direct bearing upon Knox's life or illumine the events in which he played a part. Of greatest value for the breadth of the new material are thirty-five new documents from the Marian exile that alter the interpretation of the time Knox spent within Germany, Switzerland and France and enrich the narration in Chapters 6–11. In particular, Goodman's Letter-book transforms the chronology and understanding of the Troubles at Frankfurt of 1554–5, and an entirely new account of that period in Knox's life can be found in Chapter 7. This new chronology of the Frankfurt Troubles has allowed the letter of 4 January 1555 Knox wrote and signed as 'Tinoterius' to be conclusively identified as from his pen. It has also redated to December 1554 a fascinating letter and memo written by John Bale and has proved that they were directly attacking Knox.[5]

A further forty documents in Goodman's Letter-book relate to the first two decades of Queen Elizabeth's reign and give additional context for the new letters from Knox discussed in Chapters 11–19. They chart Knox's growing pessimism because he was prepared to reveal to his close friend his inner thoughts about the situation in Scotland. The letters reveal for the first time that in 1566 Knox was contemplating accompanying Goodman on an evangelical preaching mission within Ireland that would have had the full backing of the Lord Deputy of Ireland, Sir Henry Sidney. They also demonstrate in detail how much interest Knox continued to show in the disputes within the Elizabethan Church of England and especially in the Vestments Controversy of the 1560s. In addition to providing many new insights and details about Knox's life, the Goodman papers have driven a major re-evaluation of the existing and well-known Knox material that has been in circulation since the nineteenth century.

Several other finds have added fresh insights. A new source has been recognized for the final years of Knox's life. Much of Knox's 'table-talk' during those years can be reconstructed because it was embedded within the *Memorials* written by his secretary, Richard Bannatyne. He recorded snippets of Knox's conversations, though he rarely attributed them directly. Those sayings have been identified and collected and they have added to this biography substantial additional details concerning Knox's views from 1567 to 1572. They include pithy remarks, so characteristic of Knox's descriptions of his contemporaries, and a range of short prayers or statements revealing his state of mind and his views on contemporary events. This has provided for the biography a rich vein of new sayings, many in the memorable and direct format Knox had perfected and often containing a sharp, or even vindictive, edge.

The confirmation that 'John Knox's Bible' has survived adds an interesting new facet to our knowledge of his life and of his extensive network of friends in different countries. The late Professor David Wright, my colleague at New College in Edinburgh, investigated and verified the copy of 'John Knox's Bible' currently housed in the University of Melbourne. Although it is not annotated through the text, it does have the name of those who associated with the volume. From there and with further information found in the Goodman papers, it has been possible to piece together a great deal more information about the Bible's context and the individuals involved. It was a special presentation volume Knox was given by some of his English friends around 1567, long after he had returned to Scotland. It had been printed in 1566 at Rouen, a French city Knox knew well, and was part of a bespoke folio edition. Its production is itself an indication of the complex patterns of contacts between the Reformed Protestants in France, Geneva, England and Scotland during the 1560s. The idea of a presentation and the trouble and expense of organizing a special printing demonstrated the long-lasting esteem in which Knox was held by those he had known in the London Protestant community during the reign of King Edward VI and those who had been part of his exile congregation in Geneva during the reign of Queen Mary Tudor. This provides additional evidence supporting the new insights from the Goodman papers to show how Knox remained closely involved with the 'godly' community who were pressing for further reform to the Church of England.[6]

The choice of biblical version was significant because Knox was presented with a copy of the Great Bible first produced in King Henry VIII's reign that would have been the Bible he used when he had been a minister in England from 1549. A number of those connected to the presentation, such as John Bodley, the father of the founder of the Bodleian Library in Oxford, had also been involved in the production of the Geneva Bible in 1560. That version was adopted by Knox and the Scottish Reformed Kirk, was beloved by the English 'godly', was used by Shakespeare and became by far the most popular edition in Elizabethan England. When choosing their elaborate gift, the presenters must have known that Knox had a special affection for the earlier Great or Matthews Bible, possibly because it was the English translation he had first encountered when he had been converted to Protestantism. The chance survival in Australia of this special presentation copy is a reminder that Knox's personal library has been largely lost to view, though a copy of a German chronicle that his nephew, Paul Knox, read to his uncle in 1568 now resides in Edinburgh University Library. It is possible that other volumes once owned by Knox also found their way into the library of Clement Litill, who was Knox's friend and an elder of St Giles' Kirk, Edinburgh. In 1580 part of Litill's library became the foundation for Edinburgh University Library.

No contemporary portrait of Knox, if any were made, has survived, and exactly what he looked like has been a perennial puzzle. From the nineteenth century onwards, different images of him have been suggested and have generated considerable debate. The general consensus had fixed upon the portrait in Theodore Beza's *Icones* as the best likeness. However, the recent cleaning and conservation of a painting owned by the University of Edinburgh have suggested a much earlier date of composition than had previously been thought. This portrait in oils, probably painted at the end of the sixteenth century, can now be placed among the earliest surviving images of Knox and possibly supersedes the black and white woodcut in Beza's *Icones*.[7] It depicts a man with a thinner face and longer beard than usual who appears less relaxed and certain than we find in the traditional representations of Knox. This new portrait seems to reflect some of the characteristics revealed in the newly discovered written evidence in which Knox can be seen as tired, ill and depressed.

Such significant discoveries have given a fresh perspective to Knox's life and shine extra light upon episodes, such as his visit to England in 1567, when previously his movements had been shrouded in mystery. They have brought some surprises that run counter to the popular understanding of Knox. Nothing had previously been known of the trip to Ireland he almost made at the start of 1567 to join Goodman in an evangelical mission. Similarly, the special printing of a Great Bible for Knox by his English friends had not been widely known. It had also not been recognized that his Edinburgh ministry comprised three discrete periods and that he answered three separate calls to become the preacher at St Giles', Edinburgh's burgh church.

The new material and interpretations have proved especially helpful in rounding out Knox's character. The common assumption of permanent antagonism between Knox and Mary, Queen of Scots, is challenged by evidence of their harmonious working together to prevent the breakdown of the marriage of the Earl and Countess of Argyll. In the final years of his life the extent of Knox's weariness and his thoughts about a form of retirement can be charted. On the positive side, it has become possible to determine when and where he was happiest, as in Geneva or in Ayrshire, and in the company of his spiritual 'sisters' or of Goodman. One of the most vivid new snapshots is of Knox walking and talking animatedly to Goodman as they marched round the walls of Chester or paced up and down the manse garden in Aldford.

Knox was irresistibly drawn to the Old Testament prophet Ezekiel's portrayal of God's watchman alerting the nation by sounding his trumpet, and his notorious book *The First Blast of the Trumpet* carried that sound in its title. A satirical woodcut showing him blowing a trumpet (see Plate 5) furnished the only portrait certain to have been created during Knox's lifetime. By turning up the volume metaphorically as well as literally, Knox ensured that his written and spoken words were heard. He felt diminished when his voice became weak following his stroke, but the fiery content remained. This great love of the spoken word and his understanding that in the pulpit the words flowed through him from the Holy Spirit meant that Knox did not produce a written text for his sermons. Though plenty of fragments and other evidence have survived about his preaching, in a surprising statistic only one complete text of a sermon preached by him has come down to the present. However, his intense biblicism offers a way of tracing some of the ideas that would have been incorporated into his sermons. Fascinating insights into his patterns of thought emerge from his choice of characters, incidents and verses found in the Geneva Bible, the translation with which he was most closely associated.

By comparison with other sixteenth-century commoners, a considerable quantity of Knox's writings has been preserved. The six volumes of his *Works* edited by David Laing and published between 1846 and 1864 contain nearly all of the surviving writings of Knox, and in the following decade Peter Lorimer published some extra manuscripts relating to Knox in England. The Goodman material can now be added to this corpus. Many of Knox's writings were intended for public consumption and were prepared for publication and printed during his lifetime. He regarded writing these tracts as 'preaching by pen', and his productivity was highest during the exile periods spent in Europe when he had fewer sermons to deliver. Though he preferred to preach in person, his writings enabled him to reach wider or otherwise inaccessible audiences. He was a fine writer, possessing a love of words and a great sensitivity to language and rhetoric. In all his works the subject, style and content were carefully chosen and presented. He deliberately masked this crafting of the text by telling his audience he was a plain-speaking man who addressed queen and commoner alike in simple language.[8] This was one of the many skilful strategies he employed to persuade the reader and listener to agree or to act in accordance with his message.

One of Knox's most significant works, where his literary skills are especially clear, is his *History of the Reformation in Scotland*, sometimes regarded as a form of autobiography. It was written in stages over a number of years, and in the published version Book V was the work of a continuator, probably his secretary, Richard Bannatyne. Though it most likely circulated in manuscript and an unfinished edition was printed in London in 1587, the full *History* was not published until 1644. This complex work changed its purpose and its audience while it was being written, revised and expanded. Though it revealed much about Knox, large areas of his life, such as his early years or the time spent in England, received the briefest of mentions or were not covered. Having been a notary, Knox was aware of the power and significance of formal records and assiduously collected many key documents for insertion into his *History*. A master of using documentation as proof of his interpretation of events, he did not regard a document as an end in itself; it was a tool in the great cause of persuasion and propaganda. Details about his final years not reached by the *History* were recorded in Richard Bannatyne's *Memorials*, which consciously followed Knox's lead. These chronicles were designed to present Knox's understanding of God's calling to the people of Scotland to embrace his covenant.

While providential designs on a national stage and Knox's public face can be found in his *History* and published works, his letters provide the best entry point into his personality and the more private aspects of his life. Parts of his correspondence have survived, comprising a substantial number of letters compared to other Scots of his generation, though a paltry collection when put alongside the massive correspondence of the Swiss Reformers Henry Bullinger or John Calvin. Knox had an extensive range of correspondents, though the vast majority of their incoming letters have been lost. His intelligence network was renowned in Scotland and he was generally better informed than those running the country. The surviving letters were mostly outgoing, and reveal what Knox himself was thinking. However, without the incoming letters, the reader can listen to only one half of the dialogue. If correspondence formed part of the papers Bannatyne sorted after Knox's death, that cache of material did not survive. Some of those who received Knox's letters did keep them and these letters have been preserved. The collections of three close friends provide a run of marvellous letters that forms the heart of his correspondence as we know it. Significantly, two of these three friends were women: Elizabeth Bowes, Knox's mother-in-law, and Anne Locke, his close friend, kept the pastoral letters he wrote to them.[9] Knox's best friend, Christopher Goodman, retained some of the letters he received, and their correspondence demonstrated how close the friendship was. In these letters Knox was franker and revealed to Goodman his feelings and the depression he experienced in his final years of ill health.

By drawing a wide variety of other contemporary sources into the evidential net it has been easier to examine who Knox was and what he did. A substantial quantity of contemporary comment was generated during his life: once met, he was rarely forgotten. Some material does exist within government papers, but Knox left remarkably little trace within the records of the ecclesiastical institutions in which he worked during his career. This absence of documentation serves as a reminder that he consciously maintained his distance from the administrative and institutional centres of these churches. His self-assigned role as a prophet standing apart from the 'establishment' resulted in a comparatively light administrative footprint.

While Calvin strove hard to minimize the cult of personality threatening to engulf Protestant leaders, Knox, with his showman's instincts, projected a strong personal image. He ensured that the deceptively simple role of the prophet and preacher was placed centre stage and kick-started his own legend. Within a few years of his death, and not only in Scotland, the image was already looming larger than life. When the radical Elizabethan cleric John Field was gathering all the material he could find to support the English Puritan cause, he urged Anne Locke to send anything and everything she possessed from Knox's pen. In an admiring tone Field, who had never met Knox, commented, 'What a heroical and bold spirit he was.'[10] Anne sent Field what she had, though she probably smiled to herself at the description because the man she had known had confided to her some of his doubts, fears and worries about his less than 'heroical' actions.

Knox's own words form the evidential core of this biography, and one of its main aims has been to let him speak for himself and allow the reader to listen to him. Most of his writings remain in the original sixteenth-century Scots and English and vividly convey the flavour of his thought. These words arrive in the twenty-first century full of crackles and distortions, and as listeners we filter them through our own perceptions of what is being said. Translation is required at many levels to render Knox's voice intelligible in the present. In this biography, quotations from his *History* and his 1558 tracts have been taken from the modernized, scholarly editions that render his words into a more comprehensible form.[11] The remainder are given in their original form, and Knox's sixteenth-century language can occasionally appear strange at first glance. Following normal Scots usage, he sometimes employed '-it' for the past tense, as in 'belovit' rather than 'beloved', or the letters 'quh[ilk]' where the English equivalent was written 'wh[ich]'. As with Shakespeare's English, once the text is read aloud much of its strangeness disappears and the meaning becomes plain. In this biography chapter headings have been modernized and equivalents provided for archaic or Scots words. For those anxious to track down further meanings the online Dictionary of the Scots Language is extremely useful.[12]

It is hoped the following chapters will offer the reader the opportunity to follow John Knox through his life, to see his many public and private faces and perhaps encounter a few surprises.

CHAPTER TWO

Tinoterius: The man from the banks of the Tyne

GOD WHO FROM MY YOUTH HAS PROVIDED

John Knox's own baptism in 1514 or 1515 had been a world away from that service in Geneva in 1557. The Catholic Church he entered was the great and imposing institution that bound together not only the kingdom of the Scots but the whole of medieval Christendom. In common with most Scots of this period, no record of Knox's birth or of his baptism has survived. Regarded as the essential first step on the path to salvation, baptism was never willingly omitted and Knox later acknowledged the providential hand of God from his earliest years, 'God who from my youth has provided'.[1] Baptism was the truly universal sacrament that incorporated everyone. The Church was prepared to go to considerable lengths to baptize all babies, for example each year sending a priest to the furthest point of the Scottish kingdom, the island of St Kilda. It was also willing to modify rules to guarantee that the sacrament was available whenever it was needed. Baptism was the only sacrament that anyone could perform in an emergency – lay as well as cleric, women as well as men.

Fortunately, most baptisms were non-emergency and were elaborate affairs signalling the addition of a new member within local society as well as their entry into the Catholic Church. At the start of the sixteenth century the intertwining of Church and society to form one hybrid body appeared to be the natural and permanent order of things. The Church in Scotland was by far the greatest institution in the land, whose presence was found in every corner of the kingdom and in almost all aspects of daily life. Whatever the criticisms of the running of this large, European-wide corporation, it would have been almost impossible for most Scots to conceive of life without it. To them the suggestion would have seemed laughable that in only three years' time the Church would be seriously challenged and Christendom split following one monk's protest in Germany.[2]

Knox was born in the ancient burgh of Haddington in East Lothian in 1514 or 1515.[3] He would have 'received his christendom', as it was known, when baptized in the great parish church of St Mary's, the 'Lamp of the Lothians'. This imposing building, set apart from the burgh centre and surrounded by its extensive churchyard, lay on the banks of the River Tyne looking across the water to Giffordgate, the street where the Knox family lived and where John was almost certainly born. A few days after the event the midwife would have taken this baby boy from his mother's arms and accompanied by the godparents and other friends carried him in procession to the church door. Knox's mother would have remained at home, recovering from the birth and completing her month's lying-in before she left the house. Since he had no formal role in the baptism, Knox's father might also have been absent from the ceremony. One aspect of the ritual was the creation of a symbolic separation between the realms of the sacred and profane, between the godparents and the natural parents. At the church door the priest and his acolytes would be waiting. They would receive the baby from the midwife and conduct the exorcism element of the baptism on that threshold. This involved blowing on the child, signing with the cross, putting salt in the baby's mouth and spittle on the nostrils and ears. During the baptism the godparents acted on behalf of the baby, reciting the *Pater Noster* and *Credo*, or Lord's Prayer and Creed, renouncing the Devil and affirming their faith. At the font they provided the child's name, and after anointing with holy oil the baby was immersed three times and baptized in the three names of the Trinity. A further anointing with holy chrism, the mixture of oil and balm, followed. A coarse linen cloth or *hards* was probably used to dry the baby, who would then be wrapped in a white *cuide* or chrism cloth and given a candle. At the close of the ceremony it was customary for the godparents to make their christening gift to the child they had 'raised from the font', and all would depart for a celebration.[4]

This elaborate and highly visual ceremony with its multitude of stages and symbols came to represent for the adult Knox the worst accretions that had grown over the Church's worship. Everyone in Scotland would have attended a baptism, and the higher someone's status, the more ostentatious it would have been, with a long tail of participants each carrying a particular piece of equipment or adding to the clerical presence and dignity of the ceremony with music and colour. As early as his first public debate on religious questions in 1547, Knox chose baptism as his chief example of how the Church had erroneously added ceremonies 'that God has not ordained, such as, in Baptism, are spittle, salt, candle, cuide (except it be to keep the bairn from cold), hards, oil and the rest of the Papistical inventions'.[5]

The identity of Knox's godparents is not known, though their importance is undoubted. By their participation in the sacrament they entered into a spiritual kinship with their godchild, and this relationship was taken very seriously by society.[6] It created bonds of affinity that governed social relationships, most noticeably in the choice of marriage partners and also in the field of honour. This form of indissoluble spiritual kinship was very different from the community of belief that the adult Knox wanted to foster, comprising brothers and sisters in Christ who shared a doctrinal confession. At the start of the sixteenth century the decision of who should become godfathers and godmothers, usually three to represent the Trinity, was significant for both parents and child. A great deal of thought and diplomacy were expended on this element within family strategy. Godparents, known as 'god-sibs' or gossips, would establish a long-term personal relationship that frequently made a major difference to the child's future prospects. It is possible that some of his mother's relatives through marriage were Knox's godparents, because in his first job as a notary he was employed by George Ker of Samuelston who was married to a Sinclair, his mother's family.

Knox gave very few details about his early life and in his own *History of the Reformation* introduced himself into the story only in 1545. He inadvertently revealed how much he valued his family background and place of birth by once signing himself 'Tinoterius' in a letter to the Genevan pastors.[7] In this Latin designation he demonstrated his sense of identity as 'a man from the banks of the Tyne', highly apposite since his birthplace of Giffordgate ran right alongside the river (see Plate 1). Possibly indicating its early modern pronunciation, Blaeu's map of East Lothian designated the burgh 'Hadtyntoun', further underlining how much the river was regarded as a central element within the burgh's identity.[8]

Scots were particularly conscious of their geographical roots and possessed a clear local and regional identity. In Knox's case he was proud to hail from the burgh of Haddington, centre of the shire of East Lothian. Though not in the first rank of Scottish burghs, Haddington remained of some importance in the later Middle Ages, still exporting goods from Aberlady, its port on the Firth of Forth. It lay in a fertile river valley and was within an easy ride of Edinburgh, a prime source of political news and events (see Plate 10). When Knox looked back in 1566 he remembered with some pride the Haddington he had known, seeing it as a place of beauty that produced men of 'wisdom and ability', including Walter Bower, the author of *Scotichronicon*, and John Mair, the famous professor who had taught him.[9] Knox lamented its present sorry state after the destruction caused by the English armies during the Anglo-Scottish wars of the 1540s known as the 'Rough Wooings'.

The attachment to a particular place was frequently accompanied by links of allegiance to those with power in that area. Knox's family were probably tenants of the earls of Bothwell. The Hepburn family were powerful throughout the eastern Borders and in East Lothian, and their castle at Hailes, downstream from Haddington on the south bank of the Tyne, was an important seat and the dominant power centre within the area. The Knoxes had 'looked to' the earls of Bothwell for generations and, as Knox proudly pointed out, his great-grandfather, grandfather and father had fought, and even died, under the earls' standards. In later life he retained his 'good mind' to the house of Hepburn and could never bring himself to be as bitterly critical of the earls of Bothwell as he was of other Scots nobles. His sense of 'the obligation of our Scottish kindness' persuaded him for once to leave some things unsaid.[10]

The main bulwark of any Scot's identity was their own family and kindred. In the snippets of evidence that survive, Knox took his good relationship with his elder brother William for granted.[11] Carrying their father's name and continuing in his merchant's business, William is the only sibling who can be identified for certain, though Knox probably had other brothers and sisters. Knox signed himself 'John Sinclair' when seeking to disguise his identity in the troubled times during the late 1550s, and that is the only trace of his mother that has come down the centuries. She was probably related to the Sinclairs of Northrig, and kinship might have been a factor in securing work in his first job as a notary. The value of kinship, including those ties acquired by marriage, and the loyalty or 'kindness' they should engender, were deeply ingrained within Knox. He was profoundly shocked and deeply offended by the disloyal or 'unkindly' behaviour of those he assumed were his marital kin. In 1553 as the betrothed of Marjorie Bowes he assumed he 'might have craveit kyndnes' from Sir Robert Bowes but was instead met with 'disdanfull hattred'.[12] As an adult Knox transferred this Scottish sense of 'kindness' to his close spiritual kindred. He regarded any breach of that fellowship, such as his split with later friends and fellow Protestants James Balfour or William Kirkcaldy of Grange, as a personal betrayal as well as a falling away from religious purity.

During the early years of Knox's life, Scotland was in long-term mourning for 'that unhappy field of Flodden' as he later called it.[13] Not only had King James IV died on the battlefield in the disastrous defeat in 1513, leaving a child to succeed him, but nearly every noble family in the land had lost fathers or sons, and the hundreds of ordinary soldiers who had died in the bloodbath had left countless Scottish families grieving. Later tradition has suggested that Knox's grandfather or even his father were killed in the battle, though there is no corroborative evidence for this assertion. In the immediate years after 1513, a fear of English invasion lingered and Haddington would have been a nervous place since it lay across the main invasion route from the south. The whole kingdom was afflicted by the shock of a world turned upside down, as well as by the weary and protracted process of reconstruction during the next decade as the political mess moved from crisis to crisis.

Since Knox was not the eldest son and would not be inheriting the merchant's business, he needed to find another occupation. As with many of the middling sort in Scottish society, it was probably part of Knox family strategy from an early stage in John's life that he would make his career in the Church, the best opportunity for upward social mobility. He proved an intelligent boy, and in the sixteenth century a 'lad o'pairts', as later Scots called such youngsters, could use education to climb up the rungs on the career ladder of the late medieval Church, the largest employer in Scotland. Knox probably started his formal learning at the song school attached to St Mary's, Haddington. This imposing building was the largest parish church in Scotland and provided a fitting symbol of the longevity of the burgh founded in the twelfth century. Its fine stonework and beautifully carved west door portraying the Passion were dominated by its massive ninety-foot tower. It was topped with a crown steeple similar to that above St Giles' church in Edinburgh and, to the great satisfaction of the Haddington citizens, their building was that bit longer than Edinburgh's burgh church. Although it did not formally become a collegiate church until 1540, when the young Knox was a scholar there, St Mary's would have been full of priests saying Masses for the souls of the dead at the many side altars down that very long nave.[14]

The boys of the song school were taught to read using the liturgical books on hand in the chancel and learned to sing and practise their skills as part of the choir. Knox learned and never forgot the daily round of services in the church, especially the singing of the psalms. Though he later completely rejected the liturgical round made so familiar in his childhood, all his life he retained the rhythm of moving each month through the cycle of the psalter. The Latin versions of the psalms from the Vulgate version used by the medieval Church were so deeply embedded in his consciousness that on his deathbed it was their numbering he recalled, instead of the slightly different numbers allocated to the psalms in the Protestant Bible.[15] Vivid early memories of the colourful drama and intense beauty of Catholic worship, with the singing and the incense rising into the high roof of St Mary's, probably added sharpness to his later denunciations of these liturgical practices. Precisely because it was so appealing, such 'false worship' was doubly dangerous to him. He later confessed that sometimes he could not stop the heart from making 'vane imaginationis' on the Mass even though he knew it was the 'fountane of all idolatrie'.[16]

The glory that had been St Mary's was destroyed during the Rough Wooings by the invading English army when Haddington was besieged and the church was extensively damaged and lost most of its roof, thus in Knox's

eyes fulfilling the doom-laden prophecy made in 1546 by George Wishart.[17]
Years later Knox gave the practical advice that a wall be built at the end of the
nave so that that section could be used for Protestant parish worship, with the
remainder of the building deemed surplus to the new requirements. If he felt a
certain satisfaction that his personal memories could also be walled up, he did
not reveal it nor in this instance did he take the opportunity to dance on this
particular grave of the 'idolatry' he hated so much. The burgh of Haddington
did not recover its entire parish church until 1973 when the re-roofing was
finally finished.

Once he had mastered the basics of singing and reading at the song school,
Knox progressed to the burgh grammar school, where he followed an arts
curriculum. As a young scholar he benefited from the paper revolution of the
previous century that had produced cheaper writing materials. At this early
stage of his life he seems to have acquired a sense of the importance of documents and records even though he was instinctively a man of the spoken, rather
than written, word. At school he was drilled in reading, writing and speaking
Latin and became conversant with the Vulgate Bible. The Latin text remained
permanently lodged in his memory, and as an adult when he thought of a
biblical passage he instinctively recalled that version. He would then translate
portions in his head, only sometimes checking with English translations. He
also had the habit of adding a 'double translation' incorporating alternative
meanings for some of the single Latin words to convey the complexity or
nuances within the original text.[18]

AN ORACLE IN MATTERS OF RELIGION

His studies were sufficiently successful to propel Knox to university, probably
when he was in his mid- to late teens. As would have been natural for someone
living within the archdiocese, he attended the University of St Andrews. There
he was fortunate to be able to study with one of the foremost scholastic teachers
of his day, John Mair, or Major, who had returned to Scotland after a long and
distinguished career at the University of Paris (see Plate 2). Knox was doubly
proud to be taught by a fellow 'countryman', since this distinguished scholar
was also a native of East Lothian. Though appearing stiff and formal in the
woodcut image, Mair added humour to his logic lectures and would pun upon
his own name by using the examples of horses and mares named A and B to
explain his point.[19] Knox might have learned from his master that a joke makes
a lesson easier to remember. Retaining the awe of a student for a respected
teacher, Knox in his *History* recalled Mair's theological reputation, 'whose word
then was held as an oracle in matters of religion'.[20]

At this stage in his life, Knox might not have fully understood Mair's theories, especially those advocating conciliarism. Mair's defence of the authority of the General Councils of the Church and their power over popes probably encouraged Knox to think less well of the papacy. Like many university professors, Mair might have cringed to see snippets of his lectures reappear in mangled form in Knox's subsequent writings. The highly critical attitude to papal claims found among conciliarists later served as extra grist for Knox's anti-papal mill which he ground relentlessly from 1547 until his death and which provided him with a range of examples wrenched out of context to serve his Protestant polemic. Knox probably knew Mair's major historical work, the Latin *History of Greater Britain* published in 1521. It would be linked in his mind with Hector Boece's *Scotorum Historia* first published in 1527. When John Bellenden's Scots translation of Boece came hot off the press in 1536, Knox and his contemporaries would have been fascinated by the first major work in Scots prose and would have understood how the history of the Scots could be presented in the vernacular. These histories helped shape Knox's thinking and give him the idea in 1559 of writing his own *History of the Reformation in Scotland* and turning the story of the struggle for Protestant reformation into a dramatic narrative and helping to justify the revolt against the Queen Regent, Mary of Guise.

In the debates about teaching methods and curricula that were raging across Europe's universities, Mair and Scottish teaching of this period remained within the traditional scholastic camp. Unlike other Protestant Reformers such as Martin Bucer or John Calvin, Knox did not develop into a humanist scholar and linguist.[21] But he did share the humanist celebration of the central importance of rhetoric. He loved words and language as a delicate and complex tool of communication and used them to paint pictures and convey the colours of emotions. At university he learned how to study texts carefully, and that skill served him well throughout his life. However, he probably most enjoyed the examinations held as debates between undergraduates. He grasped the use of syllogisms, the building blocks of the scholastic method, and in his later writings employed these major and minor propositions with their tidy logical proof. He relished argument and debate, especially when it was a contest. Like a boxer with his fists, he used words and phrases to score points and try to flatten his opponent. He would dance about the verbal ring, jabbing with humour or irony and throwing his opponent off balance by rapid counterpunching. In common with many lively debaters and sometimes at the expense of his own argument's consistency and coherence, he concentrated on landing blows that would damage his opponent, and he was always looking for a resounding knockout punch.

If Knox was a bruiser in debate, he was also a wordsmith in his writing and his speaking. He suffered from the orator's failing that he found it difficult to stop speaking because he relished the sound of words in his ears and a word's taste on his tongue. In his writings he frequently talked about the actual mouth and tongue, especially when describing preaching. He also thought about hearing and the ears and possessed the actor's awareness of an audience, how they were placed, whether they could hear and how they might react.[22] Knox inhabited an oral and aural world where most Scots were non-literate and nearly all daily business was conducted through spoken and heard words, normally accompanied by ritual or gestures. It remained true that it was that combination of words with actions which had the force of law and not merely the document that recorded them. A Scot did not become an outlaw until he had been literally 'put to the horn', when the royal messenger blew his horn at the market cross and proclaimed the sentence for all to hear. Knox's contemporaries expected to hear and understand and to be persuaded by words. They conveyed news by word of mouth or turned it into song. Knox thrived in such a world because of his ability to move people by his words. He became an important historical figure because he could arouse great emotion in his hearers and, of even larger significance, his words could stir people into action. Though the vast majority of his public utterances and private conversations were not recorded, his writings offer a flavour of this oratory and show why he was able to carry people with him.

In his personal correspondence and particularly in his *History*, Knox carefully constructed verbal images and dramatic scenes and filled them with vibrant colours and intense emotions. He had a scriptwriter's instinct for recognizing the dramatic in everyday life and encapsulating it in his writings. He allied this eye for a scene to the chronicler's sense of development over time. Knox's constant desire to tell a story became linked to the grand narrative of how the reformation process unfolded in Scotland. His eye and his ear were working from the beginning, seeing and hearing the details that would later be incorporated into that text. Like a modern journalist, he deliberately sought out eyewitnesses. He had probably been present at some of the incidents that took place in St Andrews during the 1530s related in his *History* and he also gathered material from those who had been there. The story of a local fisherman's dispute with the Church over paying dues on his catch sounded like a tale Knox had heard in St Andrews' harbour or in the alehouse.[23]

The oratorical skill Knox demonstrated when he was preaching had been honed at a much earlier age. The first sermon he preached, in 1547, was a highly polished performance, revealing that this was a medium in which he already excelled. Similarly, the first of his tracts penned the following year had the hallmarks of his mature style and showed a mastery of many of the rhetorical devices current in the sixteenth century.[24] Another area of study at St Andrews, canon law, contributed to Knox's later anti-papal stance. Mastering ecclesiastical law was the smart choice of subject for students intent on progressing up the ranks of the Church, whereas studying theology, the queen of the sciences, took extra years and was not a good preparation for advancement in the Scottish Church. A grounding in canon law was treated as a useful skill in both Church and royal government administration. At St Andrews Knox probably heard the lectures of the canonist John Weddell and gained enough of a legal education to allow him to become a notary.

MINISTER OF THE ALTAR IN THE ARCHDIOCESE OF ST ANDREWS

In 1536 Knox took the next step in his ecclesiastical career when he was ordained in Edinburgh by William Chisholm, Bishop of Dunblane, first as a deacon and then as a priest on Easter Eve. Chisholm, in the capital because King James V was holding a Parliament, would have been substituting for James Beaton, Archbishop of St Andrews. Ironically, several decades later the Chisholm clerical dynasty provided some of Knox's staunchest opponents. By then Knox had completely repudiated his ordination as a Catholic priest and did not mention it in his writings. Instead he regarded his call in 1547 by the congregation of the castle in St Andrews as the foundation for his ministerial role and his right to preach. Many leading Protestant Reformers had served in the Catholic Church, and it was the norm where the ruler had moved the entire Church personnel from Catholicism to Protestantism. In England when Knox was given a chaplain's post in 1549, his earlier Catholic ordination ensured no awkward questions were asked concerning his clerical status. It also meant he could be considered for the episcopal bench without any concern about his priestly orders. Although he did not care to admit it, having been a priest greatly smoothed his path during this initial phase of his Protestant ministry. In 1562 his Roman Catholic opponent Ninian Winzet taunted Knox for inconsistency because he had rejected his clerical ordination by a Catholic bishop while continuing to accept his baptism by a Catholic priest.[25]

In the short run, Knox's career stalled and he did not continue to climb the ladder of fast promotion within the Church. Theodore Beza's later suggestion that Knox was a brilliant academic prospect does not seem likely.[26] Knox did possess a quick mind and keen intelligence, and he had excellent techniques of argument and in the formal arts of rhetoric. His brief study of canon law did not give him the incisive forensic intellect that distinguished John Calvin from his fellows, and Knox had little of Calvin's humanist fascination with the anatomy of language or the skills to dissect it. As he explained in 1565 he was not one for writing scholarly treatises, because the overriding task was to preach the Gospel.[27]

A later pen portrait described Knox as a man of short and stocky build with black hair and a swarthy complexion.[28] As a priest he would have gone clean-shaven, revealing his ruddy cheeks and emphasizing his large nose and full lips. His dark-blue eyes were deep set beneath a pronounced eyebrow ridge and narrow forehead, and when he was angry his long face became enveloped in a frown. At this time, he seems to have been healthy and was strong, with broad shoulders. He was well connected in Haddington and sensibly returned to his native town to find employment. At some point before 1540 he had been invested as a notary apostolic, taking the oath of loyalty to St Peter, the Church and the Pope. This allowed him to make his living as a notary, the sixteenth-century equivalent of the country lawyer. A few of his notarial instruments have survived, several showing he was employed by James Ker of Samuelston, a relative on his mother's side. The notarial instruments record his use of the title 'Sir John Knox', a courtesy title given to priests, and the description of him as 'a minister of the altar in the archdiocese of St Andrews'. They show his individual notary's sign manual and his personal motto, 'Not to bear false witness' (*Non falsum testimonium perhibeto*). Though cast in a negative formulation, this gave an early indication of one of the fundamental principles of Knox's life: the compelling need to bear witness to what he saw as the 'verity' or truth.[29]

As he was approaching his thirtieth birthday Knox had a good steady job and was unlikely to have been worrying where his next meal might be found. He was relatively successful and a credit to his family, living in Haddington surrounded by kinsmen and people he had known since childhood. His notarial duties involved meeting and dealing with all sorts of people and their everyday problems. To judge from the number of times it appeared in his later writings, dealing with eyewitnesses was a substantial part of his work and he developed a good grasp of court procedures.[30] As their 'man of business', he frequently dealt with the local lairds and nobility and such contacts would subsequently assist him. There is no indication of whether or not he found his priestly vow of chastity difficult to keep. In the Scottish Church of James V's reign, any such lapse would not automatically have cost him his job. For most Scots a local priest discreetly keeping his 'wife' and family was relatively low on their list of the faults of the Church. They were more exercised about the lifestyle and power of the clerical hierarchy and the Church's financial exactions that they encountered in their daily lives. At least when Knox charged fees for his notarial services, his customers understood they were getting a document for their money, and his occupation was useful to them because only a written record properly produced by a notary was recognized in law.

Knox had become one cog in the large organization that was the late medieval Scottish Church. He had been brought within its embrace at baptism, and by entering its career structure he had been actively sustained by the Church through his schooling and university, then trained for his legal position and ordained. The Church had given him the elements that maintained his adult life: he was set apart from the laity in holy orders and enjoyed clerical privileges, he had a well-paid post that brought status and position within his local society and the chance of further advancement. As for his future, he was no high flyer, but he might secure a post in the Court of the Official for the archdiocese of St Andrews or obtain a benefice in the Church. Like countless other career clerics of the period, he would probably continue to live in some comfort without over-exerting himself. However much he later rejected it, Knox owed his early career entirely to the late medieval Church, and he was a churchman through and through.

CHAPTER THREE

My first anchor

At the end of 1542 dramatic change came to Scotland and to Knox's life. The death of King James V in November shortly after the Scottish army's defeat by the English at Solway Moss was an unmitigated disaster, leaving the kingdom weak and extremely vulnerable. The next decade saw a sustained struggle between France and England for the control of the entire British mainland. It was fought primarily on Scottish soil and had the kingdom of the Scots as an incidental prize. King James's heir was a week-old baby girl, Mary, Queen of Scots, and the battle to secure her marriage and kingdom provided the perfect occasion for the latest round in the Anglo-French contest for dominance. In Scotland during 1543 this produced a rapidly shifting series of alliances that were followed by long periods of warfare. The French became Scotland's protector and ally in the fight against a succession of English invading armies and against the Rough Wooing of the young Scottish Queen.[1] Over that decade nearly every Scot living between the Borders in the south and Angus in the north was directly affected by war and plague. Conquest, slaughter, famine and death, the Four Horsemen of the Apocalypse, seemed in the 1540s to be riding across Scotland, and many had their lives thrown into disarray or worse. By contrast much of Knox's turmoil in that decade was internal, as he moved from being a Catholic priest to becoming a Protestant preacher. He later suffered considerable physical hardship and illness when sentenced to enforced exile aboard a French galley. On release eighteen months later, Knox remained in exile for safety and served as a Protestant cleric within the Church of England. Religiously and geographically, the notary from the banks of the Tyne had travelled to new lands.

In 1543 Knox was continuing to witness notarial instruments as 'Sir John Knox' and was still a Catholic cleric or a 'Pope's knight', as he later termed it. There might have been a hint of which way his thoughts were turning in the unusual addition to his notarial signature of the phrase, 'a faithful witness through Christ to whom be the glory, amen'.[2] At some point during that year he began to hold some Protestant beliefs. In common with many sixteenth-century Protestant Reformers, he did not provide a narrative of his conversion to his new faith, nor did he indicate whether it was a slow rethinking of his position or a dramatic 'Damascus Road' incident that changed his views. Whatever the process, his life altered direction and within a couple of years he had become an open supporter of the Protestant preacher George Wishart, and a year later he faced the call to become a Protestant preacher himself. These radical changes to his beliefs and career gave Knox an entirely new identity and brought a new calling that shaped every aspect of his future life.

TASTE OF THE TRUTH

Scots experienced a religious tremor in 1543 when the tectonic plates underlying their ecclesiastical landscape dramatically and unexpectedly moved. Having become Regent for the infant Queen, the Earl of Arran embarked on two ground-shaking policies. He allied with England and sought to introduce limited Church reform along English lines to propel Scotland rapidly towards a break with Rome such as the English King had accomplished during the 1530s. The Regent sent preachers out on tour and the former Dominican Prior of Inverness, Thomas Gillem, arrived in his native East Lothian. According to a later commentator, Thomas Gillem was 'the first man from whom Mr Knox received any taste of the truth'.[3] However, when Knox later commented upon those sermons in his *History*, he downplayed the importance of Gillem, probably so that his hero, George Wishart, would stand out more sharply in the story of Protestantism in Scotland. As his faint praise of Gillem indicated, Knox found him worthy and boring. The friar was of 'solid judgement, reasonable letters (as for that age) and of a prompt and good utterance: his doctrine was wholesome without great vehemency against superstition'. Knox was more appreciative of the sermons delivered by another former Dominican, John Rough, who joined Gillem in a tour of East Lothian. Compared to Gillem, Rough was, 'albeit not so learned, yet more simple and more vehement against all impiety'. Here was an early indication that Knox prized zealous vehemency above solid and learned exposition.[4]

In 1543 hopes had soared among the supporters of Church reform at the Scottish royal court and wild rumours circulated as to who might join this evangelical campaign. The high moral standard and intellectual ability of John Hamilton, then Abbot of Paisley, made him a likely candidate. The euphoric bubble was soon burst that had envisaged the future Archbishop of St Andrews stepping into the pulpit to 'preach Jesus Christ'. Hamilton returned from France and persuaded Arran, his half-brother, to reverse the controversial diplomatic and religious policies.[5] The Regent's subsequent reconciliation with Cardinal Beaton ensured that Arran's 'godly fit' came to a juddering halt. The brief religious earthquake of 1543 seemed to have left little damage to the Scottish status quo.

By contrast it had cracked open the foundations of Knox's life, destroying his previous solid and secure occupation and provoking a transformation of his religious beliefs. By listening to the sermons of Gillem and Rough he had come to accept a new understanding of salvation and adopt the belief in justification by faith alone, first championed by Luther. In the 1540s adherence to this doctrine was recognized as the badge of evangelical thinking, though it was only just becoming clear that to hold it was to join the Protestant camp. When a last opportunity for an agreement over justification and reconciliation between Protestants and Catholics failed at Regensburg in 1541, it was hard to avoid the conclusion that Christendom was permanently divided. A number of prominent clerics, such as the Englishman Cardinal Reginald Pole, realized they faced the hard choice between their understanding of justification and the preservation of the unity of the Church, and most opted to remain within the Catholic Church. When a General Council was finally called to meet at Trent in northern Italy in 1545, only members of the Roman Catholic Church gathered. However, in Scotland, which did not send a formal delegate to Trent, the time for such irrevocable decisions was fifteen years away and unbridgeable boundaries had not yet emerged.

At some point following the reassessment of his religious beliefs Knox stopped practising both as a notary apostolic and as a Catholic priest. At this difficult juncture his contacts with local lairds sympathetic to the cause of religious reform helped him find work with Hew Douglas of Longniddry and John Cockburn of Ormiston. Knox was able to remain close to his home burgh and was employed on a triangular circuit with Longniddry located next to Aberlady on the Forth coast and Ormiston placed up the River Tyne from Haddington. He became the household tutor for Hew's two sons, Francis and George, and John's heir, Alexander. Douglas of Longniddry, Cockburn of Ormiston and their close friend Alexander Crichton of Brunstane were firm supporters of an English alliance and of evangelical reform. The three lairds were also clients of the Douglas family, who had returned in 1543 from exile in England. The Earl of Angus's extremely able brother, Sir George Douglas of Pittendreich, had a base near Lasswade to the west of Haddington from where he re-established the Douglas network within the region. At this early stage in their respective careers Knox probably first encountered Pittendreich's son James, later Earl of Morton and Regent to King James VI, who was to prove so important to the Scottish Protestant cause. Knox's new post placed him within this committed evangelical group, who had the political goal of achieving religious reform through alliance with King Henry VIII of England. During the subsequent Anglo-Scottish wars this East Lothian grouping became open allies of the English.

Knox had successfully made the first of his three-stage transition from Catholic priest to Protestant preacher. However, though part of an evangelical household, publicly Knox had not burned his ecclesiastical boats. The dividing lines between being a household chaplain, a notary or man of business for a laird and a tutor for the lairds' sons were very fine indeed and it would not have been obvious to the outside world that Knox had abandoned his priestly vocation. The lairds were able to offer a protective screen that might prevent him coming to the attention of the Church authorities. This was a dangerous time, especially within the archdiocese of St Andrews where Cardinal Beaton was archbishop. Beaton had chosen in 1544 to make an example by bringing to trial and execution a group of known heretics in Perth. The Cardinal's political and ecclesiastical power was increasing, making it essential for Knox to avoid any overt repudiation of his priesthood that would draw the attention of the Church courts and place his patrons, as well as himself, in danger of heresy proceedings. Following the hectic flurry of 1543, Scottish evangelical groups returned to their previous pattern of keeping a low profile by concentrating upon Bible reading and limited discussion among themselves. This was an alternative style of domestic piety that by the exercise of discretion on disputed doctrinal points was able to coexist within the institutional Catholic Church. In later life Knox possibly felt embarrassed that during this period he had kept his head firmly down and his nose buried in his books, the very model of a conscientious schoolmaster. Such behaviour was normal among Scottish evangelicals and was changed only by the arrival of the Protestant preacher George Wishart.

One achievement of Arran's reforms in 1543 was an act of Parliament permitting the reading of the Bible in the vernacular, and this immediately made biblical study safer and easier. Having accepted the sole authority of Scripture, a fundamental premise of Protestant doctrine, Knox probably took full advantage of the opportunity to study the Scriptures in the vernacular and understand the biblical message in a new way. With no translation available in either Scots or Gaelic, English versions were used. According to Knox's *History*, New Testaments and Bibles quickly appeared, accompanied by some boasting about how such copies had been kept secret when it had been heresy to read them. A Bible lying on the table became the latest fashion accessory for every noble household, as Knox waspishly observed, though he conceded that 'thereby did the knowledge of God wondrously increase'. Alongside the importation of Bibles came English anti-papal works that had justified the Henrician break with Rome and Royal Supremacy.[6]

Whether it was his own copy or one owned by Douglas of Longniddry or Cockburn of Ormiston, Knox probably had access to the Great Bible authorized by King Henry VIII. He certainly used this version during his later ministry in Edwardian England and developed a great affection for its translations, which slipped seamlessly into his thinking and writings.[7] The University of Melbourne currently holds a copy of the Great Bible, known as 'John Knox's Bible'. This was specially printed in France in 1566 as a presentation copy to Knox from Thomas Cardine or Cawarden. Such a gift indicated that Knox either had specifically chosen this translation or was known to be particularly fond of it.[8]

JOHN 17

During the early 1540s Knox made a thorough study of the Bible which must have consumed considerable time and effort. Since he employed the Bible as one of the main textbooks for his classes, such studies fitted well into his new post as a tutor. Knox has often been identified as a man drawn primarily to the Old Testament. Though he was steeped in its books and they played a significant part in his life, he was equally at home in the New Testament, especially the Gospel of John to which he constantly returned and from which he drew many of his central biblical images. On his deathbed, Knox asked his wife to read to him from the seventeenth chapter of John's Gospel, and he made the revealing comment that this was where 'I cast my first ancre [anchor]'.[9] The sea-going metaphor revealed that this was the Bible reading that spoke first to him, providing a fixed point when his mind was drifting between various possibilities. Since ships carried more than one anchor, Knox probably also meant John 17 was his most important line of safety, holding secure his sense of salvation. For him this chapter provided a summary of the good news of the Gospel.[10]

The Geneva Bible, the later biblical translation most associated with Knox, explained in its notes to John's Gospel that chapter 17 contained 'the prayer of Christ unto his Father bothe for him self and his Apostles, and also for all suche as receive the truth'.[11] In his later book on predestination, Knox specifically discussed this high-priestly prayer and explained that Christ was not only addressing the disciples who were with him but also included believers in subsequent ages.[12] Knox's initial realization that he was included in this prayer, alongside all who believed in Christ in any period, had made a profound and indelible impression upon him. At the heart of his personal faith lay this abiding sense of inclusion resting upon Christ's prayer. 'I pray not for these alone, but for them also which shal beleve in me, through their worde, That they all may be one, as thou, o Father, art in me, and I in thee . . . I in them, and thou in me, that they may be made perfect in one.'[13]

When examining the rest of John 17 Knox found it unlocked some of the central doctrines being contested by Protestants and Catholics. Through seeing that chapter anew and in the light of a Protestant interpretation, he grasped how justification, sanctification and predestination were linked. This text demonstrated to Knox how a believer could, through union with Christ, come to understand the love of God and, in the end, reach the glory of heaven. Though this Johannine passage was not normally cited as a proof text, for Knox it proclaimed the Protestant belief in justification by faith alone that he had now embraced. In particular he now understood verse 6 to provide a direct reference to the doctrines of election and justification. The Geneva Bible later appended a long note to this verse: 'our election standeth in the good pleasure of God, which is the onlie fundation and cause of our salvation and is declared to us in Christ, through whome we are justified by faith and sanctified'.[14] Christ's promise that believers would be with him and see his glory was further explained: 'that they maie profit and growe up in such sort that in the end they may enjoy the eternal glorie with me'.[15] In his later tract about predestination the assurance that believers would enter into the same glory as Christ and that God's love for the elect was immutable were two of the three points that Knox drew from this Johannine chapter. His third point highlighted another favourite theme: the close union between Christ and the believer. This mystical union was the route by which the believer understood the love of God, 'for without him we can not comprehende the love wherewith God loveth us'.[16]

The importance of these first insights never diminished for Knox and they resonated throughout his writings. During the dark days of fighting in the Wars of the Congregation in 1559–60 when he needed an anchor, his own prayer echoed themes and language drawn straight from John 17.[17] That same strong flavour was found in his great Thanksgiving Prayer in the summer of 1560.[18] When the Gospel chapter first spoke to him he might not have grasped in its totality the delicate melding of justification, sanctification and election that was expressed in the Geneva Bible and in his own later works. Over time this special chapter gathered greater weight and meaning for him. His understanding of the union with Christ grasped in John 17 was subsequently made more sophisticated by reading John Calvin's exposition and by connecting it to the practice of the Lord's Supper. However, what he took from John 17 in the early 1540s was sufficient to change his beliefs and his life and to give him a firm anchor for his new faith.

MASTER GEORGE

Another chapter from John's Gospel gave Knox one of the images he employed most frequently, that of Christ the Shepherd, with a particular stress placed upon the voice of the shepherd and how the sheep followed that voice and no other.[19] When Knox attended the sermon by the Protestant preacher George Wishart in Leith on 13 December 1545, he heard that voice and experienced a personal call to follow it. For the ensuing five weeks he became Wishart's disciple and accompanied him everywhere. From that initial encounter he never doubted Wishart's prophetic status or the divine origin of his words. In later life he might even have 'heard' the voice of God speaking with Wishart's tones. Wishart undoubtedly made an immense impact upon Knox that cut right across his life, reordered his thinking and propelled him in a new direction.

By the time Wishart visited Leith he was already a well-known evangelical preacher who had been travelling across Scotland between groups sympathetic to his message. Wishart had returned to his native land in 1543 as a result of Regent Arran's 'godly fit', having fled five years earlier and spent time in exile in Switzerland, Germany and England. His Protestant views were heavily influenced by the Swiss Reformed tradition and he translated the text of the *First Helvetic Confession* drawn up by a Swiss committee in 1536. On his return to Scotland Wishart had attracted the attention of the Catholic Church authorities and been commanded to cease preaching. His refusal to stop his semi-public sermons and his open ministry to plague victims in Dundee ensured that Cardinal David Beaton, the Archbishop of St Andrews, was determined to remove this heretical challenge. By the time Knox was accompanying Wishart, the preacher was consciously walking the road towards martyrdom. He was intent upon handing on to the Scottish evangelical movement the radical vision of Reformed theology that demanded a complete rejection of the Catholic Church and a stress upon the primacy of Scripture. He gave Knox and the other evangelicals a new ecclesiology, complete with a new view of the ministry of preaching and prophecy, a new understanding of the sacraments and new ways of worship.

Knox's meeting with Wishart marked a dramatic and vital second stage in his three-step transition from Catholic priest to Protestant preacher. In his *History* he laconically recorded his first encounter with Wishart using the third person and with minimal detail, referring to 'John Knox, who had awaited upon him [Wishart] carefully from the time he came to Lothian'.[20] Significantly, this was the moment Knox chose to introduce himself for the first time into his narrative. He desired the closest possible association in the *History* between himself and the man he called 'Master George', his hero and role model. He wanted his readers to receive their first impression of John Knox as Wishart's disciple and sword-bearer.

Wishart's sermons with their uncompromising vision of the true and false Churches were a revelation to Knox. They called him to become an open disciple of Christ, and of Wishart himself. To Knox's relief they showed him precisely where he should stand. Throughout his life he always needed to be standing firmly on one side of a fence or the other and was never comfortable with grey areas. From Wishart he grasped a new certainty of the battle between Christ and Antichrist and held fast for the rest of his life to its compellingly simple formula. Knox had stopped functioning as a Catholic priest and notary but had not openly repudiated the Scottish Catholic Church. He was a member of the evangelical groups scattered across Scotland who held unorthodox doctrinal views and shared an alternative style of private devotion. By his open preaching to such groups Wishart helped them form a loose network and changed their perspective. His unambiguously Swiss Reformed teaching with its total rejection of the Catholic Church and its new ecclesiology sharpened and defined their views. The early evangelical movement in Scotland had been given an overtly Protestant edge.[21]

For Knox, the change was far more dramatic than for his fellow evangelicals. By joining Wishart's entourage for five hectic weeks, he became an open disciple. Overnight Knox was transformed from a man on an interior spiritual journey to an enthusiastic and publicly committed supporter. To guarantee he could remain close to Wishart, he invented a new role for himself as one of the security guards. He borrowed a two-handed sword or claymore, probably from one of the lairds' households. This soldier's weapon, standing as high as a man's chest, was best used by one trained in arms. Though all nobles and many other Scots would have acquired weapons training, Knox, as a merchant's son who had entered the Church, was probably not very proficient. It is unlikely he could have been of much assistance in a real fight and on the night of Wishart's arrest the sword was taken back and probably given to someone who had experience of using it. Carrying the great sword was a grand gesture and Knox probably employed the weapon as a processional prop carried in front of Wishart, ceremonially clearing his way. These staged entrances to demonstrate the preacher's importance probably came easily to a man who grew adept at recreating dramatic scenes in words. Knox was also making explicit his own changed status because priests were not supposed to bear arms or spill blood.

What such showmanship guaranteed was that Knox would be noticed and his presence noted alongside a known heretic. News travelled to Linlithgow, on the other side of Lothian, where one of his later opponents, Ninian Winzet, was the schoolmaster. Winzet heard about the sword-carrying episode and used it in his later attacks on Knox.[22] As a former priest who had aligned himself with heresy, Knox became a marked man and his identification was made doubly sure because he accompanied Wishart through East Lothian and in Haddington where his face was well known. In Knox's hometown, the Earl of Bothwell, as sheriff of the shire, had warned people not to attend Wishart's sermons. By appearing in such a conspicuous role, Knox was defying his own 'lord' as well as Bothwell's legal authority, but he brazened it out with bravura. In addition to appealing to his heightened sense of drama, the sword he carried fitted the strong strain of military language Wishart used to describe the struggle against the Catholic Church. Such language was curiously at odds with the preacher's determined efforts during his tour to avoid direct confrontations that might lead to actual fighting. Wishart's fiery sermons included stirring metaphors of the battle against Satan, and Knox felt caught up in this cosmic struggle between the two Churches. In some of his public pronouncements the preacher could be harsh and vindictive, as in his condemnation of two Franciscan friars who had come to disrupt his sermon in Inveresk: 'O sergeants of Sathan, and deceivers of the souls of men, will ye neither hear God's truth, nor suffer others to hear it? Depart and take this for your portion – God shall shortly confound and disclose your hypocrisy: Within this realm ye shall be abominable unto men, and your places and habitations shall be desolate.'[23]

This was an example of Wishart's prophetic denunciation and the 'deadly hatred' that should be felt against the Devil and the enemies of God. Knox seized upon this idea and made it his own, justifying his own vitriolic attacks upon anyone who opposed him, particularly during his final years.[24] The explicit identification of the Scottish Catholic Church and hierarchy as a false Church left no room for compromise or for any gradual programme of ecclesiastical reform. It presented the type of black and white choice that Knox found congenial and allowed him mentally to consign to the past his time as a 'Pope's knight'. For him this amounted to far more than an intellectual acceptance of key doctrines – it was a total shift of allegiance. The metaphor of fighting under the banner of Christ was one he was to use time and time again when attempting to instil in his hearers the same sense of commitment and loyalty he had first experienced on becoming Wishart's disciple. During his own ministerial career he instinctively thought of the religious battle within a military context, explaining on one occasion that the Mass was more of a threat than if ten thousand enemy soldiers had landed.[25]

THE BLESSED MARTYR OF GOD

Writing in his *History* twenty-one years later about 'Master George', Knox was intent upon presenting a Christ-like figure. He introduced Wishart as almost beyond compare, 'a man of such graces as before him were never heard within this realm, yea, and are rare to be found yet in any man'.[26] Like the Jesus of John's Gospel, in Knox's narrative Wishart moved towards his death with a clear awareness of his fate. He preached, tended the sick and plague-ridden, protected those who would have killed him, overcame temptation alone and steadfastly endured his trial and final martyrdom. At many points Knox introduced direct parallels with Gospel scenes to make the identification impossible to escape. This went beyond conventional hagiography and placed Wishart at least on a par with the Christ-like figure of St Francis.

Knox spent a mere five weeks in Wishart's company during a preaching tour demanding constant movement between venues and different overnight accommodation to avoid detection. In his *History* he recorded only one personal conversation with his hero. On the day of the final sermon in Haddington, a letter arrived that indefinitely postponed the public debate in Edinburgh that Wishart had particularly sought. The preacher had wanted to talk and share his doubts about the future while Knox was on tenterhooks because the time for sermon was approaching and he had no wish to intrude upon Wishart's preparation. Not only was Wishart paralleling the reversals and doubts Christ faced in his last days, he foreshadowed the feelings and language Knox used in 1566 when writing that section of the *History*. Wishart's phrase 'weary of the world' became Knox's refrain in his own final years.[27]

For Knox, Wishart had put into words Christ's call to be a disciple and had made that call directly to him. It was Wishart's voice Knox had heard and to which he responded. In 1545 Knox was one of the sheep who recognized this shepherd's voice and Wishart was the shepherd he followed. When writing his *History*, Knox chose to downplay his personal experience of the call and his relationship with Wishart so that he could instead universalize the call to discipleship. He deliberately did not incorporate a spiritual autobiography into his narrative and, unlike the German Reformer Martin Luther, he elsewhere revealed little about the internal journey to reach the certainties on which he subsequently based his life. When later he employed the biblical imagery of the shepherd, he often switched between Christ the Good Shepherd and the role of pastors and ministers who were shepherds of their flocks and congregations. Being such a pastor of a flock was the duty of every Protestant preacher, though Wishart held a special place for Knox as the perfect reflection of the Good Shepherd and his personal role model.

Knox's attendance upon Wishart was brought to an end on the night of the preacher's arrest. When Douglas of Longniddry was leaving, Knox made to stay behind, but Wishart told him, 'Nay, return to your bairns, and God bless you. One is sufficient for a sacrifice.' It was a moment of great significance and emotion for Knox, and he vividly recalled that final scene in January on the frosty road to Ormiston.[28] The extreme care with which he recorded in his *History* that explicit dismissal by Wishart, and his addition of the words 'John Knox ... albeit unwillingly, obeyed, and returned with Hew Douglas of Longniddry', suggested that the incident left a painful scar. Possibly at the time and certainly upon reflection, Knox treated his leaving Wishart that night as the personal reliving of the Apostles' desertion of Christ in the Garden of Gethsemane. Once the arrest had been made, and despite the Earl of Bothwell's promise to the contrary, Wishart was handed over to Cardinal David Beaton and sent to St Andrews. In Knox's Passion-style narrative this was Wishart's Jerusalem, where he was tried, condemned and executed on 1 March 1546. The 'death of the blessed martyr of God' automatically placed all Wishart's associates in danger. At this point Knox considered leaving the country for Germany and a visit to the centres of Continental Protestantism.[29] In the end he probably laid low in East Lothian waiting for Beaton's major crackdown on heresy that did not come.

THE KINDNESS OF GOD

There can be little doubt that Wishart made a profound and lasting impression upon Knox. He gave a renewed sense of certainty and clarity of thinking to him at the turning point of his spiritual journey. Knox was happiest viewing the world in crystal-clear polarities and he thrived on unmistakable contrasts. He later explained to a friend that he needed to understand and explain religious truths in black and white terms that permitted no middle ground.[30] In 1545 he had already abandoned his priestly office and many of the beliefs of the late medieval Church. According to Wishart, that Church was a false one and those who continued to support it were 'servants of Satan' and faced the wrath of God. In its place, Wishart brought a vision of the true Church and the assurance that Knox was a soldier in the army of Christ. Under his guidance Knox rediscovered the security of belonging to the Church, catholic in the sense of universal, but opposed to the visible institution of the Scottish Catholic Church in which he had been raised.

When in 'Master George's' company, Knox probably saw a copy of Wishart's translation of the *First Helvetic Confession* of 1536. This distillation of the Swiss Reformed position had not yet been printed, but Wishart would have had manuscript copies for circulation. With the preacher probably employing the same or similar terms, the contents of Wishart's sermons and the *Confession* would have merged into one within Knox's mind. Though he did not mention it in his *History*, this lucid statement of faith might have provided a firm framework for his own emerging beliefs, and some of its key points recurred during his subsequent ministry. In Articles 5 and 13 of the *Confession*, Wishart had chosen 'kindness', a word replete with significance for Scots, to describe the believer's kinship with Christ and the saving grace received by faith. Faith was also described in this homely way: 'we hope for to come to the kyndnes of God'.

Wishart was able to give Knox a conceptual bridge joining three doctrines that were central to his theological understanding: faith in Christ, kinship with Christ and fighting under Christ's banner. Wishart's choice of language helped Knox to merge justification and election, a pairing he had first understood when reading John 17 and a link that characterized his later writings. A similar pairing coupled justification and salvation when Wishart followed Scots usage and employed the word 'safe' rather than 'saved' in his translation of Articles 12 and 19 of the *Confession*. He described the relationship between salvation and justification as 'we are safe onely by the marcie of God and merit of Christ'.[31] Though they recognized that the preacher did not mean physical safety, Knox and many of Wishart's other hearers received the assurance that they were safe as well as saved. In his later ministry Knox showed the greatest patience with those, like Elizabeth Bowes, who worried that they and their salvation were unsafe. Knox found as many ways as he could to explain that believers' safety and assurance did not rest with them but lay in the sacrifice and merits of Christ. Being Christ's, these merits were eternally safe and secure, available to all those who as believers were Christ's kin and united with him. By finding these simple terms that conveyed to his listeners a wealth of subtle Scottish associations, Wishart wrapped his Swiss Reformed theology in a cloak of recognizable colours that looked both familiar and comforting.

Throughout his life, Knox did not waver from the belief that had bound together medieval Christendom and into which he had been baptized: outside the Church there was no salvation. Yet he had been called to be a disciple of a man whose views were labelled heresy by the official Church. By giving him a new definition of the 'true' Church, Wishart had provided profound reassurance for Knox that he remained a member of that invisible body, the Church of Christ. This was not the powerful visible institution that dominated Christian Europe, but a Church that comprised a little flock of believers or was like the faithful remnant of which the Old Testament prophets spoke. Wishart explained that though this Church would continue to be persecuted and might appear to be defeated, that was all part of the divine plan. These insights sustained Knox in 1546 and remained the foundation stones for his ecclesiastical thinking for the remainder of his life. In a remarkably comprehensive way he absorbed the ecclesiological lessons Wishart had taught. He accepted the teaching about the nature of a Reformed Church and just a year later, without needing to pause for thought, he himself translated those ideas directly into practice in St Andrews.

The prophetic dimension of Wishart's preaching and ministry set him apart, and the recognition of Wishart as a prophet formed as important a motif in Knox's narrative as the Christ-like qualities. This emphasis reflected a more general Protestant search for alternative models of sanctity that broke away from medieval saints and their miracles. Knox portrayed two strands to Wishart's prophetic office, reproving and admonishing sins and foretelling future events. They were bracketed together as they had been for the Old Testament prophets on whom Wishart modelled himself. Many of the incidents recorded in Knox's *History* were selected precisely because they revealed Wishart's prophecies and predictions. There was also a pressing personal reason for demonstrating that Wishart was a prophet in the Old Testament mould because Knox sought to justify his own merging of the twin roles of preacher and prophet. He deliberately modelled his ministry upon what he had seen and heard Wishart do. After he had entered that ministry he concluded that Wishart's prophetic mantle had indeed fallen directly on to his own shoulders, just as in the Old Testament the prophet Elijah's mantle had passed to his successor, Elisha. Following Wishart, Knox combined the prophetic and preaching duties of admonition, explaining, 'therefore must the truth be plainlie spoken that the simple and rude multitude may be admonished'.[32]

Most of the ideas Knox received from Wishart would have been heard in sermons. The aural impact of Wishart's words remained firmly in his memory and he incorporated them into his *History*. Having been carried away by Wishart's language and delivery in the pulpit, Knox turned this style of denunciation into a major element within his sermons. He also acquired Wishart's fondness for contradistinctions and selected as illustrations of Wishart's preaching those occasions his mentor had moved into prophetic denunciation, as at Haddington. Wishart had been angered by the rapid diminution in attendance due to Bothwell's prohibition and felt Haddington had spurned him as the messenger of God. He launched into a condemnation of the burgh and its inhabitants.

O Lord, how long shall it be that thy holy word shall be despised, and men shall not regard their own salvation? I have heard of thee, Haddington, that in thee would have been at a vain Clerk play [mystery play] two or three thousand people; and now to hear the messenger of the Eternal God, of all thy town nor parish can not be numbered a hundred persons. Sore and fearful shall the plagues be that shall ensure this thy contempt ... yea, thou

Haddington, in special, strangers shall possess thee ... and that because ye have not known, nor will know the time of God's merciful visitation.[33]

Crucially, Wishart's sortie into such geographical expostulation had included specific predictions of the burgh's fate. He had moved seamlessly between the two prophetic strands, starting with general admonition and ending with a set of predictions. For Knox's purposes it was essential that Wishart's predictions were shown to have been fulfilled so he could demonstrate conclusively that Wishart had been divinely called and given extraordinary gifts by God. When dealing in his *History* with the damage to Haddington during the siege of 1548 Knox explicitly reminded his readers that this fulfilled Wishart's prophecies about the burgh and was direct proof of his prophetic power. 'And so did God perform the words and threatening of his servant, Master George Wishart, who said, "That for their contempt of God's messenger, they should be visited with sword and fire, with pestilence, strangers, and famine."'[34] In Knox's narrative the preacher's miraculous powers of foresight and the accuracy of his predictions were given centre stage. According to his followers, earlier in his preaching tour Wishart's foresight had saved his and their lives. When writing about the attempted ambush near Montrose Knox crafted his story with great skill to heighten the dramatic tension and emphasize the supernatural powers Wishart possessed. He underlined Wishart's Christ-like knowledge not only of his approaching death but also of its timing.[35]

Wishart inspired his disciple Knox to follow his doctrine and his ministry. With that sincerest form of flattery, Knox imitated his hero. He might have started in a superficial way by growing a black beard as long as Wishart's and for the rest of his life he sported a beard down to his chest in best prophetic style. This was probably the only aspect of Wishart's appearance he could reproduce, since his role model was tall, very thin and ascetic looking and had a sallow complexion.[36] As an ardent disciple, Knox also copied Wishart's expressions and vocabulary. Ten years later when searching for a suitable denunciation of Mary of Guise, he reproduced almost exactly Wishart's earlier phrasing.[37]

In Wishart, Knox had encountered for the first time a recognizable Protestant cleric. By carefully studying him as a preacher and prophet, he was able quite remarkably to emerge in St Andrews during 1547 with nearly all the attributes of a fully formed minister. Wishart had laid down that the central qualification for ministry was knowledge of the Bible and a willingness to preach it. This was an entirely different understanding from Knox's proud declaration a few years earlier in a notarial instrument that he was a minister of the altar, an ordained priest who could offer the sacrifice of the Mass. Wishart had rejected the concept of holy orders conveyed via an ecclesiastical hierarchy. He replaced it with preaching based on biblical study with the actual call to preach becoming the minister's warrant. Although Knox did not put this into practice during Wishart's lifetime, this new understanding of ministry made possible his final acceptance of the call to preach in St Andrews the year after Wishart's execution. In addition to the pivotal role of preaching, a minister was responsible for administering the sacraments. Wishart had taught that the seven sacraments of the medieval Church should be reduced to two: baptism and the eucharist or Lord's Supper. Wishart's guidance and teaching were made strikingly obvious in St Andrews during 1547. Thanks to his mentor, in that burgh Knox was able to administer the Lord's Supper in a 'Reformed' manner.

The targeting and removal of 'additional' ceremonies flowed from Wishart's entire approach to worship, that all its aspects should be based directly on Scripture. Knox accepted with great enthusiasm this substantial extension of the concept of the primacy of Scripture. In his later career he pushed his premise still further by accepting both the positive rule and its negative corollary. For Knox the negative aspect dominated, declaring that nothing should be present in worship which did not have an explicit biblical warrant. It was accompanied by the positive formulation that only things expressly commanded in Scripture should be practised, a step further than many other Reformed theologians were prepared to go and one that contained problems for the future. Employing the logical method he had learned at university, Knox created a syllogism and it became one of the foundations of his thinking. In more modern times, this has become known as the regulative principle.

The public nature of Wishart's preaching tour and the way in which he was able in some communities to deliver his sermons within the local parish church provided an opportunity for the first time for Scots to witness key features of Reformed worship. Particularly important for later Scottish practice were those elements that crossed over from private devotion to public worship and continued to occupy a place within each area. Wishart encouraged metrical psalm-singing among his followers and on the night of his arrest he requested that everyone sing Psalm 51, the well-known penitential psalm. This was the metrical version contained in the *Gude and godlie ballattis*, a series of Lutheran-style hymns and songs that had been circulating among Scottish evangelicals. As they were the actual words of Scripture, Wishart probably gave greater prominence to the psalms than to the hymns, following Swiss Reformed practice. Within the context of public and even private worship this created a distance between the psalms and the highly polemical adaptations of popular songs also found in the *Gude and godlie ballattis*. Probably during his time with Wishart, Knox first acquired his great love for metrical psalm-singing. He was also introduced to the use within worship of the catechetical device of learning vernacular metrical versions of the Ten Commandments, Creed and Lord's Prayer.[38] Such a heavily didactic emphasis blurred the line between worship and education in public and private settings. From its origins in Swiss Reformed practice this also became a feature of the Scottish Protestant Kirk. Though a private devotion that Wishart practised by himself, his positive use and approbation of fasting made a lasting impression upon Knox and other Scottish evangelicals. After the Protestant Reformation in Scotland, Knox wrote an *Order for a General Fast*, and as a result public fasting within a strong prophetic and apocalyptic context became a distinctive feature of early modern Scottish life.

Wishart's example through deeds as well as words gave Knox a fresh understanding of what constituted the Church. It opened up new possibilities for Knox and, less dramatically and much more slowly, for his fellow Scottish evangelicals. Little of the theological content Wishart had brought on his return to Scotland was entirely new, but his charismatic preaching and personality made an incalculable difference. He gave the Scottish evangelical groups a dynamism and sharply defined direction that produced a nascent Protestant movement. For a recent convert such as Knox, no other man could compare to his 'Master George'. Wishart was a shining living embodiment of a new vision of the Church. Having lost his Catholic anchors, once he had heard Wishart's sermons Knox was able to grasp this new certainty with relief and conviction. Wishart had proved to him that the new anchor of his Protestant faith would hold and that he was aboard the vessel of the true Church. He had given Knox a new ecclesiology and a model for his future ministry.

CHAPTER FOUR

Called by my God

Knox's future was determined by the third and final stage of his transition from Catholic priest to Protestant minister. His call to be a preacher defined him and created an exceptionally strong self-image. Throughout his life he was sustained by the conviction that he was 'cald by my God to instruct the ignorant, comfort the sorrowfull, confirme the weak and rebuke the proud, by tong and livelye voyce'.[1] Once he had stepped into the pulpit he found his metier. When looking back in 1566 as he wrote this section of the *History*, he highlighted the two things that mattered most about him during this period: his discipleship with Wishart and the call to preach. They set the pattern for everything he subsequently did and marked him out as 'a true messanger of God to whome the truth is reveled'.[2]

THAT BLOODY WOLF THE CARDINAL

After he had parted from Wishart for the last time, Knox returned to Longniddry with Hew Douglas. The news of what had happened that night at Ormiston probably reached them very quickly, and they would have been worrying not only for Wishart but also for John Cockburn and others who had been arrested. Then it would have been that wearying wait for news of further developments and the accompanying mixture of hope, despair and fear as it became clear that Bothwell had handed Wishart over to Cardinal Beaton and he had been taken to St Andrews, the base for 'that bloody wolf the Cardinal' in Knox's vivid description.[3] Seemingly unable to write directly about the painful episode, in his *History* Knox inserted the description of the trial and execution of Wishart from Foxe's *Book of Martyrs*. He concentrated instead upon portraying Cardinal Beaton as the arch-villain, and there was a strand of genuine hatred in his vicious use of the Cardinal to personify and exemplify the worst faults of the late medieval Church in Scotland. Employing every weapon in his rhetorical arsenal, Knox used humour to devastating effect to demonstrate Beaton's pride and concern for status. He inserted into the story of Wishart's final days the 'merry tale' of the fight between the Archbishop of St Andrews' clergy and those from the rival Archbishop of Glasgow during a church procession.[4]

In the months following Wishart's arrest, Knox was afraid the Cardinal's men would track him down and arrest him for heresy. He probably moved among the tight circle of evangelical households in East Lothian. When exile, the recourse of most Scottish clergy who had become evangelicals, was discussed, Knox favoured a trip to the German-speaking lands. He had probably heard critical reports about the situation in England from Wishart, who had personal experience of the Henrician Reformation. Despite the English King having broken with Rome and created the Church of England, the Latin Mass remained and Church reform was strictly limited. Getting passage on a ship for the Low Countries and then travelling to the Holy Roman Empire was complex and costly, and Knox's mercantile family had probably suffered directly when all sea-going vessels on the Forth had been destroyed during the English invasion a couple of years before. In their destructive march through East Lothian, the English army had laid waste to Seton, its fine orchards and collegiate church a few miles from Longniddry. In the Lothians there was probably very little cash or resources to fund a trip to Germany.

Some of the concern for Knox's personal safety proved groundless since in this respect Cardinal Beaton was of the same mind as Wishart – that one execution was enough. This astute politician understood that it was not an opportune moment to round up the East Lothian lairds and also-rans on an anti-heresy drive. Knox was not the only man with hatred of the Cardinal in his heart. Strongly encouraged by their English allies, some Scottish lairds had discussed how to rid themselves of Beaton as early as 1544. One of these lairds was Alexander Crichton of Brunstane, known to Knox as the close friend of his employers. In the spring of 1546 another plot was hatched in Fife with a mixture of motives and personnel. The conspirators coalesced around Norman Leslie, Master (or heir) of Rothes, who had been involved in an acrimonious property dispute with Beaton. Their number included a close personal friend of Wishart, Melville of Carnbee, who was intent upon revenge. The plan was as much a *coup d'état* as an assassination, and presumed King Henry VIII would send help for their attempt to bring Scotland back to an alliance with England.[5]

The simple and well-constructed scheme to enter the castle at St Andrews early on the morning of 29 May 1546 succeeded, and the group of eighteen men found the Cardinal in his chamber and stabbed him to death. They took over the castle and held it, thus securing the second part of their plan. Although the removal of Cardinal Beaton brought advantages to his major rival, Regent Arran, political assassination could not be tolerated. Arran brought an army to recapture the castle, but found that that was no simple task. The Regent was adept at negotiation and a past master of the very Scottish art of fighting and negotiating at the same time, a method commonly employed to defuse rebellious acts and reconstruct a workable political consensus. While it was a serious military enterprise, for practical as well as diplomatic purposes the siege was not a blockading encirclement and the leaders of the Castilians had sufficient military knowledge to defend their base. An attempt to topple the wall by undermining was foiled by those inside the castle digging a counter-mine. Arran, facing the threat of another full-scale English invasion, did not regard the capture of St Andrews Castle as his top priority. He was also constrained by the presence of his eldest son and heir within the castle walls. The young James Hamilton had been in the Cardinal's household, held as a thinly disguised hostage for his father's continued support. Given these circumstances, the siege dragged on through the winter of 1546–7.

Meanwhile Knox remained in East Lothian and continued to tutor his three charges. Beaton's murder had removed the immediate threat of arrest and he probably worked relatively normally at Longniddry. Situated among supporters of an English alliance, he would have been among the first to hear the news of the death of King Henry VIII. Edward Seymour, Earl of Hereford, the commander of the English armies that had been invading Scotland, became Protector, or Regent, for his young nephew, King Edward VI, and acquired the dukedom of Somerset along the way. Somerset placed Scotland at the top of his list of military priorities, unlike his late master, who had always seen France as the key theatre for the Anglo-French struggle. The death of Henry's great rival, King Francis I, in March 1547 brought a new regime to power in France and marked the passing of an era within European diplomacy. The emperor Charles V remained in power, the last of the three great protagonists, though so mired in the struggles in the Holy Roman Empire that he could give little mind to the small kingdom of Scotland on the periphery of Europe.

While the international scene was changing, Knox was more directly affected by the activities of the new Archbishop of St Andrews. After the Cardinal's murder, John Hamilton, Arran's half-brother, had been elevated to the primacy of Scotland. Since he was known to favour some reforms within the Church, Scottish evangelicals might have regarded this as a moderately hopeful appointment. Taking possession of a major see was a time-consuming process and was particularly protracted for Hamilton. Not yet able to exercise his archiepiscopal powers, in March 1547 he used the Privy Council's authority to start a campaign against those who were opposed to the Mass, as well as other heretics.[6] This put the pressure back on to Knox since he had accepted Wishart's views about worship in the Church and, in particular, the definition of the Mass as idolatry. As a result of discussions held at Longniddry regarding the safety of Knox and his three pupils, Douglas and Cockburn of Ormiston persuaded Knox to take their sons to the castle of St Andrews. Though a castle under siege seems to modern eyes a strange place to seek safety, the group of four from East Lothian were part of a wider influx into St Andrews Castle, increasing the total to 120 inhabitants. Shortly after Easter 1547 Knox and the boys were welcomed into the castle, possibly accompanied by William, Knox's elder brother, who was carrying letters between English Border officials and Scots supporting an English alliance.[7]

Once settled, Knox resumed his normal teaching duties, ensuring that the boys continued their Latin grammar and were reading the classical authors. He taught his pupils a catechism that set out the rudiments of faith via questions and answers. This was probably the vernacular catechism, now lost, that John Winram, the Subprior of St Andrews, had written in 1546. Following Wishart's method of employing educational tools within or alongside public worship in church, Knox rehearsed his boys so that the catechism could be recited in public in the St Andrews' parish church of Holy Trinity (see Plate 10). Alexander Cockburn, probably the brightest of the three and the most interested in his studies, was chosen for this first public performance of the catechism, a sight and sound that would became familiar in Scotland after 1560.

James Hamilton, Regent Arran's son, a boy the same age as Knox's pupils, might have joined the lessons and become acquainted with Knox at this early stage in his life. With the warmer days some lessons probably took place in the fine loggia that ran below the chapel and faced the castle's inner courtyard. There were bracing views across the sea as it pounded against the northern and eastern walls and of the cathedral on the headland beyond. Most of Knox's teaching took place in the luxurious chapel on the first floor of the eastern front that had been beautifully appointed for the Cardinal's personal use. That section of the castle overlooked the probable place of Wishart's execution a few yards from the walls and might have provided a constant reminder for Knox of Master George's martyrdom. If so, he distracted himself by continuing the reading and exposition of the Gospel of John he had started at Longniddry. Following the Swiss Reformed approach, he chose a particular book of the Bible, starting at the beginning and working his way through every chapter, giving detailed commentary on each section. This formal exposition took place at the same time every day in the chapel and attracted other castle residents who came to listen, including Henry Balnaves and the preacher John Rough, whom Knox had first heard in 1543.

IN THE NAME OF GOD

It did not take long for Rough, Balnaves and other evangelicals in the castle to decide that Knox should be recruited as another preacher. Rough felt overwhelmed by the additional duty of debating over doctrine with prominent university Catholics. Aware that his own scholarship was slender, Rough struggled to keep up his side of the debate and had persuaded Knox to supply him with study notes. Rough and Balnaves were planning to join the team negotiating with the English government and were looking for a replacement preacher for the castle. When these two men tried to persuade him, Knox refused point blank, saying 'That he would not run where God had not called him'. Interestingly, in 1566 as Knox wrote about this incident he thought it necessary to gloss his 1547 comment, 'meaning, that he would do nothing without a lawful vocation'.[8] By 1566 he was extremely sensitive to any suggestion he had not been called by God to be a preacher.

At this juncture Sir David Lindsay of the Mount was enlisted. He was Scotland's Lord Lyon, or chief heraldic officer, and a prominent playwright who had advocated reform of the Church. Since his Garleton Castle lay just outside the burgh of Haddington, Lindsay was probably already acquainted with Knox. During the siege Lindsay had been chosen by the Privy Council to conduct negotiations with the leaders of the Castilians, allowing him to move freely in and out of the castle. He joined private consultations among the evangelicals to ensure that Knox would accept this call and they agreed upon a new tactic. Within the public setting of a sermon Knox was to be confronted by the call to preach. Rough began his next sermon with a general discussion of the election of ministers in a Reformed Church and emphasized the power of the congregation. Even if the congregation were merely the biblical 'two or three gathered together', they could be proactive and call a man in whom they recognized the requisite 'gifts of God'. He stressed that the voice of those wanting to be instructed was to be heard above the wishes of the gifted man. For good measure Rough added that it was dangerous for anyone to refuse such a call. To remove any doubt as to who or what was intended, Rough turned to Knox and spoke directly to him. He formally declared:

> In the name of God, and of his Son Jesus Christ, and in the name of those that presently calls you by my mouth, I charge you, that ye refuse not this holy vocation, but that as ye tender the glory of God, the increase of Christ his kingdom, the edification of your brethren, and the comfort of me, whom ye understand well enough to be oppressed by the multitude of labours, that ye take upon you the public office and charge of preaching, even as ye look to

avoid God's heavy displeasure, and desire that he shall multiply his graces with you.[9]

To conclude, Rough asked the congregation if that had been the commission they had given him and whether they approved. Predictably, he received a ringing endorsement. It was a comprehensive piece of emotional and religious blackmail, with Rough carefully combining the voices of God, of the congregation and of himself to create a cacophony of pressure upon Knox.

Overwhelmed, Knox burst into tears and rushed out to hide in his own chamber. For many days he was miserable, his heart full of 'grief and trouble'. Normally gregarious and ready with a joke, he shunned company and could not even raise a smile, let alone a laugh. Teaching his pupils in the chapel would only remind him of the painful experience of that public call. When backed into a corner Knox's instinct was to come out fighting, but in this situation the only person with whom he could fight was himself. He was probably angry that Rough had trapped him and irked that the castle's congregation had deliberately called him by name, something he emphasized in the marginal note to this incident in his *History*. He realized he could not refuse such a call made in the names of God and Christ via the mouths of the preacher and the congregation; that was the method Wishart had taught him should be followed. In trying to persuade him, Rough made a direct reference to the parable of the talents, and in several later references to his vocation Knox underlined that he was merely a steward and would need to account to God for how he had used his talents. From the perspective of 1558, by which time his vocation had become an essential element of his identity, he was able to attribute the event to the superabundant grace of God that had called, made and appointed him 'a witness, minister and preacher'.[10]

Like all Scots, Knox would have been familiar with sermons by friars, heard on particular feast days and sometimes in the street, though not forming a routine component within Sunday parish worship. The friars had employed dramatic stories and passionate analogies to explain key doctrines and Knox mentally bracketed John Rough, the former Dominican, within that preaching style. This was creating problems for Rough as his sermons were coming under heavy academic attack in the parish church of Holy Trinity by Dean John Annand, the Principal of St Leonard's College in the university. Remaining in the background, providing notes for Rough, had suited Knox, though he probably realized too late that it confirmed he possessed the attributes needed for a preacher.

While he could give a good biblical 'lecture', as he had to his boys, it was unlikely Knox had preached before. He knew he was adept with words, but

technique was not the vital ingredient for a preacher because he believed he
needed to have the right words inspired by the Holy Spirit. He later explained,
'I consulte not with flesh and blood what I shall propone to the people, but as
the Spirit of my God who hath sent me, and unto whome I must answere,
moveth me, so I speake.'[11] As he sat weeping and praying in his room in the
castle in St Andrews, Knox was not sure if the Holy Spirit would speak through
his mouth when he stood in the pulpit. His mind was dominated by his knowledge of Wishart, who exemplified the ideal Protestant preacher and prophet.
Listening to Wishart over five weeks would have been the first extended series
of sermons he had heard. As Wishart had insisted and Knox later reiterated, it
was God's Word 'whilk aucht purelie and sinceirlie to sound fra the pastouris
mouth'.[12] It was a huge leap for Knox to accept that he should follow in Master
George's footsteps and put around his own shoulders that prophetic mantle.

A related doubt would also have assailed him as he considered the longer-
term consequences of the call. Every time he looked out of the castle's windows
he would have been reminded how Wishart's life had ended. He must have
pondered whether he would be able to make that sacrifice, should it become
necessary. In 1547 becoming a preacher in Scotland was the equivalent of a
suspended death sentence, and he was well aware that the ecclesiastical authorities already suspected he was a heretic. As he had declared to Rough and
Balnaves, he did not know if he was being called to run that race. He waited
for days to find some certainty from his private meditations; none came.

Rough needed his help immediately in the continuing sermon duel with
Dean Annand. Once more Knox found himself in Holy Trinity Church
listening and taking notes on Annand's sermon. Rough's previous points,
supplied by Knox, had pushed Annand into making his case on the basis of the
authority of the Catholic Church. The Dean ended with a flourish: 'Which
authority (said he), damned all Lutherans and heretics; and therefore he
needeth no further disputation'.[13] For Knox this was an irresistible gift, playing
directly into his hands by moving the grounds of the debate on to the nature
of the Church. Thanks to Wishart's decisive views on the subject, he knew
instantly he was on solid ground. He was probably on his feet in a flash
demanding a definition of the Church. He added immediately that it must
correspond to 'the right notes given to us in God's Scriptures of the true
church'. Not content with setting the agenda for further debate, he continued
with his own challenge by defining 'your Roman Kirk' as 'the synagogue of
Sathan' and declaring that the Pope was Antichrist. In his own highly dramatic
flourish, Knox announced he was willing to defend the proposition that the
current Catholic Church was worse than the Church of the Jews when it
condemned Christ to death.

FEED MY SHEEP

Dean Annand had refused to be provoked into a debate with Knox. That stalemate did not satisfy the people listening in Holy Trinity who themselves made an interesting plea to Knox: 'we cannot all read your writings, but we may all hear your preaching: Therefore we require you, in the name of God, that ye will let us hear the probation of that which ye have affirmed; for if it be true, we have been miserably deceived'.[14] In his decision about the call to ministry Knox had been waiting for a still, small voice, but received instead the noisy clamour of the congregation of Holy Trinity demanding in God's name that he preach. In his *History*, he drew attention to the distinct public calls to preach he had received from the two congregations in St Andrews, the castle and the parish church. They underlined the importance placed upon the call and 'election' by the church, as embodied in the worshipping community of the congregation. In Holy Trinity, the call had come again and the certainty he had been seeking accompanied it. In future, whatever doubts he harboured about his capabilities, he never doubted he had received a divine call to preach.

By including the initial 'private' call to him made by Rough and Balnaves, Knox drew a subtle parallel with Christ's three-fold commission to Peter recorded in John 21:15–17. The double or triple call to preach had perhaps given Knox the sense that, like Peter's, the shame of betraying the Christ-like figure of Wishart could be wiped away.[15] As his later writings demonstrate, he was concerned less with a personal parallel and more with establishing that all Protestant preachers had been given the command by Christ to 'fede my sheep'.[16] In a letter to Mrs Bowes he even turned Peter's name into a generic word for a preacher, commenting that God would provide 'ane Petir or uther' who would guide the sheep and break up God's Word to feed to lambs.[17] The notes on Christ's charge to Peter in the Geneva Bible made the link explicit and extended the association by tying the minister's love of Christ directly to his willingness to preach. Commenting on Christ's question to Peter, 'lovest thou me?', the side note explained, 'The minister can not wel teache his congregatioun except he love Christ effectually, which love is not in them that feed not the flocke.'[18]

From the start of his ministerial career Knox appreciated the double associations of 'call' as both the summons to the preacher by the congregation and the preacher's voice in his sermons guiding his congregational flock with the Word of God. He understood that it was not a light thing to ignore or walk away from a congregation's call and later admitted, 'I dare not cast off that burden that God hath laid upon me to preache.'[19] The imagery of the shepherd calling his flock was a constant motif in Knox's writings, drawing heavily upon

John 10, the discourse on the Good Shepherd.[20] The Geneva Bible loaded that image with extra meaning as a model for the harmony between preacher and congregation by noting at verse 3 that 'he calleth' meant 'there is mutual agreement and consent of faith betwene the pastour and ye shepe'.[21] Drawing upon both Old and New Testament imagery, Knox also frequently spoke about the hireling, the opposite of a good shepherd. If such a negligent pastor fell asleep or kept his mouth shut and did not preach, then the sheep would stray.[22] Opening with that injunction to feed the flock, Knox distilled his view of the ministerial role in 1561 when he gave the Exhortation to John Spottiswood as Superintendent of Lothian.[23]

Knox's first sermon in 1547 was a remarkably professional and assured performance, though its content has survived only in his own *History*. From the time he had heard about the two churches from Wishart eighteen months earlier, he had probably been thinking through the central issue of the nature of the Church. His study of the Bible and the preparation needed to tutor his pupils would have covered much ground that could be turned to good use in future sermons. More recently, he had honed the skill of summarizing arguments for Rough to use. This training influenced his own homiletic style because he followed Rough rather than Wishart by dividing sermons into separate points. Though he had produced written notes for Rough, he did not carry notes into the pulpit himself. He later set aside a particular day for sermon preparation when he sought to keep to his books and did not care to be disturbed.[24] Having prepared, he then preached without notes, reinforcing his sense that the right words would be supplied once the time came. Such a conviction, reflecting the experience of his first sermon, remained with Knox for the rest of his life. When he was debating with Friar Arbuckle in St Andrews he asserted, 'Christ Jesus bids us "Not fear, when we shall be called before men, to give confession of his truth"; for he promises, "that it shall be given unto us in that hour what we shall speak."'[25] Over time this solidified into a certainty that once in the pulpit God inspired him directly and that even the Kirk had no authority over the words he spoke.[26]

THAT BABYLONIAN HARLOT

Knox came to the parish church on the following Sunday and made good his challenge. Holy Trinity was a substantial burgh church boasting a considerable clerical personnel to staff its choir and say Mass at its thirty-two side altars.[27] The preaching contests had been attracting sizeable audiences, and the previous week listening to Dean Annand, their colleague, there had been a weighty collection of senior academics, including John Mair, Knox's former professor.

As it was the talk of the university schoolrooms and of the town, students and citizens attended this public forum where Knox would make his case for all to hear. Interested local lairds attended, such as James Forsyth, travelling the three miles from Nydie to hear this unknown preacher. The occasion was well organized and orderly and the niceties were observed, with Knox being given the pulpit as part of the open debates upon religious questions encouraged by John Winram. It was a most unusual freedom for someone challenging the orthodox views of the Church to be permitted to 'express his mind in the public preaching place'.[28]

In his challenge, Knox had given himself a great deal of material to cover, though his main target was the papacy and the entire Roman Church. With his military approach to debate with Catholic opponents, attack was always the best form of defence and his simple objective was to obliterate his enemies' commander, the Pope, and his headquarters at Rome. He took as his text Daniel 7, thereby placing the struggle between the true and false Churches on the cosmic stage of salvation history. By choosing the Book of Daniel, he tackled one of the most complex sets of prophecies in the Old Testament. Following Wishart, he wanted to employ the admonitory style of an Old Testament prophet. Whatever had gone through his mind between his initial challenge and the Sunday he climbed into the pulpit, he had accepted that he was Wishart's successor and was now prepared to flaunt Wishart's prophetic mantle.

Knox began with the clever debating device of treating as self-evident one of the central propositions on which he based his case. He asserted that the Church had existed throughout all ages and that Daniel's prophecies applied directly to that timeless Church. They were neither time nor context specific and the prophecies applied to the present and future as well as the past. Knox explained that, as part of his love for the Church, God ensured that Daniel, and other prophets and apostles, would give forewarning of the dangers to come in future ages. This assumed the unity of Scripture and that the Old and New Testaments were in agreement. Having inserted that essential premise at the start of the sermon, Knox could develop his points. In a conventional manner, he began with a discussion of the historical context of Daniel's prophecy when the Israelites were in exile in Babylon. The people of God were faced by the might of the great Babylonian empire, which was identified as the first of the four empires of which the prophet had spoken. There was nothing startling about Knox's identification of the Persian, the Greek and the Roman as the three empires that had followed the Babylonian hegemony. At this stage he merely mentioned in passing another of his crucial interpretative assumptions: that the papacy was the direct successor of the Roman empire and that, for the purposes of the prophecy, together they could be treated as a continuous fourth empire.

Before launching into his full-scale attack upon the papacy, Knox wanted to identify the true Church by its 'notes' or essential characteristics. Significantly, he introduced his favourite metaphor of the call of the Shepherd that would always be recognized and followed by the true Church. Rather than providing a rounded description of the true Church, Knox was intent upon depicting the false Church and quickly turned to the notes of the Beast. He shifted biblical texts and presented three alternative names from the New Testament to explain the final 'king' in Daniel. He ran together the 'man of sin' from 2 Thessalonians with the 'Antichrist' and 'that Babylonian harlot' or 'Whore of Babylon' from the Book of Revelation and carefully explained that these were not individuals but generic names for an entire 'empire'.[29] His contention was that this Antichristian empire must be the papacy, and he gave an analysis of the lives of assorted popes through the centuries to prove his point. He selected the papal opposition to a fundamental Protestant doctrine, justification by faith alone, as a prime example of the way the popes had defended doctrines against divine law and persecuted those who adhered to the law of God. Highlighting the contrast between the voice of Christ and the mouth of the Beast that could only utter blasphemous things, he declared that this must refer to the popes with all their titles. His notarial training in canon law furnished him with a ready list of papal titles and of the claims made for the supremacy of papal power and jurisdiction.

Following a final swipe ridiculing the doctrine of Purgatory, Knox ended with a boast to the learned members of his audience that, if called upon to do so, he could back up every assertion with the appropriate chapters and verses. In his *History* he recorded reactions to his first sermon from different sections of the audience. Some noted that this was a full-scale attack upon the papacy and commented that, while others had pruned the tree, Knox had hacked at its roots. The local wiseacres pointed out that Wishart had been burned, so it was clear what Knox's fate would be. Others concentrated upon the debating points and arguments and looked for a reasoned refutation from the senior members of the university before they would accept Knox's analysis. Forsyth of Nydie made a similar point in a different way, remarking that the Catholic Church should not rely upon coercion and persecution, but instead produce convincing arguments to persuade people.[30]

After the experience of preaching, Knox believed he had literally found his voice and he later recalled his first sermons in St Andrews as the time God had 'opened my mouth to his glory'.[31] His writings were peppered with references to the tongue, the mouth and the voice, and the images of the Good Shepherd and of the minister as pastor were presented almost exclusively as the calling of the sheep, feeding them and quenching their thirst.[32] Switching metaphors, his other favourite image, of the blowing of the watchman's trumpet, depended on the mouth creating a louder and more stirring sound. Following his first sermon, Knox realized that he had found his very own sword for the fight: his voice.

What was far more remarkable than the content or effect of Knox's sermon was the public platform he had been given. This encouraged an open discussion of the merits of his case by all sections of the burgh's population. John Winram, the Subprior of St Andrews, had been appointed Vicar-General of the diocese of St Andrews. This interim measure placed him in ecclesiastical control in the burgh while Archbishop Hamilton was attempting to gain formal admission and jurisdiction over his archdiocese. Winram authorized and encouraged the sermon duels and open discussion about religious questions. In many cities in Switzerland and the Holy Roman Empire during the 1520s and 1530s such public religious debate had formed the first stage of their urban reformations. In 1547 Winram seemed to be edging the ecclesiastical capital of Scotland along the path of gradual Church reform, though the ecclesiastical authorities in any other part of Scotland would have condemned as heretical the doctrines advocated by Rough and Knox. The irate Archbishop sent a sharply worded message to Winram that something must be done to counter the spread in St Andrews of heretical and schismatical doctrine.

Winram complied after his own fashion: he continued the debate in a more formal manner by summoning Rough and Knox to St Leonard's College Yards. Knox might have wondered if he were setting off to attend his own heresy trial as he made the five-minute walk from the castle past the site where Wishart had been executed and along the west front of the cathedral under the great covered pends of the priory and turned right into St Leonard's College next door. Nine statements had been taken from his sermons and set out as if they were a legal indictment for heresy. Although Winram gave assurances that this debate would follow the conventions of an academic disputation, there would have been a nervous moment as the two Protestant preachers arrived to face the ranks of Augustinian canons, Franciscan and Dominican friars and university academics. Knox, not Rough, took the lead in the disputation, trying to seize the opportunity to win support, especially from John Winram, one of the leading clerics in Scotland. Knowing that Winram favoured Church reform, in his opening remarks Knox was unusually deferential and diplomatic. However, the Subprior was far too experienced to be manoeuvred into a decisive declaration of support by such tactics.

Winram was polite in his introduction, describing the 'strangeness' of the articles instead of labelling them heretical. Avoiding any mention of the damning criticisms of the Pope in the first two articles, he began the 'reasoning' by probing Knox's views on sacramental ceremonies. This was an issue that not only divided

Catholics and Protestants, but also produced differing opinions among the Protestants, many of whom recognized that the Church could regulate some practices that were non-essential or 'indifferent'. Knox immediately used his favourite metaphor, arguing that the Church was bound to follow the Pastor's voice and could do nothing except in faith. Winram latched on to the link to faith and asserted that ceremonies, such as those in baptism, proceeded from faith and were done in faith. Knox was provoked into making a stark definition: a practice must be commanded by God 'in expressed words' before it could be deemed to be faithful.[33] Winram exposed the vulnerability of this position by asking if everything one did, including asking for a drink, was a sin unless it had God's command. Finding himself on the back foot, Knox gave a tetchy reply, accusing Winram of joking about a serious subject and inserting a sophist's quibble. He struggled back to the point he wanted to make and produced the negative formulation that became one of his trademarks. When deciding how to worship God, he turned to the injunction in Deuteronomy accompanying the Mosaic law: 'what the Lord thy God has commanded thee, that do thou: add nothing to it; diminish nothing from it'.[34]

Winram did not press Knox any further, instead handing the debate over to the distinguished Franciscan Friar Arbuckle, who assertively declared that he would prove ceremonies had been ordained by God. Knox found Arbuckle a much easier target and was able to rattle him by a series of swift verbal associations and the production of an unexpected syllogism to pull the argument back to the commandment in Deuteronomy. The friar was sufficiently off balance to make an elementary mistake by suggesting that the Apostles had received the Holy Spirit only after they had written the Epistles. Not able to let that pass, Winram rebuked Arbuckle, who had to collect himself and continue. In his *History* Knox merely provided a summary of the remainder of the debate, making no mention of any contribution from Rough or other debaters and giving the firm impression he had won the arguments.

Winram neatly avoided declaring a winner of the disputation and instead organized a programme of sermons in the parish church. This echoed once more the urban reformations of the Swiss and Imperial cities where a formal disputation was followed by a preaching campaign. Starting with his own sermon, Winram deputed one of the priory canons, friars or academics to preach every Sunday on a non-controversial topic, probably concentrating upon biblical exposition. Though Knox did not attend these sermons, he was permitted to preach mid-week. He was at liberty to refute points made the previous Sunday, though in the event he felt no need to do so. Such freedom to spread Protestant doctrine was unprecedented, enabling Knox to gather a substantial group of supporters from the burgh as well as from within the castle.

THE SAME PURITY THAT NOW IT IS MINISTERED IN
THE CHURCHES OF SCOTLAND

Remarkably, Winram was willing to permit an even greater freedom by allowing Knox to administer the Lord's Supper in Holy Trinity in a Protestant manner. Since Knox was putting into practice what he had learned from Wishart, the format of the Lord's Supper would have been along generally Reformed lines. Gazing through the rosy-tinted spectacles of hindsight, in the *History* he asserted that it was with 'the same purity that now it is ministered in the churches of Scotland'.[35] Eucharistic theology was one of the doctrines that fractured Protestant unity and generated bitter division, and Knox later became embroiled in controversy over the practices to be followed in the administration of the Lord's Supper. With sacraments accompanying the preaching, he had openly set up a fully functioning Protestant church in St Andrews. This was a long step beyond Master George's preaching campaign and was made possible only because of Winram's support and protection. Despite Winram's refusal to commit himself to such an open and unequivocal break with the Catholic Church at this stage, Knox developed an enduring trust and respect for the Subprior. When Winram did make his final break with the Catholic cause in 1559, he was welcomed. Uncharacteristically, Knox never made a critical allusion to Winram's former activities as a major figure within the pre-Reformation Church.

The establishment of this rival church in St Andrews enraged Winram's fellow clerics, who demanded that Regent Arran and the Privy Council put a stop to it before the contagion of heresy spread throughout the kingdom. However, French rather than Scottish action ended this experiment in burgh reformation. As part of the negotiations between the two sides, a papal dispensation had been procured to cover the murder of Cardinal Beaton. Those holding the castle were not satisfied with the dispensation's wording and decided to continue the fight because they hoped the English would send reinforcements. The castle faced an outbreak of plague, and Knox had used this to admonish its residents that they would be punished by God. He warned them not to place their trust in the thick walls of the castle or in the English and foretold that they would become captives and be taken into exile.[36] A French fleet sent secretly by King Henry II sailed into view off St Andrews in July 1547. It was led by one of the best commanders from the Italian wars, Leon Strozzi. His first attempt to bombard the castle from the sea was not a success, and the defenders inflicted more damage on the galleys than they received. The ships withdrew to the Tay estuary to effect repairs and ponder tactics. With the Regent bringing an army to enforce a tight siege, the main assault began. This time fourteen large cannon were landed and hauled on to the towers of the cathedral and of St Salvator's chapel to overlook the castle from both sides. The bombardment started at 4 a.m. and after six hours of pounding at relatively close range the eastern end of the castle was badly damaged. Knowing that the breached walls could not be held, and in the hope of better terms, the castle surrendered to Strozzi in preference to the Scottish Regent. On 7 August the prisoners were shipped to France along with booty from the castle. Six weeks too late for those in the castle, an English army invaded Scotland and won the battle of Pinkie Cleugh, near Musselburgh. Within Scotland, the religious changes that had occurred in St Andrews were treated as an aberration, not to be repeated and best forgotten. The new chorus to a popular song summed up the view that the clerical hierarchy should be satisfied with their victory: 'Preasts content you now; Preasts content you now; For Normond and his company has filled the galleys fow [full].'[37]

After Knox's death, John Davidson wrote in his commemorative poem that Knox loved St Andrews above all the rest because in that burgh he had first routed Antichrist and preached that only Christ could save.[38] When taken into captivity in 1547, Knox looked back at his life and saw it leading towards that brief ministry in the castle and the burgh. He identified the providential hand of God at work and the voice of the Good Shepherd heard in the tones of George Wishart and in the three-fold call to the ministry. He believed he had found his true identity as a preacher and prophet, and for the rest of his life he moulded himself into those roles.

CHAPTER FIVE

The realm of England

When the prisoners from the castle sailed from St Andrews in 1547 they must have wondered if they would ever see their native land again. Knox did not return to live in Scotland until 1559 and during the intervening years he was transformed by the experience of multiple exiles. Having watched the fate of Master George, he assumed that the captivity and possible death he was facing were part of the suffering that followed the messengers of God in particular and were the general fate of all members of the true Church. An image became embedded in his mind of the Church as the faithful few who were rejected by the world but would be protected by God and would triumph in the end. Though he survived nineteen months on the French galleys, the experience had a serious impact upon his health and for the remainder of his life he was troubled with chronic conditions such as digestive problems (the 'gravel') and severe headaches, and there were occasions when he was unable to write.[1] The unifying experience of male camaraderie and shared suffering bolstered his belief that a common faith brought deep bonds of loyalty, parallel to the 'kyndnes' so familiar within Scottish society. Time on the galleys reinforced the division taught by Wishart of the world into 'us' and 'them', and Knox never lost this mental reflex of categorizing everything into polar opposites.

On his release from the galleys Knox was fortunate to find refuge in England, ruled then by the Protestant regime of King Edward VI. He was greatly changed by the five years he spent in the Tudor state, being able for the first time to live the Protestant dream in a country that had officially adopted Reformation doctrines. Permitted to follow his vocation as a preacher, he worked within the Church of England. Having become involved with the Edwardian regime, he underwent an abrasive apprenticeship in the realities of political and ecclesiastical power. Far more welcome to him, he discovered his future bride, a secure environment in the midst of the 'little flock' of radical

Edwardian Protestants and inclusion within the strong spiritual kindred of Reformed Protestants. By the time he left England for a second exile he had become deeply attached to his new home and, alongside his Scottish identity, he regarded himself as an Englishman by adoption.[2] In the new year of 1554 with surprise and a touch of wonder, he described his feelings for the land he had just fled: 'somtyme I have thought that impossible it had bene, so to have removed my affection from the Realme of Scotland, that eny Realme or Nation coulde have bene equall deare unto me. But I take to recorde in my conscience, that the troubles present (and appearing to be) in the Realme of England, are double more dolorous unto my hert, then ever were the troubles of Scotland.'[3] During the decade of the 1550s, Knox remained within this ambit of Edwardian Protestantism, continuing to fight its battles and thinking within its conceptual framework.[4] Wherever he was in later life, he retained this awareness of Englishness and assumed the right of the insider to criticize his second home. Until he died he felt he always had one foot in England.

KNOX THE *FORSARE*

In August 1547 Knox and the other Scots captives faced an eventful voyage down the North Sea coast that included running aground on sandbanks before reaching France at the mouth of the Seine and proceeding upriver to Rouen. The prisoners had arrived in France hoping they would be released, and in his *History* Knox suggested there had been a deliberate deception. He also wrote of a clerical conspiracy, with the Pope and the Archbishop of St Andrews urging the French King to keep his prisoners locked up for a long time. In fact, the commoners among the Scots were condemned to the galleys, while the nobles were imprisoned within French castles.

Knox started his sentence as a *forsare* or galley slave rowing his ship the *Nostre Dame* round the coast to Nantes in Brittany, where they wintered on the River Loire.[5] The extremely hard forced labour ensured that a sentence to the galleys was regarded as one step above execution. When on board, the *forsares* were chained by leg irons to their rowing bench and normally split into three different shifts of fifty men and teams of four or six to man each of the oars, which measured up to fifty feet in length. In port, the prisoners were occupied with ship repairs and similar tasks and would sometimes be used as labour ashore. Convicted criminals and other prisoners of war made up the galley's 150 rowers, supervised by a hierarchy of officers who ranged from the lowly *sous-comites*, through the *comites* and up to the *argousan* or lieutenant of the galley. Free sailors crewed the ship and the commander would have been either a French nobleman or one of the mercenary experts such as

Strozzi. Thanks to royal regulations, the *forsares* were given a good allowance of clothing and they wore the heavy brown woollen over-garment sailors used and were issued with a vest, two shirts and two pairs of canvas breeches. As a device to hinder escape they were given shoes only to go ashore and had to return them when they came back on board. Though their diet was basic and not substantial enough for the amount of heavy labour they did at sea, they were allowed as much ship's biscuit and water as the sailors, had a vegetable broth three times a week, and when working ashore they received a wine ration.[6]

Conditions on board were harsh, and much depended upon the regime run by the particular *comite* and his deputies. However, as Knox later remarked, none of the Scots perished during their time rowing the French galleys and only one Scots prisoner died, and that was of natural causes. In his own writings Knox deliberately avoided giving details of his nineteen months as a *forsare*. In his pastoral correspondence he did let slip the odd mention of his galley days, but usually with only a phrase or two.[7] It was often difficult to tell whether he was more concerned with his physical pains or his mental suffering, since he tended to conflate them.[8] At the close of the 1550s Knox might have been the source for John Aylmer's description of galley life. Discussing the worst things that might befall the English, Aylmer wrote: 'Thy son's inheritance shall be chains in the galley, wherewith he shall be fettered, a whip upon his bare skin if he row not to the death, and an horse loaf and water for his daily diet.'[9] In his own *History* Knox was defensive, seeking to justify the inclusion of a discussion of those who had held St Andrews Castle by insisting that their story illustrated the theological point that God preserved his own flock when they were afflicted and, in the eyes of the world, had been defeated.

Knox was careful to present an account that focused upon keeping the faith while suffering both physical hardship and mental anguish. His retelling of how the Scots prisoners had refused to attend Mass was central to his theme about preserving their religious integrity. Both in the castles and in the galleys the Scots found ways of demonstrating their lack of respect for Catholic worship and pious practices. On a Saturday evening in the galleys during the singing of the *Salve Regina*, the anthem to the Blessed Virgin Mary, the Scots donned their caps instead of respectfully removing them and then pulled the caps over their ears to block the sound. This ostentatious refusal to participate was taken a stage further when a beautifully painted image of the Virgin was brought round the decks so that each member of the crew might kiss it. A Scot, probably Knox himself, told the ship's officer he did not want to handle the image because to him 'such an idol is accursed'. After the painting had been thrust into his face and forcibly placed in his hands, 'advisedly looking about, he cast it into the river and said, "Let our Lady now save herself: she is light enough; let her learn to swim".[10] These acts of defiance convinced the galley officers it was not worth trying to enforce Catholic observance among the Scots. A later and more unlikely story told by John Davidson, who had listened to Knox in his final years, suggested that Scottish prelates had attempted to bribe the French to throw Knox overboard.[11]

Having been called to minister in St Andrews, Knox assumed that his pastoral role should continue among his fellow prisoners. He took it upon himself to comfort those who were afraid or worried about how long their incarceration would last. He encouraged them with his insistence that God would rescue them when they least expected it and foretold that not all would be released at the same time. The Scots nobles who were held ashore also looked to Knox for moral advice about whether they might attempt escape. The experienced Sir James Kirkcaldy of Grange had told his son William and the others planning an escape that they would be putting the remaining prisoners at risk of punishment or worse confinement. Rather unfairly, Knox dismissed this advice as worrying about one's own welfare, and encouraged the escape plan with the important proviso that it should be done without killing any of the guards. When their warders were celebrating the feast of Epiphany, four Scots overpowered their drunken guards and made their escape, though it is not known if the rest of the prisoners suffered as a consequence.

In the spring of 1548 a very large French fleet was assembled, including Knox's galley, and set sail for Scotland. As soon as they reached the open sea, the ships hoisted the Scottish flag and sailed up the North Sea to the Scottish east coast – a familiar sight for Knox and his fellow Scots. In May in the Firth of Forth above the Bass Rock the fleet lost one of its major ships, the *Cardinal*, not far from Knox's former haunts of Longniddry and Aberlady on the south bank. On a fine, calm day and due to the crew's negligence, 'the fairest ship in France' ran aground on a bank between Inchcolm and Cramond. Having watched the sorry spectacle, Knox made one of the wordplays he relished, 'Scotland can bear no Cardinals.' His joke would have circulated around the Scots prisoners and amused those who had been involved in the assassination of Cardinal Beaton.[12]

Later that summer on the fleet's second trip to Scotland, Knox became seriously ill, and all thought he was dying. His galley lay between Dundee and St Andrews, and his friend James Balfour raised him so that he could look at the shoreline and asked him if he recognized where he was. Seeing the distinctive outline of the church towers of the cathedral, St Salvator's and Holy Trinity and the long sands to their west, Knox replied confidently, 'Yes: I know it well; for I see the steeple of that place, where God first in public opened my mouth to his glory, and I am fully persuaded, how weak that ever I now appear, that I shall not depart this life till that my tongue shall glorify his godly name in the same place.'[13] Balfour later retold the story long before Knox set foot back in his native land. As they served their sentence on the same galley, Knox and Balfour, the son of Sir Michael Balfour of Montquhanie in Fife, had become firm friends and Knox had helped raise Balfour's flagging spirits. The two men shared an interest and expertise in canon law and Balfour, when he was released and returned to Scotland, became Official of Lothian, the main ecclesiastical court officer of that region. If things had been different, this was precisely the career path that Knox as a notary might have expected to follow. The later bitter rejection of Balfour might have been linked to Knox's strident repudiation of the path he had not taken. While on the galleys, the two men were in harmony over their adherence to evangelical views and Knox regarded Balfour as 'the chief and principal Protestant' in Scotland. Many years later after Balfour had fallen out with Knox he asserted that he had been brought up to believe a Lutheran interpretation of the eucharist. This statement in particular roused Knox's ire and provoked the response that in 1547 Balfour had participated without a quibble in the Reformed communion held in St Andrews.[14] Probably because he was still recuperating from illness, Knox returned in 1548 with the other part of the fleet to winter quarters in France, while Balfour remained on a galley on patrol in Scotland. By the time he penned his *History* Knox could hardly write Balfour's name without adding a venomous aside; the depth of this antagonism was a measure of how close he had been to Balfour on the galley benches. Knox treated this breach of relations as a terrible personal betrayal and never forgave Balfour, whose behaviour during the later civil wars was always assumed to be inconstant and treacherous and whose name became permanently blackened.

All through his life Knox relied heavily upon his close friends and colleagues and those he regarded as his religious kindred. Their support was an essential part of his own strength, and he placed an extremely high premium upon loyalty within such relationships. In his final years another very close friend from his days in St Andrews Castle and in French custody was transformed into an enemy. William Kirkcaldy of Grange had been a firm supporter of all of Knox's policies until after Regent Moray's assassination in 1570 when they followed different parties in the civil wars. When he found his former friend on the opposite side, Knox's affection turned to hatred and no forgiveness remained in his heart. Even during this early stage in the galleys, Knox conflated the personal loyalty of friendship forged out of the sharing of hardship with the absolute loyalty to God's cause and religious commitment. At the level of personal relationships, he found it hard to appreciate that there might be competing loyalties and obligations of honour that could cut across each other. For Knox life was simple: those not for him must be against him.

During the winter of 1548 when his galley was tied up, Knox occupied his time in literary pursuits. Since his arrival at St Andrews Castle, he had admired Henry Balnaves, the cultured, evangelical diplomat. Balnaves was known to be a well-educated heretic, so the French authorities had sent other learned men to argue with him in his prison in Rouen. As a consequence of these continual debates, he had written a treatise on the Protestant doctrine of justification by faith alone. This manuscript was sent to Knox, who found it personally helpful. Thinking it would encourage and strengthen the faith of those left behind in St Andrews, he summarized Balnaves' treatise and attached his own epistle to his congregation.[15] His acceptance of this task and the automatic assumption that his ministry had continued even after the castle's fall demonstrated that Knox had already slipped completely into his vocation of preacher and prophet. In his brief accompanying letter, he adopted some of the style of the Pauline Epistles and a little self-consciously spoke of himself as also 'bound in chains' like St Paul. Buoyed up by the conviction that he would preach again in St Andrews, he offered encouragement and the confidence that God would deliver his persecuted people, giving Old Testament examples of how those sent into exile and suffering had ultimately triumphed.

RUDE BOLDNESS TO YOUR FACES

Knox's own release from the galleys came earlier than expected. The English government had made diplomatic representations to the French about their former allies from the castle of St Andrews, and Knox was freed in the spring of 1549. There must have been a sense of the miraculous when he landed on his feet and found he was far luckier than many other religious refugees in England. The Duke of Somerset's regime had given him £5 sterling as a bonus and a job that demanded he exercise his vocation as a preacher. Knox was sent to the garrison at Berwick-on-Tweed to be an army chaplain, placing him as close to Scotland as it was possible to be. While remaining safe on the English side of the border he could reconnect with the pro-English evangelical groups of allies or 'assured Scots', especially among his East Lothian friends. When he arrived in April, Berwick was the main forward base for the English war effort during the final phase of the wars between Scotland, France and England. This was the endgame of the struggle to secure the marriage and kingdom of Mary, Queen of Scots, a conflict later nicknamed the 'Rough Wooings'.[16] About a third of Berwick's population of around 3,500 were military personnel comprising English soldiers, foreign mercenaries and workers on the fortifications, with a high turnover as troops were deployed in the war zones in Scotland. This transient and diverse population with approximately four times as many men as women had turned Berwick into a rough frontier town with frequent quarrels.

Being known to have come from the galleys would have given the new chaplain credibility among the soldiers, and Knox was proud that he was able to hammer out settlements for the feuds and blood-letting that flared up in the town. The imposition of this kind of discipline by a stern preacher had been one reason for the English Privy Council sending him north. He later boasted to Mary, Queen of Scots, that he had produced a 'great quietness' during the time he had remained in Berwick.[17] He had learned how admonition in his sermons could be employed as a means of setting and maintaining moral standards. This was a different approach from enforcing morality through the formal legal system of canon law and the medieval courts spiritual. The soldiers appreciated his plain speaking, the colourful denunciations and 'ruide boldness ... unto your faces', as he expressed it. He believed he had been accepted as a simple man with no airs and graces – almost one of the boys.[18] He thrived in this military world whose society was similar to the male camaraderie and harsh life he had experienced on the galleys. A couple of years later he was at pains to explain to his fellows in Berwick that the bright lights of London had not turned his head or altered his 'simplicity'.[19]

Knox's fierce admonitory style of prophetic preaching chimed with, and offered an explanation for, the series of military disasters the English army faced between 1549 and 1550. He would have been particularly interested in what was happening to the English garrison stationed in his home burgh of Haddington. With the English failing to control the hinterland, especially the vital corridor from Haddington to the Firth of Forth, the garrison's location had proved a serious tactical mistake. The English troops stationed there could be resupplied only by armed convoy from Berwick. During the major French military effort in Scotland undertaken by King Henry II, the burgh had been placed under siege. In England, the rebellions of the summer of 1549 diverted troops intended for Scotland, and in September the English were finally forced to withdraw. They retreated from Haddington, spoiling and burning as they went and thereby fulfilling Wishart's prophecy of doom for the burgh. A succession of military reverses and the fall of Protector Somerset brought a major reorientation in English military policy. Somerset's successor, the Duke of Northumberland, pragmatically decided to end the war in Scotland and France as tidily as possible, and negotiations eventually produced the Treaty of Boulogne in March 1550. As they watched the triumph of their traditional enemies, the French and Scots, the Berwick garrison would have felt keenly their own military humiliation. The peace underscored Knox's exile status and emphasized that his immediate future lay within England and the Edwardian Church.

His ministry in Berwick was probably the first time Knox realized that his preaching and pastoral skills could alter behaviour as well as change beliefs. The whirlwind of his St Andrews experience and the unusual circumstances of the galleys had not provided him with the opportunity he had in Berwick to work for a couple of years in the same place. The preacher had his ups and downs, and at one point he had been reluctant to return to Berwick because of the opposition he had encountered there.[20] However, once he had left the garrison town he made strenuous efforts to keep in touch with his old congregation, sending at least three epistles to Berwick between 1552 and 1558. Although his first proper pastoral charge, Berwick was no ordinary English parish or congregation. In addition to the military establishment, the town was the temporary home for a community of Scots. Some were allies who had been fighting alongside the English and could not return to Scotland because they had been forfeited for treason. Others were the motley collection of immigrants, legal and illegal, found across the border in England at all periods of the sixteenth century. Over time Knox's reputation as a preacher attracted others, and a 'family' of Scots, as the Duke of Northumberland wryly named them, gathered around him, first at Berwick and later at Newcastle.[21] The English authorities were prepared to treat this odd congregation at Berwick in a similar way to the congregations of religious exiles in London and the south of England known as Strangers' Churches. Those churches were permitted to use their own language and liturgy and remained outside the normal process of episcopal jurisdiction. In a similar way, Knox was allowed far more freedom, especially in liturgical matters, than he would have found in any other parish in the Church of England. Since this special status was not explicitly stated, in his first few years Knox might not have realized just how exceptional it was. Whether aware or not, he went his own way regardless.

At Whitsun 1549, shortly after Knox's arrival in Berwick, the first Book of Common Prayer came into use as the mandatory liturgy for the Church of England. However, when he administered the Lord's Supper Knox felt at liberty to employ a different service. From the manuscript fragment that has survived, it was clear that he wrote his own prayers for at least part of the communion service.[22] Even more significant for the future, his congregation sat around a table to receive the bread and the wine. He justified these arrangements by preaching that they followed the practice of Christ and the Apostles during the Last Supper. He stressed that the Lord's Supper had no resemblance to the former service of the Mass and he derided the doctrine of transubstantiation. These attacks upon the real presence of the body and blood of

Christ in the eucharist and Knox's outspoken views would have horrified Cuthbert Tunstal, the traditionalist Bishop of Durham. Berwick lay within his diocese and was, in theory, within his jurisdiction. Knox added insult to injury when he attacked a highly conservative exposition of eucharistic theology given by one of Tunstal's senior clerics.

On 4 April 1550 Knox appeared in Newcastle before the Council of the North, the main government body in that region, which on this occasion included Bishop Tunstal and his senior diocesan clergy. There he presented a case in support of the proposition that the Mass was idolatry.[23] The arguments were couched in a conventional scholastic set of syllogisms with a major premise that was proved and a minor one that followed logically from that proof. Although the format was academic, the tone was highly polemical and was designed to appeal to a wider audience. Knox deliberately used the everyday term 'Mass' rather than discussing the doctrinal explanations, such as transubstantiation, the changing of the 'substance' of the bread and wine into Christ's body and blood, for what was happening during the eucharist.

With only Knox's side of the argument subsequently published by him, it is hard to piece together precisely what happened that day in Newcastle. In a national context the Council of the North event was of minor importance compared to the major debates that had already taken place over eucharistic theology, such as the 1549 disputation at Oxford University, Archbishop Cranmer's writings or John Hooper's sermons. Knox added vehement passion, but little else, to the theological arguments over the sacrament. He did air them in the north-east where, thanks to Tunstal's strong traditional line, little had penetrated from the debates raging in the south of England. Since the national political and religious tide was clearly flowing in the direction Knox had already travelled, the Council of the North took no action against him and Tunstal was probably warned to let him be. Knox, with his talent for identifying an enemy, put Tunstal down in the equivalent of his 'little book'.

It was probably at a later date that according to his own account Knox called the bishop a murderer and a thief to his face.[24] Such an attack might have been part of the concerted campaign waged by the Duke of Northumberland against Tunstal that eventually saw him deprived of his bishopric and imprisoned in the Tower of London. Possibly remembering his encounters with Knox, in prison Tunstal wrote a robust defence in Latin of the real presence of the body and blood of Christ in the eucharist.[25] The coming of peace on the Anglo-Scottish border allowed the military establishment and the government of the north, now including Knox, to return to its main base at Newcastle. Though continuing to visit Berwick, from 1551 Knox was preaching and living in Newcastle. The main church of St Nicholas (now Newcastle Cathedral) had its own clergy, though when he was there Knox occupied the pulpit. Despite being unwell around Christmas 1551, he complained that he was still preaching every day. Around this time he had been added to the list of King Edward VI's 'chaplains ordinary' and would have received the welcome and generous stipend of £40 per annum.[26]

THE FAMILY OF SCOTS

With a long tradition of trading links between the port and Scotland, there was a substantial group of Scots in Newcastle. As was noted later, some of his compatriots, a 'family of Scots', attached themselves to Knox.[27] Other Scots came across the border in order to hear him, swelling this 'family' around the preacher. The Anglo-Scottish peace made it easier for his blood relatives to be in open touch with him. William, his elder brother, came to visit as part of his expansion of trading links within England.[28] The mercantile grapevine would have allowed friends in St Andrews to keep in touch with Knox and his movements. In 1551–2 he began his long friendship with his fellow Scot John Willock, who was serving as a domestic chaplain to Henry Grey, Marquess of Dorset. Marquess and chaplain arrived in the Borders in spring 1551 and Willock preached in the region for the following twelve months. When he was passing through London on his way back to Scotland in October 1552 Lord James Stewart, the young Commendator Prior of St Andrews who was the illegitimate half-brother of Mary, Queen of Scots, held a meeting with Knox (see Plate 8). This was what Knox called his 'first acquaintance' with Lord James and was possibly at the instigation of John Winram, Lord James' mentor. A Roman Catholic writer later made the far-fetched claim that at this meeting the two men planned the entire Scottish Reformation. Though they would have discussed the religious position in Scotland, Lord James would have employed carefully guarded terms.[29] These connections among a broad spectrum of Anglophile Scots were to play an important role in Knox's future life.

With his confidence growing, Knox was able to exploit the Newcastle pulpit to deliver his admonitory sermons. Almost inevitably, his blunt words provoked opposition, such as his direct denunciation on All Saints' Day 1551 of the second arrest of the Duke of Somerset a fortnight earlier. In his Christmas Day sermon of 1552, he was even more explicit when he warned about 'closet' Catholics in high places and the threat posed by the possible accession of the openly Catholic Princess Mary. Knox had attached his admonition to the simile from Isaiah 5 about God's vineyard that produced only wild grapes, a warning about the lack of progress in Edwardian reform. Having experienced the consequences of the death of James V of Scotland a decade earlier, Knox had seen a ruling king die unexpectedly and be succeeded by a queen. This had automatically raised the prospect of the kingdom being ruled by her future husband, most probably a foreign prince. With the ink scarcely dry on the treaties settling the wars over the future marriage of Mary, Queen of Scots, Knox assumed that such a sequence was well understood in England, especially in the English Borders. Knox did not know or did not care how politically sensitive such matters were within England. Thanks to their experience of King Henry VIII's draconian laws and the taboo subjects of royal marriages and succession to the throne, the first reaction of Knox's hearers was that such observations were treason. Lord Wharton, Warden of the Eastern Marches, and Sir Robert Brandling, Mayor of Newcastle, produced a list of the offending passages and a possible case to answer and sent them to London.[30] In this instance Knox was fortunate that the Duke of Northumberland chose to rebuke his critics for harassing a preacher in the King's favour.

After the fall from power of Somerset, the King's uncle, in 1549 John Dudley had become the leading figure within the Edwardian regime and taken the title of Duke of Northumberland. Knox, and those who looked to Henry Bullinger and the Zurich Reformation as a model, were pleased when it became obvious that the pace of religious change was quickening. With Northumberland acting as their protector and friend and the King's personal Protestantism asserting itself, a more radical religious programme seemed to be gaining ground at the royal court. The Duke was a consummate politician, always looking for people he might manipulate or who might help him achieve his goals. When visiting the north, he had been impressed by Knox's preaching and immediately added him to the list of radical clerics who might prove useful. Being on the Borders far from London and in a military establishment, Knox enjoyed great freedom and was able to continue his ministry without becoming integrated into the Church of England. He was supported against his diocesan Bishop because it happened to suit the Edwardian regime to undermine Tunstal, and this gave Knox a distorted understanding of how the Church of England functioned. His experiences on the margin of the system ill prepared him for the power struggles at the centre of political and ecclesiastical authority.

THIS IS THE FIRST LETTER THAT EVER I SENT YOU

Knox's public role and integration into the more radical wing of the Edwardian Church were eye-catching, but the transformation of his private life was of greater importance to him. Though their courtship was far from straightforward, at the end of 1552 he was betrothed to Marjorie Bowes, a commitment which both of them believed was as binding as the subsequent marriage.

Although Marjorie's mother, Elizabeth Bowes, was very strongly in favour of the match and made strenuous efforts to ensure that it happened, her father was considerably less impressed with his daughter's suitor. Richard Bowes had risen in the world thanks to his military skills and was Captain of Norham Castle, a responsible post in border defence.[31] He was concerned about Marjorie, his fifth daughter who had been named after his mother. He regarded Knox as a poor choice of future husband: it was bad enough that his daughter wanted to marry a non-noble Scot recently released from the French galleys; what made it much worse was that this middle-aged man was an impoverished former priest with uncertain prospects. Though clerical marriage had been legalized by the English Parliament in 1548, a married cleric would still raise eyebrows in the conservative north. Many would continue to regard such a union with distaste, and names such as 'priest's whore' and worse were flung at this first generation of ministers' wives. Since clerical celibacy was a major issue within the polemical battles raging in print, some Protestant clerics turned their marriages into a declaration of anti-Catholic views rather than merely choosing a partner. However, Marjorie and Knox were deeply attached and, within the different understandings of the sixteenth century, theirs was a love match.

Knox's prospects as a future son-in-law appeared brighter to Richard Bowes by the end of 1552. Knox had become a royal chaplain and enjoyed the direct patronage of the Duke of Northumberland; he had even been considered for a bishopric. Sir Robert Bowes, Richard's elder brother and head of this Streatlam branch of the family, was a rising star among Northumberland's clients, having recently received his knighthood for his military exploits and been promoted to Master of the Rolls in the Edwardian administration. Such a conjunction of family fortunes accompanied by the heavy lobbying of Marjorie and her mother was probably enough to persuade Richard to agree to a pre-nuptial contract. At his betrothal ceremony Knox made a faithful promise before witnesses of future marriage and thereafter addressed Marjorie as his spouse and Elizabeth as his mother. He blithely assumed he had joined the Bowes family as a marital kinsman and was entitled to all the 'kindness' that that relationship would bring.

No bundle of love letters between Marjorie and John has survived and probably none existed because it was not common in the sixteenth century to conduct a courtship by letter. Even when a courting couple were apart, it was more likely that oral messages and physical tokens would be sent with the messengers who carried letters between households, and they would be expected to add all the personal greetings and details and fill any gaps not covered by the written text of the letters. A false impression about Knox's correspondence has been given by the quantity of surviving correspondence between Marjorie's mother and Knox. It was sometimes carried by George, Marjorie's brother, or by family friends, such as Roger Widdrington or Harie Wyclif and they would have been able to provide verbal updates. Marjorie was occasionally mentioned in Knox's letters to her mother because she was part of the circle who were studying the Bible together and discussing their spiritual lives, but that was not the sum of the couple's correspondence. Marjorie was writing her own letters to Knox but they have not survived because his incoming correspondence has been lost. One return letter addressed to her alone has been preserved from the time Knox was away from the north-east of England and probably in London. When Knox was about to sign it he added hastily, though not very gallantly, 'I think this is the first letter that ever I sent you.'[32]

In this particular exchange Majorie had been asking for advice, which explains why that letter was kept among the pastoral correspondence to her mother. She wanted to know, when friends came to visit her at home, how she should behave with those who remained convinced Roman Catholics, especially clergymen. In particular she wanted clarification on 2 John 1:10–11 and whether if she did extend the common courtesy of wishing Catholics 'Godspeed' she became a 'partaker of evil deeds'. Knox's reply got in a tangle, as often happened when he gave specific guidelines for a practical situation. On the one hand, he advocated an uncompromising general principle about not associating with idolaters. On the other, he fudged providing a simple guide for what was or was not religiously acceptable when mixing within the conservative society of the north-east of England. In the second part of his letter he seemed relieved to move on to the firmer ground of the spiritual doubts of Majorie's mother.[33]

Beloved Mother

From the sixteenth century down to the present, the letters from John Knox to Elizabeth Bowes have provided endless fascination and produced much speculation about the nature of their relationship.[34] With only one side of the correspondence and an incomplete run surviving, reading the letters is like listening to half a phone conversation and guessing the questions for which partial answers were given. Since the letters dealt with personal spiritual matters, it has been assumed they were private, but in this period while letters might be secret, they were rarely 'private' in the modern sense. This particular correspondence was preserved precisely because of its pastoral content and to act as a model for those suffering spiritual temptations. The letters seemed to have formed part of a composite collection gathered by Elizabeth Bowes consisting of correspondence, manuscripts and printed tracts of advice that Knox had written in the years 1552–4 when the two people were at a considerable distance apart.

At the back of his mind as he wrote to Elizabeth, Knox knew that his audience included other members of the 'faithful' and not simply the addressee. He self-consciously borrowed features from New Testament Epistles and fitted his writing into a tradition of semi-public letters of spiritual direction composed by holy men and confessors since the time of the Early Church. The homiletical style that often entered Knox's letters formed part of his attempt to generalize his advice. He also sought to prevent Elizabeth treating him as a Protestant embodiment of a private confessor. From a Protestant perspective the pastoral role had shifted because auricular confession was no longer made to a priest but instead to 'the Church'. In practice this tended to mean a conventicle-style gathering of 'two or three' faithful, an embryonic Church where the spiritual journey was treated as part of the shared experience of fellow members of the body of Christ. Knox assumed that one aspect of his duties as a pastor was to utilize such a mighty struggle against Satan as a model for others of how the true Christian could be tempted and suffer. When in London he had no hesitation handing round a newly arrived letter from Elizabeth to three other women who had been discussing their spiritual problems with him. Everyone wept at her struggles and one woman commented on how helpful it might be to talk directly to Elizabeth. Writing his reply to Elizabeth, Knox relayed all these details and turned them into an important point of comfort. From the beginning of their correspondence, he planned to incorporate his advice to her within a broader pastoral exposition, and in 1552 he started his commentary on Psalm 6 that was finished and published in 1554 and dedicated to 'his belovit Mother'.[35]

When she met Knox, Elizabeth had only recently been converted to Protestant beliefs and she had probably been a deeply devout Catholic for much of her life. She had a particular reverence for the Mass with its strong sensory appeal, which continued to draw her after she became a Protestant. Elizabeth would have meditated upon the Passion and the Holy Blood, and in his advice Knox employed these motifs, though adding a firmly Protestant gloss. Given her social status and her heightened religious sensibilities, in her Catholic days Elizabeth had probably sought assistance with her spiritual dilemmas from a personal confessor. Old habits died hard and although the entire discourse with Knox was about Protestant understandings of salvation and sin, she retained an expectation that he was on hand to give advice when she needed it. Knox frequently dropped heavy hints in his letters that he did have a number of more important calls upon his time.[36]

Though he had answered moral and religious queries for his fellow prisoners in France, Knox was still learning how to give pastoral advice and he had little experience of counselling women. He had to learn how to tread the difficult line of what was socially acceptable as well as what was religiously helpful in his dealings with women. With Elizabeth Bowes he fell into some of the perennial traps of pastoral counselling by constantly introducing his own experience as a comparison, using images and assurance that helped him rather than her and not making clear what was, and what was not, his role. Any close relationship between a Protestant preacher and an enthusiastic female convert generated comment and aroused curiosity in Edwardian England, an effect magnified within religiously conservative areas like the north-east. Knox acknowledged that his relationship with Mrs Bowes had produced gossip and in 1554 chided himself for not thinking solely of her pastoral needs rather than paying attention to their public reputation.[37] The rumours and innuendo did not disappear, and after her death Knox decided to publish one of the letters he had written to her. In the epistle, 'To the Faithfull Reader', Knox explicitly declared that the cause of his familiarity with Elizabeth Bowes 'was nether fleshe nor bloode, but a troubled conscience upon hir part'.[38] In one of the explanatory side notes he added to the letter, he summarized: 'Maistres Elizabeth Bowes, tempted still yet feghting'. He emphasized that her temptations were entirely in 'the spirit' and had nothing to do with physical matters, adding the remarkable comment that he had known no one else in Scotland, England, France or Germany who had faced such severe temptations. From the perspective of 1572, Knox could distil the central doubt she faced: 'that remission of sinnes in Christ Jesus apperteyned nothing unto her, be reason of her former idolatrie and other iniquities'. Such a lack of assurance had allowed Satan to 'buffet' her.[39]

Knox indicated that being her spiritual adviser was 'not without some croce [cross]'. He was seldom able to put her troubles out of his mind or achieve mental calm. Dealing with Mrs Bowes had also taken considerable time and effort and, employing an expressive Scots word, he described the nuisance or 'fasherie' caused by all the things he needed to do to answer her queries or attend her in person.[40] But he did acknowledge how much he had gained from the relationship. Elizabeth had become a mother to his family and himself and he had benefited greatly from her assistance. He also noted that the company of Mrs Bowes had been 'comfortable' to him and she had brought spiritual comfort and assurance during his own spiritual struggles. While taking great pains to search the Scriptures for texts to assist her, he had found answers to some of his own doubts. Knox relied heavily throughout his ministry upon the spiritual comfort given by 'belovit sisters' and he could not have done his job without their substantial religious and material support.

With unwitting condescension, Knox had told Elizabeth several times that he had been surprised to hear she was having as difficult a spiritual battle as he was fighting. On one occasion he had been sufficiently startled at hearing her speak of matters that so closely mirrored his own questionings that he leaped back and was lost for words. Mrs Bowes assumed she had shocked him by the depth of her own sin and had been upset that he appeared unable to offer any pastoral assistance. This was the 'Alnwick cupboard' incident that was later transformed into a veiled reference to some form of sexual advance.[41] As many biographers have pointed out, this is an unlikely reading of the situation and of the meaning of the text itself: 'standing at the copbourd in Anwik: in verie deid I thought na creature had bene temptit as I wes'.[42] There was nothing private or closet-like about a sixteenth-century cupboard. It was the dresser used to display the best tableware, the silver and pewter cups and plates a moderately prosperous household wanted their visitors to admire. Since the cupboard was for show, it would be located in a highly visible and public space. The relationship between Elizabeth Bowes and Knox was complex and many layered, and the gender difference undoubtedly influenced the chemistry between them. It produced a range of subtle interplays, but probably not a relationship that was 'sexual in the normal sense'.[43] Intimate and highly charged emotional relationships between women and men have had a long history within Christian tradition from apostolic times to the present. One of Knox's contemporaries, St Ignatius Loyola, had a similar close relationship with a female supporter.[44]

Elizabeth's doubts and struggles were not kept strictly private as a matter between her 'confessor' and herself. In addition to Knox sharing them with other 'faithful' whenever he deemed it appropriate, Elizabeth talked to sympathetic members of her family, bringing Marjorie and her sons, George and Robert, into her confidence. Anne Bowes, Robert's wife from another branch of the same family, was probably the 'daughter Bowes' who visited Knox in Newcastle with her own, as well as her mother-in-law's, religious dilemmas.[45] The family friend, Harie Wyclif, was sufficiently close for Elizabeth to pour out her distress over her interpretation of Knox's behaviour at Alnwick, and his intervention brought forth Knox's reassuring letter with its enigmatic phrase. There were others, though their identities are not known, who formed the inner core of the Berwick congregation and Knox's coterie in Newcastle. This was the 'company of the faithful' that gave Elizabeth Bowes some rest from her doubts. Acknowledging that spiritual friends were a lifeline to Mrs Bowes, Knox might have added that he was equally dependent upon their support. From his time in Berwick onwards, he actively sought out these close-knit groups and struggled with doubt and depression when deprived of their emotional warmth and spiritual comfort.[46]

The time Knox spent in the north-east of England marked an important and positive stage in his personal development. His vocation as a preacher, pastor and prophet was confirmed and he became a recognized member of the radical wing of the Edwardian Church. Once in the pulpit the power of his sermons could hold a large audience and sway some of his hearers. As he revealed later, he had been proud of this ability and assumed he had been doing a good job simply because he was preaching and feeding the flock with the Word of God. However, the core of his personal spiritual experience lay with the small groups of highly committed individuals, and this strongly influenced his ecclesiology. Instinctively he slipped back into the language of the 'little flock' and spoke of the badge of suffering as a mark of membership of the 'true Church'. Among these flocks he learned the art of pastoral counselling, and they formed an important strand within his understanding of discipline among a godly community and congregation. Knox found he fitted perfectly into the gatherings of the 'flock' with their strong female presence, and these 'sisters' gave him an essential support group of friends who were an immense help to him in material as well as spiritual ways. He seemed barely touched by the wider definitions of a state-authorized religious institution that encompassed the entire realm.

When Knox looked back on his time in Berwick and Newcastle he accused himself of succumbing to the spiritual temptation of pride in his ministry. He applied to himself the words he imagined Christ had spoken to Peter after the disciple's 'downsynckynge' when he had tried to walk on the water. 'Yet art thou too proude to be a pastour, thou canste not stoupe, nor bowe thy backe down to take up the weake shepe; thou does not yet knowe thine owne infirmitie and weaknes, and therefore canst thou do nothing but despise the weak ones.' Knox observed that only after personally recognizing the hidden iniquity of human nature would Peter be humble and an example of repentance to other offenders.[47]

In the years following his arrival, Knox came to identify himself with the struggle to plant the Protestant faith in England and later in London this little-known Scot joined eminent English preachers such as Hugh Latimer, Thomas Lever and John Bradford whose dynamic sermons at court epitomized the prophetic voice of the Church. By being bracketed with that company, Knox was able to recognize that he was by any standards an exceptionally good preacher and that his status as one of God's watchmen had been confirmed. He trained his preaching voice into a sophisticated and powerful instrument that would perform equally well at major public occasions and at routine services. At Berwick and Newcastle, where he ministered to a congregation for nearly four years, he realized that his sermons and ministry might change people's lives and behaviour. When he first arrived in England, being in the company of women would have been a relatively new experience for

Knox, who had previously worked in the male-dominated institution of the Catholic Church or among male prisoners and soldiers. As the 'fasherie' caused by Elizabeth Bowes revealed, it took him some time to learn how to manage a close pastoral relationship with a woman. There is scarcely any evidence of how well he coped with the development of his personal relationship and courtship of Marjorie. It was her commitment and their joint determination that ensured the wedding did eventually take place, and their marriage proved a great success, the bedrock of Knox's personal life. He had discovered women and they had discovered him and, predictably, things were never the same again.

CHAPTER SIX

Why held we back the salt?

During the final year of King Edward's reign Knox received a series of sharp lessons about the messy game of politics as he found himself stumbling along the dangerous corridors of power. This rapid education in the 'university of hard knocks' confirmed some of his fundamental assumptions as well as stripping away some of his hopes and illusions.[1] He emerged as a tougher man who was better prepared mentally for the change of regime in 1553 when Mary Tudor succeeded her half-brother Edward. Leaving England and going into exile for a second time fitted within Knox's prophetic understanding of God's providential purpose, and he was able to move more quickly than many of his English contemporaries to considering how to deal with the new situation. He remained committed to his role within the English Church, and his change of location did not alter his prophetic obligations: he turned to preaching with his pen.

From exile Knox looked back upon the situation at the end of Edward VI's reign in his powerful and hard-hitting *A Faithfull Admonition* published in the summer of 1554. He laid the blame squarely upon both those who had preached and those who had listened and summed up the preachers' efforts as too little, too late. He lamented, 'Why helde we backe the salt?',[2] and publicly berated himself and his fellow clergy for failing to denounce with sufficient fervency the vices and hypocrisy of those in government. In a beautifully compressed and powerful play on words and biblical images, he explained that God appointed preachers to be the salt of the earth. In their sermons the Edwardian preachers had failed to use the cleansing power of salt to scour away the corruption of those ruling the country in King Edward's name. Consequently, God had punished the kingdom with the death of the Protestant Edward and the return of Roman Catholicism under his half-sister, Queen Mary. The lesson of the salt burned into Knox's mind and heart. After his Edwardian experience he piled one salty denunciation upon another and blew his prophetic trumpet for all he was worth. For the rest of his life he was terrified of failing once more in his prophetic task and facing a repetition of the experience of transition between Edwardian and Marian England. In the different situation in Scotland at the start of Mary, Queen of Scots' personal rule, that fear was expressed: 'Having in mind that fearful sentence pronounced by the Eternal God against the watchmen that see the sword of God's punishment approach, and do not in plain words forewarn the people, yea, the princes and rulers, that they may repent.'[3]

When King Edward was still a healthy teenager with a great future in front of him, Knox travelled south with the Duke of Northumberland. Now designated as one of the Duke's preachers, Knox arrived at court in September 1552 confident in his abilities and proud that he had done a good job preaching the Gospel in Berwick and Newcastle. In his estimation he had delivered the bread of life without any additions or poison to the hungry souls who had cried for food.[4] He assumed that his plain-speaking sermons and oratorical power would continue to convince the hearers that he propounded the correct views on the Mass and on worship. What he had failed to appreciate as he travelled from the Borders to the capital was that he was moving into a different world. During his time as an army chaplain in Berwick and Newcastle, he had effectively been outside the institutional framework of the Church of England and had enjoyed extensive liturgical freedom. When he arrived in London he found himself inside the normal structure of the Church of England where he was expected to conform to all its practices. Before he came south he had probably heard of John a Lasco from Poland, who was the Superintendent of the Strangers' Church in London and a leader within the circle associated with Protestant Zurich and its Reformer, Henry Bullinger. When the radical Bishop of Gloucester, John Hooper, had clashed with the ecclesiastical establishment over wearing vestments, a Lasco had been a prominent supporter. Once based in London, Knox came into direct contact with the Polish Reformer. When he challenged the requirement to kneel during the Lord's Supper to receive the bread and wine, he looked to the Pole for support, despite a Lasco's failure to convince Archbishop Thomas Cranmer on that issue during earlier discussions about revisions for the Book of Common Prayer.[5]

SITTING AT THE LORD'S TABLE

On what must have been an exciting and daunting occasion in the second half of September 1552, Knox preached for the first time before the King and the assembled court at Windsor Castle. In his sermon he strongly asserted that sitting rather than kneeling was the correct posture during communion, an explicit criticism of the directions within the Second Book of Common Prayer that had just passed Parliament. As a result the Privy Council instructed the printer to halt production of the book until 'certain faults' could be corrected. The matter was urgent because the new Prayer book was due to be introduced across the land on 1 November. When he heard that printing had been suspended Archbishop Cranmer was furious and wrote a powerful letter to the Council on 7 October. Having made the substantive point that the book had been formally passed by the chief legislative body of the realm, the King in Parliament, and that the Council no longer had the authority to alter it, Cranmer then took a pot shot at Knox and his friends. They were 'unquiet spirits, which can like nothing but that is after their own fancy, and cease not to make trouble and disquietness when things be most quiet and in good order'. If they had their way, the Archbishop added, it would be a new prayer book each year and they would still find faults. He also brought his heavy academic guns to bear upon the question of posture at communion and left in rubble Knox's arguments about what had actually happened at the Last Supper.[6]

Cranmer's points about the virtues of 'good order', not to mention his other arguments, were wasted on Knox. The Scot was not adept at recognizing defeat even when it stared him in the face, and he had much to learn about the ways of English ecclesiastical politics. Unwilling to let the issue go, he and some of his fellow royal chaplains again raised the question of kneeling when making their comments upon the draft version of the Forty-Two Articles. This broad statement of the doctrinal position of the Church of England to which all clergy had to subscribe was about to be circulated.[7] One article dealt with church ceremonies, and several of the royal chaplains used their comment upon it to write to the Privy Council defending sitting to receive communion.[8] However, the Council rejected the chaplains' memo, backed Cranmer's position and ordered the Archbishop's newly composed rubric about kneeling to be inserted into the new Prayer Book. Since this was now 22 October and time very short, the rubric was not printed in the usual colour of red but in standard black and hence acquired the nickname the 'black rubric'. A more sinister connotation to 'black' only emerged later.

Cranmer had won, 'game, set and match' as his recent biographer has pointed out.[9] A demonstration of the Archbishop's success was that all six royal chaplains, including Knox, signed the draft of the Forty-Two Articles, without any qualifications.[10] Knox's oratory and black and white arguments had not worked on Cranmer or on the Privy Council, and he had been defeated on what he regarded as a key issue. Since his arrival in London his actions had given him a reputation as an outspoken troublemaker, made worse by the fact he was a 'runagate' or renegade Scot. Within a couple of years, the black rubric and its denial of the real presence were assumed to be his work and were used in the following reign to taunt Protestants. This led later historians, such as Peter Lorimer, to claim that the rubric was Knox's triumph and a victory for future English nonconformity, when the opposite was the case.[11]

Knox now faced the prospect of conforming to the ceremonies required in the Second Book of Common Prayer and established by statute. In one of the more awkward letters he had to write, he addressed his Berwick congregation who were used to sitting at the Lord's Table and instructed them to accept the legal requirement to kneel to receive communion. It took him two-thirds of the letter to reach the point and he was verbally squirming as he offered this crucial advice. With no attempt to add a positive gloss to the instruction, kneeling was presented as a necessary evil to be endured. On a personal note he emphasized that he had not abandoned his previous principles on arrival at the royal court or become proud and forgetful of his northern friends. Penning this message about conformity was like a hard pill he had to swallow and the bitter taste remained with him for a long time.[12]

Knox did not change his mind over kneeling and, even though he had told the congregation at Berwick to conform, he does not appear to have followed his own advice. This issue seemed to lie behind his refusal of a London parish in February 1553. Not surprisingly, the Privy Council wanted an explanation and summoned him. They sought answers to three specific questions: Why had he refused to serve this parish? Was he able to serve at all within the Church of England ministry? And, lastly, why did he not kneel at the Lord's Supper? Knox began his defence modestly enough, explaining that he felt he could profit the Church more outside London. He then played his trump card by revealing that he had persuaded Northumberland to countermand the appointment. Recognizing the trap within the second question, Knox did not answer directly but introduced the current apple of discord – the contentious issue of discipline and the right of the minister to excommunicate or 'to separate the leppers from the whole'.[13] Cranmer's major revision of canon law was coming up against serious lay opposition and the Council were split over how and who should administer ecclesiastical discipline. Though Knox was deeply concerned about this issue, at this juncture he seems to have been introducing the topic as a tactical move. It succeeded, and the debate moved swiftly on to kneeling, a topic on which the Council were united. After a lengthy debate Knox was dismissed with 'gentle speeches' but warned to think again about conforming and receiving communion according to the rubrics of the 1552 Book of Common Prayer.

Both sides of the kneeling debate knew there was fundamental agreement between them on the eucharistic theology of the Prayer Book. As Knox later acknowledged, Cranmer had explicitly attacked the Roman Catholic doctrine of transubstantiation and had substituted ordinary bread for the traditional wafers to underscore that key doctrinal shift. This left the Archbishop and Council puzzled as to why Knox continued to have 'a contrarie mind to the commoun order'. Knox produced the quick-fire response that 'he was more sorie that the common order sould be contrarie to Christ's institution'.[14] He held a fixed interpretation of what Christ had instituted and was impervious to counter-arguments about the participants' posture during the Last Supper. There was a hint that as he strove to remain faithful to his mentor's teaching George Wishart's ghost was haunting Knox's mind.

At a deeper level the clashes over kneeling revealed opposite views about uniformity. The Edwardian Church was rooted in the assumption that the entire kingdom should move in step along the path of religious reform and that there should only be one authorized order of worship for all to follow. It was a national Church that comprehended all the subjects of the kingdom who should form a single body with a common purpose. Bound by the legacy of the Royal Supremacy, the kingdom of England had consistently introduced major religious change through parliamentary legislation and then enforced it. Technically but a few years old, the ideal of uniformity had become more than an efficient process of implementing reform and had entered the mentality of the Church of England and of those who were running the Tudor regime. The recent rebellions against the Edwardian regime in 1549 had reinforced the assumption that obedience to the Crown and to statute law was the glue holding the realm together.

Though Knox was deeply attached to his adopted country, his thinking had not been shaped by the English experience of the twenty years since the break with Rome. The pattern of conformity was not in his bones and, having served in an unconventional post outside the parish system, it was harder for him to grasp the reality of operating as part of a national Church that was struggling to change entire communities. Consequently, he did not share the emotional attachment to the Royal Supremacy of his English colleagues and regarded uniformity as a much overrated virtue. The Scot in him also found it strange to treat statute law with the intense reverence accorded it by the English. In the long run this clash over uniformity and conformity hardened Knox's views as well as his belief that religious compromise was a disastrous, even sinful strategy. Eighteen months after his appearance before the Privy Council, his reaction to the disputes at Frankfurt over the Book of Common Prayer was conditioned by these earlier debates.

NEITHER GRATEFUL NOR CAPABLE OF BEING PLEASED

Knox was discovering the hard way that liturgical and other ecclesiastical matters were part of a much broader game of political power. He had arrived as Northumberland's preacher when relations between the Duke and Cranmer were frosty.[15] One continuing bone of contention between these two pillars of the Edwardian regime was the considerable wealth still held by English dioceses. Following the economic disaster of expensive wars in Scotland and France and the debasement of the English coinage, Northumberland fixed upon episcopal assets to help him put Crown finances back on a stable footing. In the face of this challenge Cranmer and his fellow bishops fought to retain resources for the Church and for social welfare. They wanted to prevent episcopal wealth sharing the fate of the monastic lands during Henry VIII's reign and finding its way into the purses of the English nobility. As dioceses became vacant, Northumberland tried to fill them with radical preachers who had explicitly condemned the 'lordly' lifestyle of bishops. In the autumn of 1552 his special plans for the very wealthy bishopric of Durham brought the issue into the open. With Cranmer's assistance, the Duke had finally pushed through the trial on felony charges of Cuthbert Tunstal, the serving Bishop of Durham and Knox's old adversary. When Tunstal was deprived of his see and sent back to the Tower the Duke proceeded with his plans to reconfigure the diocese and Durham's special status as a palatinate with its separate jurisdiction. He wanted to split the old diocese in two and erect Newcastle as a separate see. Both new bishops would be established on specific incomes and the other lands and assets would be gathered into the royal coffers.[16]

While sick and confined to his house in Chelsea, Northumberland set out his general plans for the dioceses in a letter to William Cecil, the rising court administrator who had become Secretary of State. He started with the vacant see of Rochester and gave three reasons why Knox should be placed there. Northumberland wanted his own client to occupy Rochester, the diocese sitting on the Archbishop's doorstep, and believed that Knox was the man for the job because he would make an excellent 'whetstone, to quicken and sharp the Bishop of Canterbury, whereof he hath need'. By being placed in Kent, Knox would also be useful against the groups of Anabaptists in that county. Further advantages would accrue by permanently removing Knox from the north-east of England where, without the preacher's encouragement, the lack of liturgical uniformity in that region would cease. Northumberland was more concerned with wider security matters and the need to break up 'the family of Scots, now inhabiting in Newcastle, chiefly for his fellowship ... wherein many resorts unto them out of Scotland'.[17] Extricating Knox from his supporters in

Newcastle and Berwick and placing him in the south of England at Rochester on the River Medway formed part of the Duke's wider plan for the Durham diocese and the entire north-east region which he detailed in the remainder of his letter.

Unfortunately for Northumberland, both the men he had picked to get the scheme under way refused to co-operate. On the terms being offered, Robert Horne, Dean of Durham, would not accept the newly configured bishopric of Durham and neither would Knox take the diocese of Rochester. When Cecil sent Knox to speak directly to Northumberland, the Scot seriously irritated the Duke, who wrote that he wanted nothing more to do with someone who was 'neither grateful nor pleasable [capable of being pleased]'.[18] Northumberland was even angrier at Horne's refusal because the Dean had implied that the Duke was not sincere in his religious protestations, a slur that provoked a robust denial. Possibly to cool things down and get him out of sight, Knox was given permission to return to Newcastle for a time.[19] In later years he explained his refusal to accept the diocese of Rochester by the enigmatic and catch-all phrase that he had foreseen 'troubles to come'.[20] Given his knowledge of the situation in the north-east, he might have wanted to help block the Duke's entire scheme for its bishops and maintain common cause with other rising stars of the Edwardian Church who were challenging the extremely dubious conditions then being attached to the acceptance of high ecclesiastical office.[21]

With considerable magnanimity Northumberland did not hold a grudge against Knox and was willing to continue to support him. In the Duke's view, 'poor' Knox needed a permanent job and at the start of February 1553 he was offered the plum London living of All Hallows, Bread Street, which had become vacant when Thomas Sampson, a well-known and radical preacher, was moved to the deanery of Chichester. Knox would be based very close to his friends in Cheapside, and the congregation of All Hallows would value another radical and vibrant preacher to replace the man they had lost. To his contemporaries Knox's rejection of this parish made no sense and was more surprising than his refusal of the bishopric; modern scholars have passed over the incident as if it had little significance. Losing the fight over kneeling had made Knox realize that if he accepted such a parish living it would severely restrict his freedom to follow his vocation as he thought fit. In the diocese of London and under the eagle eye of the impeccably Protestant, but strongly conformist, Bishop Nicholas Ridley, Knox knew he would be compelled to adhere to all aspects of the 1552 Book of Common Prayer, including kneeling at communion. He would also have to sever his ties with the congregations of Berwick and Newcastle, and his recent epistle to them revealed how keenly he felt the accusation that he was 'selling out' for the sake of promotion. In that letter he had underscored his calling to be a prophet as well as a pastor and emphasized that his main task was to concentrate upon preaching. With that clear in his own mind, he somehow persuaded Northumberland to allow him to refuse the parish of All Hallows and instead embrace a roving preaching role. Throughout his ministry this underlying tension between the role of a prophet and that of a parish minister was one that he never fully resolved. It was an irony probably lost on Knox himself that he was a strong advocate of discipline and of upholding the right of the minister and congregation to enforce obedience to the laws of God. However, he did not include within discipline the ideals of conformity and uniformity that many English prelates felt contributed to good order within society and the proper regulation of the Church.

THE LIBERTY OF THE PREACHERS' TONGUES

Knox's first and overriding call had been to preach, and when he turned in his sermons to the application of the biblical text he had the opportunity to comment directly upon current affairs. By enabling him to apply the doses of 'salt' in his admonitions, his preaching provided him with a defence against being sucked into a corrupt political regime. In the spring of 1553 he was not alone in assuming that a heavily salted message about the morality of their actions had to be given to those who held political power. A group of clerics chose the high-profile public Lenten sermons preached before the King and court to mount a co-ordinated and concerted campaign to scour and sanitize the elite with their salt-laden admonitions. The annual Lenten series attracted huge interest across London and had become one of the most significant media events of the day. One after another the sermons delivered by Edmund Grindal, Thomas Lever, John Bradford, Walter Haddon and Knox lambasted the courtiers who sat listening to them.[22] Employing similar language about purging and cleansing, Bishop Ridley later recalled how harsh the preachers' criticism of the courtiers had been: 'their tongues were so sharp they ripped so deep in their galled backs, to have purged them ... of insatiable covetousness, of filthy carnality, and voluptuousness, of intolerable ambition and pride, of ungodly loathsomeness to hear poor men's causes, and to hear God's word'.[23]

Knox later gave an account of his sermon at Westminster, the last he would preach before the young King. Starting with the Old Testament story of King David, he established that godly kings might have evil counsellors. He then specifically matched biblical characters to contemporary figures, identifying the Treasurer, William Paulet, Marquess of Winchester, with Shebna, the corrupt adviser to King Hezekiah.[24] Knox simply inferred that a direct parallel could be drawn between Old Testament Israel and Edwardian England since

for him both were kingdoms in covenant relationship with God. With deliberate calculation he employed his sermon admonitions as a method of discipline for the leaders of the kingdom and by extension for the whole kingdom;
all must be seen to be upholding the laws of God. By not hesitating to point
the finger at named individuals, once again Knox displayed his talent for
premeditated indiscretion that caused such alarm among his courtier friends.
Other radicals such as Hooper employed specific and individual admonitions,
but Knox's directness went further than theirs. If a nail needed driving home
the Scot reached for a sledgehammer; if salt were needed to cleanse and scour,
then he picked up a shovel. The Duke commented at the time, 'the libertie of
the preachers tonges would cause the Counsale and Nobilitie to ryse uppe
against them, for they could not suffer so to be intreated'.[25] In his execution
speech in the following reign, Northumberland and his Catholic scriptwriters
emphasized the impact of such admonitory sermons and their unregulated
biblical interpretations. A specific warning was given against seditious and
'lewde preachers that have openid the booke and knowe not how to shutte it'.[26]

As he witnessed the last months of Edward VI's reign, Knox shared with
other committed Protestant clergy a draining away of idealism and innocence.
The initial elation created when demonstrably Protestant measures had been
introduced was dissipated by the harsh realities of being in coalition with a
political faction that needed to maintain its power. The political art of the
possible was a concept Knox shunned and he treated compromise as another
term for lack of zeal. From this time onwards, he was deeply suspicious of any
form of gradualism, and his fear of political accommodation and the dangers
of compromise hardened into a rigid dogma. The failure of Edward's kingdom
to live up to its covenant obligations and to demonstrate to the world its determination to uphold the laws of God became in Knox's mind not only a lack of
zeal but also a failure of discipline. He stressed that the maintenance of external
godliness was a sign of covenant faithfulness and he regarded his heavily salted
prophetic preaching as a disciplinary tool.

Knox became convinced it was not enough to exhort from the pulpit; it was
also necessary for the minister to use excommunication against those who
publicly broke the laws of God. In England as elsewhere in Protestant territories throughout Europe, control over the power to excommunicate and discipline all ranks within society had become a highly contentious subject because
it constituted the new boundary zone between civil and ecclesiastical jurisdiction. Archbishop Cranmer had attempted a complete overhaul of medieval
canon law to make it fit for its new Protestant purpose within the Church of
England. Despite, or perhaps because of, his notarial background a new canon
law never appealed to Knox. Instead he was inspired by the model of how to

run a godly congregation he saw in the Strangers' Church in London led by a
Lasco. The Pole was just one of his many friends and acquaintances within the
capital's godly circle.

Away from the pressures of court, Knox found in London a parallel world
of enthusiastic lay religious commitment. He gravitated towards the intense
gatherings of Protestant enthusiasts with their Bible discussions and high
percentage of female participants. In their company he found the spiritual and
material support and fellowship he needed and became firm friends with at
least two of its impressive female stalwarts. Anne Lock, née Vaughan, and her
sister-in-law Rose Hickman, née Lock, extended their hospitality to many
radical clergy, and Knox met John Hooper and John Foxe in their houses.
These women were members of evangelical families who had been active since
the time of William Tyndale and the earliest years of English Protestantism.
The families were cloth merchants and members of the Mercers' Company
living near the Mercers' Hall in Cheapside at the heart of the City of London.
For Knox, the Haddington merchant's son, while his background might have
provided initial contacts to the capital's mercantile elite, these links marked a
social step up. He probably encountered Sir Thomas Cawarden within these
London circles. After starting his career as a mercer, Cawarden had moved
into royal service and become an important figure in the production of court
plays. His family's links to Knox were only later revealed when they organized
a special printing of the Great Bible as a gift for the preacher in Queen
Elizabeth's reign.[27] Despite his abrasive pulpit personality, Knox proved adept
at becoming part of the networks of godly in London and elsewhere in
England. A number of such significant friendships have left little trace in the
historical record and can be glimpsed only from passing comments or chance
survivals such as this John Knox Bible.

In the winter of 1552 another merchant, Thomas Ferrour, provided his house
for a meeting between Knox and an unidentified Anabaptist (the name was a
convenient umbrella term for many different groups of Protestants who dissented
from the magisterial Reformation). This anonymous Anabaptist claimed direct
divine revelation and held other beliefs that Knox regarded as heretical and
dangerous, but the Scot did not name the man either to the Edwardian authorities or later. A strong refutation of Anabaptists provided a sure signal that,
despite being critical of the establishment, Knox and other radical preachers
remained loyal to the mainstream Church. Knox had no hesitation in attacking
the Anabaptists or 'Freewillers' from the pulpit when in the Maidstone and
Faversham districts during a preaching tour in the Rochester diocese. During
these visits to Kent he met some opponents, possibly including one of their
leaders, Henry Harte, who made an indelible impression upon him. Knox was

sufficiently incensed by their views to take up his pen years later to write his longest book, in which he defended predestination against the anonymous author of *Careless by Necessity*, possibly Harte himself.[28] Knox developed a special fury against these Freewillers because he believed they had betrayed the Protestant cause from within. Such an action broke the loyalty to the common cause that should be found among all those who fought on the side of Christ against Antichrist. To those who held extreme Protestant views Knox applied his Scottish understanding of the feud against those who were disloyal.

In June 1553 Knox was fortunate that another preaching mission sent him out of London to Buckinghamshire, thereby saving him from arrest in the capital during the succession crisis caused by King Edward's death on 7 July. The attempt by the dying King and Northumberland to debar the Catholic Mary Tudor and instead place on the throne the Protestant Lady Jane Grey collapsed with remarkable speed. When the news was received a fortnight later of the proclamation of Queen Mary, Knox preached at Amersham in Buckinghamshire. His sermon on Matthew 14 was packed with warnings of divine wrath for the sins of the realm, telling how God had taken away England's godly prince and was punishing the country for its lack of zeal in the Protestant cause. He voiced the emotional lament, 'O Englande, Englande! alasse! these plagues are powred upon thee, for that thou wouldest not knowe the most happy tyme of thy gentle visitation.' Knox reminded his hearers that he had predicted this possibility and it was plain that God's anger was directed at the slow and incomplete nature of reform and not, as the Roman Catholics had been quick to say, at the adoption of Protestantism itself.[29]

Knox's personal situation was precarious. As he joked, someone was better off because he would not be returning to court to claim his salary of £40 as a royal chaplain.[30] He was now catagorised as an undesirable foreigner with no protection and unlikely to receive any consideration. Once Queen Mary's regime established itself, leading foreign Protestants who had come to the country in the previous reign, such as Peter Martyr Vermigli, were informed that they were no longer welcome in England. The message about packing his bags was equally plain to Knox as he wrestled with the dilemma of whether he should flee or remain to face persecution and probably death. While most Protestant bishops and some parish clergy felt bound to remain with their flocks, others were encouraged to follow the biblical injunction to fly to another country.[31] Having no parish, Knox was at liberty to go, though he still felt he was deserting his congregation in Berwick and Newcastle. In the autumn of 1553 he travelled to the north-east to see Marjorie.

In this affair of the heart, Knox's actions spoke far more eloquently than his words about the depth of his affection for Marjorie. His main purpose in making that dangerous journey was to talk to her, probably to say goodbye in case he should never see her again. He found it hard to accept the advice of Marjorie's brother George and those who hid him that any meeting had become too risky because news of his arrival in the vicinity had been noised abroad.[32] From the perspective of the male members of the Bowes family, Queen Mary's accession had changed everything. Having been closely associated with Northumberland and the Lady Jane Grey debacle, the family were frantically re-establishing their reputation as loyal servants of the Crown, whoever was in power. They also wanted to extract Marjorie from what had become a disastrous liaison. With the return in the autumn of 1553 of clerical celibacy, as one of the first stages in the re-establishment of Roman Catholicism, Marjorie's marriage would be illegal and any future offspring illegitimate. Knox had become a fugitive. Not surprisingly, the male heads of the family viewed going ahead with the marriage as the height of folly and the worst of all worlds. On 6 November Knox had a stormy interview with Sir Robert. Marjorie's uncle was in no mood to listen to his carefully crafted arguments and made it clear that the preacher was no longer part of the Bowes family. This lack of the 'kindness' of kinship was an unexpected and painful blow to Knox. Sir Robert probably advised him to get out of the country, and preferably right out of their lives.

Assuming that he was having to deal only with Knox and his sister-in-law, Sir Robert made the serious mistake of leaving Marjorie out of the reckoning.[33] Her actions demonstrated that she was a brave and resourceful woman, though for lack of evidence her precise character remains shadowy. In 1552 she was prepared to stand up to her father and defy local conventions by becoming betrothed to Knox. In the winter of 1553 to have broken that betrothal would have been far easier for her and would have been expected of a dutiful daughter and family member. Even if it upset her mother, she would have had the full backing of her father and uncle, who could have obtained an annulment for the betrothal and secured another marriage among the local gentry. Instead, Marjorie refused to give Knox up and bided her time. Perhaps because her brother George understood Marjorie's determination only too well, he did not risk telling her that Knox had come to the north-east late in 1553. She might already have had elopement on her mind and probably began planning so that she might seize the next opportunity.

GOD SHALL GUIDE THE FOOTSTEPS OF HIM THAT IS WILSOME

Knox was urged by friends to leave the country because keeping his movements quiet in the north-east had proved impossible.[34] Perhaps in search of a ship in a place his face was not known, he travelled to Chester where he met for the first time the man who became his closest friend and colleague. When the Catholic supporters of Queen Mary had gained control at Oxford University, Christopher Goodman had lost his place as Lady Margaret Professor of Divinity and had returned to his native town. Walking on the walls in Chester, the persuasive Knox convinced Goodman he should leave the country, thereby ensuring that he would continue to make a contribution to the Church. By arguing the case with someone in the same situation, Knox no doubt talked himself into following that advice. This momentous first meeting was etched on their memories and the scene was easily recalled years later.[35] Eventually both men left for the Continent, and during the Marian exile that Chester meeting was transformed into a strong and lasting friendship which sustained Knox until his death.

Knox suited actions to words and left England, arriving in Dieppe in January 1554. Unlike most English Protestants who travelled to Europe via the Low Countries, he went to the French port and headed for the Scots merchant community. From this first welcome and throughout his second exile, he was supported by his well-wishers from Scotland and elsewhere. He was fortunate not to encounter serious financial problems despite the extensive travelling he undertook over the next five years. He was spared the fate of other religious exiles who had to find a new occupation to feed their family, as befell his friend John Foxe, who became a printer's proof-reader. During the initial period of hiding and uncertainty in Dieppe Knox became depressed and felt his faith under assault. Though he did not doubt his prophetic insights about God's judgements, he still had to cope with the personal consequences of the loss of his betrothed, his new family, his friends and his job. Hoping for news from Marjorie and her mother, Knox remained in the French port for several weeks and was able to complete the exposition of Psalm 6 and several tracts he had been composing since the summer. Waiting did not come easily to him as he watched and pondered the destruction of Protestant achievements in England.

During these difficult days Knox's advice to anyone prepared to listen was simple and predictable: stay away from the Mass. In his terms attendance at a Catholic Mass was participation in idolatry and an automatic renunciation of one's Protestant faith, adding the sin of apostasy to the idolatry of the worship of false gods. On a national level he characterized the reintroduction of Roman Catholic worship in England as a breach of the covenant or league the kingdom had made with God during Edward's reign. In his tract *A Faithfull Admonition* in particular, he emphasized that breaking the covenant would bring upon England the same chastisement that God had inflicted upon his people in the Old Testament.

The news that many of his former congregation in Berwick, Newcastle and London were attending Mass was a considerable personal blow and left Knox feeling that his ministry had been a miserable failure. He was primarily concerned to convey to those individuals that, unless they repented, their sin was so great it would eternally damn them. In his customary strident and direct style, he demolished any 'third way'. He declared it impossible to conform outwardly to Roman Catholic worship while keeping a Protestant faith in the heart, a practice designated Nicodemism after the disciple who visited Jesus at night to avoid detection.

In 1553 English Protestant leaders with their Church now 'under the cross' had adopted this tough anti-Nicodemite line that Calvin had championed for the previous decade. A steady stream of tracts was published in the first year of Mary's reign instructing Protestants to accept the divine punishment for the sins of England and hold fast to their faith. When ordered to change their religious beliefs and practices, they must obey God rather than man and be prepared to suffer the consequences. If they could, they should flee the country; if not, they should prepare to go to prison or the stake. In particular the tracts exhorted Protestants to constancy and emphasized the value of suffering.

Thanks to his galley experience, being loyal, holding to one's faith and suffering were deeply familiar themes to Knox. They also fitted neatly into his concept of the faithful few forming the true Church. While his writings remained broadly in line with these English themes, there were some subtle differences. Knox regarded suffering as an essential tutor teaching an individual about the cycle of justification and personal salvation. It provided a reminder of the permanent human tendency to sin, of the dangers of pride and self-reliance and the need to have complete faith in, and rely exclusively upon, Christ. He was reluctant to copy his English colleagues and present suffering as the badge of an obedient subject. In however limited a way he wanted to fight back as the Scots prisoners had done in France, and he searched for some action Protestants could take in the face of the reintroduction of Roman Catholicism. While he remained in England, he had sought political support for a continued programme of Protestant preaching. Without having any clear plan he probably envisaged the type of armed protection Wishart had enjoyed during his 1546 preaching tour in Ayrshire. Knox had been half prepared to take the risk to his life such a course might entail; his English supporters were not. They believed that the unauthorized employment of military force was straightforward rebellion and that that was not to be countenanced. In an equivalent cultural misunderstanding Knox did not share the hope that the English Parliament would resist Catholic legislation. His pessimism was vindicated when Queen Mary's first Parliament swept away all Edward's religious legislation as if it had never been. That setback intensified Knox's quest for acceptable forms of political action and he continued to ponder what those holding political and military power might do for the Protestant cause.

While waiting in Dieppe during January 1554 Knox caught up with what was happening in Scotland and received the breaking news from across the Channel that a rebellion had begun in Kent. This rising attempted to prevent the proposed marriage of Queen Mary Tudor to Philip of Spain, the son and heir of Emperor Charles V. Sir Thomas Wyatt even managed to lead his army to the gates of London, though in best Tudor fashion Queen Mary held her nerve and by remaining in the capital was able to defeat the rebels. Most English Protestants frantically tried to dissociate their cause from the taint of sedition. By contrast, Knox was looking for the anti-Catholic agenda of the rebels. Ironically, in seeking a religious motive for the rebellion he found himself in step with one of his arch-enemies, the veteran Tudor politician Bishop Stephen Gardiner, or 'wily Winchester'. Knox's Scottish background not only left him free from the obsession with the terrifying spectre of treason and civil war that haunted the English, it also gave him an alternative understanding of the employment of armed force as an extreme recourse within the political process. Although emotionally caught up in the English situation, he would have examined all his options, including how safe it might be to return to Scotland. In search of direction concerning what he should do and what advice he could give to others, he undertook a long journey to Switzerland to consult the three major Protestant Reformers based there.

An answer given to a certain Scotsman

After he had travelled through France en route to Zurich, Geneva was Knox's initial stop in Switzerland. His first meeting with John Calvin was probably formal and slightly strained. This unknown Scot, who might have enthused about reading Calvin's biblical commentaries, appeared unexpectedly before the Genevan Reformer with a series of delicate political questions. Calvin was extremely busy and could manage only a brief discussion, listening politely and giving cautious and carefully worded replies. On 9 March he sent Knox down Lake Geneva to Lausanne with greetings for Theodore Beza and a letter of recommendation to Pierre Viret, who might be more sympathetic to Knox's political dilemma.[36] Viret, in his turn, seemed equally keen to pass this particular Scottish parcel, and Knox's final stop was Zurich, where he spoke to Henry Bullinger, the senior and most respected of the Swiss Reformers in this period who had been very interested in the progress of the Edwardian Church.

Knox posed the same four questions to each reformer and he received similar answers, though only Bullinger's thoughts survive in *An answer given to a certain Scotsman in reply to some questions concerning the kingdom of Scotland and England*.[37] At first glance these political queries seem dominated by the English situation, but three covered concerns common to both British realms. With little attempt at disguise, the initial question checked whether the authority of a male minor who inherited the throne had been valid. In his answer, Bullinger had no hesitation naming names, stating that Edward VI was indeed a lawful sovereign. Since Knox had shown no previous indication of doubt about this constitutional issue, the trigger might have been whether King Edward's authority was sufficient for him to make a valid will. The dying King's 'device' declaring that Lady Jane Grey should succeed him was far too sensitive to appear in either question or answer and probably had not even been directly mentioned. The legitimacy of female rule provided the basis for the next and safer question. Laws and customs on this issue varied across Europe, as Bullinger's answer was able to underline. The associated matter of whether a reigning queen could transfer regal authority to her husband was of direct relevance to both England and Scotland. Mary Tudor was proposing to marry Philip of Spain and Mary, Queen of Scots, was betrothed to Francis, the French Dauphin. Both husbands represented the more powerful partner in the alliance with the long-term prospect of absorbing a smaller realm into a larger empire. In his answer, Bullinger was able to refer again to the laws of individual realms.

For the Swiss Reformers the heart of the discussion was reached in the third query, about a ruler enforcing 'idolatry'. On this familiar ground all could agree that ungodly commands must not be obeyed. Knox's subsidiary question focused on those already in place commanding military fortresses or towns and whether they might 'repel ungodly violence from themselves and their friends'.[38] Here were echoes of the siege at St Andrews Castle in 1546–7 and of his days as an army chaplain in Berwick. Knox might have had some wild scheme relating to military commanders on the Borders but the underlying premise reflected his Scottish understanding that armed protection extended to the kindred, friends, allies and supporters of a commander or noble. This final query moved from the more passive defence against unjust force to asking about support for an active rebellion by Protestant nobles against a Roman Catholic ruler. Perhaps the lack of clarity over the religious agenda and the speed of events in Wyatt's rebellion convinced Knox that if a similar situation arose in the future he and other Protestant preachers should know where they stood and be better prepared. However, Bullinger and Calvin proved most reluctant to issue any endorsement whatsoever of armed resistance. At best they accepted there were biblical and patristic precedents that had not been 'reproved'. Instead they stressed the need for knowledge and discernment of the particular circumstances of each situation and issued a strong warning about the danger of contaminated motives when nobles rebelled. Although he might have received more encouragement from Viret, who had previously been willing to contemplate resistance by certain groups, Knox returned from his Swiss discussions having received a hefty measure of caution to quench his thirst for direct action against idolatrous rulers.

In his published tracts targeting the English Queen and the 'bak-starteris' who had returned to Catholic worship, Knox poured his frustration into extremely violent language about idolatrous rulers with a strong emphasis upon key biblical parallels, such as Athaliah and Jezebel.[39] With some loyalty towards his former patron, Knox was comparatively sympathetic towards Northumberland, whom he described as a miserable man because at his execution on 22 August 1553 the Duke had renounced his Protestant faith.[40] Knox expressed his own anger through the use of psalms of deliverance and vengeance against one's enemies, such as Psalm 79, whose first verse featured both in his *Faithfull Admonition* and as a salutation for his letter to Elizabeth Bowes.[41]

Knox's tract *A Faithfull Admonition* was his most forceful and impressive piece of writing to date, more hard hitting and containing fewer concessions to English sensibilities than the other exile tracts being printed at this time. Its language and conceptual framework carried a sharp sense of Knox's admonitory role, with the Old Testament prophet Isaiah's warnings prominent on the title page that the Lord's 'hande be stretched out styll' and 'take hede that the Lorde roote thee not out bothe heade and tayle in one day'. The main exposition concerned the Gospel story that followed the feeding of the five thousand when the disciples were caught in a storm on Lake Galilee. They saw Jesus walking on the water and when Peter attempted to do the same, Christ saved him from drowning. These miracles were used by Knox to explain the punishment being experienced by the 'professours of God's truthe in England' and to emphasize the importance of total faith in Christ, whatever the circumstances.[42] His target audience were the faithful few who comprised the true Church and he offered a message of hope and assurance that though their faith might be weak they must trust that in the midst of afflictions God would deliver his people. 'He shall sende Jehu to execute hys juste judgementes againste ydolatours' and 'Jesabel her selfe shall not excape the vengeaunce and plagues that are prepared for her portion.'[43] As the Old Testament story indicated, Knox was openly discussing 'bloud thristye tyrauntes' and was prepared to combine the charges of idolatry and treason when describing the actions of Mary Tudor. Appealing to English patriotic sentiment he accused the Queen of being 'an open traitoresse to the Imperiall Crown of England' and 'under an Englyshe name she beareth a Spaniardes herte'. With a hint of his later arguments against female rule he added, 'the saying is too true, that the usurped government of an affectionate woman is a rage without reason'. The preacher in him could not resist slipping in an 'I told you so' reference to his Christmas 1552 sermon in Newcastle.[44] He assumed a direct parallel between the history of Old Testament Israel and covenanted England and he prayed for God to raise another servant, like Phineas, Elijah or Jehu, 'that the bloude of abhominable idolaters may pacifie Goddes wrath' rather than the entire kingdom be consumed.[45] Despite the advice he had received from the Swiss Reformers, he was still thinking about the question of when active resistance was justified.

From Zurich, Knox journeyed back into France to his 'listening post' in Dieppe where he could collect the latest news from Scotland and England.[46] The port proved a useful base from which to contact other exiles from England, and Knox's writing was included in the propaganda push to publish tracts being organized at Emden on the border between the Low Countries and the Holy Roman Empire. His immediate contact was probably his fellow Scot John Willock, whose anonymous epistle from a banished man from Leicestershire was inserted into Knox's own *Faithfull Admonition* and published in Emden.[47] Knox collected letters and news from the north-east of England and replied to Elizabeth Bowes on 20 July. Since there was no prospect of returning to the region in the near future he hinted that exile might also be an option for her. Extensive travelling was costly, so he also sought funds from his friends, rather pompously citing St Paul's travels as a precedent. Though trying to maintain a light tone to jolly along his mother-in-law, Knox let slip that he was feeling dismal and directionless, commenting in an aside, 'God sall gyd the futstepis of him that is wilsome, and will feid him in trubill that never greatlie solistit for the world.'[48] Having been impressed by Geneva and Calvin, he decided to return to that city and, like many other exiles, sought to spend his time studying and improving his skills in the biblical languages. A number of the exiles were excited by the possibility of learning Hebrew in Switzerland, where some of the best teachers were based.[49] Knox settled quietly in Geneva, becoming acquainted with a number of the pastors, their wives and families, including Jean de St André, the secretary of the Company of Pastors, the corporate body of the Genevan ministers.[50] It was relatively common among European intellectuals of the day to acquire a Latin name that contained a territorial designation, and during this time in Geneva Knox probably adopted or was given the name 'Tinoterius', indicating that he was a man from the banks of the River Tyne in Scotland. Later when he was in Frankfurt, to keep his authorship secret from his opponents within the exile congregation, he signed a letter to the Company of Pastors with that pseudonym so that his Genevan friends would know who had written.

Since this was his second exile, Knox managed better than most of his English colleagues the transition from being a leading member of a powerful institution in Edwardian England to being on the run during Mary's reign. Though physically based in Switzerland, he remained mentally within the English situation. He also remained linguistically within an English context. For a decade after his arrival in England in 1549 his everyday speech was English among Englishmen and women, and when he finally returned to Scotland his English pronunciation and vocabulary would be highlighted and mocked by an opponent.[51] Written before he returned to Geneva, his *Faithfull Admonition* demonstrated that he had analysed the sins and failings that had brought God's wrath down upon the kingdom of England. Deprived of his pulpit, he preached to his congregations with his pen, asking questions and writing tracts and letters that were concerned with the difficulties brought by the re-Catholicization of England. Long before Edward's death Knox had found himself out of step with the English ecclesiastical hierarchy over liturgy and out of sympathy with the English preoccupation with conformity and uniformity. Those were the issues that would prove explosive when he was called away from his study in Geneva to serve an English exile congregation. For him the lesson of the salt from Edward's reign was that compromise in worship and reform was inherently dangerous. Knox was determined not to tolerate a weak compromise or fail in his prophetic duty a second time.

CHAPTER SEVEN

A farrago of ceremonies

Knox never found it easy to keep silent or to stay still. He might talk and dream of private study but his prophetic calling to be a watchman of the Lord militated against prolonged periods of quiet. While feeling a constant pressure to be true to his vocation, paradoxically, he was at his least decisive when sorting out the next stage in his career. During this Continental exile it was often Calvin who had to push him into accepting the next charge. However robust his public rhetoric, Knox remained vulnerable to inner doubts about his performance as a pastor of his flocks. When he was minister to the English-speaking exile congregation at Frankfurt he experienced some of the toughest and most bruising encounters of his life. Frankfurt changed him, and his battles there altered the entire English exile community. The newly discovered material in the Goodman papers reveals for the first time the full story of the 'Troubles at Frankfurt'. This dispute affected the Church of England that re-emerged in Queen Elizabeth's reign and it helped to determine the nature both of the Protestant Kirk that was to appear in Scotland and down the centuries of the Reformed tradition throughout the Anglophone world. In the short run it sent Knox into a third exile; in the long run it opened up the path that produced his lasting legacy.

THE ENGLISH CONGREGATION ASSEMBLED AT FRANKFURT

At the start of October 1554 and only a couple of months into his studies in Geneva, Knox was less than delighted to receive an invitation to become a minister to the English-speaking church being established in Frankfurt on the Main. For someone so keen to preach, he was surprisingly reluctant to take up the offer and needed a good shove from Calvin to get him on the road.[1] Although Frankfurt was a Lutheran city, the Council permitted a Reformed congregation of French exiles to use a former nunnery chapel, the Church of the White Ladies, and follow their own liturgy there. When English exiles first arrived in the city it was agreed they would use the same church on the understanding that they acted in accordance with the French congregation. Although some of the English signed the French confession, the language barrier prevented most from joining the French church. Under the leadership of William Whittingham, an exile with previous experience of travelling on the Continent, the English thought about setting up their own church and assembling the best and most rousing preachers. Alongside Knox they called James Haddon and Thomas Lever, some of the clerics who had made a major impression in the hard-hitting 1553 Lenten sermons in London. Being a congregation in exile and outside the territorial and hierarchal institution of the Edwardian Church, it was intended that the preachers should be of equal authority and operate as partners in a form of group ministry.[2] However, Haddon refused the invitation and remained in Strasbourg, and Lever spent time in Zurich before coming to Frankfurt. Though Knox had also taken his time to arrive he was still the first to answer Frankfurt's call. There he took over from John Foxe, his friend from London days, and David Whitehead, who had been covering the preaching duties.[3]

As he made his way north from Geneva, Knox probably travelled the great waterway of the Rhine, carrying him past many cities of the Holy Roman Empire. Even after this introduction to the Imperial cities, Frankfurt would have made a considerable impression upon him and he was fortunate to have friends and accommodation waiting for him in this large and cosmopolitan community on the banks of the River Main. As a place to establish an exile church, it had much to recommend it. Frankfurt was one of the most important European communication hubs where trade and news travelled to and from all four compass points. It also housed the famous book fairs at Easter and Michaelmas offering a central distribution point for the Continent's publishing trade and drawing book lovers from far and wide. When he was considering coming to Frankfurt, the English exile John Scory listed its many advantages: cheap food, benevolent magistrates, humane people, fair houses and wholesome air, only double-checking that final requirement for English comfort – whether the beer was good.[4]

Exile was a new experience for most of the English, though there were a few, like John Bale, who had fled the country in the final years of King Henry VIII's reign. The progress of the Edwardian Reformation had given them a sense of identity as an English Protestant Church, and within England the Strangers' Churches had provided models of other Protestant exiles forming their own churches. The French congregation with whom they shared the

White Ladies building contained the group that had previously settled in Glastonbury and had come from England to Frankfurt under their pastor, Vallerand Poullain. With their own Ecclesiastical Discipline which a number of the early English arrivals were happy to sign, the French were a living reminder to the English exiles of the importance of setting up their own church as a witness, and Poullain actively encouraged this goal. To William Whittingham, Thomas Wood and William Williams the city provided an ideal venue for such a beacon for English Protestantism. They wanted all the English exiles to come to Frankfurt and form a single community and church. However, this notion was not particularly appealing to those exiles who had already found places of refuge and established themselves elsewhere for study, work or other reasons. Their initial lack of enthusiasm was accompanied by a scepticism about precisely how attractive an offer was being made by the Frankfurt City Council in the provision of a church building and what form of worship would be permitted. Another group of exiles in Zurich were also suggesting that their compatriots should move to the Swiss city. With the impetus in Frankfurt coming from three laymen, there were underlying suspicions among other exiles about the Frankfurt congregation going its own way outside the supervision of senior clerics of the Edwardian Church. The exile communities of Zurich and Strasbourg co-ordinated their responses to Frankfurt's 'come hither' and employed the wealthy merchant Richard Chambers to act as a go-between.

By the time Knox arrived from Geneva around the third week in November negotiations between the three main exile communities were well under way.[5] One of the main issues being discussed was how far worship should be based upon the 1552 Book of Common Prayer. Everyone had agreed to the removal of liturgical practices that might cause direct offence to the host city or to the French congregation with whom they shared the building. Beyond that basic agreement there was a split between those who wanted minimal liturgical change and those who sought to maximize it. Those holding the minimal position believed that the 1552 Prayer Book should be followed in full with alterations made only when the local magistrate demanded them. This would align the exiles with their fellow Protestants in England and demonstrate solidarity with the Prayer Book's authors, Bishops Cranmer, Latimer and Ridley, who were in prison awaiting trial. It was argued that making significant changes would confirm the Catholic accusation that Protestants were constantly shifting their ground and might deter people from fleeing from persecution in England and joining the exile congregations. This position had strong backers within the communities based in Zurich and Strasbourg and among senior Edwardian clerics, with Richard Chambers and Robert Horne in the Swiss city and Edmund Grindal in the Imperial one helping co-ordinate the campaign and keep in contact with Richard Cox in Duisburg in northern Germany and John Scory in Emden just across the Imperial border in the Low Countries. Within Frankfurt John Bale had emerged as a keen supporter of the Prayer Book, and letters passing within this group expressed concern over the Frankfurt congregation's leaders and the need to place established clergy in authority. A broader battle was emerging for control over the English Church in exile and, in the longer term, over the future direction of the Church of England.

By contrast the other group wanted to seize the chance to amend the 1552 Prayer Book. They welcomed the freedom exile gave from the constraints of English politics, including no longer having to pace liturgical reform to suit a tardy nation. They argued that a range of ceremonies ought to be abandoned because they were remnants of Roman Catholic practice and, if King Edward VI had lived, such purification and further reformation would have taken place. They wanted to align English worship with Reformed doctrine and bring it more into line with practice in the churches in southern Germany and Switzerland. Rather than maintaining a distinctive Englishness, they preferred to demonstrate solidarity with the Reformed communities of Europe. Within the Frankfurt congregation the lay leaders had introduced a strong element of congregational participation for the management of the church that bore little resemblance to the organization of the Church of England, and Whittingham emerged as the main leader of those pushing for radical change. As his colleague Thomas Wood later recalled, it was Whittingham's critique of the Prayer Book that first persuaded him to support change.[6]

Knox's track record of criticism of the 1552 Prayer Book ensured that he became Whittingham's instant ally. Their contrasting personalities and skills made the duo a formidable team. Whittingham's flair for languages and extensive travel in the Holy Roman Empire and Switzerland during Edward's reign had made him a skilled translator. From a gentry family in Cheshire, he had educated and equipped himself to serve the Crown as an agent abroad or on diplomatic missions. He had followed his childhood friend from Chester, Christopher Goodman, to Oxford University, studying in the colleges of Brasenose and Christ Church, where he had charmed Peter Martyr Vermigli, the Regius Professor of Divinity. While on his travels he had made firm friends of Geneva's pastors, including Calvin, and had adopted a radical and critical view of the reforms in Edwardian England. His deep religious commitment and his critique of the Book of Common Prayer provided a solid foundation for the strong working relationship he developed with Knox. Perhaps a subconscious divide in Knox's mind between a minister's and a layman's vocation or

Whittingham's different character prevented greater closeness between the two men. Knox's own bond with Goodman, also developed at Frankfurt, created a different dynamic in his relationship with Whittingham, and the three men became a formidable troika.

Knox's first recorded intervention in Frankfurt was during the church meeting called at the end of November 1554 to discuss the letter and conditions brought from Strasbourg by Grindal and Chambers. One demand had been that the substance of the 1552 Prayer Book be retained. Knox and Whittingham combined to ask what 'the substance' might mean in this context. Recognizing that this was a loaded question, Grindal and Chambers ended the consultation, saying they had no authority to negotiate. Knox's influence can be seen in the more abrasive tone of Frankfurt's reply to Strasbourg. He had shifted the terms of the debate to his favoured formulation. Rather than debate what should be discarded, he started from the opposite pole – asserting that only those sections of the Prayer Book that 'stood with God's Word' should be retained. His opponents in 1554, as two years earlier in London, wanted a permissive, negative formulation that practices were allowable provided Scripture did not forbid them. By switching the basic premise of the debate, Knox ignored definitions of what might or might not be regarded as 'indifferent' or outside the irreducible core. He concentrated upon the rigid formula that everything in a liturgy must be justified directly by Scripture. The gulf between these two formulations was difficult to bridge since both parties appealed directly to the Bible. In a tone reminiscent of Knox's written style, the 3 December letter from Frankfurt to Strasbourg carried the direct warning that there was no point in the Strasbourg exiles coming to Frankfurt with the aim of re-establishing ceremonies.

The bold and defiant ring to the letter might have been a bluff since Whittingham and Knox were not convinced they commanded a majority among their congregation. They moved swiftly to strengthen their position within the Frankfurt congregation and for any future negotiation with the other exile communities. In search of a heavyweight ally, they took it upon themselves to appeal directly to John Calvin. This was a remarkably provocative move since the original letter penned by Whittingham and signed personally by Knox was written on 11 December, before Strasbourg's reply had been received. With sleight of hand the anonymous later account justifying the party of Whittingham and Knox given in the *Troubles at Frankfurt* suggested that the move to consult Calvin had been agreed by the congregation after that Strasbourg reply and after Thomas Lever's suggested liturgy had been rejected. Despite the later spin that Calvin had been consulted as a referee in the dispute, the letter was a bid by Whittingham and Knox to recruit a well-respected

Reformer to their side. The majority of English exiles would have placed Henry Bullinger and Peter Martyr Vermigli above Calvin on their list of Reformers to consult. However, Knox believed that much of the opposition to his views came from the English in Zurich, whom he presumed had Bullinger's backing. Similarly, Peter Martyr, who was resident in that city, would support the Strasbourg exiles. Both Reformers had been heavily involved in discussions over the creation of the 1552 Prayer Book, and Cranmer had directly consulted Martyr. Knox and Whittingham felt they were unlikely to receive a ringing endorsement for their stand from either Bullinger or Martyr. The content of their letter to Calvin accompanied by its Latin 'digest' of the Prayer Book constituted a pre-emptive strike against their opponents. It highlighted the ceremonies they disliked and was laced with derogatory comments, producing a caricature of the 1552 Prayer Book.

When Strasbourg's reply dated 13 December was received about a week later it was read to the Frankfurt congregation. The letter confirmed that the other exiles would not be coming to Frankfurt, at least in the short term, and implied that the Frankfurt congregation were on their own and could devise a form of worship that suited them. With Christmas a few weeks away the congregation was particularly anxious to celebrate communion together. At this juncture Knox tossed a large spanner into the works by declaring that he was not prepared to administer the Lord's Supper according to the 1552 Prayer Book and that he was equally unwilling to adopt an alternative liturgy until that was agreed by the other English communities. The English translation of Calvin's *Order of Geneva* had been suggested because sufficient members of the congregation had copies to hand. Huycke, the translator of the *Order*, was possibly also in Frankfurt at that point.[7] As a way out of the impasse he had created, Knox suggested that someone else administer the 1552 Prayer Book Communion; or, as a last resort, he was willing to resign. Neither suggestion was acceptable to the congregation.

Knox found himself in the midst of major row about Holy Communion and it brought him to the brink of despair. By the end of the year he was searching for a way to leave this ministry and possibly the city. Early in January 1555, he wrote directly to the Company of Pastors at Geneva. He signed with the pseudonym Tinoterius, possibly in an attempt to disguise the fact that he was once more in communication with Geneva.[8] By addressing his letter to the Company's secretary, Jean de St André who had recently been in correspondence with Whittingham, Knox sought an indirect way of urging Calvin to reply to the 11 December letter and the Latin digest of the Prayer Book. He urgently needed a supportive reply from the Reformer declaring that the church should not be burdened with a 'farrago of ceremonies'. He also hoped

Calvin would write to the English exiles in Zurich and 'remind them that the gospel of Christ be not disturbed on account of ceremonies dreamed up by men'. There was more than a touch of desperation in this hastily written letter, particularly in the final request. Knox wanted to escape from the stressful situation in Frankfurt and asked Calvin 'whether I may desist from this calling with conscience unharmed'. He believed that his pastoral efforts had produced the opposite effect of his intentions and that he was scattering, instead of building up, his flock. He was casting about for a way out of the nasty situation in Frankfurt and looked to Calvin for permission to leave. Calvin's overdeveloped sense of duty and self-sacrifice made it unlikely he would encourage him to quit his post merely because the going had got tough.

Whether prompted by Knox's additional appeal or just because he was clearing his correspondence, Calvin wrote to the Frankfurt congregation on 18 January.[9] He was exasperated by another bout of internal bickering among religious exiles and emphasized that it was essential the congregation coalesce into one body of worshippers and not fight over forms of prayer or external ceremonies. Having accepted the evidence of the Latin digest sent by Knox and Whittingham, he remarked that the Prayer Book had contained some 'silly things' that would have been changed in time. He attempted to rebuke both sides, urging Knox and Whittingham not to be so fierce in pushing for change, though he was harder upon those wanting to hold on to old ceremonies. He was not pleased to have been dragged into the dispute and, in a slightly weary note, commented that some of the English were not prepared to listen to him whatever he said. From Knox's perspective, Calvin's letter, while broadly supportive, did not constitute the conclusive argument or authority that might settle the storm and it ignored his question about resigning. There was little relief in this missive for the beleaguered Scot, though by the time the letter reached Frankfurt the situation had changed once more.

THE BRETHREN OF THE PURITY

In the heat of the debate in Frankfurt, accusations and counter-accusations flowed freely. Knox had been denounced as a schismatic and accused of being motivated by some personal agenda. In his turn the Scot had shown little restraint, characterizing his opponents as tantamount to Catholic priests or upholders of Jewish practices and denouncing the 1552 Prayer Book as 'unperfect, uncleane, unpure, damnable and full of superstition deservinge also death, plague and exile'. In such a contest of cumulative invective Knox had met his match. John Bale, former Bishop of Ossory, was a champion verbal prizefighter and past master of the polemical broadside. He made his own notes on the issues in dispute and drafted some satirical ripostes. In a letter to Thomas Ashley, probably then in Duisburg and on his way to Frankfurt, he also described the quarrel within the Frankfurt congregation and gave a brief summary of his counter-arguments against Knox and Whittingham.[10] He condemned the appeals sent by Whittingham and Knox to supporters of 'their factious secte' and he might have got wind of the letter they had sent to Calvin. Drawing upon his extensive studies in Church history, Bale coined a nickname for his opponents and lampooned them as 'the brethren of the purity' or the 'Catharytes'. Like the medieval heretics, the Cathars, who maintained their purity by separating themselves from the world, Bale characterized 'our new Catharytes' as boasting about upholding God's glory, maintaining the sincerity of God's Word and 'the highest puritie in religion'.

Bale had been particularly enraged by Knox's dismissal of the Prayer Book communion service as having 'the face of the popishe Masse' and provided a detailed refutation in his letter to Ashley and in a separate memo. He listed a series of comparisons between the Prayer Book service and the Mass, adding his accustomed scatological abuse about the Catholic ritual.[11] With devastating satire Bale adopted the voice of his opponents and described their perspective upon the supporters of the Prayer Book, 'what we are in your sight'. With even more bite Bale lampooned the understanding that Knox and his supporters had of themselves, 'what you are in your sight'. He commented with heavy humour that since they were 'not as other men are' it was surprising this pure brotherhood had not been taken up with Enoch into heaven; perhaps they lacked 'the fiery chariot to carry them above the clouds'. Although Bale noted 'their Scot Knoxe in his sedicious, barbarouse and scismatycall pratlynes', surprisingly he did not target Knox's status as a foreigner.

Belatedly answering Frankfurt's call to preach from the previous September, Thomas Lever arrived in the city around the end of December or the start of January. His arrival changed Knox's position and the dynamic of the debate. Having come from Zurich, Lever might have been despatched to use his position as preacher to influence the congregation in support of the 1552 Prayer Book. At a later stage Knox grew suspicious of his fellow minister and of Lever's behind-the-scenes manoeuvres. This might have been part of a personal rivalry where two intransigent men were yoked together in a team ministry. John Foxe, a friend to both, later chided Lever for being quarrelsome and blamed this side of his character on an over-zealous asceticism. Foxe's solution was simple: Lever should stop depriving himself, eat and sleep more and quarrel less. Foxe was equally prepared to take issue with Knox over the tone and arguments of his contentious 1558 pamphlet *The First Blast of the Trumpet against the Monstrous Regiment of Women*.[12] On arrival Lever found he was in the middle of the row over Holy Communion. The later accounts offered slightly different versions of the various committees and attempts to produce a new order of worship for the Frankfurt congregation. One version set out three stages: a new order by Lever that was rejected; a new order by a committee of five that was rejected; a new order by a different committee of four that was accepted. In another version, the committee of five and Lever were working on their orders at the same time and Lever did not produce a proper order, but just read some sections directly from the Prayer Book.[13]

The committee of five comprised Knox, Whittingham, Foxe, Anthony Gilby and Thomas Cole, all of whom were in favour of making changes to the 1552 Prayer Book. Foxe later described to Peter Martyr how the 'unhappy theological warfare and contention' had 'made almost the whole winter barren and unfruitful' for his own work. Being a man who loved peace and hated dissension, he had attempted to remain neutral and promote concord but had felt compelled to be a member of that committee because he 'could not be a wholly idle spectator'. Writing to Martyr, Foxe tried to present the humour in the situation, telling him how youths and even boys as young as seven had joined the fray, though the 'most vigilant fighters were the aged theologians'. He added, 'It would be an Iliad to describe the raging of the storm; you would never believe it.'[14] Foxe was trying to make the best of the major disappointment when the committee presented their order and it was rejected. His close friend Gilby, whose house Foxe shared, was deeply upset and made a tearful plea to the congregation not to condemn the order out of hand or think the authors had sought anything but God's glory. The work of this committee did bear fruit in the long run since it served as the basis in 1556 for the *Forme of Prayers* of the English exile congregation in Geneva where Knox was minister.[15]

Another committee was established with its membership carefully balanced between the two main factions. Lever and Henry Parry were paired with Knox and Whittingham, providing one clerical and one lay member from each side. They were set the task of drawing together material from the Book of Common Prayer and another liturgy, probably the *Order of Geneva*. On 6 February the committee reported back with an order the congregation was prepared to accept. A written document embodying everyone's consent stated that this order would be in place until 30 April and in any dispute five Reformers, namely the four, Calvin, Bullinger, Martyr, Viret, who were already in touch with the English exiles and also Wolfgang Musculus at Berne, would be asked to act as referees. Peace was declared, and a major effort made to bury past differences and bring the parties together was sealed by the long-awaited administration of the Lord's Supper, the visible demonstration of the church as one body.[16] Knox was greatly relieved and regarded the agreement as placing the Frankfurt church upon a proper foundation. When writing his own narrative of what happened, he began the story with this agreement and treated its breach as the fundamental cause of all the subsequent trouble.[17]

After a month when all went smoothly, the storm hit from a seemingly clear blue sky during one furious fortnight in March and it blew Knox off his feet. By the early morning of Tuesday, 26 March, Knox was setting off on the road south, banished from Frankfurt, with a treason charge hanging over his head and not entirely sure what had hit him. Though at the start of the year he had been looking for a way to leave the city, this was not what he had had in mind. The treatment of Knox split the English exiles and became part of a breach that never fully healed. As the anonymous 1575 tract proclaimed, the Troubles 'begun' at Frankfurt were a foretaste of the divisions besetting the Elizabethan Church and came to be seen as the foundation of English nonconformity and the Puritan movement. The liturgical and doctrinal stance that Knox and his supporters adopted during the Troubles led to the production of a new order of worship that was carried into the Reformed Church of Scotland and the Anglophone Presbyterian tradition. The attractive rhyming of Coxians versus Knoxians has encouraged a tendency to explain the Troubles primarily as a clash of single-leader parties. Cox's speedy victory over Knox has grabbed the headlines and disguised the longer and far less conclusive battles both before and after that furious fortnight.

THE FACE OF AN ENGLISH CHURCH

The rather airy warning made in Frankfurt's 3 December letter to Strasbourg about not bothering to make the journey just to re-establish ceremonies came back to haunt Knox and Whittingham. On 13 March, later than the February date mooted in the autumn, a large group of English exiles did arrive from Strasbourg led by Richard Cox. Alarmed by the reports from Bale (and probably Lever) in Frankfurt, Cox had travelled south from Duisburg with Thomas Ashley and galvanized a number of senior clerics in Strasbourg. A substantial party set out with the aim of regaining control over the Frankfurt congregation and establishing a recognizably 'English' liturgy. While Cox did feature on Knox's list of villains, he had plenty of company. It was probably Whittingham and Goodman who identified the hand of the Dean of Christ Church, their former Oxford college, and treated Cox as the arch-villain. Having learned his trade and kept his head in the poisonous atmosphere of Henry VIII's court during the 1540s, Cox was an excellent tactician in fights between factions. He was a determined and passionate defender of Archbishop Cranmer, the Edwardian Church and the 1552 Prayer Book that he had helped to produce.

Though based hundreds of miles away at Duisburg, Cox had been the first to alert Grindal to the threat to the Prayer Book from the Frankfurt congregation.[18] By wrong-footing his opponents at every step he achieved his goals of re-establishing the Prayer Book and controlling the congregation.

The first move was simplicity itself. After their arrival on Tuesday, 13 March, the Strasbourg party attended church for the next service and began making the Prayer Book responses out loud, though the congregation had dropped this practice. When requested by Knox and the elders to desist, they refused, declaring that they would do as they had done in England and that their church should have 'an English face'[19] – terminology that suggested careful briefing on the language of the previous debates in Frankfurt. Knox was thrown completely off balance by the support given to the incomers by Thomas Lever, his fellow minister. Such behaviour enraged him because it ignored the 6 February order that all, including Lever, had agreed to uphold. The Scot complained to Vallerand Poullain, the French minister, in the hope that Lever could be forced to adhere to the original agreement. Whether correctly or not, Knox came to the conclusion that Lever had conspired with the Strasbourg group and secretly planned this betrayal. The new arrivals also demanded that the Litany, with its series of petitions and responses, be used and the elders once more explained that this long prayer had been removed in the February order. Since the Litany with its highly traditional format carried over from Catholic worship was one of his pet dislikes, Knox's refusal was more forcefully expressed.[20]

Predictably, Sunday worship brought the major flashpoints. In a stage-managed scene, the Litany was read from the pulpit with the incomers loudly adding the responses. Lever introduced the preacher, who was someone who had previously attended Mass in England and subscribed to some Catholic articles. This was almost certainly John Jewel, who had helped Cranmer and Ridley during their disputations, but had not fled quickly enough from Oxford and had recanted and attended Mass. Though Jewel had later publicly confessed his fault, Knox and his supporters were horrified by the presence in their pulpit of one who had participated in 'idolatry'. To stir things up further, at the end of the morning service Lever threw in some extra comments and 'invectives' against opponents of the Prayer Book.

Feelings were running high as the midday meal was taken, and Knox was urged to make a stand when he preached in the afternoon service. Most secure when he was putting a case from the pulpit, on Sunday, 17 March he probably delivered one of the most impassioned sermons of his life. In a magnificent understatement William Whittingham summarized the sermon's tone: 'Knox spake his mind freely.'[21] The Scot's anger imposed a pattern upon all his past experience of the Church of England and in a single compelling denunciation he grafted his personal analysis of the faults of the Edwardian Church on to the current controversy.

Having been preaching through the Book of Genesis, Knox took as his main text the story of Noah's drunkenness and the theme of what should and should not be covered up. Running against the normal grain of the biblical text, he went for total exposure of the faults of the Edwardian Church. His attitude had hardened against the 1552 Prayer Book and in public he was prepared to call it 'superstitious, impure, unclean and unperfect'. In full prophetic mode he warned that God would punish the English in Germany if they displayed the same vices that had been prevalent in England. The ominous parallel was drawn with the Old Testament Israelites who were sent into a second exile beyond Babylon. Knox expounded in considerable detail his view of the 'slackness of religion' present under King Edward VI. He particularly selected for criticism the complete absence of discipline within Church and nation, as well as mentioning the fact that Bishop Hooper had been forced to accept the wearing of clerical vestments by Archbishop Cranmer and Bishop Ridley. He rounded off his sermon with a scathing attack upon the remaining abuses within the ecclesiastical system, in particular the holding of multiple livings or benefices, which deprived congregations of preaching and brought the Protestant faith into disrepute. This barb hit home because Cox had been Dean both of Westminster and of Christ Church, Oxford, in addition to holding other benefices. Knox was scarcely out of the pulpit before the rebukes started, led by Cox. After heated exchanges, a formal church meeting was called for the following Tuesday evening to discuss the issues.

Those who opposed Knox arrived at the congregational meeting that Tuesday evening as a co-ordinated group with a plan of campaign. Enough of them had engaged in the cut and thrust of cathedral chapters or college politics to know the group tactics of manipulating the agenda, stage-managing walk-outs and block voting. In this company, Knox was a raw novice and he made a series of tactical errors. The first item to be debated was the admission of the newcomers to the congregation instead of a discussion of the breach of the February order, as Knox had expected. The supporters of Whittingham and Knox held a majority within the Frankfurt congregation, but would lose it once the Strasbourg group joined their opponents. It was proposed that the issue of the breach of the February agreement be settled first and the newcomers admitted thereafter. That was rejected, as was another option probably put forward by Whittingham, that the Strasbourg group sign the Ecclesiastical Discipline of the French church as he and other English exiles had done the previous summer. The discussion moved to those who were rumoured to have attended Mass or recanted while in England, though when it was demanded that those under suspicion should either recant or deny the charge, Cox's group took to making noisy protests and walked out, complaining of such an 'abominable injury' to good Protestants.

With the meeting deadlocked and a majority set to deny admission to the newcomers, Knox made a serious mistake. While it was obvious the incomers wanted admission to create a majority in favour of Lever, he argued that the case over the broken agreement was so overwhelming it would triumph regardless. Over-confident about his own position, he was tactically naive and an almost inevitable sequence followed. After the newcomers were admitted, the vote on the breach of agreement was rushed through and Lever was absolved. Then Cox promptly capitalized on his dominant position by discharging Knox from preaching, thereby depriving his opponents of one of their best weapons. Since Cox had no official position in the Frankfurt congregation and was relying upon his strong personality and former authority in the Edwardian Church, his action completely undermined Knox's authority as a minister and implicitly denied the congregation's call.[22]

The following morning Whittingham tried to salvage something from the wreckage by complaining to John Glauburg, the City Councillor who was dealing with the exiles' churches. On Glauburg's orders the English services were stopped and the French minister, Poullain, was delegated to chair a committee of four to resolve the liturgical dispute. Cox and Lever faced Whittingham and Knox as they debated in Poullain's house for two days, with the Frenchman taking careful minutes. Under his expert chairmanship the committee reached agreement on most of the services until on the Friday morning the discussion turned to Matins. Knox objected to the employment of non-Scriptural texts, especially in the verse and response section that had been translated directly from the medieval Catholic rite. His fire was also directed at the inclusion of the traditional early Christian hymn the *Te Deum* or 'We praise Thee, O Lord'. Cox dug in his heels, declaring that these must remain and challenging the broader point that non-biblical material must automatically be rejected. The debate degenerated into a slanging match and the committee broke up without agreement. Knox conceded he had been 'fervent', but believed his vehemence had been in a good cause.[23]

Though the short sentences and responses following the Lord's Prayer that began 'O Lord, open thou our lyppes' proved a surprising stumbling block, the two views represent different starting points and outlooks towards the composition of a Protestant liturgy. Following Cranmer, Cox was willing – provided the doctrine expressed through the liturgy was demonstrably Protestant – to include traditional prayers translated into English. The 1552 Prayer Book had modified these short sentences by replacing the 'I' of the 1549 version with 'we', indicating that it was the congregation as a collective body rather than the priest who were making these petitions.[24] By contrast, since he believed he was defending the principle of Scriptural warrant, Knox wanted to expunge the format and words of the Catholic rites. He would include only biblical songs within a service, and the congregation prayed collectively by singing psalms and not saying responses. In terms of the text and practice of the liturgy, the division over versicles and responses was minor, but for Knox it was a deep chasm that he would not try to bridge. During subsequent years the increasing intransigence of both sides on liturgical matters justified the claim that the Troubles at Frankfurt were the beginning of fundamental splits within the Church of England.

In a last-ditch effort to regain the initiative Whittingham completed a Latin supplication to the City Council summarizing what had happened since his first arrival in Frankfurt. Stressing the breach of the February agreement, an attempt was made to invoke the clause in that agreement providing for arbitration by five leading Reformers. By this stage, however, the City fathers were exasperated and Glauburg came to the church and threatened to close it to the English unless they agreed to abide by the French congregation's doctrine and ceremonies. Reading the situation perfectly, Cox instantly accepted this offer, secured the agreement of the English congregation and begged Glauburg to continue to show favour to the English.

HORRIBLE CALUMNIES

Meanwhile Knox was facing a far more serious threat, since treason charges carrying the death sentence had been laid against him in front of the City Council. In his *Faithfull Admonition* published the previous summer, he had gone considerably further than his English colleagues in the blunt language of his denunciation of Queen Mary Tudor, her husband Philip of Spain and her father-in-law the Emperor Charles V. During the winter of 1554, among his many epithets for Knox, Bale had labelled him seditious: in an intemperate-language contest, this was the pot calling the kettle black. Crucially, it was members of the English gentry who took most offence at 'the atrocious and horrible calumnies against the queen of England', and they worried that the taint of treason would infect all the exiles and provide the Catholic government with a reason for 'overturning the whole church in England'.[25] When in March the liturgical row had been reignited, Edward Isaac of Patricksbourn in Kent came to Knox's house. He offered a choice: if Knox backed down in his attack upon the Book of Common Prayer, then the wealthy Isaac and his friends would deal favourably with him. If Knox's opposition continued, then the minister would rue the consequences. With characteristic bravado, Knox dismissed the blackmail, declaring, 'I could wish my name to perish so that God's book and his glory might only be sought amongst us.'[26] An attempt was also made to pressurize Knox's friends to persuade the Scot to leave the church or the city.

Unfortunately for Knox, Isaac did not make idle threats. Accompanied by Henry Parry and Lever's close supporter Edmund Sutton, and probably with Richard Chambers' knowledge, he made a formal complaint on 15 March to the City Councillors. The previous week Parry and Sutton had become burghers of Frankfurt and paid their city taxes, giving them considerably more standing in their appeal to the Council. On Monday, 18 March, after Knox's explosive sermon the previous day, the complainers returned to check what the Council had done. The first news of the complaint reached Knox and his supporters two days later, when the Council summoned Whittingham. When asked about Knox's character and his record, Whittingham replied that Knox was 'a lerned, wise grave and godly man'.[27] Informed about the treason charge, Whittingham was commanded to produce by 1 p.m. that day a Latin translation of nine articles drawn from Knox's tract. After Knox had freely acknowledged that the extracts were from his pen, he was banned from preaching until further notice.

The Council were in an awkward position because Knox had compared Charles V to Nero, and the Holy Roman Emperor was at Augsburg, not far from Frankfurt. If he were to hear of the slander and the charge, Frankfurt would have no choice but to deliver Knox. The following day when Knox arrived in church to listen to the sermon, his attendance provoked another walkout by his opponents. They declared that they could not be in the same place as him and probably for good measure explained to all and sundry that he was under suspension on treason charges. Over the next few days the pressure was increased upon the Council when Isaac and John Jewel demanded that Knox be sentenced. Consequently, the City fathers sent for William Whittingham and William Williams and told them to get Knox out of the city as soon as possible. Not able to attend church on Monday night, 25 March, Knox preached a farewell sermon to about fifty supporters in his lodgings. He chose as his theme Christ's death and resurrection and reminded his hearers that the elect always faced persecution while on earth, though they would receive great rewards in heaven. The following morning a group of friends and well-wishers travelled several miles down the road with Knox, and there was much sorrow and tears as they said goodbye.

To explain his precipitous departure from Frankfurt, probably about a month later Knox wrote his own *Narrative* of events. In 1574, the anonymous author of the *Troubles* had a copy of that document in front of him as he compiled his own tract. Both men automatically assumed that the treason charges were a 'dirty trick' by the opposition to remove Knox from the liturgical dispute. They knew there had been close collaboration between the gentlemen who laid the charges and the clerics who had given 'counsel'. The clergymen included many of Knox's main antagonists over the Prayer Book, with Cox, Bale, Grindal, Jewel and John Mather on the list. Knox jumped to the conclusion that recourse to the Council had been direct revenge for the personal attacks he had made in his sermon of 17 March. He was unaware that the charges had been sent to the Council two days before that sermon.[28] The obvious element of skulduggery has hidden a deeper disquiet among some English exiles about Knox's language and approach to the Marian regime. In the furious fortnight after the arrival of Cox's group in Frankfurt, that concern provided an irresistibly convenient stick with which to beat Knox. However, it was not solely the opportune creation of the moment by the skilled tacticians in Cox's party. From the dark hints in the later angry letter to Calvin from David Whitehead, it appeared there was a specific gathering of information about Knox's other misdemeanours. Though ruined by wild overstatement, that letter made the reasonable argument that Knox's *Faithfull Admonition* had damaged Protestants who remained in England. It was a fair point to suggest that possession of that tract or reading its content might put people in severe danger of accusations of treason. That had been the fate of Bartlet Green, who was arrested for sedition and later tried and executed for heresy. His intercepted correspondence with Christopher Goodman had contained the fateful phrase, 'The queen is not yet dead.'[29] It was just possible to sustain Whitehead's colourful assertion that 'that outrageous pamphlet of Knox's added much oil to the flame of persecution in England'. His case was undermined by the inaccurate cause-and-effect assertion that before Knox's tract was published there had been no burnings, and that the executions began after its publication.[30]

Over three months after Knox's banishment from Frankfurt, Richard Chambers was still expressing concern to Cox to ensure Knox 'by rashe and inconsiderat writing do in no wise molest and trouble the churche'. Chambers hoped Cox would ask John a Lasco and Peter Martyr to persuade Knox that 'he be more circumspect and less subject to his owne wilfull affections'.[31] Long before he penned his *First Blast*, there were a significant number of English exiles who had decided that his writings were potentially or actually seditious and that his tracts were bringing serious trouble to the entire Protestant cause.

Opinions about the treatment of Knox did not automatically follow the party lines of the liturgical dispute. Though a member of the Prayer Book party during the liturgical rows and friend of David Whitehead, John Mackbrair supported his fellow Scot. Mackbrair was furious with Richard Chambers because he 'had lost Mr Knoxe his good name'. In reply Chambers suggested Mackbrair was wrong because Chambers esteemed Knox. Mackbrair's source had been a member of the Frankfurt Council who had said that Chambers 'had done enough as touching Mr Knoxe to losse my head'.[32] Knox's Frankfurt supporters tended to paint the whole affair in the darkest possible colours and it was their version carried in person by Whittingham and Knox himself that reached Calvin. Such shabby treatment of a fellow minister outraged the Reformer and led to his sharp rebuke in a letter of 31 May, 'that Maister Knox was in my judgement nether godly nor brotherly dealt withall'.[33]

Some of the most vociferous condemnations of Cox and his party came from Christopher Goodman, who had arrived in their company on 13 March. Goodman subsequently became a firm believer in the theory that there had been a conspiracy to oust Knox and gain control over the Frankfurt congregation. The Englishman's stance was completely transformed. He began as one of the Strasbourg band of clerics marching into Frankfurt and ended as the individual excommunicated for his continued advocacy of the Knoxian view after the Scot's expulsion from the city. Goodman's newly discovered papers have shed an entirely fresh light upon the Troubles. The letters he wrote and papers he kept demonstrated the personal outrage he felt at the behaviour of his former Oxford colleagues and Strasbourg friends. His Oxford mentor and friend Peter Martyr Vermigli had remained in Strasbourg and amid the turmoil of the last week of March Goodman wrote letters to him bubbling with emotion and confusion.[34] In the longer run and despite Martyr's best efforts to urge reconciliation among former colleagues, the rifts created in Frankfurt did not heal. An extremely prickly exchange between Cox and Goodman in 1557 saw neither man by give much ground and at best an armed truce was achieved.[35] For Goodman, the greatest offence during the Troubles was the treatment of Knox and subsequent attempts to intimidate his party. The 'naming and shaming' of his own public excommunication reinforced his conviction that Cox and his allies had ruthlessly imposed control over the Frankfurt congregation.[36]

WITH A TROUBLED HEART

During the dispute, Knox convinced Goodman of his approach to worship and turned the Englishman into one of the most strident proponents of the 'regulative principle' in liturgical matters. Goodman also accepted Knox's analysis of the failings of the Edwardian Church and adopted the Scot's prophetic and apocalyptic version of recent English history. Of far greater significance for

Knox's future life, the Frankfurt experience turned Goodman into a close personal friend who could share and understand the trials and tribulations of following a ministerial vocation. Although this previously unknown letter found its way into his papers, Goodman was not among the addressees when Knox wrote from Geneva on 1 May to his friends in Frankfurt. Goodman had probably already left that city on a reconnaissance trip to find other cities of refuge. At the end of April, Knox had received letters from Frankfurt informing him that things had gone from bad to worse: a liturgy based directly upon the Book of Common Prayer was being used, an entirely new ministry had been appointed and Whittingham, Goodman and Gilby had been silenced. Having been comprehensively beaten, the defeated party in Frankfurt thought it best to plan to move, though they were immediately labelled schismatic.[37] Since Calvin had shown Knox the letter of 5 April sent from Cox and his supporters, the Scot already knew some of the sorry details. Before reaching Geneva, Knox had stopped in Basle where he was welcomed by Bishop Simon Sulzer, who was broadly sympathetic to his tale of woe, though wary, as he told Bullinger, of becoming entangled in any 'odious controversies' among the English.[38] Knox's letters from Basle to Frankfurt had been delayed and Whittingham or Goodman seems to have repeated some of the negotiations with Sulzer and Marbach, the pastor in Basle, concerning the establishment of an English exile community in that city.[39]

Probably in reaction to the stressful events over the past few months, Knox's health deteriorated and he was in pain and suffering once more from his chronic ailments. The Frankfurt Troubles had left him feeling mentally battered and bruised and he was depressed, signing his 1 May letter 'with a trubled heart'.[40] Despite his indifferent health, Knox was contemplating leaving Geneva again. He hoped Whittingham would arrive in the city before he left, and Knox probably deposited his *Narrative* of the Frankfurt episode with Calvin for Whittingham to collect. It had been composed in haste and without access to much documentation, with Knox even referring to his *Faithfull Admonition* by a different title. From the time he left Frankfurt Knox had probably been thinking about the possibility of returning to Scotland and finding a way of marrying Marjorie.

Though on the surface he seemed to emerge relatively unscathed, the Frankfurt Troubles changed Knox's life. Lever's lack of loyalty to the February order and agreement and the personal betrayal of his co-minister had profoundly shocked Knox. He was a firm believer in the theory of the solidarity of ministerial brethren, but its practice was harder. He had discovered that he had determined enemies among his fellow Protestants who were prepared to uphold their views with ruthlessness and polemical vigour. He had proved no match for the clergy such as Bale, Cox and Grindal or for the lay merchants and gentlemen like Chambers, Isaac or Parry. They had comprehensively defeated him and he had been fortunate to retreat from the city without further harm. The rows over liturgy and control were also struggles for power. At stake were the identity of the English religious exiles and the future direction of the Church of England. Even without the later furore over his *First Blast*, Knox might have wondered if he had a place within that institution when they all returned to England. He had discovered the hard way that he was a poor player in the tactical game of group decision-making and in detailed negotiations within committees. He became more wary of that side of ecclesiastical life and avoided committees whose members held seriously divergent views. The experience of the Troubles left him with a number of scars, including the persistent fear and half-expectation that his own side would betray him. In the future he was suspicious when he had no need to be, and unforgiving and uncompromising when challenged. For the remainder of his life he harboured a distrust of those holding senior positions within the Church of England.

As well as enemies and humiliation, Knox had found great friendship and had been given support by a significant section of the Frankfurt congregation. His friend the peace-loving John Foxe had stood by him and he had worked alongside William Whittingham, Thomas Wood and Anthony Gilby, all of whom would prove important allies and supporters in the Geneva church. The most positive consequence of that furious fortnight in March was the development of his friendship with Goodman. Although they had previously met on the Chester walls, Frankfurt turned an acquaintance into a close friend and Goodman into a passionately committed supporter of Knox. After the unmitigated disaster of his co-pastorate with Lever, Knox might have refused to contemplate joining another team ministry. However, the trust and friendship he had formed with Goodman in those few days at Frankfurt were sufficient for him to be willing a few months later to accept their joint ministry in Geneva.

CHAPTER EIGHT

Double cares

When evicted from Frankfurt, Knox was starting his third exile. He was on the road again, out of a job and with no fixed abode. He was fortunate that thanks to all his friends and supporters he quickly found his feet. During the following months he married Marjorie and brought her and her mother back to Geneva. The secret trip to collect them in Northumberland had taken him into Scotland, where he unexpectedly found himself conducting a preaching tour. When he left his native country once more, Knox carried with him a new weight of expectation that he would help to lead the Scottish Protestants out of the 'Egypt' of Catholicism. Meanwhile his Frankfurt supporters had set up a new exile church in Geneva and in his absence he was elected their minister alongside Christopher Goodman. When his new household arrived in Geneva they encountered the warmest of welcomes. Despite having plenty of new cares and concerns, Knox entered the happiest period of his life. He was a husband and became a father and he formed the special ministerial partnership with Goodman that made them such a formidable and long-lasting team.

Knox might have been describing his state of mind as he left Frankfurt when writing later about the experience of exile to his London friends Anne Locke and Rose Hickman. Exile was 'to be in suche a strait as thois that frome realme to realme, and citie to citie, seik rest as pilgremes, and yit sall find none'.[1] As he faced a third exile, Knox was fortunate to be able to return to Geneva as a city of refuge. He could look forward to a welcome from Calvin, the chance to resume his studies and escape for a while from the burden of ministry. He had arrived in his personal haven by the end of April. Either before he left Frankfurt or in Geneva, he would have collected the latest correspondence from Elizabeth and probably Marjorie Bowes, no doubt asking when he would visit. Since he no longer had a direct pastoral responsibility, he was free to plan how he might achieve this. He probably decided that the safest method was to return to Scotland and slip across the border and meet Elizabeth and Marjorie in Norham or some other safe location in Northumberland. The first stage would be to travel to Dieppe and, using the excellent communications of its Scottish merchant community with their homeland, make more specific plans there.

Knox was still in Geneva on 16 May 1555, the momentous day that marked the final stage in the long struggle between Calvin and the 'Libertine' group in Geneva. As a 'stranger' in the city, Knox might have been in danger when a large gathering of Genevans assembled against the many religious exiles who had flooded their city, especially those from France. Following the quelling of the riot, Calvin and his supporters secured the majority upon the Small Council of Geneva and dominated the city's politics. For the remainder of his life, Calvin ran the city's ecclesiastical affairs in the way he saw fit and imposed the discipline he believed held the church together. Although recognizable only with hindsight, this was the point at which Geneva became, in Knox's famous words, 'the most perfect school of Christ'. In later comments about the riot, Knox followed Calvin's own analysis and insisted that the dispute was among those who, while agreeing about Reformed doctrine, disagreed about how 'discipline' should be administered.[2]

Their fervency does so ravish me

Though he would have preferred to remain studying quietly in the 'den of my awin ease', Knox had to attend to the unfinished business of his marriage.[3] Having travelled through France and then waited in Dieppe to formalize his arrangements, he arrived back in Scotland 'at the end of the harvest' of 1555.[4] Once again the mercantile community on both sides of the sea had assisted him and he was welcomed into the house of James Sim, an Edinburgh apothecary.[5] As Knox reminded Elizabeth Bowes, he had made this journey to be with her and would not have done it for any other person. Unless he was being exceptionally tactless, this declaration included his future wife, Marjorie. The three of them understood that this was a rescue mission or a planned elopement with mother-in-law in tow. It would be a relatively speedy operation, and in December 1555 Knox was expected to be back in Geneva 'any day'.[6] Given the secrecy necessarily involved, no details have survived of his precise movements or of his meeting with the two women in the autumn of 1555. He was heartened to find that, contrary to his gloomy expectations, a number of Protestants in Northumberland had not compromised their beliefs. He cracked a biblical joke about the situation, saying there was more than one

Lot in Sodom and more than two of Lot's daughters, meaning Elizabeth and Marjorie were not alone in keeping the faith – Knox had the sense not to risk being amusing about pillars of salt.[7] At some stage, possibly during the time he spent in Ayrshire, he returned secretly to Northumberland and Marjorie eloped with him. She had probably been planning for this eventuality since the end of 1553 and certainly appeared to leave her family without regrets. The party also included Elizabeth Bowes, who flouted social convention herself by leaving her husband and the rest of her family to go into religious exile with Knox and her daughter.

Whether or not he actively encouraged Elizabeth to abandon her husband and come into religious exile, he accepted the fact. Richard Bowes took a dim view of his wife's behaviour. After her public abandonment of him, they never met again. In his will in 1558, written shortly before his death, he made no mention of Elizabeth or Marjorie. Belatedly shutting the stable door, he insisted his other daughters marry with the consent of the male members of the family or lose their inheritance. Richard could not forgive his runaway daughter and the wife who had deserted him and, for many of Knox's contemporaries, Mrs Bowes was rejecting the obedience a wife should give her husband and offering a profoundly subversive example to other women. Even in the face of persecution, the magisterial Reformers had been exceptionally cautious about authorizing the abandonment of a spouse for religious reasons.[8] In other circumstances and particularly when it suited his arguments concerning female rulers, Knox employed the principle of a wife's subjection to her husband. That central pillar of early modern social thinking was swept aside by his fixation with the need to avoid at all costs the contamination of idolatry. Where his close personal friends were concerned, their duties to their husbands were overridden by his pleas to them to preserve their spiritual safety. His worried letters to Anne Locke and Rose Hickman came close to begging them to come into exile.[9] At the same time he was more circumspect and conventional in his advice to Janet Adamson, one of his Edinburgh 'sisters', about bearing with patience the different religious views held by her husband.[10]

With Marjorie and Elizabeth preparing to make their escape, Knox returned to Scotland, assuring them that he would be back shortly. Once established among the underground network of Scottish Protestants, he discovered that his ministerial talents were in considerable demand. Not realizing how much had altered since he had been removed from his native country in 1547, he was taken completely by surprise: 'Gif I had not sene it with my eyis in my awn contrey, I culd not have beleivit it.'[11] After the battering at Frankfurt, this experience gloriously reaffirmed his sense of ministerial vocation. He was pressed to preach and teach, and found at every turn that he was 'feeding the sheep'. He described the effect of such need and enthusiasm upon him: 'thair fervencie doith sa ravische me, that I can not but accuse and condemp my sleuthfull coldnes. God grant thame thair hartis desyre!'[12] The hyperbolic language obviously reflected his amazement. It also furnished an acceptable reason for not returning to Northumberland as quickly as he had intended. In his next letter to his mother-in-law Knox was able to use the same excuse of the urgent call of God's work.

In Edinburgh some of Knox's most enthusiastic and committed listeners were the wives of merchants and court officials. As had happened in London, these 'sisters' provided practical assistance such as safe houses, hospitality and financial support alongside the less tangible, but equally vital, spiritual 'comfort and mercy'.[13] In return Knox brought his own brand of pastoral reassurance. Elizabeth Adamson, the wife of James Baron, was particularly 'thirsty' and sought out Knox's company where she gained the confidence she needed in her salvation, a certainty that sustained her during her final illness the following year.[14] Focused upon the story of the temptation of Christ, Knox's teaching had helped 'reclaim' some from 'great anguische' and they were 'brocht from the bottome of hell'.[15] The exaggerated language might reflect Knox's own spiritual struggles as well as the doubts that assailed his audience.

When recasting the account for his *History*, Knox emphasized that he was the third in a succession of preachers who were working in Scotland in 1555.[16] William Harlaw had begun the ministry and was followed by John Willock, whom Knox had known from his days in Edwardian England. Willock had returned to Scotland from exile in Emden on an embassy from the duchy of Friesland. While under a form of diplomatic protection, he was able to undertake his other task of assessing progress among the Scottish Protestant community. He found links already in place between the Lothians, the Mearns and his home in Ayrshire. Still in Scotland when Knox arrived, Willock introduced him to John Lockhart of Bar in Ayrshire and John Erskine of Dun in Angus. This neatly slotted Knox into the Protestant network that was beginning to be aware of its geographical extent and its growing strength. The movement's co-ordination and communication network transported him around the country and kept him from attracting too much unwelcome attention in any one location. Although covering the same regions as George Wishart's tours, there was no attempt to repeat Wishart's open-air or 'hedge' preaching or offer public defiance to the ecclesiastical authorities. Knox remained behind closed doors in private dwellings and met prominent people at discreet supper parties. Looking back he felt he had been in constant demand, 'for so did Sathan hunt me, upon the one part, and so did my brethren crave my deutie to be payit to thame, on the other part, that small space was thair grantit to wrytting'.[17]

Knox's first extended stay was at Dun, John Erskine's fortified house outside Montrose in Angus and the Mearns. Though the two men were like chalk and cheese, during the month's stay Knox began a firm and lifelong friendship with Erskine. The laird of Dun's urbane manners, organizational talents and diplomatic and conciliatory approach to his opponents contrasted strongly with Knox's blunt and forceful speech and 'holy hatred' of his enemies. In Erskine's company, Knox began to appreciate the strength of local networks based on kindred and alliances in addition to shared religious conviction; loyalties could be combined rather than set in opposition. The 'gentlemen of Mearns' were coalescing around Erskine's leadership. During this visit and in future years they provided a formidable body of support for Knox. The personal contacts and Protestant networks he encountered in Angus and the Mearns certainly paid dividends.[18]

At the start of the winter, Knox travelled south to his home shire of Lothian to stay with another laird, Sir James Sandilands of Calder, whom he had known from his days with Wishart. Securely based at Mid Calder Knox had easy access to Edinburgh where he 'taught' in the period before Christmas.[19] Calder House provided a convenient residence where other nobles might visit without causing remark. One feature of Knox's tour in 1555–6 was the interest shown by important members of the Scottish peerage, and three young friends dropped in to Calder to see the preacher. Lord James Stewart, the Commendator Prior of St Andrews, had already met Knox in London in 1552. He was accompanied by his friend Archibald Campbell, Lord Lorne and heir to the Earl of Argyll, and by their mutual kinsman John Lord Erskine, later Regent Mar, who would have been briefed about Knox by his relative Erskine of Dun. Although he could not have known it at the time, Knox was meeting three men who, over the following two decades, were to transform Scotland and its religious allegiance.[20] These important introductions to key members of the Scottish nobility were probably devised and encouraged by the lairds, like Sandilands of Calder, who had taken organizational control of the Protestant movement in Scotland. Whether he realized it or not, Knox was being prepared for a role as a clerical leader of that movement.

The discussions Knox held with the future leaders of the Protestant party in Scotland propelled their thinking in new directions. In a formal discussion on whether attendance at Mass was permissible, he delivered an uncompromising message to these visitors, as he had at an earlier supper party in Edinburgh. The Mass was idolatrous worship and he insisted that attendance had to stop because it was a flagrant breach of the second commandment and contaminated all who were in any way associated with the ritual. Such a simple equation was not self-evident to his Scottish listeners, and the young Maitland of Lethington ventured the teasing observation that Knox's exposition left no room to mount a counter-argument. Even during this early encounter, Knox was discomfited by Lethington's quick wit and ability to pinpoint the weak spot in any argument. The Scots were being asked to take a major step, one that carried considerable risks, and Knox either did not realize this or was not willing to prepare his listeners gradually for this new departure. During the preceding few years he had been immersed in the English confessional struggle where attendance at Mass carried with it the great sin of apostasy in addition to the pollution of idolatry. With the battle lines etched in his mind, he maintained this hard stance. The experience of his Scottish listeners was totally different. Most had come slowly to accept Protestant doctrines while remaining part of normal parish life within their Catholic country. Although they met for Bible-reading and prayers, Protestant sacraments were not available and an underground church had not been organized. Salvation and ecclesiastical reform had been the major debating points, with worship only beginning to emerge as a significant issue among this fledgling Protestant movement. Knox's tough anti-Nicodemite position gave Scottish Protestants a jolt. They did not alter their behaviour overnight, but began to act more like a church 'under the cross' than as groups of evangelical readers.[21]

The debates on the Mass also had a direct effect upon Knox's own tactics, though this has not previously received much comment. Alongside his preaching and counselling, he began systematically to 'minister the Lord's Table' in the residences of his noble supporters. Fresh from the Frankfurt Troubles he deliberately planted a self-consciously Reformed form of worship in Scotland. By bringing the sacraments to accompany the sermons he offered a complete alternative to Catholic rites. He deliberately drew the network of Protestants into embryonic congregations and separated them from the Catholic Church. These developed into the 'privy kirks' with their own structure of worship. With words backed by deeds Knox ensured that the practice of 'right' worship became a key demand of the Scottish Protestants. Liturgical reform had been a matter of debate in the Scottish Church throughout the century. This issue potentially created common ground with Catholic reformers, such as John Winram, who had remained within the ecclesiastical hierarchy. Equally it divided the Protestant movement from another strand of Catholic reform that defended the sacraments while legislating against moral and institutional failings. The Provincial Church Councils called by Archbishop John Hamilton of St Andrews from 1549 had gone down the latter route. Knox was not personally given to such calculating analysis, but other Scots might have been exploring complex tactics to achieve consensual change of liturgy and doctrine.

Knox's emphasis upon the Lord's Supper was demonstrated by his activities in Ayrshire. After Christmas 1555, John Lockhart of Bar and Robert Campbell of Kinzeancleuch came to fetch him to Ayrshire. With its proud tradition of religious dissent which stretched back to the end of the fifteenth century, this interconnected band of laird and merchant families in the parishes of Mauchline, Loudoun and Galston radiated a confident Protestant identity. This group adopted Knox as one of their own, lionizing him and surrounding him with their spiritual and material warmth and friendship. As John Davidson later noted, those in the Kyle and Cunningham districts of Ayrshire felt Knox's death sorely, 'to quhome this darling was maist deare'.[22] The peace and comfort he found during this first visit gave Knox an extra appreciation of having come home. Ayrshire acquired for him an aura of complete safety and it became his bolt-hole during future Scottish crises. If Geneva was his ideal location for study, Ayr was where he could relax.

The lairds he met for the first time in 1555–6, Lockart of Bar, Campbell of Kinzeancleuch and Chalmers of Gadgirth, as well as their lords, the Earl of Glencairn and Lord Ochiltree, became Knox's most trusted supporters. In future troubles he knew these men would never let him down and his first recourse would be to 'the brethren of Kyle'.[23] The Ayrshire women, such as Elizabeth Campbell of Kinzeancleuch, proved equally loyal and true, and ensured that he always received a warm welcome in the shire. From 1556 part of his heart remained in Ayrshire and later he was linked by marital kinship to this extended Protestant network through his second wife, Lord Ochiltree's daughter.

Knox travelled north into Renfrewshire to Finlayston Castle rather than returning to Edinburgh via the old 'Lollard trail' up the Irvine valley and across the southern uplands on what is still the connecting road, the A71. At Finlayston, the home of the Earl of Glencairn, he again administered the Lord's Supper and preached to the Earl and Countess, their sons and select friends.[24] The quickening pace generated by these sacramental celebrations was also apparent when he returned to the Mearns and found 'greater liberty' than before. Rather than the signing of a formal religious bond, he probably used the language of covenant and league as he presided at the Lord's Table and gave these Angus gentlemen an even greater feeling of communal identity, solidarity and kinship.[25] The experience of working alongside the lesser nobility in Angus and Ayrshire reinforced his linguistic and conceptual associations between the administration of the sacraments and the covenant between God and his people. In his epistles to Scotland, he called upon the deeply familiar language of noble affinities and bonds of maintenance and manrent when explaining tricky points and began his definition of baptism as 'our first entrance in the houshald of God our Father; be the whilk is signifiet, that we ar reassavit in league with him'.[26] Such a melding of the language of religious association with that of kinship helped forge the covenanting tradition that came to play a significant part within later Scottish history.

The rise in heretical activity in different parts of the country did not go unnoticed by the Catholic friars and the ecclesiastical hierarchy. A summons was issued for Knox to appear at the Dominicans' Edinburgh convent on 15 May 1556. This was the normal first stage and the venue for a heresy trial and the Protestant leadership had to decide how to respond. The confident men of the Mearns led by Erskine of Dun resolved to accompany Knox to his trial as a large, armed bodyguard. It was a common Scottish practice, especially in cases involving feuds or high-profile litigants, for a 'day of law' to be attended by considerable numbers of the friends and supporters of the accuser and of the defendant.[27] These demonstrations of support and strength emerged from the broader noble culture of kinship and bonding. Although the potential for serious armed confrontation existed, there was also the possibility that forms of private justice leading to an out-of-court settlement could flow from these semi-political demonstrations. Knox had been surprised to discover that it was an alien concept in England. During the first months of Queen Mary Tudor's reign in 1553 he had looked for just such a group of 'assured men' to defend him when he preached in defiance of her proclamations.[28] Three years later in Scotland such men would accompany him when he answered the heresy summons. The Scottish bishops, probably after prompting by Mary of Guise, the mother of Mary, Queen of Scots and the Regent of Scotland, decided not to risk armed confrontation on the High Street of Edinburgh, and a technical error was discovered in the legal summons that allowed it to be withdrawn.[29]

Knox and his supporters celebrated winning this round in the contest with the churchmen, and on 15 May and for the next ten days they held a preaching festival in a substantial lodging in Edinburgh's High Street. As the crowds increased at the morning and afternoon sermons, a major advance in the capital appeared within reach. Knowing the impact a strong Protestant presence in London had made, Knox was anxious to secure a firm foothold in the Scottish capital. With an exaggerated flourish he had declared he would die happy if he had forty successful days there.[30] Fresh hopes and dreams emerged on the back of this substantial show of Protestant strength and the rumours that Mary of Guise had restrained the bishops. Glencairn persuaded Earl Marischal and his chief adviser, Hugh Drummond of Riccarton, to listen to Knox's sermons. Marischal was sufficiently impressed to suggest that Knox put the Protestant case directly to the Regent in a formal letter. The time seemed ripe for a major political initiative to gain concessions for the Protestants and try to alter the government's religious policy.

LADY MARY DOWAGER, REGENT OF SCOTLAND

In his letter addressed to the Lady Mary Dowager, Regent of Scotland, Knox attempted to play the part of the mild counsellor employing his rhetorical skills to persuade Mary of Guise to realign her religious policy.[31] It was a less than convincing performance, with Knox at a loss to know how best to present the Protestant case and awkward in this unaccustomed role. He adopted the normal convention of self-deprecation and humility expected of authors presenting their pieces to royalty. The exaggerated avowal that he was 'a worme most wretched' struck the wrong note when it was followed by the denunciation that unless 'your grace be founde different from the multitude of Princes ... this pre-eminence wherein ye ar placed shal be your dejection to torment and pain everlasting'.[32] Attempting to gloss this warning, Knox wrote that he was merely doing what any subject would do if they saw the Regent about to drink a cup of poison.

The letter had started badly, with a slow and apparently irrelevant discourse on the suffering of the true Church: such slow starts usually signalled that Knox did not want to reach the difficult part of his message. A further problem arose from the lack of specific proposals for action from the Regent. For his own protection Knox asked for the biblical span of forty days without arrest to allow him 'liberty of tongue', to preach unhindered. However, he was prone to speaking in generalized terms about stopping idolatry and the persecution of 'the poore members of Christes body' and promoting 'the trewe worshippinge of God'. He did acknowledge that there were political constraints because 'your Grace's power is not so fre as a publik reformation perchance woulde requyre' and 'sodenly ye may not do all thinges that ye wold'.[33] This did not modify the basic message: the Regent should discard the Catholic Church and support the Protestant movement. Knox conceded that this would involve the Regent in 'a straunge and grevous battel', and in return he promised the divine blessings and joy everlasting for those who followed God's precepts.[34] In the letter's final stages Knox reverted completely to preaching and prophecy, and throughout he had proceeded by assertion with no serious attempt to convince the Regent on points of doctrine. The letter made little impression upon Mary of Guise, and Knox was stung by the report that she had made a joke of it to Archbishop Hamilton. Knox carefully recorded this in his *History* and stored it as a personal grudge for which he returned double measure in his future vicious attacks upon the Regent.[35]

Around this time Knox received letters from the English-speaking congregation at Geneva successfully formed in his absence. They reminded him that he was their elected minister and requested he return to take up his duties.

This placed Knox in a dilemma facing two conflicting 'vocations'. He felt a strong sense of obligation to the exiles who had supported him in Frankfurt. They had faced further opposition there and then had been prepared to uproot themselves and resettle in Geneva to practise the type of worship he had advocated so strongly during the Troubles. He was also the leading preacher during this upsurge of the Scottish Protestant movement. The Geneva letter might have brought him down to earth after the heady days in May. He had faced an emotional roller coaster, preparing first for a heresy trial and possible execution, then swept up in an intense ten days of preaching to jubilant supporters.

These highs and lows had been shared with Marjorie, Knox's wife. Once they had arrived in Scotland after the elopement she and her mother had rapidly made friends among the Scottish Protestant community. Having juggled the reasons in his own mind, Knox decided he should return to Geneva. He probably realized he had to consider for the first time in his life the welfare of three people, not just his own, and he wanted to live long enough to enjoy his new status as a married man. After Wishart's experience, he was aware that noble promises of protection might become fragile threads that broke under pressure. He sent Marjorie and her mother Elizabeth ahead of him to Dieppe and conducted a farewell tour of the areas he had visited. On his journey he stayed at Castle Campbell, the Lowland residence of the Earl of Argyll, eleven miles east of Stirling. He preached to the elderly fourth Earl and renewed his acquaintance with Lorne and with his Ayrshire friend Robert Campbell of Kinzeancleuch. Grey Colin, laird of Glenorchy and one of the most powerful of the Campbell cadets, was also present and lent his voice to the chorus of Campbells offering Knox protection should he face further trouble from the ecclesiastical hierarchy. Knox refused to be persuaded to change his plans and the most he conceded was that he would come back to Scotland when called. In July the preacher took ship for Dieppe. Travelling through France with his wife, his mother-in-law, his servant and his pupil took longer than his previous trips and he eventually arrived back in Geneva in mid-September, having been away over a year.

When he had left Scotland in July 1556 it was easier for Knox to depart physically than to do so mentally. It was hard to disentangle himself because as a preacher and pastor he had become immersed in the life of the burgeoning Protestant movement. He had told his countrymen he had other obligations and could not operate in Scotland as if nothing had happened since he had been sent to the galleys. He did promise that, if called, he would return to his native country. In the meantime some pastoral queries and problems remained on his 'to do' list and over the next months he wrote a series of letters to his 'sisters' in Edinburgh, general letters to the Scottish 'privy kirks' and tracts with advice on the particular issues that had arisen during his preaching tour.

THAT COMPLETE UNION OF MIND

On 13 September 1556, Knox, his wife Marjorie, her mother Elizabeth Bowes, their servant James Hamilton and Knox's pupil Patrick were formally accepted as members of the English-speaking congregation in Geneva. The event was recorded in the congregation's book which remains in Geneva to this day, and the careful keeping of records was one of many indications of how well this new exile congregation was organized.[36] As Knox would have heard in the letters exchanged while he was in Scotland, everything had gone remarkably smoothly when his Frankfurt supporters arrived in Geneva in September 1555. The English exiles shared the church building called the Auditory with the Italian exile congregation and they had officially inaugurated their new church on 1 November 1555. A new liturgy, that bone of contention in Frankfurt, had been quickly finalized and a new discipline agreed. This complete blueprint for a godly congregation was printed in English and Latin versions in February 1556 with the modest title *A Forme of Prayers*.[37] By the time Knox returned he was able to fit into a well-run organization that was growing as more English and Scots exiles made their way to Geneva. He was surrounded by a group of competent and highly committed people, and his role as first preacher and pastor was clearly defined.[38]

Knox relished the opportunity to listen to Calvin's famous sermons and consolidate his friendships with the Genevan pastors. In 1572 Theodore Beza, who became Calvin's successor, remembered 'that complete union of mind which is confirmed by the bond of one and the same spirit and faith' shared with Knox. After explaining that Geneva was not quite as Knox had known it, Beza commented that they could still share 'that same doctrine, good order and harmony between all ranks which you observed when here'.[39] Writing to Anne Locke a few months after his return in 1556, Knox had penned his own praise of Geneva. His co-minister was equally impressed by the city's order and peace and in a letter to a Lasco commented upon the 'splendid zeal' to advance the work of God shown by magistrates and ministers alike.[40]

Delighted to settle peacefully in Geneva, Knox had not anticipated how difficult it was to become the head of a household. Though accommodation had probably been arranged before he arrived, he had not bargained on the complexities of day-to-day married life. He had acquired a raft of new responsibilities, not only for a servant and a pupil, but also for his new wife and mother-in-law. During his ministerial career in Edwardian England he had received a great deal of mothering and 'speciall care' from his female friends, even those like Anne Locke and Rose Hickman who were considerably younger than him.[41] His previous life as a celibate priest and tutor, galley slave and roving preacher offered little experience to guide him and he had to adjust to living as head of a typical, ordinary household – one that contained women. As he confided to Anne Locke, he was caught off balance 'now burdenit with dowbill cairis' and scared by 'daylie trubles occuring as weill in my domesticall charge, whair with befoir I haif not bene accustomit, and theairfoir ar thay the more feirfull'.[42] In common with many confirmed bachelors who liked to study and have their books around them, he would not have been used to a normal household routine. For his sermon preparation he was accustomed to having a day without interruptions: creating that time, space, peace and quiet might have proved difficult in his new home. He was painfully aware of his new patriarchal responsibility as head of the household and complained about the complications for his 'particular care' when he had to leave 'my house and poor family destitute of all head, save God only'.[43]

Since he believed that he was occupied with the 'Lord's work' and that that must take priority over everything else, Knox probably did not appreciate the sacrifices that Marjorie and Elizabeth Bowes had made or value sufficiently their willingness to adapt. Travelling across Europe, Marjorie and Elizabeth Bowes would have expected to rough it. Once they reached their longed-for destination they needed to make adjustments and it might have been a shock to realize precisely what their new life entailed. This was the Knoxes' first taste of settled married life, and shortly after they arrived in Geneva Marjorie became pregnant. Though a joy to the couple, childbearing was dangerous in this era and it probably made Knox even more anxious. His mother-in-law was the wife of a gentleman of substance holding an important military command, and Elizabeth had been in charge of her own extensive household. She was accustomed to considerably more space, resources and servants than she had in Geneva. Adjusting to the reality of what she had given up for the sake of the Gospel and her son-in-law might have taken time, though she would have been distracted by her daughter's pregnancy and the eventual arrival of her grandson.

The transition was assisted by the warm reception both women encountered in Geneva, where they made friends within the English community and with the Genevan pastors and their wives. Marjorie created a very favourable impression upon John Calvin, who later described her as 'the most delightful of wives' and remarked to Knox that she had been a rare find.[44] Calvin would have been impressed by Marjorie's religious knowledge and commitment because she was well educated, knew her Bible and had been an active participant in the godly conventicles of her relations and friends in Northumberland. She acted as Knox's secretary and assisted him with his writings, becoming an essential contributor to his publishing activities at the end of the 1550s. She became part of the female network that had developed among the English Protestant exiles throughout the European cities and greetings and small presents were warmly exchanged. One of the few evidential traces to remain of Marjorie is the letter she wrote on her husband's behalf to John Foxe, to which she added her own postscript: 'I, your Sister, the writer herof, saluteth you and your Wief most hartlie, thanking hir of hir loving tokens which my Mother and I received from Mrs Kent.'[45] (See Plate 4) Agnes Randall, the wife of John Foxe, had asked the wife of Lawrence Kent to bring these presents for Marjorie and Elizabeth Bowes when the Kent family travelled to Geneva and became members of Knox's congregation at the end of April 1558. Knox's marriage brought him love and happiness, cut short only by Marjorie's early death. She became the perfect minister's wife and gave her husband two sons, both of whom survived. Knox had become a husband and head of household, roles that altered the pattern of his life and how he viewed the world.

Knox also encountered problems in his work life, flowing from 'the administratioun of publick thingis apperteaning to the pure flok heir assemblit in Chrystis name'.[46] While he had been in Scotland, Anthony Gilby had substituted for him, though on his return the Scot stepped straight into his position and by November at the latest Knox was occupying 'the publict place' or preaching.[47] In December 1556 at their annual election the exile congregation re-elected Knox and Goodman as their ministers and Gilby became one of the elders.[48] Preparing sermons for Sunday and weekday worship was a considerable task, especially when preaching to such a well-informed audience. Knox's undoubted talents as a preacher were much appreciated by these discerning exiles and William Fuller, one of the church elders, singled him out, declaring that he had received from the sermons 'manie heavenlie lessons and spirituall good things'.[49]

The congregation valued Knox sufficiently to allow him to respond to the various calls from Scotland and when he was away from Geneva they kept his ministerial place open for him. No evidence of the financial arrangements has survived but, unlike some other exiles, neither Knox nor his household struggled to make ends meet. When Knox considered he had been brought to Dieppe on a wild-goose chase he berated the Scottish lords for making him abandon his spiritual, as well as his natural, family, 'committing that small (but to Christ dearly beloved) flock, over the which I was appointed one of the ministers, to the charge of another'.[50] In his anger Knox was being disingenuous: the Genevan congregation had no difficulty functioning when he was away and he did not feel any need to rush back to them. What he did not miss was the conflict he had encountered as minister in Frankfurt. The credit for the marked absence of discord must go to the harmonious working of the congregation's deacons, elders and ministers, particularly the excellent relationship between Knox and Goodman that was a key to this success. On most issues the two ministers shared a similar outlook and understanding of what they were doing. With the congregation occupied by a succession of major projects, such as the Geneva Bible, little spare time and energy were left for quarrelling.

This made the Genevan congregation decidedly different from the one they had left at Frankfurt. The continued strife within the Frankfurt congregation might have concentrated minds among those who had departed.[51] In the late winter and early spring of 1556–7 a serious effort was made to reconcile those who had fallen out over the original Troubles. Having vindicated their liturgical and ecclesiological stance by running their fully reformed community, the Genevan congregation took a leading role in these overtures. John Foxe, who had remained in Basle and was a strong advocate of preserving concord, supported them. Though he had strenuously avoided being dragged into the English quarrels, Peter Martyr Vermigli was equally anxious his friends should be reconciled. A diplomat by instinct, William Whittingham regarded the healing of old wounds as a preliminary step towards a broader goal, and in Geneva he sought to achieve his original Frankfurt objective, the gathering of all English-speaking exiles into one congregation. Not often cast in the role of peacemaker, Knox was also involved and as early as December 1556 was hinting to Anne Locke that something was happening, though he tantalizingly added that he would explain properly at another time: 'Other causes moving me to desyre your presence, yea, and the presence of all sic as unfeanedlie feir God, yf possible wer'.[52] Three months later the Genevan congregation as a body sent a letter urging peace to their fellow exiles in Frankfurt.[53]

In addition to this general campaign, individual enmities were to be resolved. Probably after some persuasion by Whittingham, Goodman penned a stiff and awkward letter of apology in Latin to Richard Cox, specifically encouraging him to come to Geneva:

> if you desire to know with precision what it is to follow Christ, come to us, where you will find very many examples – and exquisite ones – of people of that sort who, denying themselves, follow Christ bravely ... If it pleases you to come here, you will never be sorry that you have done so, and you will experience how serviceable I will be to you.[54]

He received a dusty reply in Latin from his former friend and academic patron at Oxford. The invitation to Geneva was also firmly declined:

you prescribe that I should come there if I wish to follow Christ with precision. If Christ were to be found only in that place, I would hasten there, as they say, with sail and horse. I very greatly reverence the gifts of God which spring up there so abundantly. But I do not disdain equal gifts that have by the grace of God been sown in other places.[55]

Personal letters to other protagonists in the controversy were sent, and John Jewel wrote back to Goodman and Whittingham in June 1557 offering his apologies in return.[56] Curiously, in the exchanges that have survived, Knox was not specifically mentioned, though his treatment at Frankfurt had shocked many of his supporters. Many exiles did find their way to Geneva and by the end of 1558 over two hundred people had become part of that exile congregation. Even Richard Chambers and Robert Horne, who had been at loggerheads with Knox in Frankfurt, came via the Aarau congregation to Geneva in 1558. They contributed generous donations to the congregations, 'so that it appeared that the old grudge ... had bin cleane forgotten'.[57] This was true for John Bale, one of Knox's most vociferous critics in Frankfurt; he was remarkably complimentary about the Scot, whom he called his dear brother in the 1559 edition of his *Catalogue*. When news came of Queen Mary Tudor's death, the Genevan congregation made a further attempt to present a united front to carry back to England.[58]

During the summer of 1557, Knox and the Genevan congregation assisted the exiles who had left Wesel in the duchy of Cleves (northern Rhineland) in search of a place where they could pursue their trade. As a member of the original scouting party, Thomas Upcher had visited Geneva for advice and been helped by William Kethe and John Bodley to negotiate with the authorities at Aarau. While in the city Upcher had not requested a private conversation with Knox, but seeking pastoral comfort he had written once he was in Basle. Knox replied with a gentle letter of encouragement that drew upon his own experience to alleviate Upcher's anguish at the loss of the awareness of God's presence.[59] During this exchange Upcher may have sent Knox a copy of a tract written by an Anabaptist or Freewiller which had formed the final stage in a controversy about predestination that had raged within London's King's Bench prison in 1554–5 among Protestant prisoners awaiting their heresy trials. A former Freewiller himself, Upcher had been involved on the 'orthodox' side and, after his release in 1555 and flight into exile, remained in touch with John Careless who had stoutly defended predestination before his execution in 1556. The anonymous manuscript Knox received probably via Upcher was a refutation of Careless' piece and had a pun on that name in the title: *The Confutation of the Errors of the Careless by Necessity*. Upcher and other exiles pressed Knox to reply to this tract, probably written by Henry Harte, whom Knox had known in England during Edward's reign.[60] The Scot regarded the pamphlet as another pernicious example of a wave of Anabaptist ideas that had been challenging the orthodox doctrine of predestination across Europe and that were linked to the anti-predestinarian views of Sebastian Castellio, who had been condemned in Geneva a few years earlier. Having accepted the challenge, Knox probably packed the manuscript into his bag when he left in September 1557 so that he could make notes for his reply as he travelled. Anabaptists and predestination were on his mind in December of that year when he warned his Scottish brethren to be on their guard against this threat. However, his long refutation was not completed until he was back in Geneva, and was only published in 1560.[61]

OUR MISERABLE COUNTRY OF ENGLAND

Many problems, both political and theological, were clamouring for Knox's attention in 1556 and 1557. The central issue facing the exiles was how to react to the English situation. From the start of the Genevan congregation in November 1555 their prayers reflected the anguish caused by the persecution, especially the executions.

> We moste humbly beseche thee to shewe thy pitie upon our miserable contrie of England . . . And shewe thy great mercies upon those our bretherne which are persecuted, cast in prison, and dayly condemned to deathe for the testimonie of thy trueth. And thogh they be vtterly destitute of all mans ayde, yet let thy swete comfort neuer departe from them: but so inflame their hartes with thy holy spirite, that thei may boldely and chearefully abide suche tryall as thy godly wisdome shall appoint.[62]

Regular reports of what was happening in England were received that detailed which friends were in prison, who had gone to the stake or died and who had recanted. Though there was pride that fellow Protestants were bravely witnessing to their faith, the exiles also experienced the guilt felt by survivors viewing the struggle from a safe distance. That emotion was partially assuaged by the deliberate use of the language of warfare. Within the cosmic struggle between good and evil, the exiles portrayed themselves as fellow soldiers of Christ standing alongside the English martyrs. From the beginning of his ministerial career Knox had adopted the battle against Antichrist as a central motif and it came naturally to him to place the English situation within this apocalyptic framework. When the executions finally began in 1555, he felt that his earlier dire warnings had been vindicated and his prophecies had come to pass.

The strongest emotion felt by Knox and the exiles was anger, made worse by their powerlessness. It was channelled into the 'holy hatred' directed at the persecutors on which Knox had relied in the past. He had been one of the first exiles to attach epithets to those he identified as the chief persecutors. Despite bringing him serious trouble in Frankfurt, he continued using violent language and targeting specific individuals. He loved to hate 'treacherous Tunstal' and 'wily Winchester', but Stephen Gardiner had died in November 1555 and Knox failed to generate an equivalent outrage against the Roman Catholic Archbishop of Canterbury Cardinal Reginald Pole, whom he did not know. Instead he poured his anger into attacking England's Jezebel, Queen Mary, and her husband, Philip of Spain. Following the Queen's marriage in 1554 and the full reconciliation with Rome in 1555, Knox and other English pamphleteers increased their attacks upon the Spanish as foreign oppressors and imperialists as well as Catholics and persecutors. This enabled them to incorporate a patriotic plea to Englishmen to preserve their country from foreign domination.

By 1556 the high-profile Protestant clergy including the famous Oxford martyrs Cranmer, Latimer and Ridley had gone to their deaths and the English persecution had settled into a grisly routine. Many facing the stake were ordinary Protestants of relatively lowly social status, while their co-religionists higher up the social ladder were able to adopt different strategies. Some fled to the Continent or to a different part of England, some kept out of sight and many conformed sufficiently to stay out of trouble. These 'Nicodemites' roused Knox's fury and he lambasted them as backsliders and hypocrites who had betrayed Christ's cause. Other exiles were downcast on hearing news that friends had attended Mass. William Fuller, who had been part of Princess Elizabeth's household, mourned for his mistress when the news was confirmed that she was attending 'thantichristian abhomination'.[63] All the exiles were deeply affected by news of those who had recanted their faith. In the autumn of 1556 the entire English exile community was shocked and horrified by what had happened to Sir John Cheke. In exile, Cheke had been resident in Strasbourg, though he also had a base in Emden where he was organizing part of the Protestant printing campaign. While travelling in May 1556 with Sir Peter Carew he had been kidnapped and taken to the Tower of London. Chambers and Horne in Frankfurt, writing to Bullinger in September, relayed the news that Cheke had been released and they feared that he had accepted some 'iniquitous conditions'.[64] At the start of October Cheke's full recantation, including the acceptance of the real presence in the eucharist, gave the Marian regime a major propaganda triumph. Cheke's denial of his Protestant faith, compounded by his death several months later, made a profound impression on the exiles. They were concerned that the Marian regime would mount additional clandestine expeditions on the Continent and Cheke's fate reawakened the insidious personal fear of how one might react if captured.

This phase of the Marian persecution gave rise to passivity among some English exiles. Their production of propaganda tracts diminished and a mood of resignation was induced by the realization that the exile might last for many years. By contrast, the Genevan exiles seemed galvanized by the persecution. A new energy flowed through the congregation and they seemed liberated following the departure from Frankfurt by their experience of a second exile. Already in double exile from Scotland and England, and having been forced out of Frankfurt into a third exile, Knox was able to assist his congregation in channelling their anger into constructive projects. What his flock craved was action – something to do that would make a difference in this struggle. The congregation's energy was diverted into grand biblical and liturgical schemes, producing a new English translation of the Bible, a metrical psalter and further editions of their order of worship. They were intent upon forging new and lasting weapons for the fight against Antichrist. When the opportunity arose they wanted everything to hand for establishing a fully reformed Church in their own country. Confident in their apocalyptic understanding of the situation, they believed that God would provide such an opportunity. They turned to the Old Testament and the deliverance of the people of God for their hope. Even in the darkest hour, God would once again part the Red Sea and bring his people across safely and drown their enemies behind them. This was the illustration they chose for the title page of their Geneva Bible (see Plate 6).

The same woodcut was inserted inside the Bible next to the text of Exodus 14 where the miraculous deliverance was described and a long note added to prove that this was the story of the Church of God throughout the ages. The second point in particular was almost a personal description of Knox's experience. It might have come from his pen because it provided a perfect summary of his belief that in moments of greatest danger the hope in deliverance should be strongest.

In this figure foure chief points are to be considered. First that the Church of God is ever subiect in this worlde to the Crosse & to be afflicted after one sort or other. The second, that the ministers of God following their vocation shalbe evil spoken of, and murmered against, even of them that pretend the same cause and religion that thei do. The third, that God delivereth not his Church incontinently out of dangers, but to exercise their faith and pacience continueth their troubles, yea and often tymes augmenteth them as the

Israelites were now in lesse hope of their lives then when thei were in Egypt. The fourth point is, that when the dangers are moste great, then Gods helpe is moste ready to succour: for the Israelites had on ether side them, huge rockes & mountaines, before them the Sea, behinde them most cruel enemies, so that there was no way left to escape to mans iudgement.[65]

Though Knox and his congregation believed they were facing their darkest hour, they confronted it together and were striving to battle the forces of Antichrist. This intense experience of fighting shoulder to shoulder as soldiers of Christ and believing that deliverance would come even in the midst of persecution became etched on to Knox's mind. For him, the battle, the solidarity and the happiness he found in Geneva combined into one, and in future years he assumed that shared hope and zealous commitment held the key to victory.

CHAPTER NINE

Pierced with anguish and sorrow

Based in Geneva Knox became immersed in the intense and apocalyptic atmosphere generated by witnessing the Marian persecution, 'Satan's bludy clawses' as he later described it.[1] He was also caught up in the developments among Scottish Protestants and felt he had a double calling, both to his English and to his Scottish flocks. Consequently, he experienced a type of double vision as he watched the different situations and did not know which way he was called to go. He finally set out for Scotland in the summer of 1557, but was stopped at Dieppe by conflicting advice from his countrymen. In the French port he became more closely involved in the tense situation facing the persecuted Huguenots. Feeling isolated and embattled once again he took up his pen, writing a number of works and completing his most famous tract, *The First Blast of the Trumpet*. Radicalized by the English persecution in particular, Knox had chosen in that work to present arguments against female rule. Under the same pressure, his ministerial colleague Goodman in a separate tract had explicitly called for resistance to the regime of Mary Tudor. In step these two ministers of the exile congregation in Geneva crossed that particular Rubicon and achieved lasting notoriety for their revolutionary views. Their joint stance symbolized their close friendship, and for the remainder of his days Knox relied upon the support of his 'beloved brother'.[2]

THE FEARFUL CROSS OF CHRIST

It cannot have come as a complete surprise when two Edinburgh merchant friends arrived in Geneva in May 1557 looking for Knox. James Sim, his former host in Edinburgh, and James Baron carried a brief letter signed by some of the Scottish nobles the preacher had met during his Scottish tour. Gathered on 10 March in Stirling, the Earl of Glencairn, Lord Lorne and

Lord James Stewart, along with their host Lord Erskine,[3] had written requesting that Knox return to Scotland and promising that they would be 'ready to jeopard lives and goods in the forward setting of the glory of God'. They admitted that the Regent's attitude and religious policy had not altered, though they could report that the friars were not in such high favour at court. On the positive side there had not been any increase in persecution. The lords added, 'the rest of our minds this faithful bearer will show you at length', covering the sensitive information they had not committed to paper. In such circumstances it was common practice for the messenger to carry in his head the main substance of the communication and deliver it orally, with the written letter acting as his formal identification. As happens frequently in sixteenth-century history, the oral message cannot be recovered, though Knox had a copy of the original written text in front of him when he wrote the relevant section of his *History*.[4]

Whatever that private briefing covered, a major consultation followed with Knox's congregation, and advice was also sought from John Calvin and the other Genevan pastors. The result was unanimous: Knox had no choice but to return to Scotland. Reflecting Knox's reluctance, the advice was framed in unambiguous terms, 'That he could not refuse that vocation, unless he would declare himself rebellious unto his God, and unmerciful to his country'.[5] Consequently, a message was sent back with Knox's promise that he would come to Scotland once he had made arrangements for his own congregation in Geneva. During the summer Knox sent a longer letter to the Protestant nobility that was lost by 'negligence and troubles', in which he urged the nobles to do their duty and uphold true religion.[6] As before, he was trapped between conflicting loyalties, feeling obligations both to his family and to his Genevan flock, as well as to his Scottish co-religionists. He lingered for a few more months in Geneva with his new son and wife. Consulting widely and in considerable detail, he made proper plans for this visit to Scotland, devising the best strategy for its emerging Protestant movement.[7]

Knox had direct access to the most experienced team in Europe with expertise in cultivating an underground Protestant church. Over the previous decade Geneva had acted as the motor engine of the French Reformed Church. Its large and expanding population of French exiles turned the city into a printing centre, despatching French books; a training camp for clergy to be sent back into the field; and a communications hub for the intelligence network that kept in touch with the French Protestant communities, or Huguenots as they were known. The Genevan pastors would have briefed Knox on what to do, what information to collect and which types of contacts to make in Scotland. Like later resistance fighters, he was being sent into occupied territory and would be working with a network of cells. The French were experts at this type of mission: how to proselytize and survive amid persecution. Although the Scottish Regent's regime had a much lighter touch than the royal government in France, Knox remained a wanted man. Shortly after he had left Scotland he had been condemned in his absence as a heretic and his effigy had been burned at the market cross in Edinburgh in July 1556.[8] If he were arrested on his return he might be executed without further trial and even denied the public witness Wishart's death had achieved.

Although Knox had previously faced the possibility of having to die for his faith, in 1557 the odds had lengthened against a safe return. With details from the English persecution fresh in his mind, he wrestled with the prospect of his own execution. In a letter probably written in March 1557, he countered the accusation of cowardice, that 'my fleing the contrey declaireth my feir'.[9] Though addressed to Janet Henderson, Knox was talking to himself not her when he wrote about the fear 'of the death temporall'. He argued that, since everyone had to die, it was a great opportunity 'to be Chrystis witnes' in death and for the price of momentary suffering gain eternal life and joy.

> Yf we knew, I say, what comfort lyeth hid under the feirfull cross of Chryst, we wald not be sa slak to take up the same. Yf we knew that lyfe is bureit with Chryst in his grave, we wald not feir to ga and seik him in the sam. We prais and extoll the martiris and sanctis whilk by afflictionis hath overcum this warld, and yit we having the same occasioun offirit, do flie frome the battell.

Towards the end of the letter he mentioned 'my awin motioun and daylie prayer is, not onlie that I may visit you, but also with joy I may end my battell amangis yow', and he assured Janet Henderson that he would return to Scotland when properly called.[10] A few months later such ringing phrases and fine sentiments would come back to haunt him.

GRAVE MEN WEEP

Knox was facing danger long before he reached Scotland, and in the summer of 1557 the best route from Geneva to the Channel Ports was not obvious. Entering Philip II's domains was folly, especially given Knox's comments about the current King of England and his wife, and the exiles remembered the kidnap of Sir John Cheke when he had been travelling through the Low Countries. Southern Flanders and north-eastern France were currently a war zone where Philip's armies were fighting the French. The resounding Imperial victory at St Quentin on 10 August 1557 had threatened Paris, and the French were desperately drafting troops into the area to defend the capital. In addition travelling through France was more dangerous than it had previously been because of the French King's latest anti-heresy measure, the Edict of Compiègne issued on 24 July, which substantially increased the risks of execution if Huguenots were caught. As well as condemning all 'sacramentarians', the edict decreed that those found in contact with Geneva would suffer the death penalty. Henry II was determined to enforce his policy of 'One King, one faith', and that faith must be Catholic. Knox felt the pressure of these dangers and later confided to John Davidson that he faced persecution 'be all the rabill of Sathanis suddartis [soldiers] in Scotland, Ingland and France'. He felt 'not only was he hatit, and raillit on, bot also persecutit maist scharply, and huntit from place to place as ane unworthie of ony society with men'. A rumour had circulated that to 'devyse his deid' some Catholic clergy had recited the prayers for the dead for Knox.[11]

To arrive at his favoured port of Dieppe Knox possibly chose a longer western route through Lyon and across to La Rochelle on this outward journey, rather than returning this way as has previously been supposed.[12] There was a colony of Scottish merchants in the Atlantic port and he could have gone by sea from La Rochelle to Dieppe to avoid the war zone and other dangers in France. John Row's later *History* contained an account based on eyewitness testimony that when Knox was in La Rochelle he had preached in the house of a noblewoman and christened a child who had been brought many miles to the city for Protestant baptism. Some Scottish Catholics were persuaded to attend the sermon and they heard Knox predict that he would preach in St Giles' in Edinburgh in two or three years. Initially sceptical, on their passage home they faced a terrible sea storm and vowed that if they returned safely they would forsake Catholicism. They survived to tell their tale and see Knox preach in Edinburgh's parish church.[13]

A farewell party was held for Knox's family and friends on the night before he left Geneva in September 1557 and there was hardly a dry eye as they prepared to send him on his way. In the sixteenth century shedding tears was recognized as a sign of true emotion and Knox could weep with the best. He later complained angrily to the Scottish lords that it was no small matter to leave Geneva and 'more worldly substance than I will express could not have caused me to willingly behold the eyes of so many grave men weep at once for my cause, as that I did, in taking of my last good night from them'.[14] Some would have recalled the equally tearful night two years earlier when Knox had been banished from Frankfurt. For the Genevan Company of Pastors farewells had become routine as they sent another trained cleric to minister to a newly formed congregation in France. With the list of French martyrs growing each year, everyone in Geneva appreciated the high risks of being sent to serve a church 'under the cross'.[15] Knox was part of an international effort to spread the Reformed faith and he was particularly conscious of his solidarity with his Huguenot brethren.

He was probably already on the road when he heard news of the crisis facing the French Protestants in Paris. Under cover of darkness on 4 September a couple of hundred Huguenots met for prayers and worship in an empty house on the Rue St Jacques. Their secret was discovered and a large angry mob surrounded the house baying for blood. Some Protestant men fought their way out before the Parisian authorities arrived with the militia to arrest those who remained, including the women and children. They were kept in harsh conditions in prison – not normal treatment for the ladies of noble rank among their number. Three Protestants were executed at the end of September with two more a week later, while others faced torture. There was an outcry across Protestant Europe and pleas for clemency were sent to Henry II, though most fell on deaf ears. Only after the Elector Palatine, a key French ally, added his voice were the prisoners gradually released in the spring of 1558.[16]

When Knox arrived in Dieppe on 24 October he had access to the full story of those captured at the Rue St Jacques and received a copy of their *Apology* written in prison. It was possible that one of the Paris prisoners was James Hamilton, Earl of Arran, and the son and heir of the leading Scottish aristocrat, the Duke of Châtelherault.[17] Whether or not a personal link existed to the boy he had first met in St Andrews Castle in 1547, Knox wanted to do whatever he could to help the Huguenots and decided that the *Apology* should be translated and published in English. Being too busy to translate the *Apology* himself, a 'faithful brother' undertook that task while Knox wrote a preface and a series of explanatory comments within the *Apology*'s text. The notes assisted Scottish and English readers who were not well acquainted with the early Church Fathers and the heavy citation of patristic texts employed by the French apologist. In his version, Knox greatly emphasized that the French Protestants were loyal subjects of Henry II and they merely sought the right to worship in the way they believed best. The pamphlet was finished in a rush on 7 December and circulated in manuscript, though it did not appear in print.[18]

On arrival in Dieppe, Knox had been confronted by conflicting messages about his trip to Scotland. Contrary to his expectation, there was no letter waiting from the lords who had invited him to return in March, but a 'faithful brother' had written advising him to wait in Dieppe until the situation had become clearer in Scotland and the nobles had come to a decision. A separate letter sent from a Scottish gentleman to another friend in Dieppe reported that even those nobles most keen for Knox's return the previous spring had had second thoughts, while others were denying agreeing to his invitation in the first place. Reading these reports made Knox exceedingly angry and confused. His reaction was more extreme because of the effort he had made to leave Geneva and steel himself to face the prospect of a martyr's death. He was in no mood to make allowances for hit-and-miss communications or the rapidly changing situation in his native country during the eight months it had taken from the initial invitation until his appearance in the Channel port. On 27 October he wrote a furious letter to the Scottish lords, complaining, 'I partly was confounded, and partly was pierced with anguish and sorrow.' If he returned directly to Geneva he and the Scottish Protestant movement would look fools and he angrily demanded what he was supposed to say when asked 'What was the impediment of my purposed journey? judge you what I shall answer.' He foretold that God would punish Scotland for the agreement to marry Mary, Queen of Scots, to the French Dauphin and so betray 'your realm to the slavery of strangers'. While acknowledging that his words were 'sharp and indiscreetly spoken', he insisted they were friendly warnings with the lords' best interests at heart, including their eternal salvation.[19]

On a more positive tack Knox urged the nobles to go ahead with their former enterprise and expanded upon the duty of nobles. He treated them as a special category of those who held political power, the 'inferior magistrates' whose political authority was independent of the 'superior magistrate' or ruler they served. Knox explained that Scottish nobles were 'princes of the people', elevated not 'by reason of your birth and progeny (as the most part of men falsely do suppose), but by reason of your office and duty, which is to vindicate and deliver your subjects and brethren from all violence and oppression, to the uttermost of your power'.[20] The lost letter had given a more extended treatment of this theory of nobles' powers and duties and had probably explicitly employed the theory of 'inferior magistrates' that permitted armed opposition to the ruler or Emperor and had formed the bedrock of resistance ideas within the Lutheran tradition.[21] In addition to this stinging letter, Knox sent missives to the Protestant nobility and to specific individuals, such as John Erskine of Dun and John Wishart of Pittarrow, though none of these other letters has survived.

To maintain, set forward, and establish the most blessed word of God

When received in Scotland Knox's angry letter had a dramatic effect. It caused the lords to come together in Edinburgh and make a bond between them on 3 December that has become known as the 'first band'. Adapted to serve an explicitly religious purpose, it utilized the language and ethos of the bonds of manrent current in Scottish society that expressed the relationship between noble lords and their men. The Earl of Argyll and his heir, Lord Lorne, were joined by the Earls of Glencairn and Morton and Lord Erskine[22] in their promise 'to maintain, set forward, and establish the most blessed word of God and his Congregation . . . against Sathan and all wicked power that does intend tyranny or trouble against the foresaid Congregation'.[23] The nobles had done precisely what Knox had told them to do, though when he wrote again to Scotland he had not heard the news of the first band.

In addition to political news, Knox received information about unwelcome internal developments among the Protestant community within Scotland. Reflecting his discussions in Geneva, on 1 December he wrote to the Scottish brethren outlining the strategy to be followed by churches 'under the cross'. He reiterated the directive that they should separate entirely from Catholic worship and sacraments and meet 'in companyis apart'.[24] Distressed that Protestantism was getting a bad name from adherents who were morally lax, Knox urged the highest moral standards upon his flock. While the enforcement of discipline was vital, he was equally anxious to remind his readers that Christians were not 'perfect' and that the Church was an assembly of sinners, as had been demonstrated in the Pauline Epistles. His worry that Anabaptists, or Freewillers, might infect Scottish Protestantism probably reflected his past experience and the refutation he was undertaking of the tract attacking predestination more than the situation in his native land. As he awaited more news, details of Scottish political developments filtered into Dieppe during November and early December. The English declaration of war on France in June had placed the Anglo-Scottish border on to a warlike footing throughout the summer of 1557. After their defeat at St Quentin, the French wanted the Scots to open a second front, and troops were gathered in the Borders under the overall command of Châtelherault. By the time all was ready in early October, the atrocious weather had left the ground sodden and disease was rife. When the Scottish nobles decided not to invade England and disbanded the troops, Mary of Guise was furious because it weakened her negotiating position in France concerning her daughter's marriage. Knox took fright when he heard garbled accounts of what had happened on the Borders and the suggestion that there had been a rebellion against the Regent led by Châtelherault. He was particularly worried by the involvement of the Duke, whom he regarded as the turncoat who had abandoned the gospellers in 1543 and allowed Cardinal Beaton to execute George Wishart and other martyrs to the cause.

In a letter to the Scottish Protestants sent from Dieppe on 17 December, he began with a rambling and sermonized opening, a sure sign that he did not want to reach the main point about obedience to rulers. He insisted 'that nane of yow that seik to promote the glorie of Chryst do suddanlie disobey or displeas the establissit Autoritie in thingis lawfull; nether yit, that ye assist or fortifie suche as for thair awn particular cause and warldlie promotioun wald trubill the same'.[25] He conceded that nobles should ensure there was no persecution and even that they 'may attempt the extreamitie'. When clarified, this extremity proved remarkably tame: allowing nobles to 'provyd, whidder the Authoritie will consent or no, that Chrystis Evangell may be trewlie preachit, and his halie Sacramentis rychtlie ministerit unto yow, and to your brethren, the subjectis of that Realme'.[26] Knox's tone had become fearful, and he was emphasizing the importance of political obedience and the defensive containment of persecution. It was a very different strategy to the one he was contemplating for his English readers.

Knox felt alone and confused when far from his support team in Geneva. He was unsure what he should do or what advice to offer the Scots. On the one hand, despite the risks, he longed to be in Scotland and said he was willing to die there: 'I feill a sob and grone, willing that Chryst Jesus mycht opinlie be preachit in my native contrey, with a certane desyre that my earis myght heir it, althocht it suld be with the loss of this wreachit lyfe.'[27] On the other hand, he worried that religious and political agendas had become entangled and that this would be a bad time to return. In a revealing letter a few months later, he recorded the arguments that spun around in his head:

I began to disput with myself as followeth: Sall Chryst, the author of peace, concord, and quyetnes, be preachit whair weir is proclamit, seditioun engenderit, and tumultis appeir to ryse? Sall not his Evangell be accusit, as the caus of all calamitie whilk is lyke to follow? What comfort canst thou have to sie the one-half of the pepill ryse up aganis the other; yea, to jeopard the ane, to murther and destroy the other, but above all, what joy sall it be to this hart to behald with thi eyis thi native contrey betrayit in the handis of strangeris, whilk to na manis judgement can be avoydit, becaus that thay wha aucht to defend it, and the libertie thairof, ar sa blind, dull and obstinat, that thay will not sie thair awn destructioun?[28]

In this depressed and uncertain state Knox remained in Dieppe. The international situation and the war front in north-eastern France were changed by the dramatic and daring winter campaign of the Duke of Guise. In January 1558, his French troops captured the English town of Calais and completely overran the English Pale. Expelling the English from their last foothold on Continental soil was a major boost to French confidence and a devastating blow for English pride and military morale, as well as placing renewed pressure upon Philip II's forces fighting the French. It eased the travel situation for Knox by shifting the war zone further north and making the routes back to Geneva safer. He probably left early in 1558 and returned to Geneva by late February or early March, and either there he was on hand to put the *First Blast* rapidly through the press or it had already been done for him by his Genevan colleagues. At Easter Mary, Queen of Scots, was married to Francis, the Dauphin, in a magnificent ceremony at Notre Dame in Paris. It was a triumphant vindication of Mary of Guise's policies and abilities as Regent of Scotland. A few weeks later in St Andrews, Archbishop John Hamilton tried and executed Walter Myln, an eighty-year-old Protestant cleric, for heresy. The news of Myln's death had a profound effect upon Knox and confirmed his suspicions that the Scottish Catholic hierarchy were just like their English counterparts and were embarking upon a policy of serious persecution. Once back among his friends and colleagues, Knox recovered his nerve and his perspective. He was able to decide what action he should recommend to his fellow Scots, and over the following months he put together a package of tracts aimed at various audiences within Scotland in which he sought to set out his understanding of what should happen.

Beloved Brother

Though in 1556 Knox felt his cares had doubled, he came to realize he could share them with his ministerial colleague and friend Christopher Goodman and, as a consequence, halve them. The close ministerial partnership they quickly established in 1556–7 flowered into a deep and abiding friendship. Friends, colleagues and enemies recognized this Knox–Goodman team. Because of their advocacy of resistance to political rulers, after 1558 the ministers were bracketed together and their names linked in everyone's mouths.[29] In a striking woodcut image the two men were pictured side by side blowing their trumpets (see Plate 5). This double portrait found in the book of their opponent, Peter Frarin, is the only surviving image of either man made during their lifetimes. It portrays this duo as the team they were – a truth understood by contemporaries, though subsequently forgotten.

Starting in September 1556 the two men worked together for a decade, first in Geneva and then in Scotland. Tied by a spiritual as well as an emotional bond, they felt closer than blood kin, with Knox addressing Goodman as 'beloved brother' and Goodman talking about his 'dear brother in Christ'.[30] Driven apart at the end of 1565, the two men strove for the final years of Knox's life to reconstitute their working partnership. Though their efforts were in vain, Knox's letters to Goodman reveal how much he missed the presence of his closest friend. In 1568, when he realized it would not be possible to be reunited with Goodman in Scotland, he sadly wrote, 'I will the more patientlie beare his absence, weaning myself from all comfort that I looked to have receaved be his presence and familiaritie.'[31] A few months before his death when he knew he would not see Goodman again, he concluded, 'of your comfortable presence where I am, I have small, yea no, esperance. The name of God be praised, who of his mercie hath left me so great comfort of you in this life.'[32]

When talking about what Goodman meant to him, Knox deliberately chose the word 'comfort'. Meaning far more than simply feeling at ease with his fellow minister, the word carried the sense of deep assurance and spiritual security. From his earliest days in ministry Knox had been comforted sharing spiritual experiences with his godly sisters, and a few brothers. However, in these conversations he remained aware of his pastoral duty and role as a comforter. With Goodman it was different. The two ministers were on an equal footing and could share their burdens. Most of the time Goodman acted as the comforter, so in 1566 Knox strove to reciprocate and share Goodman's troubles: 'how glad wold my heart be to bear with you som part of your burthen, (how unable that ever I be) as god made you to bear with me to the comfort of many in the time most dangerous'.[33]

For Knox having Goodman literally walking by his side meant a great deal. The two men seemed to prefer to walk and talk as they had the first time they had met on the walls in Chester. During these intense private conversations as they paced up and down, they discussed key moral and spiritual dilemmas. On one occasion in Goodman's manse Knox recalled 'when in your garden at Aldford youe and I walkyng alone'.[34] Knox felt bereft when he could no longer see and talk to Goodman. In 1559, after a separation of a few months, he sent an anguished plea to Anne Locke to pass to 'my deir brother, Mr Gudman, whose presence I more thrist than she that is my own fleshe'.[35] Years later in a similarly hyperbolic comment he longed for just one day in Goodman's company before he died: 'And yet wolde I be most glaide to conferr with you if it war but one day befor that God should put end to my trubles.'[36] With Goodman prevented from returning to Scotland, Knox's melancholy increased because he sorely missed the 'familiaritie', and had to 'wean' himself from his dependence upon Goodman's presence. Though not all Knox's letters to Goodman have survived, the Scot kept up his correspondence even when he was so depressed that he could not put pen to paper for his other English friends.[37]

Being able to pour out his soul was a great benefit to Knox and he valued Goodman's role as a listening ear. What made his friend more than a confessor

was the ability to give principled and unwavering advice, and Knox singled out
this quality as the one he most valued in their friendship. 'Your familiaritie
hath bein comfortable to me for divers causes, but for non so much as for that
uprycthnes of judgement which I never did perceive to be corrupted in you for
any worldly respectes in the which integrity I pray God for Christ Jesus his
sonnes sake ye may continew to the end. Amen.'[38] For a man who gave directions quickly and easily to others, Knox struggled to take decisions about his
vocation. He found it difficult to make up his mind on his own and, especially
when he was depressed, needed his friends' guidance and direction. On such
matters he came to believe that God spoke to him through the voice of another.
Although he stood in awe of Calvin, he did not always follow his advice.
Goodman provided clarity and certainty for Knox's decision-making. Though
the Scot believed his personal faith was anchored in the Scriptures, he sometimes needed help to keep that connection taut and strong: Goodman acted
like a hawser holding Knox's anchor firm. Calvin, who had seen their friendship blossom in Geneva, understood how important Goodman was and how
much his presence mattered to Knox. In 1561 the Swiss Reformer instructed
Goodman to remain in Scotland to assist its reformation and because he was
needed to help Knox recover from Marjorie's death.[39] In his own life Goodman
could be extremely rigid and uncompromising, and he was not prone to regrets
about how he had behaved or what he had done. When defending what he saw
as the truth, as during the Frankfurt Troubles, he found apologizing difficult
and his defensive letter to Richard Cox was not conciliatory. Self-belief merged
into self-righteousness and stubbornness. John Jewel commented to Peter
Martyr that their mutual friend Goodman had an 'irritable temper' and was
'too pertinacious in any thing that he has once undertaken' making him loath
to yield any ground.[40]

From the time Goodman joined Knox's party in Frankfurt, the two men
shared a fundamental agreement about the Church and spiritual matters.
Looking back Knox celebrated this common mind: 'Now brother . . . rejos ye
with me . . . that it hath pleased the mercy of our God to mack us aggre so long
in the middest of divers tentations in the simplicitie of his trueth.'[41] From their
first meeting Knox was sure Goodman would contribute greatly to the Church
and years later that contribution had been uppermost in his mind when he had
initially urged Goodman to conform during the Elizabethan vestments controversy, otherwise 'we shold have lost youe & your comfortable doctrine in
Christ'. On this issue Goodman's uncompromising arguments altered Knox's
stance on vestments and conformity: one of the few times Knox admitted
changing his mind. When he wrote to Goodman, he knew he need not elaborate and could use a shorthand version or phrase that was mutually understood.

Knowing that his friend would fill in the gaps, he encouraged Goodman to write a pamphlet against wearing vestments setting out the basic question, 'whether the church dependith upon godes word or godes word upon the church'.[42]

During the difficult days Knox spent in Dieppe in the winter of 1557–8, he came to realize what a difference Goodman made. Being without his wife and family was bad enough, but he felt especially alone because there was no one with whom he could discuss what to do next. He described ideas whirling round his head as he struggled to decide his course of action. 'Theis and mair deip cogitationis, sa did, and yit do trubill and move my wickit hart, that as I was without comfort, sa was I almaist without consall, not onlie in that matter, but also in matteris of smaller importance.'[43] This fear, indecision and loneliness combined to give Knox an acute sense of persecution that he escaped only when he got back to Geneva.

Before Knox had departed for Dieppe, the two men had discussed the worsening situation in England. As the persecution increased, pressure built up among the exiles in Geneva to discover a plan of action for Englishmen abroad and at home. The exiles were working hard to produce good 'weapons' for the fight against Antichrist. When they 'applied' the biblical texts during their sermons, the two ministers were conscious of their duty to point a way forward for their flock. Together Knox and Goodman proclaimed the radical message that called for a revolution in England and the deposition of Queen Mary Tudor. Though it had the support of other members of the leadership team, not all the members of the exile congregation were persuaded.[44] Items from the pens of three central members of that team were printed within the revolutionary tracts of Knox and Goodman. Anthony Gilby added his discourse on Anglo-Scottish relations to Knox's *Appellation*, while William Whittingham wrote the Preface, and William Kethe a poem for inclusion in Goodman's *How Superior Powers*.[45]

Knox and Goodman discussed the doctrine of non-resistance, one of the cornerstones of Protestant political thought. Emphasizing the verses from Romans 13 that mandated obedience to the divinely ordained 'powers that be', the magisterial Reformers had underlined that resistance to rulers was also resistance to the ordinance of God. Even if faced with persecution and death, Protestants were not to rebel against their rulers. When commanded to act against the laws of God, Protestants should refuse to obey and then be prepared to suffer the consequences. Knox had encountered this strong line from Calvin and Bullinger when he had been asking his questions in 1554. An essential part of this theory of non-resistance was a conscience clause permitting passive disobedience. The attack upon Nicodemism had given this clause greater prominence and emphasized the stirring phrase of the Apostles Peter and John, 'We oght rather to obey God then man.'[46] It was employed as the justification for martyrdom, turning such passive resistance into a defiant act of witness.

Goodman chose that text from Acts 5:29 and, probably before Knox left Geneva in September, preached a sermon setting out a novel interpretation. He presented a new definition of the nature of obedience to divine commands that owed a great deal to Knox's black and white definitions of true worship and idolatry. Goodman would have heard Knox's latest formulation written to his Scottish 'sisters': 'In religioun thair is na middis: either it is the religioun of God, and that in everie thing that is done it must have the assurance of his awn Word . . . or els it is the religioun of the Divill.'[47]

Goodman combined Knox's stark approach with Calvin's logical explanation of divine commands – that a negative command automatically implied its positive corollary. In his sermon, Goodman asserted that the negative and positive meanings of a divine command were wrapped so tightly together they were inseparable; full obedience required adherence to both meanings. By applying this to his text from Acts he insisted that merely avoiding ungodliness was insufficient for true obedience to God. English Protestants must undertake positive action to uphold godliness. While martyrdom was one form of positive action, Goodman could now present resistance to the rule of Mary Tudor as another option. It was a crude argument that served as a blunt instrument to batter down the doctrine of non-resistance at its weakest point, the conscience clause. Goodman's sermon was the initial stage of a longer process of developing a more sophisticated and radical theory of resistance. Jean Crespin published it on 1 January 1558 in Geneva under the title *How Superior Powers Oght to be Obeyd*.[48]

Although Knox was not yet ready to follow Goodman all the way down this particular path, the demolition of the doctrine of non-resistance encouraged him to push ahead with his own line of thought about female rule. Goodman did briefly incorporate into his tract Knox's argument that female rule was against natural and divine law. Each man developed a different set of ideas that contributed towards a single goal: justifying the deposition of Queen Mary Tudor. Knox's departure from Geneva ensured that their revolutionary tracts would remain distinct.

THE TRUMPET HAS ONCE BLOWN

Printed in capital letters 'the trumpet has once blown' ended Knox's most famous tract, *The First Blast of the Trumpet against the Monstrous Regiment of*

Women.[49] As he was to discover, this trumpet call blew away many friends, and the two subsequent soundings he had planned were never completed. At least Knox felt he had fulfilled his duty: he had sounded the warning required of a watchman of the Lord and avoided repeating the mistake of King Edward's reign by holding back his salty denunciations. Working along different lines from Goodman, in this tract he concentrated on female rule. He had continued to chew over the problem after 1554 when he had raised the issue with the Swiss Reformers and received discouraging replies. It remained on his mind two years later as he answered pastoral queries from Scottish Protestants after his preaching tour. His Edinburgh 'sisters' had asked for guidelines about female dress, because they worried about whether it would be contrary to Scriptural commands to wear modern styles, such as the hooped petticoat or verdingale recently introduced from France. Probably after receiving clarification on the garment from Marjorie, Knox pronounced, 'verdingallis, and sic other fond fantassies that wer knawin in theis dayis, can not be justifiet'.[50] Realizing he was on slippery ground he did not make further pronouncements about specific garments. He resorted to broad instructions about avoiding luxury and ostentation and adopting moderate and sober attire. Ducking the responsibility for a final pronouncement he promised to translate one of Calvin's sermons on the subject.[51] He was out of his depth on this topic and his grumpy answer wandered as he became sidetracked into a diatribe about cross-dressing based upon the text in Deuteronomy forbidding men from wearing women's garments.[52] He finally escaped by switching to a metaphorical meaning of clothing and being 'clad' on the Day of Judgement when the wicked will be naked and the elect clothed in Christ's righteousness. The sigh of relief as he reached the familiar topic of idolatry can almost be heard across the centuries.

While thrashing around trying to explain points about female dress, Knox produced some of his most critical statements about women. He detected the 'stinking pryd of wemen' in their dedicated following of fashion and 'superfluous apparell'. Though there was no intrinsic 'uncleanness' in silk, velvet, gold and other materials, the problem was 'that uncleane personis do abuse the same to ostentatioun'. Knox highlighted three reasons for ostentatious dressing: out of pride, wanting to be the same as other women or 'to allure the eyis of men'. They played upon common sixteenth-century stereotypes of women, their pride, their stupidity and subservience, and their obsession with sex.[53] In his digression about cross-dressing, Knox went considerably beyond his text, possibly following the gloss of Tertullian, as his critic Richard Bertie noticed.[54] Knox explained that female dress was meant to demonstrate women's inferiority to men: 'The garmentis of wemen do declair thair weaknes and unabilitie to execute the office of men.' Men bore weapons to signify they ruled in the Church and commonwealth and it was, therefore, an abomination for them to abandon their authority or 'weapons' and wear female dress. Knox then launched into an attack upon those women who, 'forgetting thair awn weaknes and inabilitie to rule, do presume to tak upon thame to beir and use the vestementis and weaponis of men, that is, the office whilk God hath assignit to mankynd onlie, they sall not eschaip the maledictioun of Him who must declair himself enemy, and a seveir punisser of all thois that be malicious perverteris of the order establissit be his wisdome'. Even Knox realized that this long sentence had led him far from his brief, and he admitted it was not relevant to his Edinburgh 'sisters'.[55]

This digression revealed that in the autumn of 1556 Knox was once more cogitating the legitimacy of female rule and had the time and opportunity to collect material on women and on the question of whether they should hold positions of political power. Around the start of 1557 he had a private conversation with Calvin on the subject. Extremely cautious about meddling in these specifically political and constitutional matters, Calvin challenged the idea that there was a single divine law on this matter and cited Old Testament women such as Huldah and Deborah whose stories showed that God could use women as a special providence.[56] Despite Calvin's hefty dose of cold water, Knox continued searching classical and patristic authors, gathering quotations. His legal and scholastic training encouraged the compilation of 'case law' and 'opinions' that might be assembled to bolster his propositions. Geneva was a magnificent location for him to track such 'authorities', and many resources were to be found within his own circle such as the books of Robert Beaumont, a member of the Genevan congregation, whose booklist drawn up in February 1557 has survived on the back of a draft letter from the English congregation to fellow exiles in other cities. Beaumont possessed more than seventy volumes in Latin, Hebrew, Greek, Italian and French as well as English.[57] Knox seems to have organized his notes under three headings representing the stages of his forthcoming discussion. Choosing a favourite metaphor he described his work as three blasts on the trumpet. Not content to confine his treatment to female rule, he ranged over other aspects of political authority, as he had in the 1554 questions. His brief summary for the trumpet's *Second Blast* covered the 'lesser magistrates', definitions of tyranny and how the practice of idolatry affected oaths of allegiance.[58]

By the second half of 1557 the Roman Catholic Church was on the offensive, and Knox felt surrounded by persecution in England and France and believed it was spreading into Scotland. There was more than a hint of desperation in his drive towards radical solutions. In his criticism of the *First Blast*,

John Aylmer cited the pressure of grief engendered by the persecution as the reason Knox espoused such theories. 'Seeing this errour rose not of malice but of zele: and by loking more to the present crueltie, that then was used: then to the inconvenience that after might follow. Wherein surely doyng is somwhat to be pardoned: consideryng the grief that like a good member of that bodie which then suffered, he felte to his great sorow and trouble.'[59] Knox concentrated on female rule in his *First Blast of the Trumpet against the Monstrous Regiment of Women*, and probably finished this part of the proposed trilogy in Dieppe when he was without his Genevan support group.[60] He later insisted to William Cecil that his exile congregation had not been party to the final version before publication, 'for, Sir (in God's presence I writt), with none in that company did I consult thereof, before the finishinge of the same; and, therfor in Christ's name, I require that the blame may be upon me alone.'[61]

Compared to other possible approaches to political authority and resistance, Knox's line in the *First Blast* had one obvious advantage. Since Mary Tudor could not alter her gender, an argument based upon female rule was impossible to ignore or discount. Such a stance provided a non-confessional appeal to the English nobility to rid the country of a monarch whose gender debarred her from rule. Mary's female status automatically introduced into the discussion the disadvantages brought by her marriage and facilitated the inclusion of patriotic notes, such as freedom from Spanish rule. The attractive simplicity and directness of an argument based upon female rule dazzled Knox and prevented him from considering the wider ramifications of his proposition. Such myopia proved one of the costliest mistakes of his career.

An anxiety to offer a watertight argument drove Knox towards the universal applicability of his proposition. He was intent upon presenting a reasoned and well-sourced case that appealed to the intellect.[62] Abandoning his homiletic style, he deliberately tried to prove his case through the scholastic techniques he had learned at university. In his *First Blast* he cultivated the aura of intellectual debate, though he wrote in English and played upon popular stereotypes of women. Allowing no confusion, he began his book with a summary of his main proposition: 'To promote a Woman to beare rule, superioritie, dominion, or empire, above any Realme, Nation or Citie, is repugnant to Nature; contumelie to God, a thing most contrarious to His reveled will and approved ordinance; and finallie, it is the subversion of good Order, of all equitie and justice.'[63]

This all-encompassing thesis was a valiant effort to include as many categories of argument as possible, from natural and divine law to more general social and political order. Knox moved through those categories one by one, presenting a solid phalanx of citations and quotations from the authorities he had collected, partly as proof texts and partly as the framework for his syllogisms. Beginning with the assertion that female rule was 'repugnant to Nature', he trotted out a series of classical authors to demonstrate that this was the accepted view in the pre-Christian period of ancient Greece and Rome. The open and deliberate appeal to the wisdom of the ancients allowed the inclusion of Aristotle's theories about the inferiority of women, but was a departure for Knox, who had previously emphasized the sole authority of the Bible.

Much of the main section of the *First Blast* involved this careful rehearsal of assorted authorities combined with scholastic logic to bring the argument back to the central contention that women should not be promoted to authority. This was probably rather dull reading for many of Knox's male contemporaries, who might have thought he was making hard work of forcing an open door. In their eyes everyone knew that women had been created subordinate to men and should not normally rule men in social or political life. In common with other general principles, much of the intellectual debate about female rule had focused upon which exceptions were permissible. To strengthen his case Knox adopted the practice of dealing with counter-arguments. In this part of the book he displayed the annoying habit of disappearing down rabbit holes of biblical exegesis, such as providing excessive detail to prove that the biblical story of the daughters of Zelophehad revolved around female inheritance.[64]

Knox relied upon Aristotelian syllogisms to give logical progression to his argument. Arguing that female rule was against justice and destroyed commonwealths, he employed a hypothetical syllogism that bound together different points (if/then), refuted counter-points (but) and carried the argument forward (therefore) to a conclusion.[65] In this syllogism Knox moved back to his favourite territory of the 'express Word of God'. 'Whatsoever repugneth to the will of God expressed in His most sacred Word repugneth to justice; but that women have authority over men repugneth to the will of God expressed in His Word; and therefore mine author commandeth me to conclude without fear that all such authority repugneth to justice.' To sweep aside the objection that regnant queens were accepted by law, custom and tradition he reconfigured that conclusion into a negative formulation: 'neither may the tyranny of princes, neither the foolishness of the people, neither wicked laws made against God, neither yet the felicity that in this earth may hereof ensue, make that thing lawful which He by His Word hath manifestly condemned'.[66] This switching between positive and negative formulations removed the middle ground – the same technique that he had used discussing worship and that Goodman had employed over divine commands.

What Knox sought was to present a choice between black and white alternatives. If his readers had been dropping off to sleep with the ponderous progression through his categories, this firecracker would have caught their attention. Further radical ideas followed as he started the application of his general proposition. With the Preface and side notes, the final sections were probably added when he was preparing the book for publication in the spring of 1558. His style and tone altered, incorporating more of the denunciatory flow at which he excelled. He included specific references to current rulers, mainly Queen Mary Tudor, but also an occasional sideswipe at Henry II of France and Mary of Guise. Having established to his own satisfaction that female rule was against the laws of God and of man and against the natural order, in the 'admonition' section he applied that proposition to the current situation and discussed what action could be taken. With prophetic denunciation dominating, the focus narrowed to the main target, Queen Mary, her husband Philip and their Catholic regime. Knox shifted from general proposition to action. As his side note declared, 'women may and ought to be deposed from authority'.[67] Though there was no specific appeal to the English to resist their Queen, the nobility were instructed that they 'ought without further delay to remove from authority all such persons as by usurpation, violence or tyranny do possess the same'.[68] This was political dynamite.

The *First Blast* carried no names – neither the author, nor the publisher, nor the place of publication. It was published in Geneva by the printing house of Poullain and Rebul who did not obtain a licence to print, possibly taking the risk in order to get the work in the highly competitive and crowded Genevan printing industry. Being written in English, which Calvin could not read, the tract was able to slip through the normal checks.[69] At the time of publication, Knox did not foresee the impact the book would make. In the winter of 1557–8 it was probably one of a number of projects he needed to complete and speed through the press. Despite being anonymous the pamphlet spread quickly among the other exile communities and his authorship became an open secret, though some thought his friend Goodman had written it. It did not take long for Knox to realize just how badly the *First Blast* was being received by many English exiles. Even his friend the mild-mannered and peace-seeking John Foxe had written to him in the spring of 1558 with a rebuke about the book and its tone. The fuss made him abandon the original plan of not revealing his name until the final third blast of the trumpet. In July 1558 he publicly acknowledged the *First Blast* and published the brief outline of the *Second Blast* at the back of his Scottish tracts. The following spring he remarked to Anne Locke, 'The Second Blast I feare shall sound somewhat more sharp, except men be more moderat then I hear they are.'[70]

The four points of his proposal for this second blast explained that in a Reformed polity the criteria for kingship had changed. Rulers were to be

elected according to God's ordinance, rather than succeed by birth and inheritance. No one should hold office who was a Catholic, notorious sinner or tyrant.
Oaths of allegiance to such rulers did not count and if an unfit ruler had
mistakenly been elected, they should be deposed.[71] Printing this brief summary
so soon after the *First Blast* ensured that reactions to it encompassed the entire
package of ideas he had proposed, not solely the main tract he had printed. In
addition Knox stated explicitly in his *Appellation* addressed to the Scottish
nobility what he thought the English nobles should have done:

> I fear not to affirm that it had been the duty of the nobility, judges, rulers and
> people of England not only to have resisted and againstanded [stood up
> against] Mary that Jezebel whom they call their Queen, but also to have
> punished her to the death, with all the sort of her idolatrous priests, together
> with all such as should have assisted her what time that she and they openly
> began to suppress Christ's Evangel, to shed the blood of the saints of God
> and to erect that most devilish idolatry, the papistical abominations and his
> usurped tyranny, which once most justly by common oath was banished from
> that realm.[72]

This trumpet call for tyrannicide became indelibly associated with Knox's name.

By publishing the *First Blast* and *How Superior Powers*, Knox and Goodman
became bracketed together as resistance theorists. Their writings had been
born of an angry and defiant desperation in the face of the persecution or
'Satan's bludy clawses'. Though completed when the two men were apart, the
tracts were published within a short space at the start of 1558 and were subsequently placed into a single category. As they faced the hostile reaction, the
two friends grew even closer, and Knox's 'beloved brother' became one of the
most influential people in his life.

1 The prospect of Haddington, Knox's home town on the banks of the River Tyne.

2 Knox's teacher, John Mair, lecturing to his students.

3 Holy Trinity parish church, St Andrews, from the Geddy map c.1580.

4 Facsimile of a letter written out by Marjorie Knox and with her own postscript, from her husband to John Foxe, 18 May 1558.

5 Knox and Goodman depicted in woodcut by the Catholic controversialist, Peter Frarin, 1566.

THE BIBLE
AND
HOLY SCRIPTVRES
CONTETNED IN
THE OLDE AND NEWE
Testament.

TRANSLATED ACCOR-
ding to the Ebrue and Greke, and conferred With
the best translations in diuers langages.

WITH MOSTE PROFITABLE ANNOTA-
tions vpon all the Lord places, and other things of great
importance as may appeare in the Epistle to the Reader.

FEARE YE NOT, STAND STIL, AND BEHOLDE
the saluation of the Lord, which he wil shewe to you this day. Exod.14.13.

Great are the troubles of the righteous:

And the Lord shal fight for them and ye shal hold your peace.

THE LORD SHAL FIGHT FOR YOV: THEREFORE
holde you your peace, Exod. 14, verse.14.

AT GENEVA.
PRINTED BY ROWLAND HALL.
M.D.LX.

6 The title page of the first edition of the Geneva Bible, 1560.

7 Knox's 'Queen Mary': a composite of three female rulers.

a) Queen Mary Tudor

b) Mary of Guise

c) Mary, Queen of Scots.

8 James Stewart, half-brother to Mary, Queen of Scots, earl of Moray, and Regent of Scotland: a convinced Protestant who had a stormy friendship with Knox.

A SERMON

preached by Iohn Knox

Minifter of Chrift Iefus in the
Publique audience of the Church of
Edenbrough, within the Realme of
Scotland, vpon Sonday, the. 19.
of Auguft. 1565.
For the which the faid Iohn Knoxe
was inhibite preaching
for a feafon.

1. Timoth. 4.

¶ The time is come that men
can not abyde the Sermon of
veritie nor holfome doctrine.

*To this is adioyned an exhortation vnto all
the faythfull within the fayde Realme, for
the reliefe of fuche as faythfully trauayle
in the preaching of Gods worde. Written
by the fame Iohn Knoxe, at the commaun-
dement of the miniftene aforefayd.*

Imprinted Anno. 1566.

9 Knox's only printed sermon, preached on 19 August 1565 in St Giles' Kirk, Edinburgh.

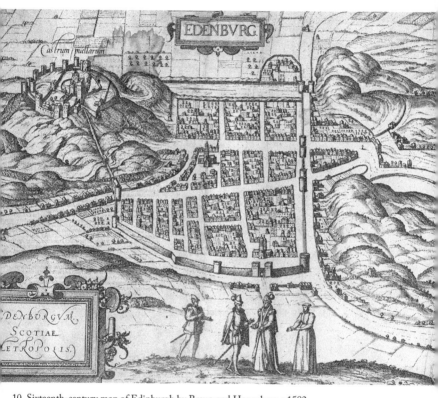

10 Sixteenth-century map of Edinburgh by Braun and Hogenberg c.1582.

11 Lord Deputy Sidney marching out of Dublin Castle with his English troops.

CHAPTER TEN

Quietness of conscience and contentment of heart

The apocalyptic pressure felt by Knox and Goodman that had produced their revolutionary tracts also drove their congregation to utilize to the full their time in exile. The great missionary endeavour by Calvin and his fellow Frenchmen to sustain the Protestant cause in France helped the English-speaking exiles to find their own purpose. The congregation saw their mission as preparing for the future throughout the British Isles and witnessing in the present. They became a working model of a Reformed community embodied in Word, sacraments and discipline resting upon a strong spiritual core. In a remarkable undertaking they produced a community of texts, the Geneva Bible, the metrical psalter and their new liturgy. The 'example of Geneva' which they created with the help of their zealous congregation became the model for everything Knox subsequently did. This time in Geneva was the shining beacon that remained with him for the rest of his life. The dynamism of the common effort generated additional writings, including the only publication by a woman, Anne Locke, Knox's close friend. Knox was also busy writing, and in the summer of 1558 produced his three most significant tracts for different elements within his Scottish audience and then another addressed to his old English congregations in Newcastle and Berwick. He was not alone in his planning for a Protestant future in Scotland, and the Anglo-Scottish leadership of the congregation became involved in developing a wide-ranging strategy that encompassed both the Tudor state and Stewart Scotland.

HAVE MERCY, GOD

In a delightful irony, while Knox was away from Geneva working on his *First Blast* in Dieppe, his friend Anne Locke was developing her authorial voice and discovering a means to subvert the inferior position of women within the

Church.[1] By writing for publication, Anne joined the male members within the Genevan congregation in their common enterprise. As she explained in her Preface, she was adding her 'basket of stones' to help build the wall of the new temple, as the Jews had done at the time of Zerubbabel.[2] In November 1557, possibly accompanied by her friend Marjorie Knox, Anne had listened to John Calvin's sermons on the Book of Isaiah. She had probably travelled part of the way to Geneva with the Bodley family, and they also attended Calvin's sermons. Their teenage son, Thomas Bodley, possessed a copy of Calvin's sermons on Genesis, keeping the manuscript continually with him and ensuring that it was eventually deposited in the Oxford library that carries his name.[3] Many of the city's exiles came to listen to Calvin, and a system had been organized with a speed writer to transcribe his sermons as they were preached. The text was copied and circulated and, after Calvin had revised it, formed the basis of his printed biblical commentaries.[4]

Anne availed herself of this 'semi-official' French text on the prophet Isaiah where over four sermons Calvin discussed the Song of Hezekiah. She translated them into English and dedicated them to her fellow exile, the intrepid Katherine Willoughby, Duchess of Suffolk. At the back of her edition Anne added her own sonnets based upon Psalm 51. When she returned to England the volume was printed and was the only publication by a woman within the Genevan congregation. With their heavy emphasis upon ecclesiological, biblical and political tracts, it was one of the few products of that congregation to deal with personal devotion. It provides the best mirror in which to view the importance of female participation in Knox's congregation and see previously hidden aspects of the community's devotional life. As Locke was Knox's closest female friend, her work also reveals the nature of the 'comfort' that supported him in his 'dolour' and the spiritual struggles he shared with his small group of close confidants.[5] It was possible that Anne wrote with Knox in mind, since Psalm 51, being the psalm sung on the night of Wishart's arrest, might have acquired a particular resonance for him as the expression of the experience of the Garden of Gethsemane and the facing of suffering. Anne's meditation, 'Have mercy God for thy great mercies sake', was well known to both the congregation's ministers. Several years later, Goodman had her poem with him when he was minister in St Andrews. He requested a composer friend, Andro Kemp, to set this metrical meditation into four singing parts, and it was copied into Thomas Wode's Partbooks and entered the Scottish tradition of Protestant devotion.[6]

Anne wrote her extended meditation upon one of the seven penitential psalms, the 'Miserere', Psalm 50 in the Vulgate Bible and Psalm 51 in Protestant numberings. This psalm had held an important place within Catholic liturgical and devotional practice and by her strong Protestant emphasis Anne sought to reclaim it for the Reformed community and their spirituality.[7] Her devotional writing formed part of the broad tradition of singing psalms characterizing the Reformed churches and enthusiastically adopted by the exile Genevan congregation with their own metrical Psalm Book. Sung, read or as a focus for meditation, psalms provided an important link between worship in church and household and private devotion. Anne's poem was located in this liminal area, allowing her to contribute to the congregation's devotion without infringing the taboo against women leading public worship.

In her poem Anne broadly followed the lines of interpretation given in the short 'argument', possibly written by William Whittingham and placed at the start of the psalm in the Geneva Bible and the Psalm Book:

> When David was rebuked by the Prophete Nathan, for his great offences, he dyd not only acknowlage the same to God with protestation of his naturall corruption, and iniquitie: but also left a memoriall thereof to his posteritie. Therefore first he desireth god to forgive his synnes and renewe in him his holie spirite: with promesse that he wil not be vnmyndefull, of those great graces. Finally fearinge lest god wolde ponishe the whole churche for his faute: he requireth that he wolde rather increase his graces towards the same.[8]

Anne reflected upon the nature of sin and repentance, and, like Knox, dwelt upon the sense of being a 'cursed wretch' whose sins deserved the divine judgement 'and damned downe to depth of hell to go'.[9] As the preacher had reiterated in his own writings, it was only when 'lost with panges and passions of despeir' that one could then crave God's mercy and find 'The face of comfort in extremest grefe'.[10] Anne enjoyed wordplays just as much as Knox and in one sonnet employed 'justice' and 'just' in a complex poetic sequence. It allowed her to affirm justification by faith alone, that doctrinal badge of Protestant identity. Another strong Protestant message was woven into Sonnet 14, where Anne moved considerably beyond the base text of Psalm 51:12. She dealt with that loss of the sense of God's presence that had been the subject of Knox's 1557 letter to Thomas Upcher. Commenting on the 'swete retorne of grace that I have lost', she concluded the verse with her 'anchor': 'To hold my faith from ruine and decay, With fast affiance and assured stay'.[11]

For both Anne and Knox, the congregation in Geneva provided a secure anchor. As the 'first preacher' to this large community of deeply committed Protestants, Knox later boasted that his congregation were a model of 'peace, concorde, sober and quiet livinge'.[12] Through the tinted lens of memory, his Genevan ministry developed an even warmer and rosier glow, and he looked back with longing to his flock, 'amongst whom I once lived with quietnesse of conscience and contentment of hart'.[13] His experience had been enhanced because of the high esteem in which he was held by the city. In June 1558, he and Goodman were presented before the Council in Geneva and freely granted citizenship of the city as a mark of respect for their ministry to the English-speaking exile church. At the ceremony, Knox probably thought of his father as he gave the name for the register, 'John Knox, son of William Knox, Haddington'.[14] For the rest of his life Goodman remembered his Genevan citizenship, repaying his adopted city by collecting funds for them in the 1580s and in 1603 leaving a bequest in his will to Geneva.[15]

THE EXAMPLE OF GENEVA

The greatest achievement of Knox's congregation in Geneva was their production of a 'community of texts'.[16] These covered the broad spread of a public order of worship, private devotions, the metrical psalter, ecclesiastical discipline, catechisms and a new translation of the Bible accompanied by a complete interpretative apparatus. At its core were two separate volumes, *The Forme of Prayers and Psalmes of David*, and the Geneva Bible. When combined these parts formed a greater whole: the essential tools for a newly Reformed Church. It conveyed a distinctive vision of the godly Church organized and packaged into a concrete, printable form that was easy to reproduce, transport and disseminate and was to prove of incalculable worth when Knox returned to Scotland. Equally significant, by its own well-organized running and the exercise of discipline over its members the congregation proved that they had developed between 1556 and 1559 a workable template for a godly church. This 'example of Geneva' combined practice with theory into a single package that exerted immense influence upon the Reformations of Scotland and England and entered the mainstream of Protestant culture for the Anglophone world. Much of what today is recognized as the English-speaking Reformed or Presbyterian tradition was first assembled in Geneva between 1555 and 1560. Though Knox's name is often attached to this package, the Scot knew it was primarily the work of his friends. It is impossible to quantify the level of his personal contribution since no authors' names were provided and the volumes were published when Knox was away from the city. However, he was a passionate supporter and user of that community of texts and led the dissemination of the entire example of Geneva.

The congregation's achievement was possible only because they were working in Geneva during a remarkable few years. Writing the Preface to his 1557 New Testament, William Whittingham explained that he was 'moved with zeal, counseled by the godly, and drawn by occasion, both of the place where God hath appointed us to dwell, and also of the store of heavenly learning and judgment, which so aboundeth in this City of Geneva, that justly it may be called the patron and mirror of true religion and godliness'.[17] The English were one constituent within an extended exile community that was producing new biblical editions in Greek, Hebrew and Latin as well as translations into English, French, Italian, Spanish and Dutch.[18] Those biblical scholars pooled their scholarship and manuscripts, drawing upon exciting discoveries such as new readings from the Greek New Testament manuscript still known as the Codex Bezae after Calvin's successor.[19] Since Knox spent lengthy periods away from the city and his central task when in Geneva was to be the congregation's first preacher, others led these projects, though all shared the same vision of a fully Reformed Church. His most substantial contribution was to the order of worship in the *Forme of Prayers* that used the drafts hammered out by him in the committees that had sat in Frankfurt during the Troubles.[20] When Whittingham, Goodman and Gilby had arrived in Geneva in the autumn of 1555, the new congregation they formed needed its own order of worship. They had brought with them from Frankfurt a selection of drafts of services and metrical psalms. While Knox was still away in Scotland, they assembled an entire order of worship and put through the press the first *Forme of Prayers*, published in English and Latin on 10 February 1556. From the beginning it was recognized as providing a model for the future.[21]

When Knox wrote to Anne Locke in December 1556 he explained why he thought Geneva was 'the maist perfyt schoole of Chryst that ever was in the erth since the dayis of the Apostillis. In other places I confesse Chryst to be trewlie preachit; but maneris and religioun so sinceirlie reformat, I have not yit sene in any uther place.'[22] For the Scot it was the public maintenance of the laws of God and the consequent reformation of behaviour that were so impressive and in his view unique. Arriving shortly after Knox and also joining the congregation with his wife and children, Thomas Hancock wrote of his first impressions of the Swiss city in his autobiography: 'I dyd se my lord God moste pewrly and trewly honored, and syn moste straytly punnisshed: soo hytt may be well called a holy citie, a citie of God.'[23]

Though Knox could write with wonder about what Calvin had achieved in Geneva, he did not follow to the letter Calvin's ecclesiological understanding of discipline. He rejected the Frenchman's very careful distinction between the Word and sacraments as the two marks of the true Church leaving discipline to be described as the sinews that held the Church together and were vital for its good functioning. Knox had no hesitation in recognizing that discipline was a third mark of the true Church. Though Knox was not present at that first service of the newly formed exile congregation, his co-minister Goodman had emphasized how difficult it was to preserve godly order in a Church and maintain the unity and mutual love of the congregation. The best way to guard against the Devil's attempts to sow discord in this flock was to uphold discipline. Already a clear and close association had emerged that associated a pure and settled polity for a Church or congregation with the enforcement of a high moral code and this became the double meaning of discipline in the future Protestant Scotland. Though no records have survived of discipline meetings by the ministers, elders and deacons of the exile church in Geneva, a passing reference in a letter to Goodman indicated that Michael Gill, a member of the congregation, had been excommunicated, or barred from receiving the Lord's Supper. Once he had acknowledged his fault, publicly repented and been reconciled with the man he had wronged, Gill was able to return to full fellowship among the English exiles.[24] The very matter-of-fact way in which this had been mentioned in the letter suggests that the exercise of discipline had rapidly become a fact of congregational life. In subsequent years discipline was one of the distinctive hallmarks of the example of Geneva as it was received in England and Scotland.[25]

In common with the congregation's other major production, the Geneva Bible, it was not deemed appropriate to name the authors of the *Forme of Prayers*. Those involved in producing the community of texts were Knox's close friends and comprised a markedly Anglo-Scottish group. William Whittingham was the mastermind behind both the metrical psalter and the biblical translations. He was one of those who remained in Geneva to see the Bible through its printing in 1560. William Kethe, a Scot, probably took over the psalter project when Whittingham was working on the Bible and was helped by John Pulleyne, who arrived in Geneva in 1557. On the commercial side, John Baron, from an Edinburgh merchant family who was married to an Englishwoman, Anne Goodacre, helped with the Geneva Bible and remained with Whittingham and Kethe to see it and Knox's predestination tract through the presses. Anthony Gilby, a noted Hebraist and advocate of Anglo-Scottish unity, played a prominent role in biblical translation, probably taking the lead in the Old Testament section. William Cole, who was another member of the biblical team and probably also remained in 1559, showed a strong interest in Scottish affairs.[26] Miles Coverdale, with his Scottish wife from Perth, was the most experienced biblical translator and psalm versifier in exile. He would have been consulted about the Geneva Bible and the psalter, though he did not settle in Geneva until the autumn of 1558. The close relationship between Knox and Coverdale was emphasized when Miles became the 'witness', formerly a godfather, at the baptism of Eleazer, Knox's second son. Thomas Sampson, who did not remain long in the city, probably had more of an advisory role. As a former Oxford professor, Goodman was well qualified to assist and had long experience of working with Whittingham. Like Knox his ministerial duties probably prevented too heavy an involvement in biblical translation, though he would have helped supervise the revision of the *Forme of Prayers*.[27] John Bodley and William Williams, elders of the congregation, were the main financial supporters of the projects, establishing a printing office in Geneva in 1558 and commissioning Rowland Hall to print the Bible.[28]

Knox was proud of the new biblical translation, and his predestination tract of 1560 contained the first direct quotation in print from the Geneva Bible. Given that he regarded the Word of God as the route of salvation, nothing was more important in his eyes. Making that Word available to listeners and readers in sermons and as a printed vernacular text was central to his evangelical message. The production of the up-to-date English translation of the Geneva Bible by the congregation laid the foundation for a godly Church and a pure reformation. Knox was adamant the Word of God must be properly understood, and the Geneva Bible brought the 'true sense' to the reader and listener. Whittingham and his team devised its most important attribute of combining the biblical text and interpretation into one seamless entity.

The Geneva Bible's revolutionary format created the first English study Bible with all the necessary apparatus and commentary lodged within one set of covers. The division of chapters into numbered verses was adopted from the French translations that were being printed in Geneva, and this simple but dramatic change in layout transformed the reading and citation of the Bible and dictated how that book is understood today. The Geneva translation provided a full critical apparatus with carefully structured additions placed to guide the reader at all stages. At the start of each biblical book was placed an 'argument' or summary of the contents, and each chapter had a short list of main points and key verses. Down the margins, side notes explained difficult ideas, alternative readings, linguistic points and cross-references. They also gave explanations and interpretations of the biblical message. Maps and diagrams were inserted within the text, making the experience of the people of God real to the eye, with a diagram of a Jewish priest's garments or maps of the places in the Gospels or the early churches, while tables and indices allowed the text to be searched. As an immensely user-friendly book, the Geneva Bible became a bestseller and by far the most popular version for the people of Protestant Scotland, Elizabethan England and the early American colonies. Down the generations and across the seas, this Bible transmitted the specific vision of Knox's exile congregation.

The same attitude to the Word and the corresponding apparatus were found in the metrical psalters produced by the Genevan congregation. Like the

Bible, the psalter contained 'arguments' to give the context for each psalm. The Psalm Book, as it became universally known in Scotland, incorporated in one volume both the *Forme of Prayers* and the *Psalmes of David in Metre*. Being smaller and cheaper than the complete Bible, the Psalm Book offered a more accessible and affordable section of the biblical text. It was extremely popular, running to many different editions in Scotland and England, and approximately a million copies had been printed by about 1640.[29] Within the biblical canon, the Psalms were regarded as containing the essence of the Bible. This understanding was mentioned in the prefaces to the Anglo-Genevan psalters produced by Whittingham and his team. They presented the metrical psalms as translations of the Word of God and not as mere biblical paraphrases.[30] Singing the psalms formed an essential component within public worship and private devotion and made a bridge between those two poles of the spiritual life. Knox's daily devotional routine was built around the Psalms, and throughout his life he followed the liturgical practice, acquired as a child in Haddington's church, of moving through the entire psalter every month. Like Anne Locke he often turned to the Psalms to help him express his own spiritual struggles. His fellow Scot William Kethe wrote the metrical version of Psalm 94, and Knox printed this at the end of his *Appellation* as the best reminder of how to face persecution and hold fast the belief that God will rescue his people and confound his enemies.[31]

When he returned to Scotland, Knox had the substantial advantage of bringing with him the 'example of Geneva' with its combination of texts and practice. Having been achieved in that Reformed city, this model could be presented as being in complete accord with Calvin and the best Reformed churches in Europe. In addition to the practical advantages of having a pre-packaged foundation for church building, their existence imbued him with confidence and the pride of ownership: these were the products of his own congregation. This community of texts also encouraged greater rigidity in Knox because he was firmly convinced they embodied the Word of God, leaving little room for adaptation or amendment to fit other perspectives.

YOU MAY PROVIDE TRUE TEACHERS FOR YOURSELVES

Knox was on the periphery of the production of the texts during 1558 because he was occupied with his own series of tracts. This was the most intense period of writing and publication during his life and reflected his double focus on the situation within Scotland and within England. In the *First Blast* he had become distracted from his main argument while 'talking with my God in the anguish of my heart' and had made the plea 'To thee, O Lord, I turn my wretched and wicked heart; to thee alone I direct my complaint and groans; for in that Isle to thy saints there is left no comfort.'[32] The emotions he had experienced when confronting the persecution in England and in France became transferred to Scotland, though his advice as to the appropriate course of action in the three countries remained very different. The burning of Walter Myln in St Andrews in April 1558 in particular caused him to view the Scottish ecclesiastical hierarchy in the same light as he regarded the English and French Catholic clergy. Despite their meagre record of actual persecution, Knox spoke in highly emotive language of Scottish bishops as priests of Baal who exercised their tyranny or as wolves intent upon the blood of Protestants. Such intensely aggressive language disguised the comparative limitations of the programme of action he proposed.

By July 1558 when he published his three tracts addressed to Scotland, Knox had a strategy and a list of demands. He set out a common programme, though he approached his three Scottish audiences with separate arguments and an agenda to fit each group. For himself, he wanted his death sentence quashed and freedom to return to Scotland without fear of legal process. He also demanded 'liberty of tongue' giving him freedom to preach and to present his own case against the Catholic hierarchy, their doctrine and liturgy. More generally, he demanded an end to the persecution of Protestants and the 'tyranny' of the Scottish bishops. He sought toleration for Protestant preaching and worship, at the very least in noble households and private gatherings. Though short passages in the tracts had more radical hints, they were not yet developed. Closing his *Appellation*, he summarized the demands:

> For in the name of God I require of you that the cause of religion may be tried in your presence by the plain and simple Word of God; that your bishops be compelled to desist from their tyranny; that they be compelled to make answer for the neglecting of their office, for the substance of the poor which unjustly they usurp and prodigally they do spend; but principally for the false and deceivable doctrine which is taught and defended by these false prophets, flattering friars and other such venomous locusts.[33]

Within this Scottish context Knox's message was far more cautious than the one he sent to England in his *First Blast*. In the first of his three Scottish tracts he addressed the Regent with an augmented version of his 1556 Letter. He abandoned his failed attempt at conciliation, and his 'additions' to the text introduced more denunciations and warnings of divine punishment if the Regent did not change her religious policy. The tone was sharper, verging on the cruel, when Knox characterized the early death of Mary of Guise's two sons followed by that of her husband as divine punishment.[34] There were indications that the Regent's gender might be used against her and her rule was dismissed as 'borrowed, extraordinary and unstable for ye have it but by permission of others. And seldom it is that women do long reign with felicity and joy.'[35] Though rebutting the slur that Protestants were seditious and rebellious, Knox added the ominous aside, 'Neither yet is every tumult and breach of public order contrary to God's commandment.'[36] The language of threat had not yet moved into political resistance against the Regent's authority but continued as religious denunciation. Knox's personal pique showed through: 'I did not speak unto you, Madam, by my former letter, neither yet do I now, as Pasquillus doth to the pope … But I come in the name of Christ Jesus, affirming that the religion which ye maintain is damnable idolatry.'[37] In his 1558 *Letter to the Regent* and his *Appellation* Knox sought a public disputation in Scotland to settle the question of what was 'true religion' and what 'heresy'. More in hope than expectation, he demanded that the case against 'idolatry' should be presented in open debate. He went so far as to indicate which Church Councils might be cited as subsidiary authorities to the Bible. Showpiece disputations had been a feature of the early reformations within Swiss and Imperial cities and were used in England in 1559 and France in 1561. Though Mary of Guise was unlikely to stage such a disputation, Knox's offer to debate strengthened his appeal. He projected a remarkable confidence in his own ability to win that type of stand-up contest.

Knox had much higher hopes of the Scottish nobility. As the title indicated, in his *Appellation* he made a judicial appeal for protection from his condemnation as a heretic two years earlier. Donning his former notary's hat, he may have started compiling this section as soon as he arrived in Geneva in September 1556, drawing up a specific list of legal precepts to justify an appeal from his sentence of death for heresy and from the jurisdiction of the Church court. Linked to this legal appeal, he requested a guarantee that he could return to Scotland without fear of arrest and execution, and it was probably connected to the call home received in May 1557 and might have been a plan for a quasi-legal challenge to the heresy conviction. In this section Knox argued that the entire Catholic hierarchy were 'unjust judges' and should not decide his case.[38] Medieval civil law recognized the claim that an accuser's 'mortal hatred' against the accused invalidated the legal process, and it had been accepted as a valid argument in heresy trials before the Roman Inquisition. For good measure, Knox threw in the procedural point that his prior accusation against the Scottish bishops should be heard before their counter-case.

After these technical legal points Knox shifted his legal ground. He began to argue that civil rulers had the right to override the sentence of an ecclesiastical court, not simply hear appeals. Leaving the niceties of the legal challenge far behind in the main part of his tract, he expounded the proposition 'it is lawful for the servants of God to call for the help of the civil magistrate against the sentence of death, if it be unjust'.[39] The links between the two parts of the *Appellation* were tenuous, suggesting that the sections were drafted at different times. Knox was not necessarily intending to develop a single, internally coherent theory. Instead he was trying to score a succession of polemical hits and pile up arguments with the cumulative effect of making a compelling call for action. This approach encouraged his habit of going off at tangents and introducing ideas that did not fit the main thrust of his argument.

Within the *Appellation* Knox inserted comments drawn from arguments Goodman had developed in his *How Superior Powers*.[40] He appropriated Goodman's view of covenant obligations to punish idolatry extending to every member of the people of God, 'the punishment of idolatry doth not appertain to kings only, but also to the whole people, yea, to every member of the same according to his possibility'. Instead of expanding this covenant theme that later became so important to him, Knox reduced it here to a rhetorical device to goad the nobility into action.

> If this be required of the whole people, and of every man in his vocation, what shall be required of you, my Lords, whom God hath raised up to be princes and rulers above your brethren, whose hands He hath armed with the sword of his justice, yea, whom He hath appointed to be as bridles to repress the rage and insolence of your kings whensoever they pretend manifestly to transgress God's blessed ordinance?[41]

Knox concentrated upon the Scottish nobility and in a flattering tone he explained the origin of their authority and their duties: 'Consider, my Lords, that ye are powers ordained by God . . . and therefore doth the reformation of religion and the defence of such as injustly are oppressed appertain to your charge and care.'[42] Nobles were 'lesser magistrates' and were included in St Paul's description in Romans 13:1 of the powers (in the plural) that were to be obeyed. Although owing obedience to the 'superior power' of the monarch, they had their own duty to uphold true religion. Knox was adapting ideas developed by the Lutheran opposition to Emperor Charles V which he had encountered in the Magdeburg *Confession* that had been written by the Lutheran clergy of the city in 1550 to justify their stand against the Emperor.[43] A number of Reformed churches fighting against Catholic rulers formulated theories justifying their resistance by reference to the power of these 'inferior magistrates', expanding the original theory to suit different constitutional frameworks. Knox's friend Theodore Beza was already developing his version to fit the French situation, where the Protestant position was rapidly changing. By May 1558 Huguenots were attending open-air gatherings, singing metrical psalms and listening to sermons, and in Paris the armed retinues of leading nobles protected Protestant crowds.

In his tract Knox encouraged Scottish nobles to offer similar protection. Rather than confining themselves to defending and maintaining their kin and friends, he wanted nobles to recognize the religious obligations of their office and to their spiritual kindred. Throughout the *Appellation* he suggested actions already familiar to the Scottish nobility and he may already have heard about the exchange he later incorporated in full within his *History* between the fourth Earl of Argyll and Archbishop John Hamilton of St Andrews at the end of March 1558. The Archbishop had asked his brother-in-law to hand over John Douglas, Argyll's household chaplain, for a heresy trial. The Earl had returned a forthright answer, defending Douglas and his Protestant doctrine as well as warning the Archbishop that there were plenty of other noble houses 'that profess the same God secretly'.[44] By requesting the type of protection and 'maintenance' being given by Argyll to his preacher, Knox's appeal fitted into this Scottish context.

Towards the end of his tract Knox suddenly appeared hesitant. Having demanded that the Scottish nobility do their duty, he ended lamely with a request merely to be vigilant and careful.[45] However, in a final flourish he reverted to his prophetic mode and issued a personal challenge, combining the language of noble honour and personal combat with prophetic admonition:

> I have offered unto you a trial of my innocency; I have declared unto you what God requireth of you being placed above His people as rulers and princes; I have offered unto you and to the inhabitants of the realm the verity of Christ Jesus; and with the hazard of my life I presently offer to prove the religion which amongst you is maintained by fire and sword to be false, damnable and diabolical. Which things if ye refuse, defending tyrants in their tyranny, then dare I not flatter ... so must I cry to you that you shall perish in your iniquity.[46]

In addition to the Scottish Regent and the nobility, Knox directly addressed the common people of the kingdom. His *Letter to the Commonalty* with its strong pastoral tone was one of his gentler works, and he gave the impression he was speaking to each individual, adding the personal touch by signing the letter, 'Your brother to command in godliness'.[47] He was almost tender as he sought to persuade his listeners of the importance of their religious duty. The argument was simple: everyone was equal in the eyes of God and salvation was offered irrespective of rank or social position; therefore obtaining access to salvation was a basic religious duty. He summed up the point in a side note:

'Reformation of religion belongeth to all that hope for life everlasting.'[48] Since salvation came through hearing the Word of God, everyone should have access to this spiritual food for their souls found in biblical preaching and teaching. However, it would be freely available in Scotland only once Protestant preachers were allowed to function. Though the ordering of religion was primarily the duty of rulers, subjects were not relieved of all responsibility. While there were distinctions regarding 'the regiment and administration of civil policies, yet in the hope of the life to come He hath made all equal ... [therefore] it doth no less appertain to you, beloved Brethren, to be assured that your faith and religion be grounded and established upon the true and undoubted Word of God than to your princes and rulers'.[49]

As in his sermons Knox juxtaposed the promise on the one hand and the prospect of divine punishment on the other, emphasizing that in the Old Testament punishment fell upon the entire people of Israel, not only their rulers. He satirized the array of excuses commonly used: 'We were but simple subjects; we could not redress the faults and crimes of our rulers, bishops and clergy. We called for reformation, and wished for the same, but lords' brethren were bishops, their sons were abbots, and the friends of great men had the possession of the church, and so we were compelled to give obedience to all that they demanded.'[50] When urging action, he suggested a limited set of objectives. The common people should demand that their rulers, both Crown and nobility, provide preachers and expel those clergy not doing their job. Knox did venture on to more radical ground: 'And if in this point your superiors be negligent, or yet pretend to maintain tyrants in their tyranny, most justly ye may provide true teachers for yourselves, be it in cities, towns or villages; them ye may maintain and defend against all that shall persecute them and by that means shall labour to defraud you of that most comfortable food of your souls, Christ's Evangel truly preached.'[51] He offered the more modest practical suggestion that there should be a tax strike, with people withholding their tithes from the Church, thereby targeting the Catholic clergy. He wanted religious change and sought pressure from below to help achieve it. He stopped short of demanding that the people establish public Reformed worship because that remained within the province of the superior and inferior magistrates. In prophetic style he drew his *Letter to the Commonalty* to a conclusion by summarizing the perilous situation in Scotland. If nothing were done about the Catholic clergy and the idolatry that defiled the kingdom, he asked his rhetorical finger-pointing question, 'Will God in this behalf hold you innocents?'[52]

In the three 1558 tracts aimed at Scotland, what Knox did not demand was as significant as the plan of action he did propose. Directing his violent language at the Catholic clergy, he scrupulously avoided calling for outright rebellion or the overthrow of the Regent's regime. Expecting little from Mary of Guise, his 1558 *Letter* read more like a final warning. The nobility were his key audience and he wanted a policy of increasing pressure to change Scottish religious policy. Looking to the model of defiance offered and open gatherings taking place in France, he wanted toleration of Protestant worship and doctrine in Scotland and hoped the nobility would take direct action to achieve it. Even the common people had a role in maximizing the pressure. In practice there was a high chance such behaviour would have led to violent confrontation, though Knox's arguments still fell considerably short of revolution.

GIVE EAR THEREFORE BETIMES, O BRITAIN

When in Geneva, Knox was able to discuss the Scottish situation with his close colleagues. Christopher Goodman and Anthony Gilby gave him their full backing and he could share his concerns with William Kethe, his fellow Scot. Both Gilby and Kethe added contributions to his *Appellation*. Gilby wrote an *Admonition to England and Scotland to Call Them to Repentance* while Kethe appended his metrical version of Psalm 94. At the start of his *Admonition*, Gilby mentioned a range of the writings produced by different members of the Genevan congregation. They were part of a single Anglo-Scottish or 'British' campaign to present the Protestant cause to their English-reading audience, and Gilby warned, 'Give eare therefore betymes, O Britanie, (for of that name both rejoyseth) whiles the Lord calleth.'[53]

The fate of both kingdoms occupied Knox's mind at all times. In his *First Blast* he had recognized that God had 'most justly punished the proud rebellion and horrible ingratitude of the realms of England and Scotland. For when thou didst offer thyself most mercifully to them both, offering the means by which they might have been joined together forever in godly concord, then was the one proud and cruel and the other unconstant and fickle of promise.'[54] Knox's colleagues shared the memory of that 'Edwardian moment' when a marital union between the two realms had seemed possible.[55] They were equally convinced that the future fate of the two countries was bound together, and Gilby expressed these ideas at length in his *Admonition*. This Anglo-Scottish perspective recognized an important convergence under way as the two kingdoms shared similar experiences. Though Knox had deliberately not exploited the parallels in his Scottish writings, a queen ruled in each realm and a female Regent was in charge in Scotland. As a consequence of the marriages of those queens, both countries faced domination by the 'strangers' of the husband's country, with England under the control of Spaniards and Scotland under the French. Each country had a Catholic Church subservient to the papacy in Rome, practising 'idolatry' in its worship and persecuting Protestants at home. By the middle of 1558 Knox discounted the vast gulf between the religious enforcement practised by the Scottish and English authorities and assumed that the Scottish clergy would increase the level of persecution by emulating, if allowed, their counterparts in England and in France. One critical difference remained between the two realms: England had once embraced the Gospel and made its public covenant with God, while Scotland had not. Having rejected the 'light', the English were apostates as well as idolaters.

Within the apocalyptic framework in which Knox and his colleagues were operating, they were convinced they had entered a critical juncture when God was calling England and Scotland to obedience. Gilby summed up this view: 'O England and Scotland, both makinge one Island, most happie if you could know your own happines.'[56] He adapted the biblical parable of the two sons sent by their father to work in the vineyard. The first son, Scotland, refused to go, and Gilby gave a brief survey of the opportunities offered to the Scots in the period of the Rough Wooings. The Scots having rejected the chance of union with Protestant England in Edward VI's reign, God was now offering them a second chance. When Gilby spoke about England, the other son who had said he would work in the vineyard but had done nothing, he was unsparing in his criticisms. He attacked what had happened under Henry VIII, calling it a 'deformation' rather than a reformation, and took the unusual step of being intensely critical of the Royal Supremacy. Although the reign of Edward VI had witnessed a major improvement, two things had been lacking: a fully Reformed liturgy and the imposition of discipline. These were the central points that Knox had emphasized and that were at the heart of the Frankfurt dispute, and they were the two things first supplied by the exile congregation in Geneva. Gilby and Knox agreed that behind the Edwardian failure and the disaster of Mary's succession lay a fundamental lack of religious commitment. They both employed the same text from Matthew 6:22: 'If the eye be single, the whole body shalbe clere.'[57] The phrase about a single eye developed into an abbreviated slogan for Knox and his friends to describe the need for total commitment to the godly cause. In best Knoxian style, Gilby presented a stark choice between life and death: both sons, England and Scotland, must work together in the vineyard of the Lord.[58]

Knox amplified these themes of repentance, choice and imminent judgement in one of his most impressive pieces of forceful writing. On 10 November 1558 he printed his *Exhortation to the inhabitants of Newcastle and Berwick*, the third open letter he had addressed to his former congregations in the north-east of England. Knox was at his best admonishing people he knew, conscious of a continuing pastoral responsibility for them, and the tract was full of anger and

sorrow because so many had returned to Catholicism. He described this transformation: 'But oh, alas! howe are ye changed? how are ye corrupted? whitherunto
are ye fallen? and how have ye deceived the expectation of those that dyd labour
in planting and watering yow, and now do sobbe unto God for your ingratitude,
callinge with tears unto his mercie for your conversion, and that unfayned repentance may sodenly appeare in yow?'[59] Exaggerating for maximum effect, he wrote
of a total defection: 'O consider, deare Brethren, what grief it is, that in such a
multitude none shal be founde faithful, none constant, none bolde in the cause
of the Lorde Jesus, whome so boldlye before they had professed.'[60]

Knox was unsettled and upset that his ministry in Berwick and Newcastle
appeared to have been a failure. He confided that he was 'wounded almost to
the deathe' and in great desperation because he believed God had cursed him
by not rewarding any of his labours.[61] The New Testament examples of St
Paul's lack of success had drawn him up 'from the bothome of hell, to the
whiche some tymes I sinke for remembrance of your fall and for my other
offences against God committed'. Employing a favourite sermon technique, he
turned his personal experience into a spur on his readers.[62] As he had with the
Scottish 'commonalty', he satirized the weak excuses of those who had
conformed:

> Alas! we can not redress the iniquitie of these tymes, we have no pleasure in
> idolatrie, we are sorye that the blood of innocents is shed in our lande; we
> woulde be content that true religion shulde be used; but wicked men now
> beare dominion, and therfore must we serve and obey the tyme: when god
> shal please to restore his truth, we wilbe gladd of it, but in the mean tyme, we
> must obey the lawes set forthe by our superiours: God knoweth our hartes,
> and we trust he wilbe merciful unto us.[63]

Knox was implacable: no excuse would suffice and God would send further
plagues and vengeance because 'the bloode of God's innocent children, which
cruelly is shed in your lande (wherof ye are all giltie by reson of your permission
and silence) dothe continually crye in the eares of our most juste God'.[64] In this
prophetic sentence pronounced against the towns of Berwick and Newcastle
can be heard the almost unbearable pressure felt by Knox that had been built up
by the shedding of innocent blood in the persecution. The fall of Berwick's
sister garrison of Calais allowed Knox to underline how little time was left.
Through the repetition of the word 'now' he stressed the urgency: 'Now he
offerethe himself unto yow; now he is neare; now he is to be founde, whyle he
callethe you to repentance by his Messingers and Worde.'[65] The only solution
was repentance, and Knox summarized what that required: 'professe the trueth

which ye have denyed, remove to your power iniquitie from amongste yow, and abstayne in your bodies from idolatrie committed and maynteyned by your wicked rulers.' This was not an incitement to rebellion, but a programme of limited resistance similar to that given in his *Letter to the Commonalty of Scotland*, which he mentioned. During the previous six months his views had merged on what to do in England and Scotland where 'the dayes are so wicked'.[66]

In Geneva Knox found great support among his friends and congregation as they confronted together the anguish generated by the persecution in England. They turned to the Psalms, like Locke's poem on Psalm 51 and Kethe's metrical setting of Psalm 94, to give voice to their misery and affirm their belief in divine deliverance. The active production of 'weapons' to be used in the fight against Antichrist gave them a strong sense of purpose and a focus upon the future. Acutely aware that they were living within an apocalyptic moment, they believed that the situation within the two kingdoms of England and Scotland was about to reach a climax with God calling both realms. The heightened sense of a crisis building in France, of which Knox was particularly conscious, added to the immediacy created by their Anglo-Scottish outlook. In 1558, a sense of urgency fuelled both by desperation and by hope was building within him and his friends. The confidence that God would deliver his servants, as he had the psalmist King David, bolstered Knox and helped keep at bay his personal fears and anxieties.

CHAPTER ELEVEN

England, in refusing me, refused a friend

To Knox and his congregation the death of Queen Mary Tudor represented the divine deliverance for which they had prayed. They could now look forward to the end of their exile and returning home. Knox probably thought he faced a complicated balancing act between conflicting calls. Having been based among the English exiles during his period on the Continent, he recognized a prophetic role in helping England to return to the covenant with God forsaken under Queen Mary. At the same time he was committed to pushing forward the Protestant cause in Scotland. In the longer run and in line with the grand Anglo-Scottish strategy developed in Geneva, he hoped a shared Protestant faith would bring together in friendship his adopted and native countries. He was convinced God had given both kingdoms a second chance to answer this particular call to unity, rejected first during King Edward VI's reign. However, any dilemma he might have had about which task to attend to first was solved by the virulent reactions to his *First Blast*. After a long wait in Dieppe, in the spring of 1559 his only option was to return directly to Scotland. The new Queen of England refused to permit him to set foot in her kingdom and extended her displeasure to his Genevan congregation and their hosts. Queen Elizabeth's assumption that everything to do with Geneva, including Calvin and Beza, was tainted by association with Knox's views had profound consequences. This turning away from Geneva helped alter the re-established Church of England and changed its outlook for generations to come.

After the debacle of his previous attempt to visit Scotland, Knox was wary about planning another trip. During the summer of 1558, Calvin extracted a commitment from him enabling the Swiss Reformer to assure the Earl of Arran on 1 August that Knox would willingly dedicate his services to his native country once arrangements had been made to disengage him from his Genevan congregation.[1] The formal call from Scotland took several more months and Knox made no attempt to pre-empt the summons. Marjorie was pregnant again and gave birth to another son, who was christened Eleazer on 29 November with Miles Coverdale as witness. During that month John Gray had arrived in Geneva on his way to Rome to expedite the appointment of Henry Sinclair as Bishop of Ross. It was an incongruous combination of tasks – the summoning of the Protestant Knox back to Scotland alongside the continuation of routine appointments to the Scottish Catholic hierarchy. Gray carried letters from the Protestant nobles calling Knox and requesting that Calvin ensure he answered that call. Gray brought news and details of Scottish events over the previous six months, and they were probably the source for *Truthful Tidings* published in the city early in 1559. William Cole had heard the news from Knox and the next day relayed it to John Bale in Basle. The letter was published in Low German or Dutch as *Warhafftige Tydinge*: an indication of how much interest existed throughout the international Protestant community in the spread of their faith in Scotland.[2]

Gray may have brought rumours of another major European news story: Queen Mary Tudor had died and Elizabeth had become Queen of England. Whenever the exiles first heard the news, they rejoiced to know that 'Jezebel' was dead and that Cardinal Pole had died at about the same time. Mary's death transformed the prospects for the Genevan exiles. After 'they had geven to God hartie thankes for his great goodnes', the church held a major consultation.[3] The first task was simple. A copy of the new 1558 psalter was rushed through the press and dedicated to Queen Elizabeth.[4] As a personal gift William Fuller had special small copies made for the Queen of the French Bible, a New Testament and the Genevan *Forme of Prayers* finely bound, gilded and enamelled, though in the end he did not present them.[5] The congregation decided who would remain in Geneva to finish their major projects of seeing the Bible through the press and continuing the work on the metrical psalter. Keeping to their annual routine, on 16 December, Knox and Goodman were re-elected as ministers alongside a full complement of elders and deacons.[6] The initial euphoria in Geneva had been tempered when William Fuller, one of the congregation's elders, received an update that the new Queen, his former mistress, had yet to show signs of a Protestant policy. He recalled, 'my first good hope and great rejoysing was quite quenched and extinguished, and was turned into so great heaviness, mourning and lamentation'. He was so downcast personally that he did not want to leave Geneva, and Calvin had to instruct him to return to England.[7] However, most of his fellow exiles were longing to return home.

The trickiest issue the Genevan congregation faced was relations with the other exiles. For the previous eighteen months bridges had been built with the other communities to remove past 'jars' over the Book of Common Prayer and liturgical ceremonies. To consolidate that reconciliation the congregation sent letters on 15 December to their fellow exiles urging unity and suggesting a common policy once in England. William Kethe carried the letters to Aarau and Frankfurt, and copies were also sent to Basle, Strasbourg, Worms, Zurich and other centres.[8] Everyone was aware that speed was essential, and Kethe quickly brought back replies from Frankfurt and Aarau.[9] The Frankfurt letter mentioned that many English exiles had already left for home, and some of the Genevan congregation were equally anxious to be on their way and were given formal leave to depart by the Genevan Council on 24 January.[10]

BRIEF EXHORTATION TO ENGLAND

Knox had been preparing to leave for Scotland, but rearranged his plans. He stayed in Geneva long enough to pen his *Brief Exhortation to England* printed on 12 January 1559. While this tract addressed the entire kingdom, it was linked by Knox to the letter directed specifically at his old congregations at Newcastle and Berwick that he had completed a few weeks before Queen Mary died. The two pieces were held together through their unifying theme of repentance. Following the accession of Queen Elizabeth, Knox had turned the plea for repentance within his *Brief Exhortation* into a call to renew England's covenant with God. Initially made under King Edward, the covenant had been forsaken under Queen Mary, but God was now offering England another chance; if it were not taken, divine vengeance would inevitably follow. In line with the traditional understanding of penitence Knox first sought to ensure that his readers were fully aware of their guilt. In his condemnation he made no concessions at all, declaring all those who had acquiesced in the Marian regime's re-Catholicization of England to be guilty of apostasy, idolatry and murder. At the end of his tract Knox had attached his list of those who had died for their Protestant faith in Queen Mary's reign. He spoke of the cry for revenge from the blood of 'your brethren and sisters'; in his mind this was a blood feud as well as a holy war.[11] He warned that only true contrition and repentance would prevent God's vengeance from falling upon England.

On the traditional cycle of penitence, contrition had to be accompanied by amendment of life, and this would be demonstrated by the country's return to Protestantism. Knox set down in precise terms what such a 'reformation of religion' entailed. In succinct form he gave a distillation of the Reformed ideal worked out by the leaders of the exile congregation in Geneva during the previous year. They had drawn upon their experiences during the Marian exile to develop this blueprint for full reformation and in Frankfurt and especially in Geneva they had crystallized what they believed had been wrong or lacking within the Edwardian Church of England. The second chance offered by the accession of Queen Elizabeth was the opportunity to move decisively to create a fully Reformed Church. Knox set out two fundamental requirements: applying the regulative principle to worship and staying true to God's covenant through the exercise of discipline and instruction in Protestantism.[12] He presented a simple set of logical steps from repentance to covenant renewal. Like Old Testament Israel, England would become again a covenanted people.

First and foremost was the purification of worship: 'Let God's Worde alone be the rule and line to measure his religion. What it commandeth, let that be obeyde; what it commandeth not, let that be execrable.' Next came instruction in the Protestant faith, best achieved through preaching the Word by ministers based in cities and towns. This was elaborated into some remarks on the Church's polity and a specific set of criticisms of the Edwardian Church of England such as holding multiple benefices or placing lordly bishops in charge of unwieldy dioceses, remarks that had been part of Knox's final inflammatory sermon to the Frankfurt congregation. The targets could also be relatively minor, such as reliance upon the printed sermons in the *Book of Homilies*. Predictably, Knox gave high priority to the exercise of discipline, which included the exclusion of Catholics from all offices and rule within the realm and punishment of those involved in the persecution. Finally, the development of a new academy in Geneva that opened in 1559 probably inspired an explicit section on the provision of schooling and higher education as key to the long-term instruction in Protestantism necessary to sustain obedience to the covenant. By employing the Old Testament model of a covenanted people Knox emphasized the common duty of both secular and ecclesiastical authorities working together for the temporal and spiritual welfare of the people of God. This distinctive and uncompromising vision of the godly Christian commonwealth had developed from his own covenant thought, to which had been added the insights of Goodman and the other leaders of the Genevan congregation. In his *Brief Exhortation* Knox was addressing England, but the ideal of a full reformation and the covenanted people were clearly in his mind when he finally returned to Scotland, and echoes of the tract appear in the *First Book of Discipline* of 1560.

When Knox set off for Dieppe on 28 January 1559 he left Marjorie and her mother behind in Geneva in Goodman's care and with Anne Locke for company. Though the winter was severe enough for the Rhine to freeze and travelling was difficult, he arrived at the Channel port on 19 February.[13] Once there he sent a request to Sir William Cecil, who had become Queen Elizabeth's Secretary of State, for a passport to enter and travel through England. There was plenty to occupy him in Dieppe while he waited. With no resident pastor for the Huguenot community, Knox offered to help and found himself in the middle of a major expansion in support of Protestantism. He baptized and preached at open-air assemblies and on 1 March presided when a number of Picardy notables, such as the Sieur de Senarpont, publicly declared their Protestantism.[14] With the French Reformed Assembly organized to meet in Paris in May, Knox probably heard about the forthcoming production of the French Confession of Faith: more material for future church-building.[15] Though Anne Locke had sent several letters from Geneva (with one taking five weeks to arrive), he only had time to reply on 6 April. He apologized and reassured Anne that, even if he had not managed to write, their friendship was as firm as ever.[16]

Once the news of Mary Tudor's death had been confirmed, other exiles had rushed back to England to become involved in the new regime as quickly as possible. Sir Anthony Cooke, urged on by his son-in-law William Cecil, left Strasbourg on 20 December.[17] The Strasbourg view of their compatriots in Geneva had been captured in Thomas Randolph's wry comment to Nicholas Throckmorton: 'The Genevians repent their haste; they blew their triumph before their victory.'[18] Having been shocked by the contents of Knox's *First Blast*, Cooke, as one of the most influential English exiles in Strasbourg, had earlier written to Beza to check if the Genevan pastors had approved the book. Beza brought the letter straight to Calvin and he investigated. In his previous private conversation with Knox in the spring of 1557, Calvin had made his own views on female rule plain and warned the Scot about the dangers of raising such issues. Although personally annoyed that Knox had disregarded his earlier advice, Calvin pragmatically recognized that the damage had already been done. In the summer of 1558 he decided that little could be achieved so many months after publication and was mindful that any public fuss ran the risk of Knox and the rest of the English exiles being banished from Geneva with nowhere else to go.[19] Knox's earlier expulsion from Frankfurt was a nasty precedent. Calvin warned him explicitly about future publications, and it was no coincidence that the Scot's long tract on predestination demonstrated at length and in detail how closely the author agreed with Calvin. Even so, the City Council would not license its printing in 1560 until they had carefully checked a Latin summary of its contents and Whittingham had personally vouched for its orthodoxy.[20] After he had complained to Calvin, Cooke and other exiles had consulted in Strasbourg about who might rebut the *First Blast*. Bartholomew Traheron, who had opposed Knox during the Frankfurt Troubles, was probably the author of first choice, though he died during 1558. John Aylmer instead took up the challenge, starting work on *An Harborowe for faithfull and trewe subiectes*, which was printed early in 1559 by John Day in London.[21]

Another of Knox's adversaries, Richard Cox, made full speed to London and was back in time to be involved in the planning for the new Elizabethan Church. Encountering the *First Blast* had probably given him a satisfying 'I told you so' moment. His passion for order had been deeply offended during the Frankfurt Troubles by Knox's rejection of the Book of Common Prayer and by the Scot's violent language in his *Faithfull Admonition*. Cox regarded the *First Blast* as a seditious tract that threatened political and religious order, and on his arrival in England the future Bishop of Ely might have briefed Matthew Parker, the new Archbishop of Canterbury.[22] Not having been in exile, Parker was horrified at the threat to the social and political system posed by the ideas of Knox and Goodman and lamented:

> If such principles be spread into men's heads, as now they be framed and referred to the judgment of the subject, of the tenant, and of the servant, to discuss what is tyranny, and to discern whether his prince, his landlord, his master, is a tyrant, by his own fancy and collection supposed, what lord of the council shall ride quietly minded in the streets among desperate beasts? What master shall be sure in his bedchamber?[23]

Parker's hand-wringing over the writings of Knox and Goodman added to the fearful atmosphere that prevailed during the early months of Elizabeth's reign.

To make sure neither Knox nor the 'precisian' attitudes of the Genevan congregation established themselves in England, Cox might have considered reusing tactics that had worked so well in Frankfurt to secure an orderly Protestant settlement.[24] The Queen needed no prompting to recognize the subversive nature of the *First Blast*. Thanks to their resistance tracts, Elizabeth had Knox and Goodman firmly in her sights and seized any opportunity to launch her retaliatory blasts. Refusing Knox's request for a passport and denying him entry to England did little to assuage her anger – everyone associated with Geneva became tainted by the *First Blast*. Goodman was deemed as bad as Knox, and he was forced into hiding on his return to England. For the rest of her reign the Queen hounded him and blocked his career.[25] In the spring of 1559 John Pulleyne, a member of the Genevan congregation and newly provided to the archdeaconry of Colchester, was arrested. In a sermon he had unwisely indicated his support for his Genevan colleagues and had to explain himself in front of the Privy Council. Despite his experience and his talents, Pulleyne rose no further in the Church of England. In April there were reports of house-to-house searches which caused the returning Genevan exiles to be afraid, even of other members of their congregation.[26] William Fuller, who had disagreed with Knox's revolutionary stance, was

accused of being an informer for the Privy Council and was shunned by
Knox's and Goodman's supporters.[27]

Waiting in Dieppe, Knox heard of the troubles his former congregation
were encountering. In a letter to Cecil he tried hard to take full responsibility,
declaring, 'the poore flocke is innocent' and adding a barbed parenthesis
possibly directed at Fuller, '(except soche as this day loudest crye treason)'.[28]
Beginning to appreciate the extent of his disgrace, he told Anne Locke in
Geneva, 'for to me it is written that my First Blast hath blowne from me all my
friends in England'.[29] A few months later he reminded her of his gloomy
predictions to the congregation, now being fulfilled: 'after our departure frome
Geneva sould our dolour beginne'.[30] The Queen also blamed Calvin and
the city of Geneva for permitting the publication of the tracts. She refused
Calvin's accession present of a biblical commentary and did not even send
a polite reply. Calvin's hurt and confused letter to Cecil explained that he had
not authorized or known about Knox's *First Blast*. It did no good. Years later,
Beza explained that those revolutionary books had blighted relations between
England and Geneva.[31]

Knox was becoming increasingly frustrated and found it hard to believe
that his passport request had been refused and that William Cecil, his friend
from Edwardian days, was unable or unwilling to sort out the problem. He
wrote for a third time on 10 April and re-sent the same letter a fortnight later
in case that copy had been lost. Hurt and surprised at Queen Elizabeth's
furious reaction, he levelled his fire at Cecil, reminding the Secretary that
repentance was needed because in Queen Mary's reign he had betrayed God
by his willingness to conform to Roman Catholicism.[32] Knox indulged in the
classic refuge of wounded pride: those who opposed him would be sorry in the
end, and in dramatic fashion he declared, 'Englande, in refusing me, refuseth a
friende.'[33] Not being permitted to travel to the north of England disrupted his
travel plans. He had intended to pay a pastoral visit to his former congregations of Berwick and Newcastle. Following the *Exhortation* he had addressed
to them the previous November, he had probably been busy preparing repentance sermons and deciding on the most appropriate form of discipline and
reconciliation for those among his north-eastern flock who had attended
Mass. In the medium term, he seems to have envisaged an itinerant preaching
ministry that operated across the Borders, using Berwick as a safe haven if
things became too dangerous in Scotland. He later told Cecil it was essential
to station a preacher in Berwick who would be able to secure the allegiance of
most of the lairds in the East and Middle Borders. A common Protestant faith
was the best way of overcoming centuries-old hostility: Knox assured Cecil
that those who 'professed them selves ennemies to superstition within Scotland'

would not 'lift thare handis against England, so long as it will abyd in the puritie of Christes doctryn'.[34]

The Berwick placement might have been part of a grander scheme hatched in Geneva that planned for Anglo-Scottish religious amity. In his April letters from Dieppe, Knox told Cecil he needed to talk to him face to face because there were matters he dared not commit to paper or trust to most messengers.[35] With an exaggerated flourish he reminded Cecil that he had never offended anyone in England, 'except in open chare [chair meaning pulpit] to reprove that which God condemneth can be judged offence'.[36] For the remainder of his life Knox dropped hints that he had played an additional secret role in the Anglo-Scottish amity.

Despite appearances Knox was a man capable of keeping secrets. His deliberate lack of discretion in the pulpit disguised this talent and it has been overlooked down the centuries. When someone shouted his opinions as loudly as Knox did, listeners failed to note what had not been said. Like hiding an object in full view, Knox's noisy public persona was a good cover for the things he did want to keep quiet. Though he felt he had been badly treated in 1559, he did remain a friend to England and committed to Anglo-Scottish friendship, but he became permanently suspicious of the Elizabethan regime's motives. At the end of April he gave up hope that he would be permitted to visit England and took ship directly for Scotland.

THE TERRIBLE BLAST OF THE TRUMPET

At the time of its publication, Knox was blissfully unaware of the difference this 'terrible Blast of the Trumpet' would make to his life.[37] John Aylmer, with his talent for stating the obvious, explained that in the *First Blast* Knox had 'cracked the dutie of obedience'.[38] Whether justified or not, Knox had been labelled an advocate of violent resistance. By the end of 1558 all his readers knew that England's next ruler was another queen. While Mary Tudor's comparatively early death could not have been anticipated a year or so earlier, Knox's apparent lack of foresight or consideration of Princess Elizabeth puzzled contemporaries, as well as future generations. The closest to an explanation Knox managed was in his reply to John Foxe. He had written the *First Blast* 'not so much to correct common welthes as to delyver my own conscience, and to instruct the consciences of som semple [simple or ordinary people], who yit I fear be ignorant in that matter'.[39]

That kind of explanation was never going to work with the Elizabethan regime. The Queen had either read Knox's work herself or knew enough about its central tenets to be profoundly and permanently enraged by its message and the man who had composed it. Elizabeth saw the book not only as directly threatening her royal dignity but as a personal insult. The attack upon her 'just right' to rule by descent undermined her pride in being her father's daughter and its timing highlighted the extreme sensitivity of her succession. Questions about the legitimacy of the daughter of Anne Boleyn, Henry's wife after his divorce from Catherine of Aragon, were openly raised in Catholic Europe. Mary, Queen of Scots, backed by her father-in-law Henry II of France, asserted that she was the true and legitimate heir to the English throne and quartered the arms of England with those of Scotland and France. At this stage there was no suggestion of female solidarity between Mary and Elizabeth in the face of Knox's attack upon regnant queens, though in 1561 there was a rumour that Mary, Queen of Scots, wanted a united front against the *First Blast*.[40]

When charged by Cecil in the spring of 1559 with writing a treasonable book, Knox was prickly and defensive: 'The writinge of that booke I will not denye; but to prove it treasonable I think it shall be harde.' As his proof text concerning the problems of female rule, he made a most odd choice, especially in the context of an unmarried queen: 'this was the voice of God, the which first did pronounce this penaltye against Women, "In dolor shalt thou beare thy children."'[41] Having tried defiance with a touch of hauteur, Knox reached the wounded protestations of loyalty: 'And yet if any think me ennemy to persone, nor yet to the regiment of her, whome God hathe now promoted, they are utterly deceived in me.' Knox probably felt magnanimous when he explained his major concession: 'if Quene Elizabeth shall confes, so that the extraordinary dispensation of Godes great mercy maketh that lawfull unto her, which both nature and Godes lawe denye ... then shall non in Englande be more willinge to meintein her lawfull auctority then I shal be'. Reading this, Cecil probably put his head in his hands and filed the letter well out of his mistress's sight.[42]

A couple of months later the Secretary dropped a large hint about how Knox might retract his views. Cecil had hoped to speak to him in person about the Scottish situation and probably brief him on a suitable apology for the *First Blast*. Unfortunately the secret meeting at Stamford between Cecil and Knox planned for the autumn of 1559 did not take place. At the top of his letter, Cecil placed, in Latin, the verse from Galatians in which Paul proclaimed that there was neither male nor female, but all were one in Christ. Cecil's letter came too late – Knox had already written his own letter of apology to the Queen a week earlier. Even if he had received this new proof text, Knox would probably not have used this biblical escape route to retract his views.[43] Several copies of his letter of 'apology' have survived and one contains a series of marginal annotations that reflect the Queen's indignation.[44] Knox never stood before Queen Elizabeth to explain himself, but the annotated letter gives a flavour of the confrontation that might have occurred. One comment summed up Knox's attempt at an apology with the exclamation, 'O vile purgation, false, lewd, dangerous, and the mischefes therof infinite! Is this to purge or to excuse? It is to put a firebrand to the state.'[45] More succinct, though equally damning, was the verdict, 'your purgation worse than your boke'. Other comments noted further 'lewd' propositions and indicated logical points or questions that could be raised against Knox's reasons. In general there was 'Too much fansie to mainteine former follies escaped yow by zelous hatred of an evell Quene. This is but patcherie.'[46] Knox never mastered the skill of apologizing. This attempt was the one that mattered most and proved his least successful. Queen Elizabeth, who was an expert at nursing a grudge, never forgave Knox.

Those who rushed to Queen Elizabeth's defence over the debate about female rule did not necessarily calm her anger. The most obvious attempt at damage limitation was John Aylmer's book which had been organized by the Strasbourg exiles. He protested that he was not attacking Knox personally and assured his readers of 'the mans honestie and godlynes'.[47] In a comment that would have provoked laughter among Knox's Frankfurt opponents, he added, 'this man therefore I dowbte not wyll paciently heare what may truly be sayd against him'.[48] In what was a remarkable admission, he conceded that if Knox had restricted his fire to Queen Mary Tudor 'he could have said nothing to[o] muche, nor in suche wyse as could have offended any indifferent man'.[49] Queen Elizabeth would not have been impressed by that line of argument and would have relished even less some of Aylmer's other assertions about her gender. One of his reassuring arguments was that in England with its Privy Council and Parliament her male advisers would hold a regnant queen to a straight and narrow path. Aylmer's main theme called upon an English patriotism through which he could obliquely attack Knox for being a Scot. He began his work with the description of the *First Blast* as a 'lytle booke strangely written by a straunger' and continued that, even though Knox loved England, he was not English. Though foreigners might state their views in the pulpit, Aylmer warned Knox, 'being a straunger you disturbe not our state'.[50] Such patriotic rhetoric often carried a xenophobic edge and contained anti-Scottish and anti-French elements.[51] Aylmer chose the character of 'Mother England' to deliver an emotional appeal to her subjects and in one famous side note concerned with the threat posed by the Franco-Scottish alliance summed up his view: 'God is English.'[52]

Aylmer had also made the simple point that the Scriptures taught obedience but did not provide a blueprint for constitutional arrangements.[53] By challenging the Scriptural basis for Knox's arguments, the unpublished tract by

Richard Bertie provided a far more sophisticated refutation.[54] A fellow religious exile, Bertie was the husband of Katherine, Duchess of Suffolk, and had served as an elder in the exile congregation at Wesel before the couple had eventually made their way to Poland. On their journey back to England, Bertie had written extended notes on the *First Blast*. With his library packed in boxes for the journey, he felt himself 'teddred by the shorte lyne of my memorye', but offered a strong counter-case to Knox. Adopting a similar gladiatorial style of argument, he sought to demolish Knox's points by reducing them to the absurd. Having obtained a copy of Knox's augmented 1558 edition of the *Letter to the Regent*, he taxed him on the differences between the 1556 and 1558 versions in their treatment of Mary of Guise. He highlighted another inconsistency, questioning why Knox had not preached against Queen Jane, 'to speake playnely fowle flattery yeasterday and fonde furye to daye'.[55]

Bertie's substantial argument was found in his reinterpretation of the passages from Deuteronomy upon which Knox and Goodman had relied. He put his finger on one of the cornerstones of their view of a Christian commonwealth: for contemporary Christian kingdoms the judicial rules of the Mosaic Law were as binding as its moral commands. Bertie observed, 'what an intrycate mysmase the Author hathe to treade owte before this place of Deuteronomy will frame to his purpose'.[56] This biblical challenge to Knox's view of the law of God and the 'expresse word of God' came from someone equally committed to a Reformed Protestant cause and a friend of Anne Locke. It is not known if Bertie's refutation ever reached Knox and there is no trace of a response to his challenges. However, his arguments demonstrated that Knox's black and white views were most vulnerable to those who shared many of his premises and yet challenged his conclusions.

For Knox's Roman Catholic opponents, his *First Blast* offered plenty of ammunition with which to mount an attack. At the funeral of Queen Mary, Bishop White warned, 'the wolves be coming out of Geneva . . . and have sent their books before them, full of pestilent doctrines, blasphemy, and heresy, to infect the people'.[57] Peter Frarin seized upon Knox and Goodman as the perfect examples from Scotland and England to demonstrate that all Calvinists were rebels and worse. For those unable to read, he simplified the message into a rhyming couplet placed beneath the woodcut of the two preachers blowing their trumpets (see Plate 5).

> No Queene in her kingdome can or ought to syt fast,
> If Knokes or Goodmans bookes blowe any true blast.

In addition to making life difficult for Knox, Goodman and their Geneva congregation, the *First Blast* had major consequences for the reformations within the island of Britain and for English relations with the broader Reformed movement in Europe. Throughout her reign Queen Elizabeth linked Geneva to sedition and never extended any warmth in that direction. Bullinger and Zurich were given the chance to be the main conduit of Reformed thinking into England, and this created a significant difference from the close relations the Scottish Kirk had with Geneva. The veterans of Knox's Genevan congregation found themselves marginalized and alienated during the making of the Elizabethan Settlement and in the longer-term management of the Church of England. As the reign progressed they provided one of the core components of the Elizabethan Puritan movement.[58] With the coming of a second generation of bishops, such as Whitgift and Bancroft, the tracts of Knox and Goodman provided an excellent stick with which to beat their Puritan opponents. Following Aylmer, this emerging 'Anglican' view also chose to castigate Knox for being a foreigner, the father of Scottish Presbyterian views and, by definition, not truly English.[59] The reception of the *First Blast* gave birth to the enduring myth of John Knox as a revolutionary.

SATAN'S BLOODY CLAWS

The Marian exile had changed Knox, and the man wanting to re-enter England in 1559 was a tougher, wiser and more secure person than the one who had landed in Dieppe five years earlier. On the positive side, marriage had brought him a happy family life and delight in his wife and two sons. In Geneva he was part of a circle of close personal friends, such as his male colleagues Goodman, Whittingham, Gilby and Kethe, and he enjoyed friendship and spiritual support from women such as Anne Locke. The comfort they gave made him stronger and helped him face some of his fears and take crucial decisions. Having been selected from among distinguished competitors, Knox had gained additional confidence as a minister to a congregation where his preaching was greatly valued and pastoral skills were in demand. He felt fulfilled as 'first preacher' to the remarkable Geneva congregation that had realized in practice his ideal of a properly functioning church. As a pamphleteer, he had found his voice and addressed a wider audience with great assurance. Written at the end of his exile, the *Brief Exhortation* was probably his most dynamic pamphlet, full of forceful and compelling prose that swept the reader along with its drive and emotion. These successes reinforced his awareness of his vocation as a prophet chosen by God to be a special messenger for the perilous times faced by England and Scotland. Such confidence made it harder for him to distinguish between his own insights and what he believed was the voice of God speaking through him. Once he had recognized a certain meaning in a biblical text and fitted it into a collation of texts to form a single unit and point, he did not acknowledge alternative interpretations. He became increasingly dismissive of those who opposed his presentations of Scriptural demands.

Knox found it particularly difficult and painful to watch helplessly from the sidelines as the martyrs were caught in 'Satan's bludy clawses',[60] and the experience left a deep scar. His survivor's guilt was channelled into an intense anger and hatred for Roman Catholic clergy, and in his mind their hands would always carry the stain of blood. Inspired by the death of his first hero, George Wishart, he admired all the English martyrs and carefully collected a list of names, including those who died in prison, which was published in 1559.[61] Among the names was John Rough, the minister who had called Knox to preach in St Andrews. He had been caught and was executed shortly after he returned from exile in the winter of 1557 to minister to the underground congregation in London.[62] Knox found it difficult to live with the ever-present threat of capture and a martyr's death, and knew he would struggle to find the cold courage to embrace that form of witness. His spirit was willing to fight to the death, but he was afraid he would lose his nerve at the end. Several times when called back to Scotland he seemed to freeze, unable to take the next step himself. When pushed out of his safe haven by Calvin and other friends, he did find the courage to march 'towards the sound of the guns'.[63] Once in the midst of real danger, as he was in Dieppe in 1557 and 1559, he found the mettle to get on with his job of being a minister.

Knox and the rest of the exiles understood the Marian persecution as a terrible plague sent by God to punish England for its failures under Edward and its apostasy under Mary. Interpreting Edward's reign had been an essential part of the exile and produced a broad consensus among the exile writers. Knox and the more radical group based in Geneva went further in their rewriting of the narrative of Edwardian England and identified the central problem as a lack of total commitment that left 'reformation' half finished. The pre-Reformation Church structure and much of its personnel had been allowed to remain and the Book of Common Prayer had not removed all 'dregs of popery' from worship. Crucially, there had been no discipline to uphold morality and maintain the obligations of the covenant. In their analysis political contamination had undermined a full religious commitment and the drive to measure all things by the plain Word of God. Failure had been inevitable because the extent and pace of Church reform had been dictated by 'carnal wisdom and worldly policye'.[64] After Mary Tudor's reign, Knox could not rid himself of the fear that it might happen all over again. The ghost of the English 'Jezebel' haunted him and he became convinced that the rule of any other regnant Catholic queen would inevitably follow the same course.

CHAPTER TWELVE

Restorer of the Gospel among the Scots

Knox arrived in Scotland in the middle of a crisis. His famous sermon at Perth triggered an iconoclastic riot that rapidly escalated into full rebellion against the Regent, Mary of Guise. The fighting drew into Scotland French and English military forces to contest the latest round of the long-running battle for dominance in Britain. During 1559–60 Knox served as an army chaplain to those Protestants who had rebelled against Mary of Guise and had called themselves the Lords of the Congregation, and experienced at first hand the campaigns they fought. Thanks to the death of Mary of Guise and a combination of unusual factors, the Congregation and its English allies emerged triumphant. Knox was sure he had witnessed the hand of God bringing Scotland's deliverance.

The man who landed at Leith in May 1559 was unlike the prisoner bundled into the French galleys a dozen years before. Having managed only a short and whirlwind preaching tour in the winter of 1555–6, Knox had become distanced from his native country. The Scotland of 1547 was long gone and even the kingdom he had left three years before had changed a great deal. After his departure in May 1556 he had endeavoured to keep in touch, but communications with Geneva and even Dieppe had been hit and miss. From the summer of 1557 he had been rehearsing the moment of his return and had spent much time thinking of Scotland and discussing the situation there. Calvin and the Genevan Company of Pastors had briefed him on a strategy for a church 'under the cross', and his friends had developed their Anglo-Scottish vision. Despite this preparation, Knox was caught off guard by the situation he encountered on landing, and spent his first weeks finding his feet.

In the spring of 1559 with the signing of the peace of Cateau-Cambrésis European politics were at a turning point. The treaty between the Valois monarchy and its Habsburg opponents ended the warfare that had overshadowed international relations since the end of the fifteenth century. Slowly during the coming decades confessional fault lines would replace dynastic alignments within Europe. In the long run, this made more convincing Knox's stark descriptions of the world as divided between the forces of Christ and Antichrist. In the short run, the peace highlighted a new phase in the struggle over control of the mainland of Britain following the death of Mary Tudor and accession of her half-sister. As Knox knew from his stay in Dieppe and from his London correspondence, the French and English courts assumed they had entered another round in the struggle for Britain, with Scotland as the immediate battleground but England as the final prize. Though no longer King of England, Philip II remained interested in this battle for Britain. However, he had a low estimate of England's value to the Habsburg cause and was heavily pressed by other problems, especially in his Mediterranean territories. The last thing he wanted was to reopen the wars with France on Scottish soil, and his attitude prevented the Scottish crisis escalating into a full-scale European conflict.[1]

Knox had a simple strategy when he arrived in Scotland: he had come to further the Gospel in whatever form that might take. As he wrote to Anne Locke as soon as he arrived, 'be life, be death, or els be both, to glorifie His godlie name'. What he had not anticipated was finding himself in the middle of a crisis about to reach its climax. Hearing of the Regent's summons to his fellow preachers to appear on 10 May in Stirling, he decided to accompany them. As a condemned and wanted man, this increased the chances that he might be glorifying God by his death in short order. He admitted to Anne he was scared and asked her to pray that he would 'shrink not when the battell approacheth'.[2]

There was no time for Knox to ponder options because he had been recognized and his presence reported to the Scottish clerical hierarchy, who were meeting in the capital's Dominican priory, so he prudently left for Dundee. The Scottish bishops wanted to capture this 'old condemned heretic' as he came back into the country and once more had him proclaimed an outlaw.[3] Knox needed to catch up fast. He heard of the Beggars Summons posted on the doors of Scottish friaries on 1 January 1559 supposedly written by the poor or 'real' beggars who, adopting the legal language of giving notice to quit, had warned the friars, or 'false' beggars, to leave their properties by the traditional moving day just before Whitsun. 'Flitting Friday' would fall that year on 12 May, less than ten days after Knox left for Dundee. Knox would also have been briefed about the last Provincial Council of the Scottish Catholic Church that had been held in March and had witnessed another failure to secure institutional reform. For those who had remained inside the Catholic Church during the 1550s, like John Winram, it marked a watershed, and Winram himself left the Catholic Church together with Lord James, the Prior of St Andrews. On a national level the Regent's instruction to enforce the celebration of Mass at Easter brought a choice: many Protestants voted with their feet by attending Protestant worship or failing to make their Easter Mass. When rebuked by the Regent, the Protestant Lord Ruthven, Provost of Perth, had defiantly replied that he could not, and would not, force the consciences of the people of the burgh by demanding they attend Mass.[4]

Knox arrived in Scotland with a deep distrust of Mary of Guise. Since writing his 1558 *Letter*, his attitude had hardened, not helped by the reputation among the Huguenots they attacked of her Catholic brothers, the Duke of Guise and the Cardinal of Lorraine. Knowing that she was a skilful politician, Knox assumed that that indicated a capacity for deception. He was afraid political compromises would sully the purity of the religious cause. On his sea voyage to Leith, he had secretly been shown the new Great Seal of Scotland being brought to the capital. It incorporated the arms of three kingdoms, those of France and Scotland to which were added the English arms representing the claim that Mary, Queen of Scots, was the rightful Queen of England. Viewing the Seal reinforced Knox's conviction that the long-term aim of the Regent and, indeed, of Henry II of France, his son and daughter-in-law was a fully incorporated Roman Catholic Franco-Scotland that could invade England, and he repeatedly warned the English government of the danger.

MONUMENTS OF IDOLATRY

Long-term strategies seemed out of place as Knox was caught up in the immediate crisis. Protestant supporters of the preachers Paul Methven, John Willock, William Harlaw and John Christison decided to accompany them to Stirling for their 'day of law' on 10 May. Drawn from across Angus and the Mearns, they assembled in Dundee and moved west to Perth. Although unarmed, such a large group might appear threatening so their representative, John Erskine of Dun, was sent to seek a continuation of the summons in the expectation that negotiations could then begin. Knox preached to the supporters as they waited in Perth. Though Erskine of Dun returned with an optimistic report, hopes were dashed when the preachers were outlawed because they had failed to answer their summons. Knox immediately interpreted this development as an example of the Regent's inherent duplicity. On Wednesday, 11 May in the parish church of St John in the centre of the burgh, he preached a sermon 'vehement against idolatry' and that day witnessed an iconoclastic riot in Perth. This famous occasion has subsequently been designated the start of the Protestant Reformation in Scotland.[5]

In addition to Protestant anger about the Stirling decision, a highly volatile situation already existed within Perth. The burgh's craft guilds had pushed for religious and other reform in the past, utilizing direct action to achieve change. Even if he had been warned about this background, Knox probably would not have altered his behaviour. As was his wont, the language of his sermon was extremely violent and he probably took as his starting point the biblical story of Christ cleansing the Temple. Conflicting accounts make the precise sequence of the day's events difficult to establish. After Knox's sermon had finished, the riot started when a priest came into the church to prepare for Mass, probably at one of the side altars. A boy, possibly an apprentice, challenged the priest, who cuffed him round the head. In retaliation the boy threw a stone, missing the priest but breaking an image close to the tabernacle. In his *History*, Knox added, 'And immediately the whole multitude that were about cast stones, and put hands to the said tabernacle and to all other monuments of idolatry.'[6] Craftsmen formed the core of the iconoclastic group who destroyed Catholic objects within the parish church. With a pre-existing plan to hold a forceful demonstration, the craftsmen seemed to have attended the sermon with stones in their pockets.[7] They later declared that the entire community had been united behind this direct action to reform the burgh: 'God sterit up our haill communitie of merchandis and craftis be assistance of His Holy Spreit to be joinit in ane congregatioun of Crist.'[8] After the iconoclasm in the parish church, attention turned to the burgh's friaries, possibly on the following day, it being the date set in the Beggars Summons for the friars to quit. All three buildings lay just outside the walls, with the Greyfriars or Franciscans to the south, the Dominicans or Blackfriars to the north, and the royal foundation of the Charterhouse to the west. Each building was attacked and looted, and within two days only the walls were left standing. The pro-Protestant Provost Lord Ruthven and the Perth Council filled with his supporters did not intervene to stop the destruction – though, possibly attempting a retrospective authorization, they banned the celebration of Mass within the burgh.

Neither Knox nor the other leaders of the preachers' supporters who had gathered in Perth had been prepared for the extent or fierceness of the riot. Knox had frequently been 'vehement' in his sermons, but never before had this provoked a full-scale riot. Not averse to playing the prophet Elijah inciting the destruction of the altars of Baal, he would have been gratified by the smashing of such idols. He was probably taken aback to discover that once his prophetic words had been spoken he retained little control over subsequent actions. His reaction and his precise role in the events of the two days have been confused by the account found in his *History*, laden with the benefits of hindsight. This version of what happened and who was responsible for the iconoclasm conflicted with his letter in June 1559 to Anne Locke. To her he made a direct link between the Stirling decision and the brethren's violent reform in Perth: 'after complaint and appellatioun frome such a deceitfull sentence, they putt to their hands to reformatioun in Sanct Johnstoun'.[9] In the *History*, however, Knox offered a detailed story replete with propaganda spin in which the iconoclasts had become the 'rascal multitude' and there was no involvement from respectable members of the congregation.[10]

The Perth riot was a serious tactical mistake for the Protestants because it left their noble supporters unprepared and wrong-footed. As Lord Herries later described it, 'a seditious sermon stirred up the people to furie and madnes'.[11] It was a gift for the Regent, who treated the incident as an unacceptable breach of law and order that required punishment from those holding civil authority. Leading Protestant nobles such as Lord James Stewart and the Earl of Argyll supported the Regent, and even Perth's Provost, Lord Ruthven, made his peace with her. An agreement was negotiated allowing the Regent to enter Perth with her soldiers to demonstrate that royal authority was not being challenged. Uncharacteristically, Mary of Guise made enough political errors during that reoccupation to justify a switch of allegiance by Argyll and Lord James Stewart. When they rejoined their co-religionists it healed a potentially dangerous rift among Protestant supporters. Led by the two young nobles, the armed Protestants now named themselves Lords of the Congregation and defied the Regent.[12]

Whether or not this was his intention, Knox's Perth sermon changed Protestant tactics. The Protestants were a small, though committed, minority and only some of those supporting religious reforms were prepared to countenance rebellion. As well as fighting to introduce religious reform and defend those burghs where it had been implemented, the Lords of the Congregation faced a major propaganda battle. After the mess at Perth that left the burgh occupied by royal troops, the Lords needed a success. They looked to bring religious change to St Andrews, the ecclesiastical capital of Scotland. The burgh had held a special significance for Knox from the time of his declaration that he would preach there again when he recognized the distinctive St Andrews skyline while lying sick on the French galley. Anxious to fulfil that prediction, he was not going to let the opportunity slip even after the Archbishop of St Andrews threatened that 'a dozen culverings [guns] should light upon his nose' if Knox preached in the cathedral city.[13] Bringing their noble retinues to give protection to their preacher, Lord James and Argyll were also prepared for the aftermath of the sermon. Knox chose as his text Christ's cleansing of the Temple, and the congregation duly followed his exhortation and 'cleansed' the church. Having support from the Burgh Council, the university authorities and the Augustinian canons under the direction of Lord James and John Winram, the burgh of St Andrews was 'reformed'.[14] Considerable care was taken to turn the iconoclasm into an orderly ritual with the wooden statues and furnishings being carried to where Walter Myln had been executed the previous year and symbolically burned on that spot. The saying about the friars, which Lord Herries attributed to Knox – 'Pull down the nests that the crows might not build again' – did have a Knoxian ring to it, and he was a man to identify enemies.[15] At some stage the Dominican and Franciscan friaries were also neutralized.[16]

Having lost control of his cathedral city, the Archbishop went straight to Falkland Palace to get help from the Regent. She despatched a contingent of troops under a French commander and ordered lodgings to be found for her in Cupar, the burgh controlling the strategic crossing of the River Eden. Hearing that the Regent's soldiers were on their way, the Protestants in St Andrews marched quickly to intercept them. Cupar had already reformed its own churches, and if the Regent occupied the burgh, that situation would be reversed and St Andrews would be in considerable danger. Knox travelled with the small contingent of Congregation soldiers, hoping the frantic call for reinforcements would be answered in time. It was a sticky moment for the Congregation. Knox later recalled the confrontation at Cuparmuir as one of the three crisis points of the entire summer campaign. In his *History* he said of the timely arrival of reinforcements from Dundee, Angus and Fife that 'God rained soldiers.'[17] Divine intervention was probably assisted by local knowledge: the Hill of Tarvit rises steeply above the burgh, and by placing soldiers against the skyline the Protestants might have bluffed the French commander into thinking their force greater than it was. Once their reinforcements had arrived, the Regent's commanders were brought to the top of the hill to sign a truce and were able to look down on the camp in Cuparmuir and verify that their troops were outnumbered. This 'battle that never was' provided a turning point in the Wars of the Congregation because the Regent's forces missed the chance to nip the rebellion in the bud, regain St Andrews and achieve a significant symbolic and strategic victory. In the event, throughout the Wars of the Congregation the Protestants held north-east Fife and they were able to consolidate their changes within this locality.

St Andrews became the eastern headquarters for the Lords of the Congregation and Knox was based there during most of the fighting of 1559–60. Thomas Wode, a monk at Lindores Abbey who came to St Andrews, made a particular point of recording that Knox was not the first settled minister in St Andrews: that accolade went to Knox's friend Christopher Goodman. Wode explained that Knox was on the move with the Lords as an army chaplain: 'Albeit maister Knox for the maist part maid his residence heir (as the cheiff lords of the congregation often did) he read and preachit quhair the lordis wer.'[18] Feeling that his place was with the Congregation's troops, Knox may have opted at the back of his mind for the prospect of dying on the battlefield, like the Swiss Reformer Ulrich Zwingli, rather than facing the stake. He shared the dangers and identified with the fears of the Congregation's troops during the campaigns. In sermons in 1559 and 1563 he related with some pride, 'I have not yet forgotten what was the dolour and anguish of my own heart when at Saint Johnston, Cupar Muir, and Edinburgh Crags.'[19] Neither an experienced nor a natural soldier, he was filled with conflicting emotions when on campaign, as he explained to Anne Locke: 'we stand universallie in great feare, and yit we hope deliverance'.[20] Believing it was his duty to stay with the troops, he did not take Anne's advice to withdraw from the front line to St Andrews.

Knox's strong sense of divine providence at work in everyday life gave him a form of double vision during the military campaigns. On the one hand, like Oliver Cromwell in the next century, he trusted in God and kept his powder dry. Though no military commander, he understood the practical problems of keeping troops supplied and fighting, and he sought aid from all quarters to hold men in the field to fight the professional French soldiers. On the other hand, he treated the struggle as a re-run of Old Testament warfare where it was essential for the Israelites to trust completely in God and not rely upon their own military strength. When faced with defeat in battle, Knox interpreted this as a lack of faith in God's power. As he acknowledged in his letter to Anne Locke, 'We trusted too muche … in our owne stren[g]th.'[21] He used his preaching to rally the soldiers by convincing them God was on their side and the reverses were a test of their faith and commitment. His voice was capable of carrying to the troops and they heard his magnificently stirring rhetoric. Thomas Randolph described the energizing effect of Knox's battlefield sermons as like having five hundred trumpets blowing in one's ears.[22] Knox demonstrated what a sharp and ruthless weapon his sermons could be, capable of wounding those who fought alongside him, such as the Hamilton kindred, as well as attacking the enemy. By being able to boost morale when it reached its lowest ebb, he made a considerable contribution to the Congregation's military effort. As Winston Churchill did with his 1940 oratory, Knox found the words to ensure that the Congregation did fight on the Fife beaches and did not surrender during their 'darkest hour'. A Knox sermon was a magnificent asset during wartime but could become a liability when peace and diplomacy were the order of the day.

During the summer of 1559 the Congregation were on the crest of a wave and swept along, retaking Perth, reforming Stirling and marching into Edinburgh. In the capital they found they had overreached themselves. The Captain of Edinburgh Castle whose cannon commanded the city was Lord

Erskine, one of the signatories of the first band of December 1557. Unwilling to break his oath of loyalty to the Regent, he refused to join the Congregation. Knox, calling this 'treasonable defiance', found it impossible to comprehend how Erskine could place his code of honour above his religious convictions.[23] The Congregation faced a crisis on Edinburgh Crags or Calton Hill and were forced to make a disadvantageous agreement at Leith links and leave Edinburgh at the end of July. It was a major reverse and punctured the optimistic hope that the momentum of reform could carry the day by itself.

THIS COMMON CAUSE

Once the rebellion against the Regent got under way, it became clear that support for religious reform was not enough on its own to secure the Congregation's objectives. Those with military experience, like Knox's old friend William Kirkcaldy of Grange, knew that help was needed to counter the professional French troops the Regent had at her command and the re-inforcements she could expect from France. She did not need to take the offensive, but could contain the rebellion and wait until the Protestant levies had to disband for lack of resources. Since many Protestants had been strong Anglophiles during the Rough Wooings, they turned to England for help. Kirkcaldy of Grange was in touch with English border officials at the latest by the end of June 1559. Since they were denied at the time, in his *History* Knox disguised just how early such contacts had been made.[24]

Seeking English help for the Congregation fitted neatly with the Anglo-Scottish strategy devised by Knox and his friends in Geneva. Working towards the long-term goal of the spread of Protestantism throughout the islands of Britain, they had directed the Genevan congregation's liturgy and its translation of the Bible towards 'our beloved in the Lord the brethren of England Scotland, Ireland, etc'.[25] When Knox was in correspondence with Gregory Railton, a former Frankfurt exile who was acting as an English agent, they used the biblical allusion 'yf your eis be single' almost like a code word. In his letter to Railton in October 1559, Knox employed it to express the imperative need to focus upon one single goal: the achievement of a Protestant unity between England and Scotland.[26] He interpreted what was happening in Scotland with reference to that Anglo-Scottish strategy and was determined to push ahead with religious and political amity between his native and adopted countries. The rebuff he had received from the Elizabethan regime stung more sharply because he knew he had worked tire-lessly for England's good, and in his letters to Cecil he made veiled references to the benefits such efforts had already brought during Mary Tudor's reign.[27] Knox was convinced the current 'uproar for religion' in Scotland was the providential moment when perpetual friendship between the two realms might be achieved. Interpreting the current circumstances within an apocalyptic and prophetic context, he believed that God was offering a second chance for the kingdoms to come together and that the missed opportunity of union during Edward VI's reign could be redeemed. England and Scotland would be able to base their friendship upon the solid rock of a shared Protestant faith, understanding 'what love, cayr, and solliciteud, Christ Jesus requireth the memberis of his body and trew professoris of his nam to bear on[e] towardis another'.[28] Knox was sure this final opportunity had to be grasped: God would not endlessly offer additional chances.[29]

Not relying on confessional solidarity alone, Knox made a strong political case for armed intervention serving England's best interests. The argument was simple: if French troops defeated the Scottish Congregation and took complete control of Scotland, they would be free to invade England and place Mary, Queen of Scots, upon 'her' English throne. England should, therefore, fight a preventative war on Scottish soil and do so while it still had Scottish allies. Cecil, who had been writing memos along these lines for months, hardly needed Knox to tell him that 'Our destructioun war your greatest loss and that when Fraunce shalbe our full maisteris (which God avert), thei wilbe but slender freindis to you'.[30] Despite berating Cecil for his backsliding during Mary Tudor's reign, Knox treated him as a committed Protestant and Cecil signed his replies as a fellow 'member of the body of Christ'.[31] With his own well-developed British strategy, the English Secretary was prepared to employ the language of Protestant amity in his Scottish correspondence.[32] However, when he faced the delicate task of persuading Queen Elizabeth to support the Scottish Protestants, he chose different arguments. Any associations with Knox were a liability, and he reminded the English commanders at Berwick Sir Ralph Sadler and Sir James Croft to keep Knox completely out of sight in their despatches.[33]

Though a pariah in England, from the Congregation's perspective Knox's up-to-date knowledge of many key people in the English government and his extensive network of English contacts in London and the Borders offered a valuable addition to their fledgling intelligence network. During the summer of 1559 he was heavily involved in communications and negotiations with England. The military situation in July prevented the secret visit to Stamford to talk to Cecil, but the next month Knox slipped down the east coast by sea to Lindisfarne. When he went for talks in Berwick, his face was sufficiently well known in those parts to be recognized. With his cover blown, Knox returned by sea to Scotland two days later. His companion on the Lindisfarne trip, Alexander Whitelaw, travelled overland from Berwick with William Knox. On the road, Lord Seton's men – assuming they had both Knox brothers in their sights – hotly pursued the pair for three miles until they reached safety at Ormiston. That scare made Knox withdraw from field work as a secret agent. His fellow minister, John Willock, proved more successful in his undercover career. Knox let his pen do the work and became an extremely busy correspondent and secretary to the Congregation, at one point managing only four hours' sleep a night. While he was writing his letters at midnight with sleepy eyes, his wife Marjorie was also hard at work being a clerk.[34] Knox told Anne Locke, 'the rest of my wife hath been so unrestfull since her arriving heir, that skarslie could she tell upoun the morrow, what she wrote at night'.[35]

Knox once more adopted Sinclair as his surname to keep secret his correspondence with the English commanders at Berwick.[36] Former Marian exiles who knew Knox, Thomas Randolph and Gregory Railton, were used by William Cecil and Nicholas Throckmorton, the English Ambassador in Paris, and the Scots Alexander Whitelaw and Henry Balnaves were also recruited. They formed part of an undercover Protestant network with international contacts that later became such an important feature of the Elizabethan regime.[37] When trying to run a secret operation, Croft complained bitterly, the Scots were hopelessly open in their dealings, and Knox had to apologize and excuse the leaks as best he could.[38] Knox's role in these negotiations remained in the shadows because he was adept at covering his own tracks. Growing desperate in October 1559, he suggested some subterfuges to allow the English to send military assistance while denying involvement and disowning their own troops. Croft told him tartly that the French were not fools and would recognize a blatant breach of the Anglo-French peace treaty when they saw it.[39]

Knox bombarded his other English friends and contacts with requests for aid. He called upon members of his former congregation in Geneva to make collections to support the Scottish cause and used Anne Locke and Thomas Wood to organize these efforts. The rich merchant John Bodley received letters from Knox, as did Miles Coverdale, probably with similar pleas for help. When Anne Locke wrote that the former exiles had not contributed because they thought the English government was about to intervene, Knox was annoyed and pointed out that money was still urgently required. The Protestant nobles were in dire financial straits, with Lord James Stewart close to ruin having spent 13,000 crowns and another noble having to reduce his retainers from forty men to two.[40] Knox warned that if the Protestant cause failed in Scotland, not long afterwards London would suffer.[41] In addition he sent specific requests to his family contacts. His wife's brother, Sir George Bowes, at Berwick, and his mother-in-law were entreated to secure good horses in England so he could sustain his role as army chaplain.[42]

Knox knew that once an appeal went to the English government the assistance they gave would be on their terms. Although he enjoyed being in the know and closely involved in the Anglo-Scottish strategy, he was ambivalent about being sucked into 'civill effares' and wary of the political contamination which this brought. Knowing he was unsuited to diplomatic negotiations he expressed considerable relief in late autumn 1559 when William Maitland of Lethington, who had been Mary of Guise's Secretary, took over the task of travelling to London for talks.[43] From an early stage Cecil had advised the Scottish Protestants to produce some constitutional authority to justify their actions and at the least form a Council. One obvious issue was the attitude of the second person of the realm, the Duke of Châtelherault, heir presumptive to the Scottish throne. In a successful English undercover operation in France the Earl of Arran, Châtelherault's eldest son, was rescued before he could be arrested and was helped by Thomas Randolph to escape the country. Having secretly travelled via Geneva and London, and having had meetings in those cities, Arran returned to Scotland in September. As a deeply committed Protestant, he was a welcome addition to the Congregation, becoming a co-leader alongside his cousin Argyll and Lord James, and his return enabled Châtelherault and the Hamilton kin and allies to join the Congregation.[44] Knox remained highly suspicious of Châtelherault, whom he regarded as the epitome of an inconstant and insincere magnate.[45] In his sermon at Stirling on 8 November, he explained that the Congregation's recent defeat was because they had trusted the numerical strength brought by the Hamiltons instead of relying upon God. He queried whether Châtelherault had made a full enough confession for having previously supported the Regent, and declared that God was testing the Hamiltons. Knox's analysis must have made hard listening for the Duke and his kin, though Lord Herries later credited the sermon with being the reason why the Congregation 'recouvered spiritt' after its reversals.[46]

Knox disapproved of Arran's extreme quest for military glory and raised the subject in a sermon during the Congregation's darkest days. In mid-January 1560, after a serious defeat at Kinghorn on the Fife coast that threatened the loss of St Andrews, he preached to the dispirited Congregation soldiers in Cupar. Although brave to the point of recklessness in battle, in camp Arran was withdrawn and refused to mix with the troops. Citing the Old Testament King Jehosaphat, Knox specifically commended that king for fraternizing with his men, and the contemporary parallel was obvious to all listening. Since Arran was hypersensitive, took criticism badly and was inclined to see insults even if they had not been intended, Knox's gibe verged on the malicious. If Arran had indeed been among those arrested at the Rue St Jacques and imprisoned for six months in 1557, Knox should have made greater allowances for a damaged young man. Whatever the cause of the Earl's sensitivity, Knox's remarks would not have enhanced the cohesion of the demoralized army. A couple of years later the extent of Arran's vulnerability was revealed when the Earl lost his sanity. While Knox was not a direct cause, his carping did nothing to strengthen the Earl's fractured sense of his own worth on his return to Scotland.[47] The preacher's persistent sniping at the Hamiltons and his insistence on a policy of no compromise were probably significant factors in Knox's removal from the inner counsels of the Lords of the Congregation.

Too extreme

Knox was sent to St Andrews on 29 January 1560 explaining to Gregory Railton, 'I am judged amongis ourselves too extream, and be reason thereof I have extracted myself from all public assemblies to my privat study.' This did not prevent him adding a further criticism, probably of Arran's rashness: 'yet can I not cease to signifye unto you, that onles wisdom bridill the foolishe boldnes of some, all that favour the good success of this great and godlye interprise will one day murn'.[48] A week later as plans were being finalized for a meeting between the Lords of the Congregation and English officials, Knox penned a highly critical letter to Châtelherault and the rest of the Lords based in Glasgow. He berated them for suggesting that the eastern contingent of Lords who had been fighting the French non-stop should be obliged to travel to the western Borders to suit those who had hardly seen combat during the previous months.[49] Knox linked his irritation with Arran to his deeply embedded distrust of Arran's father and his Hamilton kin who were entrenched within the Scottish Catholic hierarchy, including the Archbishop of St Andrews. Over future years Knox's profound dislike of Châtelherault and the Hamiltons festered into hatred, even before 1570 when he demonized the entire kindred for their involvement in Regent Moray's assassination.[50]

Knox would have been one of the voices in October 1559 urging the Congregation not to reinstate Châtelherault as Regent following Mary of Guise's deposition. The Duke's pre-eminent status was recognized but, probably to his own relief, he was given no additional title or power. His nominal leadership of the Congregation provided a constitutional figleaf, making it easier for Queen Elizabeth to support the Scottish rebels. The English government eventually signed an alliance at Berwick in February 1560 with the Congregation, technically acting as the Duke's representatives. From the summer of 1559 English financial aid had been coming in dribs and drabs, but it was not enough, as Knox did not tire of reminding his correspondents. Cecil had hoped to start aid to the Protestants with words, before progressing to money and, as a last resort, the provision of military support. Knox labelled this incremental approach as 'drift of tym' and was sure it would lead to disaster – help would arrive too late to save the Protestant cause in Scotland.[51] At the English court, Cecil faced an uphill struggle to convince Queen Elizabeth to intervene militarily in Scotland and in December 1559 narrowly won the argument in the English Privy Council.

As a consequence, an English fleet set sail in midwinter for Scottish waters, and the sighting of those ships in the Forth in January 1560 was the turning point of the Wars of the Congregation. The Regent's troops had been moving through Fife raiding the countryside and burning the houses of Protestant lairds, such as Kirkcaldy of Grange, and the Congregation were in retreat and losing engagements. Though guerrilla tactics were slowing the French advance, the Congregation's soldiers were fighting every day, sleeping in their armour and, as Knox noted, had not pulled their boots off for three weeks.[52] The ships seen off the Isle of May in the outmost reaches of the Firth of Forth were first thought to be French supply vessels. Much encouraged, the Regent's troops pressed forward to within six miles of St Andrews. When it was realized this was an English fleet, the French beat a hasty retreat to avoid being stranded on the wrong side of the Forth away from their main base in Leith. Meanwhile Knox was in St Andrews 'with sorrowfull heart' amid a fearful population who 'quaiked for a time' because they had few illusions about what would happen when the French captured the burgh. Even friends were telling Knox to his face that the cause was hopeless and 'the support of England will cum when we that now suffer have no nead of it'.[53] The news that the English navy had been spotted from Fife Ness caused them to 'praise God, who suddanlie diverted frome them that terrible plague devised for them by the ungodly . . . We have had wonderful experience of God's mercifull providence.' In this letter to Anne Locke, Knox admitted he had 'that little sparke of hope which the Holy Spirit did kindle and foster in my heart'.[54] He treated their deliverance as a further example of how one should be thankful for the workings of Divine Providence. He did not mention in this letter that he had known ships had been despatched thanks to his English contacts, though he had not known when the navy would arrive.

The troops of the Congregation did not need a preacher to persuade them of the Isle of May miracle. For one young man fighting with the Congregation alongside his elder half-brother, Lord James Stewart, the sight of the ships was the first time he could forgive the English for the death of his father at the battle of Pinkie in 1547.[55] The arrival of the English navy had a profound effect upon many Scots and helped them regard the English, their 'auld enemies', in a new light. The citizens of St Andrews gave a particular welcome to Admiral Winter and his men, knowing they had braved severe storms to arrive in time to save their burgh, their cause and their kingdom. The Admiral and other naval officers attended the parish church, heard Knox preach and were present to witness the recantation made by John Wilson, vicar of Kinghorn and canon of Holyrood, a prominent local Catholic.[56] As Knox understood, this type of direct contact, as well as English military assistance to remove the French 'occupation' of Scotland, could change hearts and minds and might make possible his vision of amity between the two peoples based upon their shared Protestant faith.

The navy's arrival was the first instalment of English military aid. In April an English army marched into Scotland and was treated to an unprecedented welcome with much backslapping as Lords of the Congregation met the English commanders at Prestonpans. Knox noted as a marvellous sign for future goodwill that the Scots were happy to supply the English army at reasonable prices, though experiencing a dearth themselves.[57] The euphoria of greeting their rescuers dissipated when the combined Anglo-Scottish forces failed to capture Leith, where the French had expertly fortified themselves.

Knox remained in St Andrews until the end of April. By then Mary of Guise, who had taken shelter in Edinburgh Castle, was seriously ill. As she lay dying from dropsy, four leading Protestant nobles of the Congregation visited her to make their farewells to a woman they respected, though they had fought against her. John Willock had a lengthy conversation with her and, though making no concession on the Mass, she seemed to accept that her salvation was through the merits of Christ alone.[58] Knox rejected all touches of chivalry towards his fallen enemy. In his eyes the Regent had fought under the standard of Antichrist and was an object of his 'holy hatred'. He gloated over her death, insisted she should not be buried with Catholic rites and added a prayer that God rid Scotland 'from the rest of the Guisian blood. Amen. Amen.'[59] The previous October he had self-righteously declared that he held no personal hatred for Mary of Guise, although the letter he wrote offended his fellow Protestant Robert Lockhart so much that he refused to deliver it to the Regent. The fervency of his denunciations and the innuendoes attacking Mary of Guise's morality and character belied his declaration. In his *History*, he poured out his venom towards her and did not find one redeeming virtue in her.[60] His hatred seems to have been in direct proportion to his fear that she was capable of thwarting the establishment of a Reformed Church.

Once the Regent had died, the negotiating teams got to work. William Cecil came in person to Edinburgh to conclude a treaty between England and France, including some 'concessions' for the Scots. All foreign troops left Scottish soil as quickly as could be arranged. Due to an unusual set of international circumstances, the rebellion of the Lords of the Congregation had succeeded with English assistance. The French were sufficiently concerned with their domestic situation to settle for damage limitation in Scotland, assuming they could at a later date recover control over Mary, Queen of Scots' kingdom. The rest of Europe was relieved that this peripheral conflict had been contained instead of escalating into international warfare. When Knox had stepped off that boat in Leith, no betting man would have backed such a result.

THY WONDROUS WORKS LATE WROUGHT IN OUR EYES

At the great setpiece of a Thanksgiving service for victory in front of the 'greatest part' of the Congregation assembled in St Giles' in Edinburgh, Knox delivered a sermon 'made for the purpose'. He then launched into a great prayer narrating the story of deliverance they had experienced and encouraging his hearers 'to meditate thy wondrous works late wrought in our eyes'. The Scottish Protestants had faced great dangers and like the people of Israel in the Old Testament had been carried through all the miseries by the hand of God. He provided a dramatic litany of the horrors warfare brought. They had been delivered not by their own 'wit, policy or strength', but because they had cried to God and he had saved them, even though they did not deserve such mercy. Scots would be able to preserve in perpetual memory the way God 'has partly removed our darkness, suppressed idolatry, and taken from above our heads the devouring sword of merciless strangers'. Given Knox's deep-rooted fear that Scotland might emulate England in accepting and then rejecting God's call, he was vehement about the danger of apostasy, urging Scots never 'to forsake or deny this thy verity which we now profess' and praying for the grace of continuance.[61]

Such a prophetic exhortation was to be expected, but Knox spent the closing part of his prayer urging the congregation to be particularly mindful of the debt they owed to the instruments of God's deliverance, the English. The alliance with their neighbours was a 'most godly league contracted in thy [God's] name', and he prayed that the Holy Spirit would keep it firm and Satan not be permitted to sow discord between the allies. He suggested that this Anglo-Scottish friendship was a model and example for a new peaceful phase of international relations in which there would be no 'ungodly war'; war against Antichrist or the forces of Roman Catholicism did not fall into that category. Knox had placed Anglo-Scottish amity firmly into the prophetic narrative of Scotland's journey into the light of the Gospel. He was developing that narrative into his *History of the Reformation* and he focused in Book III upon the league with England. In the summer of 1560 it appeared as if the hopes and plans that had been formed in Geneva for the evangelization of Britain were beginning to be realized.

CHAPTER THIRTEEN

Churching it like a Scythian

The Congregation's military and diplomatic triumph in the summer of 1560 brought to the fore of Scottish politics the daunting task of creating a new Reformed Kirk across the whole country. This was a matter of considerable interest among other Protestants, especially Knox's fellow exiles and associates in England, France, Switzerland and Germany and of concern among many Roman Catholic observers in Europe. When in Geneva, Knox had discussed with Calvin and the other pastors the problems of establishing Protestant churches and watching how it was being done 'under the cross' in France. With the leaders of the English-speaking exile congregation, he had constructed a British strategy aiming for the long-term goal of shared Protestantism and friendship uniting the Tudor state with the Stewart kingdom. That team had also produced the community of texts that any English-speaking Reformed church would need to start functioning: a Bible, a psalter and a form of prayers alongside the experience and practice of the 'example of Geneva'. Even if he had done nothing else, this package of essential items Knox introduced to his native land would have transformed Scottish Protestantism.

Once he had returned to Scotland in 1559 many of Knox's earlier plans were left on the drawing board or overtaken by events. Both in the heat of the moment during the Wars of the Congregation and in its immediate aftermath, Scottish Protestants reacted to the situation in which they found themselves. In this context, however loud and assertive, Knox's voice was one among many. In the business of construction, Knox worked best with his clerical colleagues. He became one member of the team of six Johns who produced the defining documents of the Scots *Confession of Faith* and *First Book of Discipline*. Haunted by his experiences of England and exile, he was adamant about what must be avoided in this newly emerging Kirk. He was constantly looking for the 'single eye' of zealous Protestants and quick to identify as hypocrisy any slackening of the total and unwavering commitment he demanded of those who should be building the house of the Lord in this newly covenanted nation.

THE PEOPLE TO BE ORDERERS OF THINGS

John Jewel enjoyed his Latin jokes and liked to enliven with amusing comments the news he sent from London to Peter Martyr Vermigli about the doings of their mutual friends, the returned Marian exiles. At the start of August 1559 he gave Martyr a summary of what had been happening in Scotland:

> Every thing is in a ferment in Scotland. Knox, surrounded by a thousand followers, is holding assemblies throughout the whole kingdom. The old queen (dowager) has been compelled to shut herself up in garrison. The nobility with united hearts and hands are restoring religion throughout the country, in spite of all opposition. All the monasteries are everywhere levelled with the ground: the theatrical dresses, the sacrilegious chalices, the idols, the altars, are consigned to the flames; not a vestige of the ancient superstition and idolatry is left. What do you ask for? You have often heard of *drinking like a Scythian*; but this is *churching it like a Scythian*.[1]

Among the ancient Greeks the Scythians had been renowned for not watering their wine, something the classical world regarded as uncivilized and dangerous. Jewel was probably also making a less than complimentary reference to the Scottish origin myth which asserted that the Scots had originally come from Scythia. He certainly believed that the undiluted reform Knox and the Scots were imposing upon their churches was as potent, risky and uncivilized as a drink of neat alcohol. Having opposed the radical approach in Frankfurt, he characterized the Scottish reforms as an example of Knox's uncompromising stance and turned it into a shared joke with Martyr. The Archbishop of Canterbury, Matthew Parker, who had a tendency to fret, revealed his own serious alarm at the details of events in Scotland. Unlike Jewel he did not highlight the role of the nobility, being horrified instead by the actions of ordinary Scots. He observed to Cecil, 'God keep us from such visitation as Knox have attempted in Scotland; the people to be orderers of things.'[2] The opinions of English bishops were not of great consequence for Scotland, but they expressed the profound concerns of European social elites about any direct action taken by 'the people'. As was proved a few years later in the Netherlands, the contagion of an 'iconoclastic fury' was capable of sweeping across the whole country. Rulers at national and local levels, who had no police forces to maintain order, were constantly fearful that overnight a riot might become full-scale revolution. Knox was sufficiently swayed by such concerns to adapt his descriptions of 'people power'. Between the correspondence he wrote as it was happening and the editing in 1566 of his *History*, he altered his terminology. The actions accomplished by the 'brethren' became those perpetrated by a 'rascal multitude'.[3]

The experience of Knox and the Lords of the Congregation at Scone Abbey in June 1559 had demonstrated how easy it was to lose control of a crowd with destruction on its mind. Scone was the residence of Bishop Patrick Hepburn, its abbot. At the end of the month after the Protestant forces had retaken Perth, a large contingent travelled a couple of miles up the road to the abbey intent upon seizing it. On the first night, Knox's intervention prevented the burning of the granary, and Argyll and Lord James Stewart had succeeded in calming the crowd. Not to be denied, angry local people, who had suffered as the tenants of Abbot Hepburn and his sons, attacked and looted the building complex on the following night. This destruction led to a serious rift in the ranks of the Congregation, and in his *History* Knox, making the best of what had taken place, rewrote this serious loss of control by the Congregation's leadership as an example of divine vengeance upon an ungodly prelate. He introduced the testimony of an elderly local woman about the immoral goings on at Scone to suggest that the attack was morally justified and in accordance with God's will.[4] As he discovered, revolution was easier to write about than to experience and he was beset with the persistent fear that the pure, unadulterated religious motivation for iconoclasm would degenerate into popular violence.

FACE OF A PERFECT REFORMED KIRK

The split within the Congregation reflected conflicting views of the purpose of violence and religious reform. In addition to their concerns about the social consequences of uncontrolled rioting, the Lords of the Congregation sought to restrict the violence to specific targets. Since nobles' kinsmen staffed the upper levels of the Catholic Church, the Congregation wanted to tread carefully where prelates' lives and property were concerned. To do otherwise would seriously jeopardize their chance of support from the rest of the Scottish nobility as well as involve them in possible blood feuds. Judicious cleansing was one thing. Killing churchmen or wholesale destruction and appropriation of property was quite another. Such an attitude ran counter to Knox's religious imperatives with their black and white alternatives. He wanted the suppression of idolatry because it was an abomination and polluted the realm. When he and his fellow five Johns were working in the spring of 1560 on the draft of the *First Book of Discipline* they produced a definition of 'idolatry'. They explained that it covered the Mass, the invocation of the saints and the adoration of images and extended to the 'monuments and places of the same' – ecclesiastical buildings where Catholic liturgy had been conducted. Added in a typical Knoxian formulation was that catch-all phrase concerning worship: 'all honouring of God not contained in his holy word'. The entire panoply of Catholic worship was condemned as so lethally unclean that it contaminated the kingdom and its people; wherever it was found it had to be suppressed. If they permitted idolatry to continue, the Lords of the Congregation would face divine judgement because God had 'armed their hands with power to suppresse such abhomination'.[5]

During the actual fighting this clash within the Congregation over the extent of reforms had been disguised because of the nature of the struggle. Since it had started and continued as a rebellion against the Regent, religious change was accomplished in particular places at particular times. It was a localized process happening when the Congregation's forces achieved temporary ascendancy over specific regions and was reversed if the Regent's troops regained control. In these contested localities the 'cleansing' of the churches or the restoration of the Mass was the visible indication of the area's current religious allegiance. The conduct of worship was the litmus test to distinguish Catholic from Protestant. Large areas of Scotland were untouched by the fighting, and they watched and waited to see who would emerge victorious and which form of worship would become the norm.

In one of his more breathtaking understatements, Knox described the process of reform to Cecil: 'The Reformation is somwhat violent, becaus the adversareis be stubburn.'[6] Where the Congregation were able to seize control they had a list of targets in an effort to neutralize their stubborn adversaries. As in Perth and St Andrews, the churches and friaries were 'cleansed' and the parish church adapted for Protestant worship. Located outside the burghs, the monasteries experienced differing fates. Most were forced to abandon their liturgical round but otherwise escaped relatively unscathed.[7] In addition to destroying the friaries, the system of Church courts presented another specific target and where they had the authority the Congregation forced these courts spiritual to stop functioning. That removed the likelihood of future heresy trials, and a condemned heretic like Knox might have been able to breathe a little easier.

Knox's animus against the Catholic hierarchy and his vitriolic language when describing them made him ready to accept any collateral damage when reforms were violently implemented. When discussing the prelates he routinely added the adjectives 'bloody' or attached them to 'Satan their father' or mentioned that they 'bore the beast's mark' and were persecutors. With his experience of the intense English persecution, he assumed that the Scottish senior clergy, if given the opportunity, would have acted in the same way. They were the local representatives of the Pope, and since his very first sermon he had identified the papacy as the Antichrist.[8] Such language surfaced in the October 1559 declaration by the Lords of the Congregation.[9] The Archbishop of St Andrews had reported that the new preachers had called upon the nobles 'to putt violent handis, and slay all kirkmen that will not concurr and tak their opinion'. He knew that 'Master Knox . . . esteemeth me an enemy' and that the preacher would not have hesitated to urge Châtelherault to begin with his stepbrother the Archbishop 'to use the rigour on me be slauchter, sword, or at the leist, perpetuall prison'.[10] Holding Hamilton responsible for the persecution of Scottish Protestants, especially the burning of Walter Myln, Knox wanted blood for blood.[11] He had few qualms about using intimidation and pressure upon Catholic clergy to induce a recantation. When he was based in St Andrews, a number of Catholic priests gave their recantations in front of the congregation on Sundays during February and March 1560. The most prominent was the detailed recantation given by the Provincial General of the Dominicans, John Grierson, who was in his eighties and probably in fear of his life or of imprisonment.[12]

Other Catholic kirkmen who had equally been involved in the heresy trials but had subsequently joined the Protestant cause received completely different treatment from Knox both at the time and in his *History*. Knox's striking lack of criticism of his past record was most noticeable in the case of John Winram, the Subprior of St Andrews. He had supported Knox in 1547 and they seemed to have resumed a friendship in 1559 that lasted until Knox's death. By contrast, the minister of Ballingry held the opposite view of Winram's last-minute switch to Protestantism and pointed out that the future Superintendent of Fife had 'smoored [smothered] and held down the Kirk' and had converted merely to hold on to his possessions.[13] Winram and other canons in St Andrews had made their 'notable' confessions of faith in July 1559 and Knox probably felt that that wiped the slate clean. With repentance occupying such a central role in his preaching and his spiritual life, Knox was conditioned to accept the idea of a new beginning or 'conversion', when amendment of life followed contrition. However, he seemed to accept the genuine penitence of certain individuals far more easily than others.

Winram's was not an isolated case. Of the six Johns who worked on the *Confession of Faith* and *First Book of Discipline*, three had been active in the Catholic Church at the start of 1559. John Row, the youngest in the group, had been the last to switch and had been converted by Robert Colville of Cleish in the autumn or winter of 1559. This canon lawyer was the type of cleric about whom Knox was particularly scathing, perhaps because it was a career he had himself rejected. Within a few months of Row's acceptance of Protestantism the two men were working amicably together. In his *History*, Knox opted for minimum comment about the timing and nature of such high-profile conversions while he quietly sidelined the contributions of the three bishops, Orkney, Caithness and Galloway, who had been happy to join the Protestant cause. Bishop Alexander Gordon of Galloway had been the first to defy the Regent's government and preach openly in 1559 and was a member of the first religious committee advising the Lords of the Congregation. The two men became firm friends, and Knox leaped to Gordon's defence when Mary, Queen of Scots, later suggested he was untrustworthy.[14]

St Andrews was able to provide a safe and congenial haven for Knox and his family during the Wars of the Congregation. Since the Regent's forces did not recapture the burgh, the dramatic changes that Knox had provoked by his June sermon had never been reversed. The band signed in July 1559 by 334 individuals in support of the Congregation was an indication of the strong core of knowledgeable and committed Protestants within St Andrews who were capable of creating and sustaining a Reformed congregation. Fitting his prophetic role and desire to accompany the Congregational troops, Knox was afforded the unusual and considerable luxury of being able to leave his ministry in the burgh, as he had done in Geneva. His personal life and comfort improved considerably in the late summer when his wife Marjorie, probably accompanied by their two boys, joined him. Serving as a secretary, Marjorie made a significant contribution to Knox's workload and nursed him through the fevers and other illnesses he suffered in these months. In the autumn, Elizabeth Bowes joined her daughter and son-in-law in St Andrews. Possibly accompanying Marjorie on part of her journey, Christopher Goodman had also arrived in Scotland to join Knox so that they could work together again. Although his friend was based on the other side of the country in Ayr, Knox took great heart from Goodman's presence in Scotland.[15]

St Andrews rapidly developed a fully functioning Reformed church. As it boasted five years later, since 1559 it had displayed 'the face of ane perfyt reformed kyrk' with 'the sacramentis deuly ministrat, all thingis done in the kyrk be comly order establesched, disciplyn used and resavit wythowtyn contempt or ony plane contradiccione of ony person'.[16] Knox preached and administered the sacraments in the large parish church of Holy Trinity, which was sufficient for the burgh's needs, and left the cathedral surplus to requirements. Having the practical experience and texts from his Genevan congregation as his basic equipment, he had made an immediate start to Reformed practice in worship and sacraments. With similar speed St Andrews was able to establish the third mark of the true Church, the exercise of discipline. By October 1559 at the latest, elders and deacons had been elected and a Kirk session was functioning.[17]

Their supreme confidence in their authority and right to control the moral direction of the community was shown in the willingness of Knox and the session to pronounce on marital cases. This precocious new Protestant court simply assumed they should exercise parts of the consistorial jurisdiction of the suspended courts spiritual. In March 1560, amid legal and political uncertainty, Knox with a Kirk session augmented by some senior university figures passed judgment in a request for divorce. Such a remarkable step was probably driven by Knox's own experience in Geneva within Calvin's 'holy city' and of exercising discipline within his exile congregation. They combined to give him a strong sense of what authority ought to belong to a fully Reformed church. The Scottish Protestant courts rejected the canon law and its procedures and made their decisions based upon a new set of rules, what Knox and his fellow Protestants presumed were the 'laws of God'. When the situation in Scotland was finally regularized by the creation of the Commissary Courts in 1564, the commissaries accepted the new Protestant divorce, though they took back much of the jurisdiction in marital cases that the Kirk sessions had grabbed in 1559–60.[18]

When in the following year Goodman replaced his friend and became the first 'settled' minister of St Andrews, he ensured that their Genevan practice became thoroughly entrenched in the burgh. To Knox, St Andrews appeared capable of imbibing undiluted the strong wine of Reformed Protestantism: in the ecclesiastical capital of Scotland they were 'churching it like a Scythian'. Unfortunately, the superficial ease and speed of this limited urban reformation in St Andrews were atypical and gave Knox a false impression of the scale of problems to be faced in establishing a Reformed Kirk throughout the rest of his native land.[19]

Less happily, Knox started on the wrong foot in his first Edinburgh ministry and he never quite fell into step with the burgh. Over the years he developed a complicated love-hate relationship with the capital. During the first rush of enthusiasm when the Lords of the Congregation appeared to be sweeping all before them, the Edinburgh Protestants, who had previously operated as an underground movement, felt bold enough to meet openly in the Tolbooth or Town Hall, where on 7 July 1559 they elected Knox as their minister.[20] He understood the importance of a capital city and in 1556 had boasted that if he were granted forty days' preaching in Edinburgh he would die happy.[21] He hoped the pulpit at St Giles' would become like the media hotspot of Paul's Cross in London where preachers and their sermons influenced the court as well as the city. Unfortunately, within a few weeks of his election the Congregation were in retreat and had to abandon the capital. It was 'found dangerous' for Knox as a convicted heretic to remain in the city. Instead, the courageous John Willock stayed behind while Knox accompanied the departing Lords of the Congregation. Willock continued to minister to the faithful in Edinburgh for the next year. Knox was thrown off balance and felt ashamed that, when danger threatened at the end of July and again in November 1559, he had left the city with the army of the Congregation. There was a defensive note in the way he described the episode in his *History*, implying he had merely obeyed when the Lords of the Congregation had made the decision he should leave. Remarkably similar explanations were later attached to two subsequent departures in 1566 and 1571. Knox was careful to acknowledge Willock's courage in 1559–60, declaring that 'for his faithful labours and bold courage in that battle, [he] deserves immortal praise ... [because] he preferred the comfort of his brethren, and the continuance of the Kirk there, to his own life'.[22] Predictably, Willock's prestige increased and he was recognized as the 'primate' of the Reformed faith in Scotland.[23] When Willock moved to the west of Scotland in the summer of 1560, Edinburgh's Burgh Council were generous in their appreciation of 'the greit travell sustenit be him this haill yere bigane in preching an ministering of the sacramentis within this burgh' and gave him the substantial bonus of twenty gold crowns.[24]

At the start of May 1560, Knox finally returned to Edinburgh in the closing stages of the Wars of the Congregation, when the English army and the Lords were besieging Leith. His position as the capital's minister had been confirmed when the Lords reallocated the limited preaching resources at the disposal of the fledgling new Kirk, and at this point most of the major burghs were provided with a minister. Knox welcomed his placement in Edinburgh because it offered the ideal setting for his prophetic role as God's watchman. With the capital frequently serving as the home of the royal court, the administration and major political players, Knox was conscious that his preaching would always attract a wide and influential audience. His Edinburgh pulpit allowed him to fulfil his self-appointed prophetic task as Scotland's Ezekiel, the watchman of the Lord, or Jeremiah, the prophet of tough political choices. Though his ministerial experience had been spread over more than a decade, his post in Edinburgh was his first proper attempt at parish ministry. In England he had been an army chaplain or been given special preaching appointments and he had refused the offer of the London parish of Bread

Street. The calls he had answered in St Andrews Castle, Frankfurt and Geneva had been from highly unusual congregations, not territorial parishes but similar to a gathered church comprised of the religiously committed. When based in St Andrews in 1559–60, Adam Heriot had been serving as the parish minister while Knox was the army chaplain to the Congregation's troops. Edinburgh was a fresh challenge for Knox, though he was also part of the national effort to establish a new Protestant Church in Scotland.

BEAR THE BARROW TO BUILD THE HOUSES OF GOD

Before the messy endgame of the Wars of the Congregation had limped to its conclusion, the leading Protestant ministers had started the planning process for a new Protestant Church. Around the start of May 1560, Knox moved from St Andrews to Edinburgh and became part of the committee of six Johns who drafted the *First Book of Discipline* and the Scots *Confession of Faith.* Knox and Willock were retained from the original religious advisory committee to the Lords, while Christopher Goodman and Alexander Gordon, Bishop of Galloway, were dropped. Goodman had remained in Ayr as the burgh's minister – being English probably disqualified him from this committee. Location in the west might have been a factor in the exclusion of Gordon. Another long-term Protestant, Spottiswood was added along with three churchmen who had recently been active members of the Catholic establishment: Winram, Douglas and Row. On paper the committee's composition looked like a compromise, with three from the old establishment to balance the three from the new faith. If Knox experienced qualms about the committee, he rapidly discovered he could work well with his team of fellow Johns. Whatever their background, they were committed to a radical vision of the new Church and rejected the advice Archbishop Hamilton gave Knox that it was safer 'to retain the old polity', at least until a new one had been introduced.[25] From its initial draft, the committee produced a radical plan for a new institution.

The post-exilic period of the Old Testament when the Temple needed rebuilding had come to encapsulate for the Marian exiles the goal of reconstructing Protestantism in Britain. With only two chapters, Haggai is the second shortest book in the Old Testament and highlights the contrast, beloved by Knox, between obedience and disobedience, the former bringing blessings, the latter curses. Though many people said the time was not ripe to build the Temple, the prophet Haggai addressed them and Zerubbabel, prince of Judah, insisting that the Lord's House be given top priority because there would be no prosperity in the land until it was built. James Pilkington, who had been a member of the Geneva congregation in 1556, had published an entire commentary on Aggeus (or Haggai) addressed primarily to the English situation.[26] In the Preface to her book, Anne Locke had referred to bearing a barrow of stones as her contribution to the construction of the Temple, and Zerubbabel's difficulties were mentioned in the Dedicatory Preface of the Geneva Bible addressed to Queen Elizabeth.[27] At this transition stage from military struggle to forward planning for the ecclesiastical organization, Knox was able to draw upon the vision for building a Protestant Britain that had been developed during his exile in Geneva.

While those attending Parliament were assembling in Edinburgh, on 11 August Knox chose Haggai for his sermon text, 'in application whereof he was so special and vehement'.[28] The text perfectly suited his message that the new Protestant Kirk must be erected and must take precedence over all other considerations. Though some would directly oppose the rebuilding of the Temple, as the Geneva Bible's note on Haggai 1:4 warned, there was also danger from those who had a different set of priorities and preferred 'policie and private profite to religion'.[29] One of those listening to the sermon was William Maitland of Lethington, who had been chosen as Speaker or 'Harangue maker' to Parliament. In a typically witty quip Maitland joked, 'We must now forget ourselves, and bear the barrow to build the houses of God.'[30] Knox was intensely prickly over anything he construed as undermining his prophetic role and reacted badly to levity on this serious subject. In the *History*, having stressed that Maitland had spoken 'in mockage', he retaliated with a prediction about the speaker: 'he shall have experience that the building of his own house (the house of God being despised) shall not be so prosperous, and of such firmity, as we desire it were'. With the subsequent death of his son in exile and poverty bringing the loss of Maitland's lineage or 'house', these words of Knox were treated as a prophecy that had been fulfilled.

Edinburgh was especially full for the Parliament because in an unusual development one hundred lairds arrived and petitioned to be allowed to join proceedings as barons of the realm. Largely drawn from the areas of Protestant strength in Angus and the Mearns, Fife, the Lothians and the south-west, they joined the third estate. Working with Protestant commissioners of the burghs they formed a religious pressure group lobbying the first estate of the Catholic clergy and the second estate of the nobility. They presented a petition replete with Knoxian phrases and themes requesting redress against the Catholic clergy, the condemnation of Catholic doctrine and worship, and the abolition of papal authority in Scotland.[31] The last-minute decision to place a Confession of Faith before the Parliament was another consequence of this pressure group's activities. The 'barons' were instructed to produce a summary of doctrine with the help of the ministers and, according to Knox, the Scots

Confession was composed in four days.[32] Although doctrinal issues would have formed part of the committee's discussions, there were traces in the text of the *Confession* indicating that it was a rush job. In a broad sense the *Confession* followed the pattern of the Apostles' Creed, and most of the first half was relatively uncontroversial in sixteenth-century theology. The language and tone within the second half of the *Confession* were more combative and possibly had greater direct input from Knox, featuring some of his favourite phrases, such as the 'synagogue of Satan'.[33]

The production and content of the *Confession* demonstrated how well the team was working and its ability to integrate the insights and experiences of all six members. Consequently, the *Confession* did not simply reflect Knox's views nor can it be classified as exclusively Calvinist. In his *History*, Knox did not reveal the debates that had taken place, and what was discussed in the committee remained confidential. Here as elsewhere, Knox and his fellow committee members exercised a sense of collective responsibility for their team decisions and products. The returned Marian exile Thomas Randolph, who was serving as English Ambassador in Scotland, sent information concerning some of the revisions and excisions in his reports to Cecil. Predictably, Knox's views on the monarch or 'civil magistrate' were controversial, and John Winram and Maitland of Lethington revised those sections, removing any mention of the circumstances when disobedience to a ruler was permitted.[34] Knox did not cavil about this or other possible omissions and was happy to support the final draft in its entirety.

The presentation of the *Confession* became the first item of business for the Parliament. Not being members of the legislature, on 17 August, Knox and four other committee members stood at the fence that demarcated the parliamentary chamber prepared to answer any questions. In his capacity as Prior of Portmoak, Winram was entitled as a member of the first estate to sit within the chamber and to add his contribution there. Instead of a normal debate the occasion turned into an enthusiastic religious meeting with a number of lairds giving a testimony to their Protestant faith. From among the noble estate, Lord Lindsay from Fife declared, 'I have lived manie yeres; I am the oldeste in thys companye of my sorte; now that yt hath pleased God to lett me see this daye, wher so manie nobles and other have allowed so worthie a work, I will say with Simion, *Nunc dimittis*.' The speed with which the *Confession* had been written gave no time for the Catholic hierarchy to make a response and they were placed under immense pressure to conform. The Earl Marischal seized upon their silence to condemn them and, with the mood of the chamber so fervently in favour, very few Catholic clergy or nobles were prepared to vote against the *Confession*.[35]

The 'Reformation Parliament' ignored the provision of the peace treaty that had expressly forbidden that religion should become a topic of debate. While Knox scorned such views, doubt remained about the legality of the Parliament's proceedings and procedure, though King Francis and Mary, Queen of Scots, had authorized its initial calling. Since the 1560 legislation did not subsequently receive the royal assent, among the legal profession its official status was at best uncertain.[36] After the overwhelming Protestant fervour had been released by the acceptance of the *Confession of Faith*, parliamentary business settled into a more accustomed routine. The other religious legislation concentrated upon the removal of the Pope and Catholic worship rather than attempting a programme of construction. Papal jurisdiction was abolished within Scotland and the celebration of Roman Catholic sacraments and other forms of worship banned. In August 1560 everyone realized that Scotland had moved decisively out of the Catholic fold and was accepting Protestant doctrine. Little else had been decided, leaving a great deal to do and agree.

The order of Ecclesiastical Discipline

During the autumn, work began in earnest to ready the *First Book of Discipline* for the next meeting of the Estates. Revisions were made and three major interpolations inserted on educational matters and the role of the superintendents. At the heart of the debates was the key financial question of how the new Church was to be funded. The committee of six Johns made the radical bid for the new institution to take over the entire patrimony of the old Church. They needed resources to finance the newly erected Protestant Kirk, to provide for an educational programme at school and university levels and to assist the poor. This ambitious vision for full-blown reform to create a covenanted kingdom entirely rejected a gradualist approach. While sympathetic to their aims, the English Ambassador was worried about this unwillingness to compromise; he found them 'so severe . . . so lothe to remytte anie thing of that that thei have receaved, that I see lytle hope therof'.[37]

In the wider sense of discipline signalled in its title, the *First Book of Discipline* incorporated a blueprint for the polity of the Kirk and an outline for the Christian commonwealth it was hoped Scotland would become. Within these broad goals was included upholding a moral code that constituted discipline in its narrower sense. The two senses were linked in that section of the *First Book* when it asserted that 'no Commonwealth can flourish or long indure without good lawes and sharpe execution of the same, so neither can the Kirk of God be brought to puritie, neither yet be retained in the same without the order of Ecclesiastical Discipline'.[38] Discipline also constituted the third mark by which a true Church might be recognized, and its inclusion placed the Scottish Kirk in line with many Reformed churches in Europe but out of step with Calvin's tighter ecclesiological definition containing only two marks, preaching the Word and the right administration of the sacraments. The *First Book* specified the process by which discipline should be upheld and adopted the Reformed 'consistory' comprising the minister and elders. When Knox had been in St Andrews such a consistory, or Kirk session as it became known in Scotland, was functioning as early as October 1559 and included deacons in its meetings. The Kirk session's personnel and methods probably reflected the practice of Knox's Genevan congregation that had already given him the experience of how to exercise Church discipline, and this model was carried across into the practice of the Scottish Kirk.

It was noticeable how much in the *First Book* reflected the congregational perspective that had characterized Knox's experience and ecclesiology. Eighteen months earlier in his *Brief Exhortation* addressed to England, he had employed the same broad themes such as discipline, the importance of preaching and religious instruction and a rejection of the medieval benefice system and large dioceses. When considering a whole kingdom, he thought of a covenanted people based upon the Old Testament kingdoms of Israel and Judah. His understanding revolved around the necessity of the people remaining obedient to the covenant and hearing the prophetic messages delivered by their preachers. Such a framework did not lend itself to thinking about structures or organizations and when considering the whole of Scotland Knox struggled to conceptualize them. He was clearer about what he did not want within a new national Church than the mechanics of establishing the Scottish Reformed Kirk. The other Johns probably supplied a number of ideas that tackled the problems of running a national ecclesiastical organization, such as the superintendents. There proved to be no time to iron out inconsistencies between different sections and conflicting aspects drawn from different models of Church organization. Consequently, the *First Book* did not offer a fully coherent and integrated structure for the new Reformed Kirk. It comprised an unusual mix of practical organizational details alongside a broad and radical vision.

No small heaviness

After the euphoric summer of 1560 the midwinter months blew an icy wind through the hopes of Scottish Protestants. During December 1560 and January 1561 Knox felt powerless to prevent his world from disintegrating. His personal life was rocked to the core, Scotland's Reformation had stalled before completion, and the new political and diplomatic alignments were under threat. Bowed down by the weight of troubles, he found it difficult to find hope for the future. The experience of losing his wife magnified his streak of pessimism and encouraged his tendency to dwell upon the worst possible consequences: for him the glass became permanently half empty.

The most devastating event happened during the first half of December 1560 when Marjorie died. Knox's wife was only in her twenties and the cause of her death is not known, though sudden death from disease or accident was not unusual in the sixteenth century and women faced substantial extra risks during pregnancy and childbirth. Knox would later be buried in the churchyard at St Giles', and probably his wife had also been laid to rest there. In his own will, he augmented Marjorie's previous legacy of money, silver cups and spoons to their two sons. He also recorded her benediction for her boys, full of faith and hope, 'that God, for His Sone Christ Jesus saik, wald of His merci mak thaime His trew feireris and als upricht worshcipperis of Him as ony that evir sprang out of Abrahames loynes'. Marjorie's faith had quietly helped Knox's own, and she had brought him great personal happiness in their five years of marriage. She had become the perfect minister's wife and gave her husband two sons, both of whom survived. Despite his initial trepidation, Knox had relished his roles as husband, father and head of a household. To the end of his own life Marjorie remained in his heart as his dearest wife of 'blissit memorie'.[39] As was frequently the case with his deep emotions, the more he felt, the less he wrote. In his *History*, he merely included the laconic phrase 'no small heaviness' to describe his devastating sense of loss following the death of his 'bedfellow', a common term of endearment for one's spouse.[40]

Knox never fully recovered from the shock of Marjorie's death, which left him rudderless and depressed for months and struggling to recover any sense of optimism for the rest of his life. He had lost his close companion, secretary and spiritual confidante in addition to being without a wife and the mother of his sons. Several months later Calvin sent gracious condolences to Knox and in a separate letter to Goodman urged him to give his friend as much support as possible during this difficult time. On the domestic side Knox found it hard to cope, and in 1562 Elizabeth Bowes came to Edinburgh to help her son-in-law look after his two boys, both less than five years old.[41] Knox remained a widower for over three years, a relatively long time by sixteenth-century standards. Possibly as a means of comforting and strengthening himself as much as his congregation, he was preaching through his favourite Gospel of John and by October 1561 he had reached the penultimate chapter. In a deeply depressed letter to Anne Locke written in that month, Knox confessed that 'my inward and particular dolour releaseth nothing'. He looked for his release from his 'earthlie tabernacle' in death and headed his letter with the melodramatic phrase, 'I dalylie long for an end of miseries.' He also expressed the hope that he might pass away as soon as he had completed those sermons on John's Gospel.[42]

Shortly after Marjorie's death, news reached Scotland that Francis II, the young husband of Mary, Queen of Scots, had died on 5 December of an ear infection that had turned septic. With his impressive news-gathering network, Knox was the first in Scotland to receive the tidings, courtesy of one of his reliable French contacts. He went immediately to Hamilton House, at Kirk o'Field just outside Edinburgh's walls, to tell Châtelherault, the senior person in the realm. When Knox arrived, the Duke was in consultation with Lord James, and the two nobles took the opportunity to offer their condolences and comfort to him on the loss of his wife. Despite his similar bereavement, Knox treated the Queen's loss of her husband, childhood friend and companion strictly as a political matter. Seeing the hand of God in this event, he rejoiced that a threat to the Protestants of France and Scotland had been removed.[43] While they digested the news and its implications for Scotland, confirmation of Francis II's death arrived in a message from the English commander at Berwick, Lord Grey of Wilton.[44]

In Knox's analysis of the consequences of the French King's death his first thought was that the disruption of France's power would remove the immediate threat of French troops being sent to Scotland to regain full control over the kingdom. There was the added relief that, with their niece no longer Queen of France, the influence of the Guise brothers, the Duke and the Cardinal of Lorraine, would be restricted. Knox was convinced the timing of the King's death had prevented the execution of a group of French Protestants trapped in a Guisian plot.[45] Since Catherine de' Medici was already the Queen Dowager in France, the position of Mary, Queen of Scots, in her adopted country was unclear. However, on the broader European stage she immediately became an extremely eligible widow. While her husband's death did not technically affect her rule in Scotland, it did raise questions about a new marriage alliance and possibly a new home for the Queen.

THE WORDLINGS REFUSED

An emergency Convention of Estates was summoned to Edinburgh for 15 January 1561 to discuss the new situation facing Scotland and Mary, Queen of Scots. The meeting provided an opportunity to present the revised version of the *First Book of Discipline* to the Estates for approval. Around Christmas a relatively small number of ministers and laity had met, with Knox and the

Edinburgh commissioners heading the list of recorded participants, and this gathering of 'particular' churches into a national or 'universal' Church became the first General Assembly of the Church of Scotland. At its meeting, two lists were compiled with the positive one containing those deemed suitable and qualified to serve the new Kirk as readers or ministers. On to the negative 'little list' were put those priests who continued to celebrate Mass and the lairds who protected them, carrying the implied assumption that they 'never would be missed'. This encouraged a vindictive attack against John Sinclair, Dean of Restalrig, possibly instigated by Knox who deemed him a traitor to the Protestant cause for advocating reform and then deciding to remain loyal to the Roman Catholic Church. The Assembly sought the destruction of Sinclair's collegiate church as 'a monument of idolatry' that should 'be razed and utterly cast down and destroyed'.[46] Knox was still pressing for sharp and complete breaks with past practices and personnel.

In a couple of small but significant steps, the Assembly continued to act on the assumption that the Kirk was taking over the main resources linked to the parish churches – the teinds or tithes, the 10 per cent tax on all forms of income. The commissioners were instructed to bring to the next meeting the names of those receiving the teind income in their respective parishes. The Assembly also proposed to treat Catholic clergy, who had served the old Church but would not in future have a salary, in the same category as the poor. Such measures were whistling in the wind: it had already become clear there could be no straightforward transfer of parish church resources from the old to the new ecclesiastical institution. The complex area of ecclesiastical finance was never going to lend itself to simple solutions and would require instead delicate political negotiations.

For decades the resources of the Scottish Church had been propping up royal finances and subsidizing noble incomes. Untangling these threads was both extremely difficult and a political minefield. Knox could not, or would not, understand how complex the finances of the old Church had become. Like St Francis, another merchant's son, Knox was extremely sensitive to the corrosive effects of the love of money. Though he rejected the Franciscan ideal of holy poverty, he believed his watchman's role included a duty to sniff out the slightest smell of greed. Within the different context of the Edwardian Church, he had been caught up in the struggle over diocesan finances when he was himself suggested for the see of Rochester and there were plans to dismember the wealthy diocese of Durham. He had criticized the courtiers' greed in his sermons, and this vice became associated in his mind with their betrayal of the Protestant cause when Queen Mary Tudor came to the throne. In exile Knox had developed a logical progression that assumed the nobility were solely motivated by self-interest and greed in their dealings over Church property. This deadly sin of avarice was a symptom of a lack of religious zeal that also disguised a time-serving hypocrisy. These vices had undermined the Edwardian Reformation and brought divine punishment. In Geneva, when Knox and his friends discussed their strategy for a Protestant Britain, they had devised a single remedy for those past mistakes to ensure they would not to be repeated in the future: the maintenance of the zealous 'single eye' of complete commitment.

Knox believed that this commitment produced a willingness to finish the job whatever the cost. Those who had fought during the Wars of the Congregation had been prepared to die for that cause. The soldiers' flamboyant gesture of donning their 'St Johnstone ribands', a rope noose worn round the neck to proclaim that they would die before surrendering, was precisely the kind of zeal he sought. He applied his 'all or nothing' principle to the other aspects of Church organization, not only to worship. Almost before the ink had dried on the *Confession of Faith*, to Knox's fearful gaze there were signs of a lack of total commitment to establishing a 'perfect reformation'. He therefore analysed the reception of the *First Book of Discipline* in the simplistic categories of total failure or success: it failed because the Convention of Estates did not endorse the entire book. By treating it as an undivided entity, Knox presented the refusal of the financial claims as a rejection of the entire blueprint for the organization of the new Kirk. He subsequently inserted the unpublished text of the *First Book of Discipline* into his *History* with the explicit aim of heaping coals on the heads of his opponents. He underscored the moral: 'posterity to come may judge as well what the worldlings refused as what Policy the godly Ministers required; that they ... may either establish a more perfect, or else imitate that which avariciousness would not suffer this corrupt generation to approve'.[47] Unintentionally undermining his own case, Knox had included the Act of the Council in January 1561, endorsing the *First Book* with the proviso that those who held benefices in the old Church should sustain ministers in their parishes.[48] The Scottish nobility wanted to continue the slow transfer of ecclesiastical resources from the old Church to the Crown that had been under way since the reign of James IV. A quick transition would have precipitated a minor social revolution.

Knox singled out Lord Erskine as a noble who would not forgo his revenues from monastic property. Having signed the 1557 band and the letter recalling Knox, Erskine had been a firm supporter of Protestantism when it was an underground movement. During the Wars of the Congregation he had held Edinburgh Castle neutral and, at the end, given shelter to Mary of Guise. Rather than recognizing that Erskine was following the noble code of honour,

Knox castigated such behaviour as a lack of fervency. The Catholic beliefs of Erskine's formidable wife, Annabella Murray, also aroused his ire and provoked the unpleasant aside '(a sweet morsel for the Devil's mouth)'.[49] Of Erskine he commented, 'he has a very Jezebel to his wife, if the poor, the schools and the ministry of the Kirk had their own, his kitchen would lack two parts, and more, of what he unjustly now possesses'.[50] This heavy-handed and malicious humour against Erskine for his dependency upon monastic property was an example of how the subject of ecclesiastical finance made Knox even more strident.

The first half of 1561 had for Knox the nightmare quality of watching impotently as Scotland repeated the mistakes made by Protestant England. In the summer he faced the final piece that completed the pattern: the return of idolatry. Having abolished the public celebration of Roman Catholic rites in Scotland and urged the destruction of the settings and equipment for celebrating Mass, he realized that the return of Mary, Queen of Scots, jeopardized that achievement. The Scottish kingdom had entered into the covenant with God to be his people through their public declaration of the Protestant faith and worship. It had begun the radical reform of 'churching it like a Scythian' and then within a few months that zeal had gone and the country failed to remain true and obedient to the laws of God. Knox knew that such disobedience would bring divine punishment: he had seen it all before.

CHAPTER FOURTEEN

Sorrow, dolour, darkness and all impiety

Knox's outlook was darkened by sorrow and depression during the opening years of Mary, Queen of Scots' personal rule. He believed that the fervency and commitment to the Protestant cause of the Lords of the Congregation, with whom he had fought in the Wars, had been quenched.[1] Still full of grief after Marjorie's death, he struggled to run his household and learn his job as Edinburgh's minister. In the middle of August 1561 one of the worst sea mists in living memory settled over the Firth of Forth and Edinburgh and this gloomy 'haar' perfectly matched his mood. His interior world was clouded with depression as he looked outside upon the sunless, dripping-wet world where in that mist he could only see as far as 'the length of two pairs of boots'. To sixteenth-century people particular weather patterns might signify the hand of God working in the world to warn his people of things to come. When cannon boomed out on the Forth, Knox and the rest of Edinburgh realized that the ships carrying Mary, Queen of Scots, to Scotland had arrived earlier than expected. God's message was plain to Knox: 'The very face of heaven, the time of her arrival, did manifestly speak what comfort was brought unto this country with her, to wit, sorrow, dolour, darkness and all impiety.'[2] Long before Mary stepped back on her native soil, Knox had made up his mind about her. She was a regnant Queen, and he knew what he thought about that; she was the daughter of Mary of Guise, so she would have inherited her mother's craft and guile and expertise in political management; worst was her Roman Catholicism, and he was convinced it was the persecuting kind, following the practice of her uncles the Duke of Guise and the Cardinal of Lorraine. He was certain, whatever the outward appearances, that there must be a hidden agenda: she was a Catholic Queen Mary and would revert to type.

Since the news of King Francis' death the nobility's main concern had been with the possible return to Scotland of Mary, Queen of Scots. Her half-brother,

Lord James Stewart, had been commissioned to go to France to put the case of the Lords of the Congregation as tactfully as possible in the hope they would continue holding political power and their policies would not be discarded. Looking for a Roman Catholic resurgence, John Leslie, later Bishop of Ross, had also been lobbying the Queen of Scots. Knox and some fellow ministers had warned about the dangers of a Roman Catholic Queen in the country, but were dismissed as 'unquiet spirits'. No one was sure whether when Mary returned to Scotland she would be prepared to hear a private Mass or insist upon a public celebration. It was little consolation to Knox that this was not the wholesale apostasy that England had committed in 1553. In an attempt to stem the tide he saw flowing fast against him, his sermons became increasingly severe and uncompromising, filled with warnings of the plagues and punishments God would send upon his people when they failed to obey him. Knowing he was the messenger of God, he felt he had no option except to trumpet his message. The English Ambassador Thomas Randolph commented that Knox 'thonderethe owte of the pulpet, that I feare no thynge so muche, that one daye he wyll marre all. He rulethe the roste, and of hym all men stande in feare.' He added that Knox's thundering was effective, adding tongue in cheek to his friend Throckmorton, 'Woulde God you knewe how myche I am amended myself.'[3]

To put in execution God's judgements

The sound of the guns from the French galleys had put the capital in a frenzy of preparation. Knox acted swiftly, alerting his Protestant supporters and gathering some musicians. Having disembarked at Leith on 19 August, Mary was conveyed to Holyrood Palace for her first night back in Scotland. Knox and his friends went to offer their own style of greeting. Gathered outside the palace they sang metrical psalms to the accompaniment of fiddles and other instruments. This was never intended to be a friendly serenade, though the Queen made the perfect diplomatic response by saying the music was agreeable and perhaps they should return on another night. While her French entourage judged the music to be terrible, they understood exactly what was being done.[4] In France, the Protestants defiantly and aggressively sang metrical psalms on the streets. Psalms and riots went together in French minds in the sixteenth century in the same way as soccer fans' chanting and violence did in the twentieth. By singing their 'battle hymns of the Lord', Knox and his friends were making a noisy declaration about whose supporters were in control: Knox got his retaliation in first.

Edinburgh became crowded with nobles and many others rushing to greet the Queen. There was considerable tension on 24 August, the first Sunday after Mary's arrival, because it was known that Mass would be celebrated in the Royal Chapel. While Knox was preaching in St Giles', zealous Protestants led by Patrick, Master of Lindsay (heir to Lord Lindsay of the Byres), and other Fife 'gentlemen' went to the Queen's palace at Holyrood with the intention of stopping the Catholic service. They caught and beat a server who happened to be carrying a candle through the palace's close. However, they could not break into the chapel to attack the priest, whom they threatened to kill, because they would not force their way past Lord James, their Fife Protestant hero, who was standing at the door to deny entry. After the Mass, the priest was whisked to safety by Lord James' two Protestant half-brothers. That afternoon a large Protestant demonstration went down to the palace to protest. For Knox and the godly, the celebration of Mass on Scottish soil was a deeply offensive and terrible breach of the covenant the Scots had recently made with God. It was a national disaster and these Protestants 'could not abide that the land which God by his power had purged from idolatry should in their eyes be polluted again'.[5] Throughout Europe, the fear of pollution caused by heresy or idolatry galvanized Catholic and Protestant activists alike to employ violence to rid themselves, and their kingdoms, of its taint. For centuries people had believed the purity and health of Christendom should be preserved at all costs and they were prepared to cleanse religious contagion by fire if necessary. When Knox employed the Old Testament language of the covenant he was tapping into this same fear of communal religious pollution.

To calm the situation, a royal proclamation was issued the following day promising that the next Parliament would debate the religious issue. In the meantime no one should change the religion that the Queen had found 'publicly and universally standing' at her arrival, and special protection was extended to the Queen's household.[6] The Earl of Arran took exception to this final part and issued his own protestation that every subject in the realm, including the royal household, should obey the law against idolatry passed in 1560 and found in God's word. Knox was impressed by Arran's bold move and tough Protestant stance and it brought the two men closer.[7] In the pulpit the following Sunday, Knox delivered a hard-hitting sermon against idolatry and warned that it would bring plagues from God. He added a comparison that became famous: 'one Mass ... was more fearful to him than if ten thousand armed enemies had landed in any part of the realm, of purpose to suppress the whole religion'.[8] He reminded his listeners that during the recent wars victory had been theirs when they relied entirely upon God. He warned, 'when we join hands with idolatry, it is no doubt but that both God's amicable presence and comfortable defence leaveth us, and what shall then become of us?' Mary's advisers, who were trying to maintain stability, told Knox to stick to his text and not give 'a very untimely admonition'. That was water off a duck's back to Knox and confirmed that he was doing his job as a watchman of the Lord.

Knox was not merely employing his love of an arresting phrase when saying he was afraid of the Queen's Mass: he knew he was fighting a battle but was unsure about his strategy. Several years later when writing and revising this section of his *History*, he berated himself for not being 'more vehement and upright in the suppressing of that idol in the beginning'.[9] He revealed that secret discussions about tactics had taken place among the 'earnest and zealous'. Despite his pulpit thundering, it was Knox who had persuaded them not to adopt a more aggressive strategy, 'to put in execution God's judgements'.[10] He was already regretting that advice a couple of months later when he wrote to Cecil that he should have been more forceful from the start about Mary's Mass.[11] At that time he had been genuinely unsure and tentative, not knowing when to send people on to the streets or to man the barricades. Contrary to the modern image, Knox was not a revolutionary 'action man'. Though an excellent army chaplain, he was not a military commander or an urban freedom fighter.

When the Queen made her formal entry into Edinburgh on 2 September 1561, the preacher heartily approved its religious content. Though the burning in effigy of a priest saying Mass had been vetoed, Mary had been presented with the central text of 'right worship', a Psalm Book or *Forme of Prayers* including the metrical psalms devised by Knox's Genevan congregation. The capital city had delivered an unequivocally Protestant message to its monarch.[12] In an attempt to defuse the situation and introduce the Queen to Knox within a private and non-confrontational setting, the preacher was summoned to Holyrood Palace on 4 September. In common with his other interviews with Mary, Queen of Scots, evidence for what happened comes almost exclusively from Knox himself in his *History*.[13] By the time Book V was written, Knox's view of Mary, Queen of Scots, had set in stone and he had a specific set of objectives when setting down his narrative. Since he would have made a magnificent screenwriter, these confrontations with the Queen are brilliant pieces of dramatic dialogue that have fascinated readers over the centuries. He deliberately gave the Queen short or one-line feeder comments that allowed him to expand at length and Mary was also scripted with dramatic gestures, such as bursting into tears or staying quiet for fifteen minutes. As Knox admitted, discussions with the Queen were not brief and he was merely recounting the highlights.

MY SUBJECTS SHALL OBEY YOU, AND NOT ME

On the first occasion he met Mary, Queen of Scots, only Lord James and two gentlewomen, stationed at the far end of the room for propriety's sake, were present. At the start of his account Knox summarized the topics he was including. They all focused upon charges that had been made against him: raising rebellion against the Regent and the Queen; his views on female rule; his seditious behaviour in England; and, finally, being a necromancer. What followed was a series of justifications by Knox aimed at the audience of the *History*. He chose the first three accusations to demonstrate that he was not a rabble-rouser but a loyal subject who had the best interests of Queen and country at heart. He was equally anxious to make clear he had apologized to Mary over the *First Blast* and had made as many concessions as it was possible for him to make about female rule. He could not understand why neither Queen Elizabeth of England nor Mary, Queen of Scots, had been satisfied with his apologies on that subject. He felt he had bent over backwards to explain that his main target had been Queen Mary Tudor. Despite his belief that female rule was wrong in principle, he assured the Scottish Queen that if the realm were happy to accept her authority, he was prepared to keep his contrary opinion within 'my own breast'. He would refrain from preaching or speaking against a form of government with which he disagreed, in the same way as the Greek philosopher Plato had done in his day. Knox sought a biblical equivalent to clarify his position and used the example of Paul, one of Rome's two Apostle saints, who had been a loyal Roman citizen appealing to the authority of the pagan Roman Emperor. Given that the Emperor in question was Nero, this concession sounded far from gracious on Knox's part. It was not improved by a ponderous attempt at a humorous aside – that if he had intended to threaten the Queen's position, he would have done so long before she returned to Scotland.

Later in the interview the Queen raised the issue of obedience to monarchs and their religious commands. Knox became tangled over the difference between passive and active resistance, and then produced a comparison between a tyrant and a mad father who needed to be restrained by his children. He jumped over several logical steps by making an association between madness and persecution, asserting that princes who 'would murder the children of God' were in 'a very mad frenzy'. In that instance the princes should be stripped of the sword of justice and put in prison until they came to 'a more sober mind'. Knox produced his checkmate line, possibly added in 1567, that this was 'no disobedience against princes, but just obedience, because that it agreeth with the will of God'.[14] After this discourse, the Queen concluded, 'my subjects shall obey you, and not me . . . and so must I be subject to them, and not they to me'. Knox ignored or missed the sarcasm, declaring that everyone was to obey God and queens had the role of being nurses to the Church.

The Queen voiced the nub of the problem: 'ye are not the Kirk that I would nourish'. For her the Roman Church was the true Church. Assuming that the Queen was debating and not seeking conversion, Knox's reply was exceptionally dismissive and included a string of abusive terms to describe 'that Roman harlot'. He told Mary she was ignorant and deluded and had failed to recognize the plain word of God. For good measure he launched into an attack on the Mass and ridiculed his Catholic opponents for failing to meet Protestants in debate. It had reached noon and the Queen was probably most grateful to be called to dinner. Despite the abrasive tone in the main interview, Knox's parting words were remarkably conciliatory: 'I pray God, Madam, that ye may be as blessed within the Commonwealth of Scotland, as ever Deborah was in the Commonwealth of Israel.'[15] For one moment it appeared as if Knox was surprised by the hope that this Queen Mary might be different.

The previous account given in his *History* did not fit with those final words nor did it accord with the different interpretations following this first interview, probably supplied by Lord James. The Catholics were reported to be fearful and the Protestants hopeful, expecting that the Queen would consent to hear some preaching. Knox's own verdict – that Mary displayed 'a proud mind, a crafty wit, and an indurate heart against God and his truth' – seemed equally at odds with the discussion he recorded. This was not simply the wisdom of hindsight when he wrote his *History*, as later in 1561 he had told Cecil he had 'espied such craft as I have not found in such age'.[16] Before he entered her presence the previous September, Knox already possessed a pre-existing picture of the Queen he expected to meet and everything Mary said was slotted into that preconceived character. As the English Ambassador graphically, if sarcastically, remarked of Knox's view of Mary, he

> hathe no hope (to use his owne termes) that she sall ever come to God, or do good in the common welthe. He is so full of mystrust in all her doyngs, wordes, and sayenge, as thoughe he were eyther of God's privie consell, that knowe howe he had determined of her from the begynynge, or that he knewe the secretes of her harte so well, that neyther she dyd or culde have for ever one good thought of god or of his trewe religion.[17]

The attempt by Lord James and Lethington to facilitate a greater understanding had backfired, merely confirming Knox's prejudices. There was no meeting of minds and Knox did not want to engage in dialogue. Mentally shaking the dust from his sandals, he left the royal court, which he said was 'dead to me, and I to it'.[18]

From all sides Knox was receiving advice to moderate his stance, especially in relation to Mary, Queen of Scots, and he explained to Cecil why he would not heed such counsel. He acknowledged that 'Men deliting to swym betwix two watters, have often compleaned upon my severitie' and stated baldly that he would not do evil for good to come of it. In relation to the Queen's Mass, he deeply regretted 'that I did not mor zelouslie gainstand that Idol at the first erecting'. He regarded the softly-softly policy of winning over the Queen as counter-productive since 'by permission Sathan groweht bold', and his understanding was that 'the Quen neyther is neyther shalbe of our opinion; and in verray dead hir hole proceadings do declayr that the Cardinalles lessons ar so deaplie prented in hir heart' that only death would separate them.[19] It was a profoundly pessimistic assessment.

Having detected the Scottish nobles' backsliding over the financing of the new Kirk, Knox looked for the presence of hypocrisy, the vice that had accompanied greed in Edwardian England. Those who had been the Congregation's chief supporters were no longer following his guidance and Knox felt personally betrayed. Not knowing how to deal with this challenge, he found the struggle debilitating and depressing. He confessed to Calvin, 'I never before felt how weighty and difficult a matter it is to contend with hypocrisy under the disguise of piety. I never so feared open enemies when in the midst of troubles I could hope for victory. But now this treacherous defection from Christ ... so wounds me that my strength daily diminishes.'[20] In his main request to Calvin, Knox was on difficult ground since he wanted the Swiss Reformer to pronounce that it was lawful to prohibit Mary, Queen of Scots, professing her own religion in Scotland.

In support of their own position, Knox's Protestant opponents were citing the strong line on obedience to political authorities emanating from Calvin and the other major Reformers. The issue had been debated in early November 1561 after Knox's sermon attacking the solemn Mass that had been celebrated on All Saints' Day. In the house of James McGill, the Clerk Register, six leading royal councillors lined up against four ministers, including Knox, to debate the proposition 'Whether that subjects might put to their hand to suppress the idolatry of their Prince?' It was decided to refer the matter to Geneva, and Knox offered to write. With his political brain, Maitland noted that the answer might depend on how the question was put to Calvin – an insightful observation that, as usual, irritated Knox. The preacher chose to be economical with the truth and failed to mention that he had written to Calvin the previous week posing the same question.[21] Guessing what Calvin's answer was likely to be, he was probably stalling for time. He also used Maitland's offer to write to Calvin as a reason for subsequently doing nothing.

MY LORD ARRAN AND MY LORD BOTHWELL ARE AGREED NOW

Things seemed to go from bad to worse in the months following Mary's return and Knox felt everything he tried to do or say went wrong or was misconstrued.

He confided to Anne Locke that he had had the most humiliating experience of his life around the Easter period in 1562.[22] Despite his misgivings and previous refusals to become involved, he had agreed to attempt to end the bitter feud raging between the Earls of Arran and Bothwell. Both men were Protestants and Knox was finally persuaded by the argument that a public reconciliation would benefit the Kirk by demonstrating that it could bring peace among its adherents. Knox had complex personal links to the various protagonists within the feud. As he proudly declared to Bothwell, he had a 'good mind' to the house of Hepburn because of the long tradition of service to the earls stretching back to his own great-grandfather. One of the original disputes in the current feud had arisen during the Wars of the Congregation. Despite his Protestant beliefs, Bothwell had remained loyal to the Regent and made a significant seizure of English gold on its way through the Borders to the Congregation. During that incident the laird of Ormiston, Knox's old friend, was injured and his cause had been taken up by Arran. Ormiston's son, Alexander Cockburn, who had been Knox's pupil many years earlier, was once again associating with the preacher. Despite some friction during the Wars of the Congregation, following Arran's assertively Protestant stance over the Queen's proclamation six months earlier the Earl and Knox had become allies. Conversely, Knox had been shocked and offended by Bothwell's drunken antics and the fights on Edinburgh streets between groups of Hepburns and Hamiltons.

As often happened in Scottish feuds, though Knox had loyalties to both sides, in his clerical role he had to act impartially and bring peace to both parties. Being good at admonition, he performed the 'knocking heads together' part with success and boasted to Anne Locke that it had been little short of miraculous. Following normal practice, the kinsmen of the two Earls then hammered out the hard negotiations over the conditions for the reconciliation. At the important reconciliatory meeting, Arran moved directly to Bothwell to embrace him, bypassing the penitential rituals of recompense Bothwell had agreed to perform. Knox then supplied an impromptu homily to underline the moral message about forgiveness and reconciliation. Though giving no details, he mentioned that he had already been misreported and left shortly afterwards to avoid making things worse. The following day both men attended Knox's sermon, dined together and travelled to Kinneil, the Hamilton residence on the Forth, to meet the Duke, Arran's father, and complete the reconciliation of the kindreds. Everything appeared to be going according to plan. The ending of the feud rapidly became the talk of the town, causing one man to make a merry jest on Edinburgh's High Street that landed him in serious trouble. A cook, Ninian McCrechane, suggested the world must have turned upside down and exclaimed, 'Loving to God, my lord Arrane and my lord Boithwile ar aggreit

now; Knox quarter is run, he is skurgeit [scourged] throw the toun.' For slan-
dering Knox, even in jest, McCrechane was whipped and placed in the branks
or stocks.[23] The ending of this major feud was no laughing matter.

Having thought his job was done, Knox was startled on Friday, 27 March,
when Arran came to his lodging after the sermon with a wild tale of how
Bothwell was plotting to kill Lord James and Lethington and kidnap the
Queen so that she would marry Arran. Knox attempted to calm the Earl and
persuade him not to tell the world or take any precipitate action. Convinced he
would be accused of treason, Arran continued to tell people and wrote down
the accusations. The Duke tried to restrain his son, but Arran escaped and
headed for the Queen in Fife. Knox sent a frantic warning to Lord James
recently created Earl of Moray that Arran's words should be discounted
because he was 'stricken with frenzy'.[24] With accusations and counter-
accusations flying around the royal court, the affair mushroomed into a major
political crisis. Following further strange behaviour, Arran was diagnosed as
mad, though this did not prevent Bothwell being placed in prison on suspicion
of treason.[25]

Knox felt besmirched and deeply humiliated because he had effected the
reconciliation that led to the crisis. Bothwell and his supporters were blaming
him for the disastrous outcome and Knox felt he had inadvertently broken 'the
obligation of our Scottish kindness' that had stood for so long between his
family and the Hepburns.[26] After the Council had met to discuss the affair,
Dumbarton Castle was removed from Hamilton control. Given his highly
critical stance in the past towards the Hamiltons, Knox was blamed by them
for his intervention and the mess in which they found themselves. The disgrace
of two potential rivals ensured Moray and Lethington gained most from this
affair. They became even more powerful following the fall of the Roman
Catholic Earl of Huntly, who was manoeuvred into a full rebellion in the
summer of 1562. Their policies for a Protestant Scotland were in the ascendancy and Knox was in the political wilderness.

The preacher was also battered by the experience of driving through a
national Reformation. He passionately believed in undiluted and uncompromising Church reform. The euphoria of the Reformation Parliament in the
summer of 1560 and the success of planting the face of the Kirk within the
burgh of St Andrews had given him a false impression of the completely
different challenge posed by building the house of God throughout the land.
He had brought with him the preconceptions of his English experiences and
he struggled to fit Scotland into the template devised in exile. In the midst of
the deep depression caused by Marjorie's death, he lashed out against his allies
during the Wars of the Congregation, the Protestant nobility. Their failure to

accept the new Kirk's claim to the entire patrimony of the old Church enraged him. He was overtaken by the fear that Scotland was repeating the mistakes of Edwardian England with greed and hypocrisy destroying the 'single eye', the fixed purpose driven by religious zeal. The arrival of another Queen Mary, accompanied by her idolatry, seemed to complete the parallels with England. Locked into an incorrect analysis of the actual situation in Scotland, the pessimistic Knox was blinded to many of the real challenges of establishing the Reformed Kirk within the realm.

Painful preacher of his blessed Evangel

Hanging in the capital's church tower beneath its impressive crown steeple, the Great Bell of St Giles' was inscribed in Latin, 'I lament the dead; I summon the living; I subdue thunderbolts'.[27] As the minister in Edinburgh, Knox heard it ringing out over the burgh to summon the city to worship in St Giles' and to warn and protect its inhabitants during thunderstorms and man-made crises. It was part of his job to explain to his parishioners that the tolling of the bell at the death of one of their number had a new Protestant meaning: the Catholic practice of praying for the dead had been forbidden and the bell was only a method of communication.[28] In attitudes to the dead as in many other traditional religious practices, Knox was determined to remove or reinterpret them and replace them by a Protestant culture. The attempt to establish Reformed beliefs and habits across an entire community was a different type of ministerial task for him. He was faced with the specific challenge of reforming the Scottish capital, where he had to deal with all of Edinburgh's living and its dead. He brought to this new task his own line in thunderbolts – his preaching. He took great pains over his work, describing his job as being a 'painfull preacher of his blessed Evangell'.[29] Knox assumed that his prime purpose was to be a prophetic preacher and that sermons would be the central driver of religious change in Edinburgh. Lacking previous experience of parish ministry, he had not appreciated the range of other skills needed to alter the burgh's religious landscape. In this unfamiliar context he confronted the tension in his own ecclesiology between the faithful few and the undifferentiated mass of a national, territorial Church.

By being confirmed as the Edinburgh minister Knox got what he wanted in the reshuffle of 1560 and avoided one of the new roles as a superintendent over a region of Scotland, with its considerable administrative and organizational burdens. His Kirk colleagues did not try to force him to don the Superintendent's mantle, though on an ad hoc basis the General Assembly frequently employed him as a commissioner, the stopgap solution to not having enough superintendents. As minister at St Giles', Knox was exceptionally fortunate that the Superintendent of Lothian was John Spottiswood, whom he had inducted into that role in 1561. Spottiswood was based in the capital because it was the 'best reformed kirk' at the centre of his region and its Kirk session formed the basis of his own Superintendent's Court. Being a man of great tact and generosity of spirit, Spottiswood was able to work in close harmony with Knox and there was no tension over their respective jurisdictions and roles. In the heated atmosphere of the early seventeenth century, William Scot asserted, 'Mr John Knox his ministry did more good then all the superintendents.' By reading back into the 1560s the later bitter debate over presbyterianism versus episcopacy, Scot implied incorrectly that by remaining a parish minister Knox had rejected a post with ministerial oversight. Scot's interpretation ignored the warm working partnerships that existed between Knox and all five superintendents.

In the early stages of his Edinburgh ministry Knox might have assumed that the job would be akin to serving his exile congregation with the addition of parts of Calvin's role in Geneva. He had already witnessed a series of mature burgh reformations among the Swiss and Rhineland cities and had become aware of the great advantages of an urban community for the advancement of Protestantism. He perhaps had not fully appreciated that working within a city also entailed severe restrictions. Anything that threatened the merchant oligarchies who ran these cities would be blocked or resisted. The years of struggle and diplomacy that Calvin had expended had not been in evidence in the Geneva of Knox's memory with its fully functioning discipline and aura of godly mission. Social rank and the maintenance of the existing order were as important to the wealthy merchants of Edinburgh as they were to the Scottish nobility, and radical religious changes would not be permitted to spread into other areas of public life.[30] The Edinburgh Council might have a Protestant majority, but it remained opposed to 'severitie' and kept in check the repression of Roman Catholicism through penal taxation or the removal of burgess rights, and limited any excessive coercion of individuals for religious nonconformity.

As the minister at St Giles', Knox faced three substantial challenges in dealing with his congregation and parish, the Burgh Council and the royal court – challenges for which he was ill suited in outlook and temperament. In 1560 only a small minority in his parish would have firmly identified themselves as Protestants. Some parish residents were directly antagonistic towards the new faith, and many were ignorant about the religious controversies or were little moved by them. Knox had always found the religiously committed the easiest people to understand because they were either supporters or enemies. The rest he regarded as indifferent, uncommitted, ignorant or even hypocrites for failing to live up to their protestations, and he easily slipped into a dismissive attitude that identified them as 'not one of us' or potential enemies. With the embattled radical's innate suspicion of numerical majorities, he felt that a popular view was by definition not the correct or godly one. His past experience of uncompromising stands made it extremely difficult for him to woo the undecided or indifferent and gently persuade them to change their minds.

As the burgh's minister Knox needed to develop a good working relationship with the Council. Thanks to civic pride and major financial contributions, long before the Reformation crisis most Scottish burghs had exercised substantial control over their burgh churches and the clergy who staffed them. Edinburgh was proud of its fine parish church of St Giles' and after 1560 was equally proud it had secured for that pulpit the most famous Protestant preacher. As a matter of the burgh's honour, whenever Knox's status as its leading clergyman was threatened the Council backed their celebrity preacher, though that was a long way from full support for whatever he did or said. Knox did not recognize the need to emulate Calvin by undertaking the painstaking political process of establishing a party capable of running the Council. That frustrating process required a willingness to negotiate and compromise over some issues in order to achieve long-term goals. It was a skill that eluded Knox. The same deep aversion to compromise and what he denigrated as political contamination also hampered the minister in his dealings with the royal court and administration, the other substantial political power in the capital. His single solution to all three problems was to be more strident in the pulpit and increase the level of his admonitions to his listeners.

In his previous career Knox had become accustomed to having the liberty to come and go where and when, in his view, God called him. He had opted for a roving preaching mission instead of the Bread Street parish in London in 1553, and in Geneva Goodman covered his extended absences. In addition to the stop-go start of his Edinburgh ministry in 1559–60, Knox later left the burgh for long periods because of his political stance. He was formally called to St Giles' on two further occasions, in 1567 and 1572, and his time in Edinburgh can best be viewed as three different ministries. The persistent pattern of absence suggested that he was not entirely comfortable within the confines of a single parish, however large and significant. Mentally, he found it hard to adjust to the day-to-day routine and the internal rhythms of parish life dominated by pastoral concerns. He was torn between a longing to proclaim his prophetic message at the centre of affairs and a desire to be free from political contamination and surrounded by his close 'brethren' in the cosier communities of Ayr or St Andrews.

Although Knox liked to pretend he was just an ordinary burgh minister working in his parish, this was far from the case. He received more privileges than other parish ministers and was treated on a par with the superintendents. His substantial salary was paid regularly, at least by sixteenth-century standards. Initially it was paid by the Edinburgh Council and after 1562 under the system of the Thirds of Benefices. Knox was vociferous in his criticism of the Thirds, a royal tax of a third levied upon the benefices of the old Church that was divided between the Queen's household and stipends for Protestant clergy. With his talent for soundbites, he described it as two-thirds remaining with the Devil and one-third split between the Devil and the Kirk.[31] He complained bitterly about the arrears and failures in the payment system for most ministers, though his own stipend was given top priority and drawn from whichever district had funds. His annual stipend was worth £566 6s 8d in 1566 and was paid in cash and in kind, with allowances of wheat, barley and oats – substantial remuneration that many lairds would have envied. A fragmentary account for 1564 indicated that he was given the extremely unusual privilege of two servants being funded from the Thirds, £20 and £40 a year respectively being paid to Margaret Fowlis and John Reid.[32]

As part of their generous package of benefits, the Burgh Council provided Knox and his household with good accommodation inside the city. From the start of September 1560 he was placed in a large house in Trunk Close, off the north side of High Street, previously used by the Abbot of Dunfermline. It was called a 'mansion' and had a garden and some extra ground and was a sufficiently desirable residence for John Durie, one of the burgh's prosperous tailors, to be compensated for moving out to accommodate the minister.[33] In 1567 Knox moved into a different house and shifted again in 1572 when he probably occupied the property standing on High Street near to Trunk's Close now known as John Knox's House.[34] The Council also sought to make Knox's job more manageable by easing his preaching load of five sermons a week. Having close colleagues made a substantial difference to him, especially after he struggled to cope following Marjorie's death. A strong clerical support team was created for him, with John Craig being funded to act as a second minister for the large Edinburgh parish from April 1562 and John Cairns paid to act as its Reader. When ministerial resources were so scarce, this represented a considerable luxury for Knox.

OF A GRAVE BEHAVIOUR, SINCERE, INCLINING TO NO FACTION

The self-effacing John Craig proved a good foil for Knox. When he returned in 1559 having been out of the country for twenty-four years, Craig's vernacular had been rusty and at first he preached in Latin to scholars in Edinburgh's Magdalen Chapel. A year or so later his Scots was back and he became minister in Canongate, the neighbouring parish that lay on the other side of the Edinburgh city walls and contained the Palace of Holyrood. The following year he was persuaded to assist Knox at St Giles'.[35] In some of the key debates and confrontations, Craig proved a strong supporter of Knox and they developed a warm partnership. Like Goodman before him, Craig worked with Knox on liturgical orders. Completed after Goodman had been forced to leave Scotland in 1565, the Knox–Craig team produced the *Order for a General Fast* and *Order for Excommunication* that were added to the *Book of Common Order* (as the *Forme of Prayers* was known in Scotland).[36] Craig's high intellectual standing gave his views independent weight, and in the General Assembly debate concerning obedience to the ruler he made a telling point in support of Knox based upon his knowledge and study in Italy.[37] As the historian Spottiswood, son of the Superintendent of Lothian, commented, Craig 'was held in good esteem, a great divine and excellent preacher, of a grave behaviour, sincere, inclining to no faction, and, which increased his reputation, living honestly, without ostentation or desire of outward glory'.[38] As he was more diplomatic and able to work with all sides, his emollient presence was a major asset to Knox and Edinburgh, though it was that talent for compromise which later provoked criticism during the Marian civil wars. In 1566 it was Craig who carried the burgh through the crisis period at the end of Mary's personal reign and was brave enough to refuse to proclaim the banns for the Queen's marriage to Bothwell, declaring them 'altogether unlawfull'. Similarly, in 1571 when Knox departed, Craig remained at his post in Edinburgh. He finally moved from the capital in 1572 to minister in Montrose and then Aberdeen.[39]

In a burgh like Edinburgh, Protestant worship and three weekday sermons were available in addition to a Sunday service. Every day the 'common prayers' would be said, the Bible read and psalms sung in St Giles'. The Reader, John Cairns, provided this solid fare of worship through the week as well as the initial part or 'readers' service' on a Sunday, between the second and third bell before the minister came into the pulpit to preach the sermon. The heavy burden of catechizing the children and congregation fell primarily upon Cairns. Craig and Cairns also organized the major effort needed to examine those attending communion by testing their knowledge and their faith. With one parish covering the entire burgh, the numbers were considerable and there were well over a thousand communicants, approximately one in five of Edinburgh's adult population. As the numbers not taking communion indicated, adherence to Protestantism did not come quickly or universally within the capital. The requirements of Protestant worship put different demands upon the inhabitants of Edinburgh, and one challenge was organization. Possibly under Craig's direction, the burgh was divided into four quarters that developed into separate congregations, though Edinburgh's official team ministry did not appear until after Knox's death. A start was made on the division of the interior space within St Giles' giving the congregations a definite spatial identity. When his voice became too weak to carry at the end of his life, Knox was able to preach in the smaller space of the Tolbooth Church within St Giles'.[40]

Both Knox and Craig were excellent preachers, and the Sunday sermons in particular became significant events, part of the burgh's religious, social and cultural activities and provoking much discussion and debate. Unlike the ordered progress of Calvin's biblical expositions from the pulpit, Knox's preaching and the texts used for his sermons are not easy to reconstruct. It is known that during his first year in Edinburgh he preached his way through his beloved Gospel of St John. Some of his hearers were opponents, such as the highly intelligent schoolmaster from Linlithgow, Ninian Winzet. As well as mocking Knox's English-sounding accent, Winzet made a joke about how Knox had explained John 19 in his sermon. Expounding the Johannine description of the crucifixion, Knox had discussed the passage where Jesus' side was pierced by the spear, producing a flow of blood and water. The Roman soldier who had used the spear was traditionally identified as Longinus, whose blindness had been miraculously cured by drops of that blood and water. In medieval theology his spear and the blood and water that flowed had been used to emphasize the parallelism between the crucifixion and the Mass. In Winzet's judgement Knox had become excessively entangled discussing Longinus. If the preacher had taken the opportunity to challenge traditional eucharistic theology and advocate a Reformed understanding of the sacrament in his sermon, the schoolmaster had been neither impressed nor persuaded.[41]

Attending the sermon in St Giles' automatically carried a political dimension and usually indicated a basic alignment with the Protestant cause. This ensured that the presence or absence of different members of the royal court and nobility was noted with great interest. Knox was quick to exploit the appearance of any such arrivals and to add comments to his sermon directed specifically to them. The most famous occasion occurred when Henry, Lord Darnley, newly married to Mary, Queen of Scots, was treated to Knox's comments about how the Old Testament King Ahab should have dealt with his wife, the idolater Queen Jezebel. Making the exception to prove Knox's rule about not printing his sermons, this particular sermon was published because of the furore it created; it is the only complete text of a Knox sermon to have survived.

More than most preachers Knox had a habit of ranging across a variety of texts or biblical examples, though following standard Reformed practice he did strive to preach through a biblical book from start to finish. Believing he understood the 'sense' of Scripture, he felt he could bring together different texts to form a new composite whole. While it was a commonplace that one text could interpret another, Knox carried this practice to extreme lengths and became a master of the composite text. Giving the impression of being a single unit, his constructed texts were drawn from a number of different biblical locations. One famous example of this technique was his distinction between true worship and idolatry. 'You shall not each do what seems good to yourself but what I command you, this only should one do for the Lord: neither add anything, nor take anything away.' This ran together passages from chapters 4 and 12 in Deuteronomy to create a single, compelling divine instruction.[42]

In the Scots *Confession of Faith*, the sacraments were placed alongside preaching as a mark of the true Church. For Knox the administration of the Lord's Supper was an essential part of the congregation's life and it held profound significance for him in his personal spiritual life as well as in his theological thinking. His insistence upon sitting to receive communion or paring down the order of service to 'essentials' had created great controversy in the past. Both the liturgy and practice introduced into Scotland conformed to the model Knox had brought with him from Geneva, and they were duly practised in Edinburgh. Since they created no public fuss, they also generated little direct evidence about this central sacrament. One noticeable statistic concerning the Lord's Supper was that while a substantial minority did communicate, four out of five adults did not. At Easter 1561, the English Ambassador reported that there were about 1,300 communicants in St Giles'. The prosaic records of the purchase by the Burgh Council of substantial quantities of bread and wine for communion note the regular provision of the Lord's Supper within the burgh. They signal the profound change in the experience of the congregation in St Giles' with the laity receiving the wine for the first time and sitting to drink that wine from ordinary domestic vessels. In the course of the third communion administered by Knox, six and a half gallons of wine were distributed, costing £3 10s, alongside twenty-four loaves, costing 28s, and great candles and other candles for the door were bought to provide the lighting. Sacramental practice had been transformed in Edinburgh, though how well the nuances of Reformed theology were understood and received by the bulk of the population is much harder to gauge.[43]

Discipline, the third mark of a true Church in the *Confession*, was established in Edinburgh with the election of a Kirk session. For the period of Knox's ministry its records have been lost, though occasional glimpses of its

activities appear in other records and some of its actions with regard to matrimonial cases were recorded in the decisions of the new Commissary Court of
Edinburgh. Not surprisingly, given his high profile and outspoken views, Knox
attracted criticism from residents of the burgh and this was punished both by
the burgh court and by the Kirk's courts. In 1563 the prominent widow and
successful businesswoman Euphemia Dundas accused Knox of being a
common harlot all his days, possibly a reference to his broken vow of priestly
celibacy. She also alleged on one occasion he had been found with a prostitute
in the drying chamber of a corn kiln. Having had the General Assembly write
to the Burgh Council, Knox also began an action for slander against Euphemia.
He defended his good name with great legal vigour.[44]

His reaction to Dundas' allegations indicated that he was willing to employ
the ecclesiastical disciplinary process to protect his own reputation as well as
seeking redress in the civil courts, tactics he used in his final years when his
sensitivity to criticism increased. He seemed to be evolving a double standard,
expecting his listeners to accept the admonitions they received but demonstrating little forbearance himself in the face of public criticism. Some of his
friends and acquaintances probably shrugged and joked about Knox being
Knox, but others would have found this forthright speech a major barrier to
working alongside him. Abrasive leaders who do not suffer disagreements tend
to be surrounded by those whose job is damage limitation. John Craig was probably kept busy pouring oil on troubled water within Edinburgh, and the superintendents, such as Spottiswood, Erskine of Dun and Winram, can occasionally
be glimpsed soothing the recipients of some of Knox's sharper observations or
calming a tense situation at court.

Within a pastoral setting Knox constantly emphasized that discipline was
primarily concerned with repentance and ultimately reconciliation. In the
broader social and political context, discipline was presented as upholding the
laws of God, and the emphasis rested upon enforcement and punishment. Both
understandings were necessary, but Knox's experience of conflict and criticism
pushed him further towards a pessimistic legalism. It encouraged the besieged
mentality of treating those who did not support him as enemies to be attacked
or punished, rather than forgiven and reconciled.

My Meg

On occasions duties given by the General Assembly sent Knox away from the
capital and gave him the freedom of the roving preaching role he missed. In the
summer of 1562 he left Edinburgh, probably with relief, to fulfil his commission
from the Assembly to visit parts of Ayrshire and Galloway. Roman Catholics

such as Ninian Winzet and René Benoit were urging him to debate in the capital, something Knox always managed to sidestep. Instead, he relished the chance to spend time in the company of his ardent supporters, especially the 'brethren of Kyle' who had been part of the original backbone of Protestant support in the 1550s. Since his visit during the 1555–6 preaching tour he had felt at home in Ayr and its environs, especially when staying with close friends such as Robert Campbell of Kinzeancleuch and his wife, Elizabeth Campbell. Queen Mary's arrival had made no difference to Robert's Protestant commitment and he had tartly observed how 'the holy water of the court' had quenched the heat in other Protestants' anger against idolatry.[45] Knox knew he could rely upon the godly zeal of the 'gentlemen of Kyle' and the Earl of Glencairn 'not to suffer the enemies of God's truth to have the upper hand'.[46] He incited them to organize within Ayrshire against the regional power of the Earl of Cassillis, his Kennedy relations and the Roman Catholic enclave that surrounded the Earl's uncle, Quintin Kennedy, Abbot of Crossraguel, identified in the first General Assembly as upholders of the Mass. Rumours of a meeting in Paisley between the Abbot and the Archbishop of St Andrews increased the level of concern and, on 4 September in Ayr, a great gathering of Protestant supporters signed a religious band to give their full backing to preaching and the preachers and all other members of the Congregation. With a nostalgic twinge, Knox might have felt he was back once more with his brethren as it had been in the early days of the Wars of the Congregation.

Quintin Kennedy had been vigorously defending Roman Catholic doctrine since 1558 and in a series of treatises had provided a coherent and careful explanation of Catholic eucharistic theology.[47] He had paid particular attention to refuting Knox's views on the Mass, especially the syllogism defining idolatry first used in 1550.[48] He had challenged Knox to refute his writings and John Davidson and George Hay had taken up their pens to reply to him, though their works were not yet in print at the time Knox travelled west. In his final tract, *Ane Compendious Reasoning*, Kennedy had challenged Knox and seven other leading Protestants by name, giving each individual a topic to debate alongside a humorous quip or pun about them. His list began with Knox and his ministerial vocation, with Kennedy pointedly addressing him by his former title of a Catholic priest, 'Schir Johne Knox'. Kennedy joked that Knox was a high priest, not according to the order of Melchizedek as in Roman Catholic tradition, but according to 'the order of Calvin'. The Abbot wanted his opponent to debate priesthood in general and in particular to discuss the oblation made by the Old Testament priest Melchizedek that had formed part of Kennedy's defence of the Mass.[49] Within late medieval Christianity the discussion about Christ being a high priest according to the order of

Melchizedek in Hebrews 7 was well known both as a theological concept and in visual representations in contemporary paintings.[50]

In a curious decision, the General Assembly had sent George Hay as Commissioner to Carrick, the part of Ayrshire dominated by the Kennedys, at the same time as Knox was sent to neighbouring Nithsdale and Galloway. This did not prevent Knox tangling with Kennedy. Accompanied by a considerable following, he appeared unannounced at Kirkoswald church to challenge Kennedy on the content of his sermon the previous Sunday. The Abbot was not willing to be bounced into debate by such tactics. He wrote instead suggesting an academic disputation the following week in front of a restricted audience. A flurry of tetchy letters followed, sorting out the arrangements and the role of the Earl of Cassilis, Kennedy's nephew. The debate was held over three days at the end of September in Maybole, the adjoining parish to Kirkoswald, within the Provost's house. As the company assembled at 8 o'clock on the first morning, Knox grabbed the initiative by launching into a long, public prayer and could not be interrupted. The debate that followed contained a mixture of spoken and written elements and focused on the original story in Genesis of Melchizedek meeting Abraham. In particular, the argument turned on the phrase 'brought forward bread and wine' and whether this implied that Melchizedek made an offering or sacrifice to God. Kennedy carefully rested his arguments upon biblical interpretation and so took the fight to the Protestants on their own ground of Scripture as the sole authority. After much sparring over technical points, the debate became deadlocked. Kennedy was not in good health and he had to stop from time to time. On the third day the debate was postponed because local provisions for men and horses had been exhausted. Kennedy had promised to complete the debate in Edinburgh in front of the Queen, but due to his illness there was no further reasoning. He did take part in the defiant open celebration of the Easter Mass in Ayrshire in 1563 but died in the following year.[51]

Kennedy's supporters asserted that he had won the debate with Knox and were looking for a 'wolter' or upset and overturning of the religious situation.[52] To counter any such impression, Knox published the records of the Maybole disputation and added a prologue full of mockery about the Mass.[53] The hard-edged tone was part of his normal desire to flatten an opponent in a public fight, though it possibly also reflected unease about exactly how well he had done. A more ruthless Protestant policy emerged in the polemical works published in 1563 and 1564. Roman Catholics were denied access to Scottish printers and a chilling biblical verse was printed in the Protestant tracts and in Knox's account of the Maybole disputation. It encapsulated the newly aggressive attitude: 'Everie plant which mine heavenlie Father hathe not planted shalbe rooted up.'[54] Even in Knox's safe haven of Ayrshire there was an embat-tled feeling. When Mary, Queen of Scots, came on progress in the summer of 1563, bringing the celebration of her private Mass, Knox described its delete-rious effect to Cecil, in 'those quarters which longest have bein best reformed hath so dejected the hartes of many, that men appear not to have the coraige thei had befor'.[55]

Quick to seize upon the darker implications of each event, these small signs confirmed Knox's fears about the fragility of what had been achieved in 1560 and the assumption that more battles were round the corner. He employed the daily prayers inserted into the *Book of Common Order* to highlight the danger. In the thanksgiving at table the prayer also sought deliverance from idolatry, preservation from tyranny and the continuation of quiet and concord 'for a season'. When challenged to explain why he had prayed for quiet for only a limited time, Knox retorted that there could not be permanent peace when idolatry was permitted to return where once it had been suppressed.[56]

There had been a lighter note to Knox's visit to Ayrshire. He had spent some time at the home of his great friend the modest and peace-loving Andrew Stewart, second Lord Ochiltree.[57] At Ochiltree, Knox became better acquainted with Margaret, the daughter of the house, and probably started the courtship of his second wife. He married Margaret in the spring of 1564 when she was seventeen and he about fifty. Large age gaps in second marriages were not uncommon during this period because older men often sought wives among women of child-bearing age. To sixteenth-century observers it was the social gap between the couple that was more shocking than the age difference. It especially incensed the Queen because Margaret Stewart's royal connections meant she was 'of the bludde and name'. Mary, Queen of Scots, had angrily declared that Knox would not remain in Scotland, though Randolph wryly observed, 'ther wilbe myche a doe before he leave yt. In thys, I wyshe that he had done otherwise.'[58] Knox came to rely heavily upon 'My Meg'.[59] As well as being the mother of their three daughters, Martha, Margaret and Elizabeth, she became his secretary, companion and latterly his nurse. Marital kinship further increased his contacts with Ayrshire, where the radical and uncompro-mising Protestantism of the faithful brethren flourished.

Knox brought his second wife back to the capital where as a noblewoman she could mix easily with the court and the burgh's elite. She appears to have been a good household manager and hostess and probably attracted a wider range of friends and visitors to the family home. In his *History* Knox provided remarkably little comment or detail about his Edinburgh friends and allies. Similarly, his surviving correspondence offers few clues since sixteenth-century people did not normally write letters to those living in the same burgh. A tantalizing glimpse of Meg's influence can perhaps be viewed in records of the neighbouring parish of the Canongate in October 1564. A John Knox, probably the preacher, was witness for the baptism of Margaret, the daughter of William Robesoun.[60] With the baby sharing her name, it is probable that Knox's wife had also been acting as a godmother or witness. The Robesouns were a prominent Edinburgh family, with John serving as a notary and William was probably the Edinburgh butcher who was Deacon of his craft in 1557–8 and 1570–1.[61] These hints of otherwise unknown relationships suggest that much of what the Knoxes did in Edinburgh and the networks they created have disappeared from historical sight because no evidence has survived.

Within the burgh there were many different views of Knox. For Edinburgh Council, Knox was a successful celebrity preacher, though on occasions the content and tone of his sermons brought them trouble. For those outside his line of fire, the sermons provided weekly edification or entertainment and endless talking points, and his thundering reached legendary status. For those hit by his admonitions or thunderbolts, the sermons brought fear or consolation. However, a number of the citizens of Edinburgh did not hear him preach or did not care. During Knox's time as minister, the majority of the adult population did not participate in the Lord's Supper, and his success in 'converting' the burgh from Catholic to Protestant beliefs is hard to assess with such limited evidence. Much of the daily pastoral work and provision of worship was undertaken by his fellow minister, John Craig, and the Reader, John Cairns. As with his other congregations, Knox's pastoral attention appeared to be focused upon the groups of religiously committed. In his more general dealings and involvement in the public and political life of the burgh, he found it hard to move outside the groups who supported him or seek alliances with a broad spectrum of Edinburgh's elite. On many levels, he struggled to embrace the whole of his parish in a territorial ministry serving an entire community. He believed with his head that the Scottish Kirk encompassed the whole kingdom and every parish was a microcosm of that ideal of the people of God. His heart told a different story, and led him back to the comfort provided by the faithful few who shared his uncompromising zeal.

CHAPTER FIFTEEN

What have you to do with my marriage?

During the first few years of Mary, Queen of Scots' personal rule, none of Knox's dire predications were fulfilled about the consequences of welcoming a Catholic Queen and permitting her to attend her private Mass. The Queen's closest advisers were Protestants intent upon an alliance with England and Mary was pursuing a conciliatory religious policy that permitted the Reformed Kirk to establish itself.

Mary's Protestant half-brother Lord James had been created Earl of Moray and was in high favour alongside the Secretary, William Maitland of Lethington, and the Earl of Argyll. In national politics Knox found himself relegated to the sidelines. His sense of being a lone prophetic voice blinded him to the possibility of gathering allies within Edinburgh and creating an alternative party to support his cause.

LOVE GOD ABOVE ALL AND THY NEIGHBOUR AS THYSELF

As the capital, Edinburgh was subject to far greater scrutiny and control from the Crown over its affairs than other Scottish burghs. During the see-saw period of the Wars of the Congregation, the coups and rapid change of councils severely complicated political alignments within the city. Once Queen Mary had returned, the Council needed to steer a course between working with the royal administration and defending its independence and its privileges. To Knox such a policy smacked of political accommodation and he was inclined to judge all actions in terms of such moral absolutes. He had a habit of shooting first and asking searching questions later. He found it particularly difficult to resist the compulsion to issue his verdict and was especially prone to jump to conclusions concerning the motivations of others. If their actions did not follow the course he had laid out, he assumed that the motivation was a base one, springing from self-advancement, greed or lack of zeal. In addition to his high-profile rows with leading politicians, in his *History* Knox pronounced a series of dismissive verdicts, many of which he would have voiced in Edinburgh. In 1562, John Shairp decided to pursue a legal career, though he had been designated as 'fit' for the Protestant ministry in the first General Assembly of 1560. Knox was quick to criticize him for becoming an advocate: 'some ministers, such as Master John Shairp, had left their charges and entered into other vocations more profitable for the belly'.[1] Among Shairp's legal colleagues in Edinburgh were a number of convinced Protestants, though Knox missed an opportunity to exploit their unified support. If the preacher had assiduously cultivated this professional group, he might have achieved a firmer foundation for operations within the capital. Protestant lawyers had played a part in the success of the Reformation in other European cities and in the following decade the legal profession provided significant help to the King's Party. Some Edinburgh lawyers like the zealous Protestant Town Clerk, Alexander Guthrie, were willing to take radical actions to attack the enemies of the Kirk or to gain greater Protestant control.

Another lawyer who served the Edinburgh Kirk as an elder and was a regular commissioner to the General Assembly was Clement Litill, a convinced and well-read Protestant. Knox's bitter opposition to Litill's Catholic patron and friend, the Lord President of the Court of Session, Henry Sinclair, might have kept Litill and the preacher at a distance. Despite his own notarial training, Knox had a cavalier attitude towards correct legal forms, though in the 1558 *Appellation* he was happy to exploit them because it suited him. He had been particularly angry with the brothers Henry and John Sinclair, Catholic clerics serving in the Court of Session, and much of the Edinburgh legal establishment when they had raised doubts about the constitutional legality of the acts passed by the 1560 Reformation Parliament. In 1563 when the next Parliament was called, Knox was among those agitating strongly for a full legal settlement of the religious question, while at the same time declaring that the Protestant faith had already been legally established. With Litill and Knox keenly interested in the latest Protestant theology it would have been possible for a closer relationship to develop between them, especially after Henry Sinclair's death in 1565. As a commissary on the new Consistory Court of Edinburgh created in 1564, Litill was involved in the regularization of Scottish Protestant divorce and would probably have discussed the issue with Knox. The preacher might later have given Litill two books on the subject he had received hot from the press with a courteous covering note from Theodore Beza, his Genevan friend.[2]

Knox seemed ill at ease operating among the committees and male power networks of public life. However, he was more successful influencing people through the small coventicle-style meetings that possessed a large female component. The wives of members of the 'militant tendency' within the Edinburgh Kirk often supplied the crucial link with him. Guthrie's wife, Janet Henderson, was one of Knox's 'sisters' to whom he had written when in exile.[3] As had happened in his previous congregations, he made firm friendships with women who had sought his spiritual guidance. His Edinburgh 'sisters' gave him an advocate within the households of some of the merchants, lawyers and craftsmen and helped ensure that their husbands were firm Knox supporters. This placed the preacher at one remove and Knox does not appear to have attempted to organize or channel this support.

If Edinburgh's minister had mounted such a charm offensive, he might have started close to home. One of Knox's near neighbours living in a fine house on the north side of High Street near the Netherbow was James Mossman, a prominent goldsmith, and his wife, Mariota Arres. The couple had redesigned and redecorated their house at the end of the 1550s, proudly displaying on the exterior their initials and coat of arms and a prominent biblical motto. They chose to carve Christ's summary of the law along the front of their house, 'Luve God abuve al and yi nychtbor as yersel'.[4] Beneath a finely carved sundial a figure of Moses was shown receiving the law on Mount Sinai and looking at the sun, with the name of God carved in Greek, Latin and English. These biblical motifs were carefully integrated into the classical themes and decoration in the Doric pilasters of the first-floor window, or the garlands and urns displaying a French Renaissance style similar to work of the same date at Holyrood Palace. In 1561 to celebrate the Queen's return to Scotland, the Mossmans added a splendid interior panel with a lion rampant. Being craftsmen of the highest order, the Mossman family were prepared to pay for the best work for their home. Knox would frequently have walked past the impressive frontage and seen the goods displayed in the open booths of Mossman's jewellery shop. The house proclaimed Mossman's core values, loyalty to the Crown and a strong Christian humanism that valued civic virtues such as respect for the law, moral discipline, literature and learning. The Mossman family were representative of the merchant and craft elite who ran Edinburgh. They were steeped in the attitudes of civic and Christian humanism, and patronized artists and writers like the Bannatyne and Bellenden family grouping of lawyers and royal administrators based in the capital.[5]

Moses receiving the law was one of Knox's favourite biblical images and should have given him plenty of common ground with James Mossman and other members of Edinburgh's ruling elite. However, his unwillingness to compromise, his strident tone and particularly his direct attacks upon Mary, Queen of Scots, and her court made it hard for him to gather support from individuals such as James Mossman. During the civil wars James emerged as a prominent Queen's Man and used his talent to mint coins for the Queen's Party, a decision that led to his execution for treason.[6] Deep rifts emerged in those civil wars among Edinburgh's leading families and their politics, with James' younger brother, John, becoming a King's Man. James' craftsmanship in silver was employed to make for Rosneath the first Protestant communion cup that has survived. Before that fracturing caused by the civil wars, a more tactful minister than Knox might have been able to attract both brothers to his cause. By harnessing the biblical humanism and desire for moral and social order present among Edinburgh's elite, he could have drawn together a broad base of support. Today tourists gaze at the fine frontage built and decorated by the Mossmans and, in an ironical twist, assume that this was what Knox chose for the house that now bears his name.

A SUBJECT BORN WITHIN THE COMMONWEALTH

The effect of Knox's abrasive style was most noticeable in his dealings with the Protestant nobility and in particular in his relationship with the Earl of Moray. Since the Queen's return their friendship had been under considerable strain, and after a serious disagreement the two men stopped speaking for eighteen months; 'neither by word nor write' was there any communication between them.[7] The final break in 1563 had been provoked at the first Parliament of Mary's personal rule. A full legal settlement for the new Kirk did not appear on the parliamentary agenda, as Moray had earlier assured Knox it would. The preacher regarded the omission as additional proof of the loss of religious commitment among those who had been the chief Lords of the Congregation. He deduced that Moray had been corrupted by his half-sister and had become so involved in his private concerns that he was failing to give the Queen good counsel or the Kirk the support it needed. In his *First Blast*, Knox had warned that female rule would weaken a queen's royal counsellors because men, who should be taking command, would become increasingly sycophantic and unable to withstand the wishes of the monarch. A regnant queen was thus deeply subversive of the natural order, upsetting the gender roles that held society together and undermining the exercise of authority.

Another serious concern voiced in the *First Blast* focused upon a regnant queen's choice of husband. If the queen followed the 'natural' pattern of wifely subjection to her husband, this would place her kingdom at his mercy. When the husband was a foreigner, he would introduce his own countrymen and it was likely the kingdom would be absorbed into his own territories or, at best, exploited for his own ends. Knox assumed that Scots understood such dangers because following Mary's first marriage they had experienced what it was like to live in Franco-Scotland. In 1563 he gave specific and dramatic warnings in a sermon attacking the possibility of a Spanish match for Mary. This was the setting for his final stormy interview with the Queen and heightened the tension between the preacher and her counsellors.

After Knox's initial unsuccessful meeting with the Queen in 1561, their three subsequent interviews had brought nothing to change his mind. In the dialogues he recorded, he continued to place the main emphasis upon justifications for his own words and actions and gave little coverage to what was said by Mary, Queen of Scots. In the second and third meeting the exchanges remained polite and edged towards civilized behaviour as Knox ended the third meeting with what, for him, was a gracious farewell. Thanking the Queen for enforcing the law against the public celebration of Mass that had taken place in Ayrshire at Easter in 1563, he assured Mary 'that ye shall please God, and enjoy rest and tranquillity within your Realm; which to your Majesty is more profitable than all the Pope's power can be'.[8]

In his narrations of the royal interviews, Knox did not highlight the remarkable fact that, once away from contentious matters, he co-operated perfectly amicably with the Queen. On a matter of mutual concern, he and Mary were happy to join forces, and they briefly worked as a most unlikely pair of marriage guidance counsellors. They were both concerned by the breakdown in the marriage between the Earl and Countess of Argyll. Before Mary's return to Scotland, Knox had reconciled the couple and had not heard of further problems until the Queen requested his help. The task of restoring marital relations between the Argylls was divided between them, with Mary speaking to her half-sister, Countess Jane, while Knox tackled the Earl. The sharp and forceful letter Knox wrote to Argyll produced a change in the Earl's behaviour. It was probably inserted in his *History* to prove the inclusiveness of discipline, with those of the highest social rank also being rebuked for their sins. The Queen's intervention was private, though it involved a warning to the Countess of a withdrawal of royal favour if she did not co-operate. By these means the marriage was held together for several more years, though eventually the Earl and Countess were divorced.[9] As this co-operation demonstrated, provided there was no religious element it was possible for Knox and the Queen to work together. On Mary's side there was also a willingness to listen to Knox on religious subjects, and she offered him the opportunity to become a personal religious adviser. He was extremely wary of 'private' conferences and refused point blank to accept any such position at court. As well as the deep, and probably justified, suspicion that this was a plan to blunt his public criticism, such a role did not accord with Knox's self-understanding as a watchman of the Lord.

The conciliatory note on which their third meeting had ended was broken from the start of the Queen's final interview with Knox a couple of months later. In this encounter Mary lost the composure and civility she had maintained during their previous meetings. Knox had been summoned because he had preached upon the subject of Mary's marriage negotiations and the strong rumours circulating about a Spanish match during the 1563 Parliament. The prospect of a union between Don Carlos, the heir to Philip II of Spain, was for Knox the worst of all possible matches. He assured his hearers that the Cardinal of Lorraine had already provisionally agreed to the proposal and told the Scottish nobility that they were enemies to God if they agreed to this marriage.[10] A Spanish match had a horrible aura of familiarity for Knox and it was the final piece of the pattern he had traced in English affairs during the reign of Mary Tudor. He remembered only too well that a regnant Catholic Queen first reintroduced the Mass and polluted the realm with idolatry, then married the Catholic heir to the Spanish throne leading to the full-scale persecution of Protestants and the suppression of their faith. Having walked each step of that path ten years earlier, Knox was determined to proclaim an unambiguous warning that action had to be taken now before it was too late for Scotland.

He began his sermon with a highly emotional appeal to the times of the Wars of the Congregation when together the Protestants had faced desperate days and yet kept their trust in God and final victory. He instructed his listeners to hold fast to God's cause whether or not the Queen agreed. Echoing his 1558 tracts, he asserted, 'Ask ye of her that which by God's word ye may justly require, and if she will not agree with you in God, ye are not bound to agree with her in the Devil.'[11] His main admonition was reserved for the prospect of Mary's marriage: if the nobility agreed to a Catholic husband 'ye do so far as in ye lieth to banish Christ Jesus from this Realm; ye bring God's vengeance upon the country, a plague upon yourself, and perchance ye shall do small comfort to your Sovereign'.[12] Protestants and Catholics alike were outraged by his sermon. Some of his closest friends were angry with him and it was a Protestant, Robert Douglas of Drumlanrig, Provost of Lincluden, who laid charges against him.

The Queen was furious that Knox had assumed the right to dictate whom she might marry. When she demanded, 'What have ye to do with my marriage?', Knox launched into a discourse about the role and duties of a preacher and why he had refused in an earlier interview to act as the Queen's private religious adviser. To Mary this gave no answer at all and was completely off the point. A second time she repeated her question and then demanded to know what role Knox had in the Commonwealth. He produced his famous riposte, 'A subject born within the same, Madam. And ... a profitable member within the same,' and reiterated that his prophetic duty was 'to forewarn of such things as may hurt it, if I foresee them . . . for both my vocation and conscience crave plainness of me'. When he recapitulated the central message of his sermon, the Queen wept angry tears and stormed at him.[13] While John Erskine of Dun attempted to repair the situation, Knox kept his mouth shut and stood with a neutral expression, though he made a bad situation worse when he attempted an apology. He was dismissed to the outer presence chamber where the only person prepared to talk to him was his father-in-law, Lord Ochiltree. The preacher did not improve the occasion by attempting some 'merry quips' with the Queen's ladies sitting there. Having remarked upon their court finery, he could not resist adding the moralizing point that when Death came neither beauty nor the latest fashion and jewellery could be taken on that journey. It probably caused some amusement later at his expense as his crass remarks were relayed among the royal household. In his *History*, Knox seemed blissfully unaware of how his attempts at light-hearted chat might be received. Fortunately for him, while he had been passing the time of day with the ladies-in-waiting in the outer chamber, Erskine of Dun and Lord John of Coldingham had persuaded the Queen not to press legal charges against him. She was more lenient than Queen Elizabeth, who reacted extremely badly to any public discussion of her potential marriages, and the unfortunate John Stubbs lost his right hand for putting his views into print.

Few doubted it was in Scotland's, as well as in Mary's, best interests for her to remarry and produce an heir. Since the Queen's return, Moray and Lethington had persuaded her that her marriage was the trump card in the negotiations with Queen Elizabeth over recognition as the heir to the English throne. By 1564 the Scottish Queen and her counsellors were pressing Elizabeth to name an acceptable suitor for Mary. Moray and Lethington expected the subsequent marriage alliance to achieve their goal of a lasting concord between the realms of England and Scotland and to secure the position of the Scottish Kirk, the two objectives for which they had fought the Wars of the Congregation They also hoped the marriage would lead to Mary's conversion to Protestantism. Knox's outbursts were doubly unfortunate because the Protestant leaders shared with him the aim of amity with England and the ultimate goal of a united Protestant British Isles. From their perspective, his constant harangues and repeated attacks upon the Queen only made their task harder. Little common ground seemed to remain with him when he routinely prayed in St Giles' about the impiety of the realm because 'the most part, alas! following the footesteps of the blynde and obstinate Princesse, utterly despise the light of thyne Evangel, and delyte in ignorance and idolatrie'.[14]

An additional irritation for Moray and Lethington was that with his extensive news-gathering network Knox was exceptionally well informed about political and diplomatic happenings. He regularly received updates from

England, France and Flanders and sometimes heard from his contacts before news arrived through official channels. Thomas Randolph, the English Ambassador, benefited from Knox's intelligence network and was himself one of his informants. The two men normally discussed affairs face to face in Edinburgh, frequently taking dinner together in Knox's manse, Randolph's lodgings or the house of one of the Anglophile burgh councillors, such as Alexander Guthrie. A great deal of this information concerned sensitive negotiations that the royal counsellors would have preferred to remain confidential. However, if Knox decided there was a threat to Scottish Protestantism, he did not hesitate to broadcast his fears via the pulpit, as he had over the rumours of a Spanish match. His desire to 'publish in the public interest' was radically different from the perspective of Lethington, a diplomat to his fingertips. Though willing to exploit Knox's pro-English stance for his diplomatic mission, Randolph also worried that the preacher might ruin delicate negotiations by proclaiming sensitive information to the world.

Broadcasting via an open letter to the Protestant 'brethren' brought Knox a summons to appear before the Privy Council to investigate whether such a letter constituted an illegal convocation of the Queen's subjects and, therefore, treason.[15] On 15 August 1563, during one of the Queen's absences from Holyrood, Edinburgh Roman Catholics attended the Mass that was held in the Chapel Royal. This was regarded as especially provocative because the Lord's Supper was being administered on the same day in St Giles'. Egged on by Knox, Protestant stalwarts, sent to note the names of those who attended, burst into the chapel to stop the Mass. In the scuffles that followed, the Queen's frightened French ladies had the presence of mind to send for the royal Comptroller, Sir John Wishart of Pittarrow, who was receiving communion in St Giles'. He arrived with Edinburgh's Provost and burgh officers to restore order at Holyrood. As a result two burghers, Patrick Cranstoun and Andrew Armstrong, were charged with breaking into the palace. They were well known to Knox, who fully supported their action in attacking the celebration of Mass. He decided to use the day of their appearance in court as an opportunity for a Protestant show of strength. On 8 October he wrote a circular letter to the 'brethren' with a great rallying call about withstanding the reintroduction of the Mass and opposing violence against ministers, citing an injury received by Robert Pont, one of his colleagues. Deliberately invoking the 'public promise and solemn band' that many Protestants had made, most recently in the Ayr band of 1562, Knox called for supporters to converge on Edinburgh on 24 October, the date fixed for the trial of Cranstoun and Armstrong.

A number of moderate Protestants judged Knox's communication to have overstepped the mark and they took the initiative in reporting the letter to the legal authorities. From there it progressed to the Queen and Council. When advised by fellow Protestants that the Queen was angry and an apology would be in order, Knox predictably and adamantly refused. His argument on the matter with the Master of Maxwell, a Protestant noble from the western Borders, was sufficiently bitter for them to become permanently estranged. Knox was similarly defiant and abrasive when visited by Lethington and Moray. The Earl stayed behind to speak further and attempted to re-establish their relationship, but Knox was dismissive and would make no reciprocal gesture of reconciliation. Knox turned his own summons before the Council into a 'day of law' and was accompanied to Holyrood between six and seven in the evening by a considerable body of 'assisters' who crowded into the courtyard. Thanks to his own legal training reinforced by the opinion of John Spens, the royal Advocate, Knox knew that his letter was not technically treasonable. He was fortunate his enemies, especially the chief legal officer, Henry Sinclair, the Lord President, were sufficiently upright that they were prepared to defend this legal point, even at the cost of royal displeasure. Proudly admitting authorship of the letter, Knox declared he had written it at the command of the national Kirk. He then deliberately embarrassed the lords sitting at the Council board by reminding them that during the Wars of the Congregation they had made no objection to his summons to the people to fight on behalf of Protestantism and against the French. Knox launched into a succinct exposition of his belief in a grand Catholic conspiracy to destroy Protestantism and exterminate Protestants. Having been reminded by the Queen that he had made her weep, Knox took the cue to summarize that interview and his warning that the nobility were enemies of God if they consented to a match with a foreign Catholic prince. Despite Lethington's attempt to steer the Council into a guilty verdict and the unusual demand for a second vote, the Council absolved Knox. He raised the issue at the next General Assembly, seeking retrospective justification and threatening to resign if he had exceeded his remit. After a long debate, the Assembly did back Knox, but would not personalize the duty of sending warnings, seeing it rather as a function of all ministers. This subtly downgraded Knox's emphasis upon the prophetic character of his warnings and his special role in the capital to keep watch upon national events. Despite the existence of written minutes, he was not simply checking the record when he appealed directly to the memory of those present and revealed that his purpose was in fact personal vindication.

KEEP THEIR LAND CLEAR AND UNPOLLUTED

Nothing daunted by his brush with the Privy Council, Knox continued to employ his prayers for the Queen as a form of offensive weapon. During the

General Assembly in June 1564, Maitland of Lethington challenged him on the subject: 'moderate yourself, as well in form of praying for the Queen's Majesty, as in doctrine that ye propone touching her estate and obedience'.[16] Knox freely admitted that his normal prayer to God for Mary's conversion to Protestantism was conditional, 'if thy good pleasure be', and called for her deliverance from the bondage of Satan. He ended his prayer, 'that this poor Realm may also escape that plague and vengeance which inevitably follows idolatry, against thy manifest word and the open light therof'.[17] Lethington commented that he had never agreed with the implications of that final section, which contained Knox's repeated insistence that all Scotland was collectively responsible and therefore guilty of allowing the Queen's idolatry. As a consequence of this guilt, the entire community would suffer divine punishment because the covenant had been broken. This was the cornerstone of Knox's view of Scotland as a newly covenanted nation: when it had adopted the Protestant faith the kingdom publicly entered into a covenant with God to become his people, 'suppress all kind of open idolatry and ... keep their land clear and unpolluted'. Like the Old Testament Jews when they entered the Promised Land, the Scots had received the same commandment to be a 'holy people unto the Lord thy God'.[18] Knox developed the parallelism between the deliverance of the Jews from Egypt and the Scots from the tyranny of the Catholic Church and French rule. Being a covenanted people, the Scots had agreed to obey the laws of God, including the commandment 'The idolater shall die the death.' That law needed to be enforced without respect of persons, and Knox asserted, 'to me it remains a constant and clean commandment to all the people professing God and having the power to punish vice'.[19]

As usual, Lethington identified the crucial question: who might punish rulers if they were idolaters? The previous day Knox had preached upon Romans 13, the proof text for political obedience, and had endorsed the right of resistance when rulers commanded unlawful things.[20] This was a considerable advance on the statements he had made in his 1558 tracts, and he expounded the ideas further during the debate with Lethington. He had come wholeheartedly to adopt many of Goodman's theories and accepted the sharp distinction between obedience due to political authority and obeying the particular person who held that authority. He also accepted Goodman's reasoning about the rights and duties of a covenanted people of God. By these means Knox waved aside the difference between a persecuting Catholic Queen and one who privately practised her own religion. He demanded that Mary's Mass should be forcibly removed, thereby extending his resistance theories to justify direct regulation of royal religious policy. That major conflation alarmed many fellow ministers and they were not prepared to endorse all of his conclusions.

WHAT HAVE YOU TO DO WITH MY MARRIAGE?

For Moray and Lethington the marriage negotiations with Spain had offered a lever to pressurize Queen Elizabeth into being specific about her wishes over Mary's marriage. Eventually, in March 1564 London sent the name of Lord Robert Dudley, created Earl of Leicester to guarantee his aristocratic status. The identity of the suitor raised plenty of eyebrows in Scotland since the courts of Europe had been gossiping for years about Dudley being Elizabeth's lover. Knox supported the proposal while remaining studiously silent about any possible scandal attaching to Leicester. He had known the Duke of Northumberland's younger son in Edward VI's reign and in 1563 had written a deferential letter to him urging him to continue to 'advance the puritie of religion' and particularly to help the 'true preachers' within England.[21] A couple of months after Dudley's candidature had been proposed, Knox picked up news that the Earl of Lennox had been negotiating to end his long-term exile and some reports were suggesting the Countess and their son would come to Scotland before long. In his letter to Randolph, Knox commented 'that jorney and progress I lyke not' and added he had heard a whisper that Lennox's permission to return had already been granted.

In his letter Knox had also made an enigmatic reference to the 'salt man' who had despatched well-equipped workers and would be sending more to manufacture salt upon salt (producing top-quality refined white salt). Although its precise meaning is now lost, this was probably a reference to a more secret Catholic threat. Knox had already relayed to Randolph rumours flying around the Edinburgh markets that the Mass would be restored, that the Archbishop of Glasgow and Abbot of Dunfermline would arrive as ambassadors from the Council of Trent, that the Earl of Bothwell would return to act as the Queen's enforcer, and 'then shall Knox and his preaching be pulled by the earis'. 'Maddye', the fictitious female character personifying market gossip, was exclaiming every day on these subjects, but Knox declared he was not worried.[22] However, Randolph decided that the news was important enough to be relayed directly to Queen Elizabeth and with his report enclosed Knox's letter, along with another from Kirkcaldy of Grange. As it transpired, the intelligence about Lennox and his son proved accurate, while the rest of the predictions failed to materialize.

In September 1564, Lennox was permitted to return to his native land after his twenty-year exile and was restored to the lands and honours stripped from him during the Rough Wooings. His Countess, Margaret Douglas, was not permitted to accompany him to Scotland. Although she was a prominent Catholic and had been a close friend of Queen Mary Tudor, Lennox had conformed to the Elizabethan Church of England and was willing to attend St Giles' and listen to Knox's sermons. Lennox's sustained charm offensive at the

Scottish court obtained permission for his son, Lord Darnley, to join him the following February. With remarkable speed, about a month later Mary, Queen of Scots, had decided she would marry her cousin. More significant than Darnley's height and boyish good looks, this decision was probably provoked by an unusually clumsy and blunt letter from Queen Elizabeth refusing to settle the English succession until she herself married or chose not to do so. At a stroke the English Queen had destroyed the careful Anglophile policy Moray and Lethington had constructed since Mary's return to Scotland.[23]

THE BOYS SERVED HIM WITH HIS EASTER EGGS

The Queen's determination to marry Lord Darnley destabilized Scottish politics and increased fear and speculation, especially among her Protestant subjects. In the spring of 1565 the 'brethren of Kyle' heard rumours that the Roman Catholics were planning a demonstration by celebrating Masses at Easter, as they had done in the shire in 1563. Using the old networks developed in the 1550s they sent letters to Dundee, Angus and the Mearns, Fife and Edinburgh. This provoked a major incident in Edinburgh and showed how Protestant direct action within the capital could provoke a serious backlash and fuel a Catholic revival. Having been tipped off by their Ayrshire brethren, Edinburgh's Protestants were on the prowl during the Easter period for signs of the celebration of Mass. Riding away after completing the Mass, a priest and his two assistants were recognized, chased and caught. James Tarbot, the priest, was seized and taken to the Tolbooth to be charged with breaking the law against celebrating Mass. At this point Protestant vigilantes intervened and dressed Tarbot in his Mass vestments, tied the chalice to his hands and him to the Market Cross in the middle of High Street. They then encouraged young boys to pelt the priest with eggs and other missiles. The following day, this time properly accompanied by the burgh hangman, Tarbot was sentenced to stand at the Market Cross in the branks or pillory. When a large group of Catholic craftsmen attempted to rescue the priest, fighting started between the rival parties. The Provost and the burgh's guard had to intervene to get the priest safely back to the Tolbooth prison and try to calm the situation. Reports of the full-scale riot on the streets of the capital were relayed to Stirling where the Queen was holding court. Given the extremely tense political situation over the forthcoming Darnley marriage, rumours flew around Edinburgh of armed contingents being despatched to restore order. Instead the Lord Advocate carried out an investigation, the Burgh Council received a severe reprimand for permitting vigilantes to undermine the law and the priest was released several days later. In his *History*, Knox blackened the priest's reputation and attempted to pass off the egg-throwing incident as a prank by a group of boys who had 'served him with his Easter eggs'.[24]

On the one hand, Knox's words applauded direct action, and on the other hand, he stood back from it. His violent rhetoric encouraged such aggression, though with little planning or forethought about the consequences. In this instance a large number of Catholic supporters took to the streets to fight Protestant intimidation and deliberate provocation. Edinburgh came close to the violent confrontations that had been common within French cities before the start of the religious wars. Knox did not seem to be in control of what was happening among Protestant radicals in Edinburgh or to have any clear plan of action. Some of his friends and Edinburgh supporters, such as Alexander 'King' Guthrie, were operating independently of him and pursuing their own agenda within the arena of burgh politics.[25]

BE MERCIFUL TO THY FLOCK, O LORD

Though for the wrong reasons, Knox had been proved right in his gloomy predictions about Moray's political future. The Darnley marriage had driven the Queen's brother into the political wilderness. His dramatic fall, the rise to political power of the Lennox Stewarts, combined with Elizabeth's open disapproval of the proposed marriage, left Anglo-Scottish friendship in tatters and split the Protestant, Anglophile consensus that had dominated Scottish politics since 1560. As sincere Protestants, Moray and his close ally Argyll worried about the repercussions for their faith of the Darnley marriage and raised the cry of 'the Kirk in danger'. The Earls' sudden call for militant action met with a mixed response from their co-religionists because they had been hearing for years from Knox that the courtiers were betraying the Protestant cause. The gap between the preacher and the Protestant magnates was not easily bridged. Hopes of reassembling the coalition that had won the Wars of the Congregation were not realized, and the Scottish Protestants were divided and confused. Crucially, Knox did not lend his voice to urge military action nor did he take any obvious lead in organizing the opposition. Despite his exceptionally confident assertions in 1564 of the rights and duties of resistance to a ruler, a year later he was not a recruiting sergeant for rebellion. He remained in the capital preaching at St Giles' when the lords were pushed into open defiance in the summer of 1565 and were joined by his father-in-law, Lord Ochiltree.

Knox's sermon on 19 August made Darnley so 'crabbit' the King could not eat his dinner. When the irate man stormed off to go hawking before ensuring that Knox was 'dischargit from preaching', the position was left unresolved. Amid the 'terrible roring of gunnes and the noyce of armour', at the end of August 1565

Knox broke with normal practice and wrote out the offending sermon for publication (see Plate 9).[26] Though his right to preach had been strongly supported by Edinburgh's Council, he had been banned from preaching when the King and Queen were resident in the capital and he had understood this as a form of discharge from his ministry at St Giles'.[27] With the royal couple gleefully pursuing the rebel lords across the country and driving them into exile, the King and Queen were rarely in Edinburgh during the next few months. An uneasy compromise was reached over Knox; he was not prosecuted but neither was he functioning properly as a minister, and he found himself in a curious limbo. After Edinburgh Castle's cannon had fired upon the rebel lords and they were forced to leave the burgh, Knox did not accompany them. Having given his support to Moray, Knox's close friend Goodman had to leave St Andrews and Scotland. Neither man could have known that this would be the last time Goodman would set foot on Scottish soil and that in future the friends would have to rely on letters to keep in touch. Goodman possibly carried the text of Knox's sermon with him and ensured it was published in London the following year, and in November he was preaching to the lords in their exile in Newcastle. While remaining in Edinburgh, Knox made no secret of his approval of the rebel lords and openly prayed for God to comfort them in their afflictions. Maitland of Lethington stoutly defended Knox's prayers and sermons before the King, Queen and Privy Council. Risking his own precarious political position, the Secretary demonstrated his integrity and considerable generosity towards the preacher who had been constantly abusing him as a 'clawback' of the court. Knox, who could never bring himself to trust Lethington, showed no signs of gratitude.[28]

During the second half of 1565 Knox was in poor health and had ended the written version of his August sermon with the prayer, 'Be mercifull to thy flocke, O Lorde! and at thy good pleasure put an end to my miserie.'[29] Word of his discharge from the Edinburgh ministry reached St Andrews and their commissioners requested the General Assembly to translate Knox to their parish church of Holy Trinity because Goodman had fled to England. Though the Assembly told St Andrews to find a replacement from its own university, it immediately appointed Knox as a Commissioner to the south of the country to preach and plant kirks 'so long as occasion might suffer'.[30] This had the appearance of a tactful posting to get Knox away from Edinburgh and out of further trouble. To keep him fully occupied, Knox was also given a more sedentary task. Alongside his colleague John Craig, the Assembly commissioned Knox to complete the form of service to be used for a national fast that could be printed and circulated through the country.[31]

Knox had turned exclusively to spiritual weapons when facing this latest round in the struggle against the forces of Satan. Until the preaching ban at the end of August, he had wielded the powerful sword of the Word of God with his normal routine of sermons packed full with warnings and admonitions. After the departure of the rebel lords into exile, he urged his fellow Protestants to arm themselves with prayer, fasting and repentance. He reassured them of the past efficacy of such 'spiritual weapons, to wit, earnest invocation of God's Name, by the which we finde the proude tyrannes of the earth, in tymes past, to have been overthrowen'.[32] The General Fast was devised as a new weapon for this fight and the *Order* written by Knox and Craig revealed how much had changed since the Wars of the Congregation. Just as in 1559, Knox called Protestants to stand up and be counted and fight under the banner of Christ. However, at the end of 1565, rather than inviting them to join the army of the Congregation, Knox's call was to band together in a public fast as a witness to the rest of the kingdom and as a demonstration of repentance and humiliation before God. The target audience had reverted to the 'faithful few' and Knox was primarily addressing the small group of committed Protestants rather than Scots in general.

An inherent tension within the *Order* reflected the contradictions within Knox's own mind. The Fast was a public ritual to be undertaken by the whole Kirk and yet the language and many of the assumptions within the *Order* addressed the 'faithful remnant'. They were to witness to their fellow Scots and intercede with God on the kingdom's behalf. The immense importance of the little flock of 'deare brethren' within Knox's experience and his ecclesiology were transferred to this *Order of the General Fast*.[33] However, while addressing the faithful few, Knox did not abandon the concept of Scotland as a covenanted nation and in the *Order* maintained a close parallelism between Scotland and Old Testament Israel. The concept of having real religious zeal or being 'affectually moved' was employed to distinguish between the external calling of the entire kingdom and the internal call of the elect: 'The rest were externally called, but obeyed not: they heard aswel mercy offered as threatninges pronounsed, but nether with the one nor with the uther were affectually moved.'[34] Such a double personality, with a national territorial Kirk held alongside a zealous, persecuted minority, became embedded within the consciousness of the Reformed Kirk in Scotland for many centuries and more widely influenced how the Scots have understood themselves.[35]

The calling of the Fast for the last week of February and start of March 1566, just prior to the meeting of Parliament, demonstrated the self-conscious intention to make a serious, though passive, political protest.[36] By positioning the Fast week to run through Ash Wednesday, it coincided with the start of the great penitential season of Lent. While Lent was no longer officially observed in Protestant Scotland, it retained a powerful presence in Scottish life. The

Order drew heavily upon the traditional rituals and performance of penance, though it declared that this Protestant Fast was different from previous Catholic practice. Strong themes of moral regeneration and social justice helped broaden the Fast's purpose and appeal, and it was intended to be a communal ritual demonstrating that the entire community was subject to discipline. Stressing repentance and the hope that God would 'creat in us new heartes' pulled the separate aims together. Reflecting the dominical command to honour God and love one's neighbour, the Fast showed 'the right way of God, aswell concerning his trew worshipping as in doing of your dewties one to another'.[37] The title page with its quotation from Joel 2 summed up the purpose of the exercise: 'Turne yow unto me with al your heart, and with Fasting & with weeping, and with murning.'[38] The specific aim of averting the wrath of God and preserving Protestantism was immediately stated: 'we may yet so convert to our God, that we provoke him not to take from us the lyght of his Evangel, which he of his mercie hath caused so clearly of laite dayes to shine within this Realme'.[39]

In the months following her second marriage the actions of Mary, Queen of Scots, gave the appearance that she was about to reintroduce Roman Catholicism into her kingdom. This was placed in the context of a Europe-wide initiative led by the papacy and the monarchs of France and Spain. Knox had probably supplied the details of this assumed Catholic conspiracy to kill Protestants, as well as the figure of one hundred thousand who had already suffered in France and the text of a fictitious decree from the Council of Trent.[40] In the winter of 1565–6 his earlier predictions seemed to be coming true in 'these our last and wicked days'. As he had prophesied, this was precisely because Scotland had chosen 'to shake hands with the Devil and with idolatry' and had welcomed home the Catholic Mary, Queen of Scots.[41]

By his unshakeable conviction that Mary, Queen of Scots, would at some stage revert to type and become another persecuting Catholic Queen Mary, Knox had almost made it happen. He had split the Protestant political consensus first forged in 1560 and created a gulf between the zealous brethren who hung upon his words and the Protestant political leadership. Throughout the 1565 crisis the Queen had cleverly exploited this split among the Protestants and she had successfully portrayed her opponents as Anglophile rebels and not as defenders of the Protestant faith. Despite Knox's fighting talk about Mary's Mass and his open espousal of resistance theories, the preacher had proved remarkably passive in 1565. Overcome by the old fears of political contamination, he had chosen to fight with spiritual weapons alone.

CHAPTER SIXTEEN

Unthankful (yea alas miserable) Scotland

The new material discovered in the Goodman papers and elsewhere has removed much of the mystery that previously shrouded the 'hidden years' of Knox's life, between 1565 and 1567. In March 1566 Knox went into self-imposed internal exile to Ayrshire and then contemplated going across to Ireland to join his friend Goodman. Instead he met Goodman once more when he travelled in 1567 to England and found himself embroiled in the vestments controversy and in contact with early separatists in London. Knox's links remained strong with his former Genevan congregation, who presented him with a special Bible, though other plans for reunions or relocations did not come to fruition. After Mary, Queen of Scots, was imprisoned in Lochleven Castle Knox finally returned to Edinburgh and accepted a second call to minister at St Giles'. He had been a passive observer during the dramatic crises that ended Mary's personal rule in Scotland and yet had spent much of his time writing his *History* to explain to Scots the meaning of their recent history. Its vision of the covenanted kingdom had a lasting impact upon Scottish identity.

In the *Order of the General Fast* one revealing phrase summed up the para-lysing effect of doubt upon a Christian's life: 'the murtherer of all godly exer-cise is desperation'.[1] Although Knox appeared to have few doubts about his personal salvation, he was deeply afflicted by what had happened in Scotland since the return of the Queen. His withdrawal in 1565 from his previous style of political engagement placed much greater stress upon the spiritual weapons of preaching, penitence and prayer. His own inner spiritual strength was tested when he was banned from preaching and the first period of ministry at St Giles' came to an end. As one disaster followed another during that year, Knox lost his decisiveness and slid into doubt and desperation. In his charac-teristically dramatic fashion, he described his mood swings in a deeply gloomy letter written on 12 March 1566 and concluded that he had learned little from the experiences of his long life and many troubles. 'In youth, myd age, and now, after many battelles, I find nothing into me bot vanitie and corruption. For, in quyetnes I am negligent, in trouble impatient, tending to disperation; and in the meane state, I am so caryed away with vane fantasizes, that, (allace), O Lord, they withdraw me from the presence of thy Majestie.'[2]

TENDING TO DESPERATION

Years earlier Knox had confessed to Elizabeth Bowes that when life had been going smoothly he had not been as diligent as he should have been and he knew he had not employed those periods of quietness to best advantage. When faced with extreme trouble, he assumed he had been equally remiss because he failed to find the patience to bear his misfortunes with fortitude, becoming instead totally miserable. He finally berated himself for his behaviour during those times between peace and conflict – the Aristotelian 'golden mean' – where harmony should be found. Then he feared that a frantic 'busyness' filled his life to the exclusion of his most important duty, to stand in the presence of God. In 1566 he viewed his keen interest in politics and plans for action and engagement as 'vain fantasies'. He admitted he had lost the comfort of God's presence, the affliction that he had helped Thomas Upcher face in 1557 and that Anne Locke had described in her meditation on Psalm 51. When he penned these lines he was beset by troubles and unsure what to do for the best. In such crises, Knox became weighed down by 'dolour', one of his favourite words, and sometimes sank into a profound depression, when he would pray for release from this life. He even convinced himself that writing to close friends was pointless or a form of vanity and sin.[3] At the end of this letter he made the agonized plea, 'Now Lord put end to my miserie.'[4] To early modern men and women, desperation was the forceful term used to describe an intense state associated with depression and often linked to thoughts of death. At its most extreme it characterized Judas' mental state after he had betrayed Christ and was driven to suicide, regarded in this period as a terrible sin. In March 1566, Knox hit one of the lowest points of his life.

One unexpected consequence of his withdrawal from the world of direct action was that he found himself guilty by association when others took decisions and actions in the name of the defence of Protestantism. Though not joining Moray and Argyll in their rebellion, Knox had given them vocal support. He had prayed for the exiled lords and reminded doubters that fears for Protestantism were proving justified. As power within the Burgh Council drained from the Protestants and Anglophiles during the winter of 1565, he was not the only Edinburgh Protestant to be growing more desperate. Catholicism was gaining strength in the capital and Darnley had been heard boasting that the Mass would shortly be set up in St Giles'. In more measured language, the Queen had discussed liberty of conscience and legal toleration for different forms of worship. She had been encouraging nobles to attend Mass with her and had introduced four friars to preach openly at court. At the start of February, the feast of Candlemas was celebrated with considerable pomp, with a great procession including the King and Queen carrying their candles. These celebrations were combined with the arrival of a French embassy bringing the prestigious Order of St Michael for Darnley.[5] On the night before Darnley's inauguration, four men attacked Friar John Black when he was walking along the Cowgate, probably on his way back from the palace at Holyrood. He was stabbed between the shoulders but survived the attack, though he lost a great deal of blood. All the assailants were leading Edinburgh Protestants and Knox's supporters and friends. The preacher had made no secret of his animus against the court's 'flattering friars' and had called Black a whoremonger as well as an idolatrous priest.[6]

All priests who continued to celebrate Mass in defiance of the Queen's proclamation and the Burgh Council's edict were guilty of a capital crime, in Knox's opinion. He held a radical and uncompromising view about the right to punish infringements of divine law. Upholding God's law was a collective responsibility and the central covenant obligation of the entire people of God. Whenever God's law had been broken it was essential for punishment to follow to demonstrate that the covenant remained intact. Though normally delegated to those with due authority, when they failed to act, the right to punish devolved to the lower levels of command and finally filtered down to individual Christians. Knox believed that in 1560 the Scots had accepted this obligation to uphold God's law and punish those who broke it, and he possibly stretched this theory of punishment to excuse the knifing of Friar Black on an Edinburgh street. He was certainly willing to voice his strong approval of another, higher-profile stabbing: the murder of David Riccio in front of the Queen in Holyrood Palace. On that same night of 9 March and within the palace, Friar Black was also murdered, probably by his original attackers intent upon completing the job they had initially botched.

When writing his *History* a few months later, Knox launched into an explicit justification of the nobles who had carried out Riccio's assassination and were languishing in exile. With no sympathy for the victim, the incident was discussed as if it had been an unconventional execution of a low-born, foreign and corrupt favourite. 'And to let the world understand in plain terms what we mean, that great abuser of this commonwealth, that poltroon and vile knave Davie, was justly punished . . . for abusing of the commonwealth, and for his other villany which we list not to express.' The final phrase referred to the allegation that Riccio had been Queen Mary's lover. Knox named Morton, Lindsay and Ruthven and their assisters 'who all, for their just act, and most worthy of all praise, are now unworthily left of their brethren and suffer the bitterness of banishment and exile'.[7] In other parts of the *History*, Riccio's demands for bribes and his 'over great familiarity' with the Queen were emphasized to add substance to the accusations against the Italian.[8]

In common with a substantial proportion of the Scottish nobility and the English Ambassador, Knox and his fellow minister John Craig most probably had foreknowledge of the conspiracy against Riccio. It had initially been planned as a coup to realign power at court and engineer the return of the rebel lords exiled in 1565. At least in the version conveyed to the Edinburgh ministers, the additional aim of upholding 'true religion' was added to the removal of Riccio and reinstatement of the exiles. The plot was devised as a desperate remedy because conventional political methods had proved unsuccessful. By feeding Darnley's jealousy of Riccio, the danger and volatility of the enterprise were greatly magnified. In the event, Queen Mary's resourcefulness and her ability to convince Darnley to change sides enabled her to escape from the palace and flee to Dunbar. This produced the worst possible outcome for those who had directly, or indirectly, been involved in the murder. Assuming that Darnley had spilled all their secrets, the murderers along with the exiled lords who had ridden into Edinburgh the following day had to escape before the Queen returned with troops at her back. A sense of panic spread through the capital, and on 17 March the nobles left at 7 a.m. while Knox departed for Kyle at 2 p.m. the same day 'with ane greit murnyng of the godlie of religioun'.[9] He headed for Ayrshire, his place of safety, and as justification for his sudden departure might have cited the General Assembly's order to visit the south. By the time he left the capital, he had been fully discharged and that first period of ministry at St Giles' was at end.[10] The Burgh Council probably strongly encouraged Knox to leave, possibly indicating that they could no longer protect him. They had taken the precaution of sending a placatory delegation to meet the King and Queen before the royal couple re-entered the burgh. With no time to plan, Knox left behind his pregnant wife and two sons and, shortly before he departed, wrote the letter expressing his depression and desperation. In such a situation his own death appeared to him the greatest mercy, despite having a loving wife, family and another child on the way. Knox was on the run once more from another triumphant Catholic Queen Mary.

HISTORY OF THE PROGRESS OF THE RIGHT RELIGION WITHIN THIS COUNTRY

Once in Kyle safe within 'the receptacle of God's saints' and surrounded by the warmth of his supporters, Knox recovered from his desperation. He reached instinctively for his pen as the alternative method of continuing to preach and prophesy, exactly as he had at the beginning of the Marian exile in 1554. For most of 1566 he concentrated upon the revision and writing of his *History of the Reformation in Scotland*. He found a path out of his depression using an intellectual activity on which he could focus, by engaging his mind with understanding the unfolding of God's providence. Through his literary work, he traced the hand of God guiding the faithful through all the triumphs and tragedies of the past years. By telling the story of the Scottish Protestants, he reinforced in his own mind the providential pattern revealed within those historical events and confirmed his reading of them. He drew comfort and reassurance from the knowledge that God was controlling the communal life of the kingdom. Since they formed an episode within the cosmic struggle between Christ and Satan, the events of the past decade also held an eternal significance. His heightened apocalyptic awareness allowed Knox to draw upon his confidence in the ultimate triumph of the forces of Christ. Whether adopted consciously or not, writing the *History* was the best therapy he could have found. In the Preface to Book IV, the text he took from Isaiah became a personal affirmation as well as an uplifting call to the faithful: 'They that wait upon the Lord shall renew their strength.'[11]

Knox's *History* had begun life in 1559 as an extended justification for the rebellion mounted by the Lords of the Congregation. During the dark days of November when defeat was looming, Knox completed what became Book II of the final work and he ended that section with the prayer 'Look upon us, O Lord, in the multitude of thy mercies; for we are brought even to the deep of the dungeon.'[12] This first effort was not published because it had been overtaken by events and the shift in the Congregation's fortunes and its propaganda following the alliance with England. As he declared in the original Preface, the *History*'s purpose was to explain why the Lords of the Congregation had taken up 'the sword of just defence against those that most unjustly seek our destruction'.[13] Following a chronological line, Knox had placed together a series of documents from the Congregation and their enemies, and through an extended commentary he had woven them into a justification of the Congregation to convince his fellow Scots to support the Lords.

Knox had not stopped gathering relevant material and subsequently decided to continue his story of the 'progresse of the richt religion within this cuntine'.[14] In the spring and early summer of 1566, he was busy revising

Book III which covered the period from November 1559 to the return of Mary, Queen of Scots in 1561.[15] He altered the central message of the *History* by adding a second section with the triumphant end to the 'Reformation of religion' in Scotland. The new Book III and revised Book II, spanning 1558 to 1561, proclaimed for posterity 'how wondrously hath the light of Christ Jesus prevailed against the darkness in this last and most corrupted age'.[16] Knox expounded the story of Scotland's deliverance and how, like the Old Testament Israelites, God had brought them forth from the bondage and tyranny of 'Egypt'. When all appeared lost, the Scots had been granted their own 'Red Sea' experience, and the final sequence within Book II fitted perfectly the awareness of being beset by danger on every side. With conscious parallelism to the drowning of Pharaoh and the Egyptians, at the start of Book III Knox inserted the 'drowning of the French', when 'the righteous God who in mercy looketh upon the affliction of those that unfeignedly sob unto him, fought for us by his own outstretched arm . . . God fought for the defence of Scotland'.[17] The Scots had been guided through their own Exodus and brought to victory in the summer of 1560, and through this dramatic and mighty deliverance they had been transformed into a people of God. They had entered into a covenant relationship with God, and when the *Confession of Faith* was affirmed and other legislation passed in the Scottish Parliament of August 1560 the kingdom had publicly recognized that divine bond. Following the Old Testament template, divine deliverance had been followed by Scotland's public acceptance of the law of God.

Written shortly before the *History* revisions, the Preface of *Order of the General Fast* had emphasized this interpretation of recent Scottish history. Knox had highlighted the miraculous transformation of ordinary, humble Christians during the Wars of the Congregation:

> then we followed God, and not carnall wisedome, and therefore made he few in nomber fearfull to many, fooles before the world to confound the wyse, and such as before never had experience in armes, made God so bolde and so prosperous in all their interpryses, that the expertest souldioures feared the poore plowmen; yea, our God faught for us by sea and by land, he moved the heartes of strangers to supporte us, and to spend their lives for our relief.[18]

In his *History*, Knox hammered home the message that the Protestant triumph did not rely upon the power, numbers or skill of the Lords of the Congregation. He chose to express his points in a series of rhetorical questions, mentally ticking them off on his fingers as he was wont to do in the pulpit. 'For what was our force? What was our number? Yea, what wisdom or worldly policy was into us, to have brought to a good end so great an enterprise?'[19]

Knox stressed the completeness of the transformation as God established a religion of 'great purity' in Scotland and the kingdom moved from darkness into light. In describing the Protestant triumph, he indulged in some ecclesiastical one-upmanship. While other Reformed churches possessed sincere doctrine equal to that of the Scots, they also 'retain in their Churches, and the ministers thereof, some footsteps of Antichrist, and dregs of papistry'. By contrast there was 'nothing within our Churches that ever flowed from that Man of Sin' because everything 'followed only that which we found approved by himself [God]'. In Knox's portrayal, it was strict adherence to the regulative principle, for which he had fought at Frankfurt, that placed the Scottish Kirk at the top of the Reformed league.

Establishing the perfection achieved in that moment of triumph was particularly significant for Knox's argument. Regarding Protestant doctrine and sacraments within Scotland, he went as far as saying, 'we are bold to affirm that there is no realm this day upon the face of the earth, that hath them in greater purity'.[20] In the final sections of Book III, he had inserted the texts of the major Protestant documents of 1560 including the entire *Confession of Faith* and full formal extracts from the parliamentary record of the legislation. At the end of the book, and more in the nature of an accusation, he had placed the complete text of the unpublished *First Book of Discipline*. He made it available so 'the posterities to come may judge as well what the worldlings refused, as what Policy the godly Ministers required'.[21] By isolating the years 1558–61 in his *History* and providing his narration of deliverance, he created the concept of a speedy 'Scottish Reformation' as a transformative event rather than a gradual or organic process. This hugely influential idea passed into Protestant and national historiography and retains its significance to this day.

In 1566 Knox's original intention had been to narrate Scotland's 'exodus' and thereby fulfil his prophetic task to explain to his fellow Scots their covenant duties to God in response to that great deliverance. As the closing pages of Book III made abundantly clear, even at the time of triumph he recognized that there had not been full obedience to God and his Word. As a further token of his faithfulness to his people, God had sent 'a wonderful and most joyful deliverance' with the death of King Francis II, who had been threatening the Protestants in France as well as in Scotland.[22] Her husband's death had prompted the return of Mary, Queen of Scots, and this provided the major test for the Scots in their new covenant relationship with God. That furnished the direct link with Knox's situation in 1566. Once again using a question, he demanded, 'From when (alas) cometh this miserable dispersion of God's people within this realm, this day, anno 1566, in May?' His answer was plain: 'Because that suddenly the most part of us declined from the purity of God's word, and began to follow the world; and so again to shake hands with the Devil, and with idolatry.'[23] In his Ayrshire retreat, Knox was full of anger and bitterness about the divine punishments brought by this lack of obedience and faithfulness to the laws of God. There could be no excuse since God 'made his truth so to triumph amongst us that, in despite of Sathan, hypocrisy is disclosed, and the true worshipping of God is manifested to all inhabitants of this realm whose eyes Sathan blinds not'.[24] Knox felt the imperative to drive home the lesson that Scotland was not keeping God's covenant.

In the style of the Old Testament prophets, he admonished the Scots for failing in their duty by detailing the precise nature of the backsliding, starting from the return of Queen Mary in 1561 and continuing up to 1564. This formed Book IV of his *History*, and contained direct and bitter attacks upon Moray and Lethington, who had allowed the Queen to retain her private Mass. In this book Knox employed fewer contemporary documents, instead replacing them with the powerful dramatic dialogues he had held with the Queen and with Lethington. Such scripts allowed Knox to explain the duties of a faithful Protestant living under a Catholic queen and had the effect of directing the narrative spotlight on to him and his views. He brought the book to a close a year before the disasters of 1565, concluding with his debate with Lethington which demonstrated the clash between two irreconcilable understandings of the situation. In a little note at the very end of Book IV, he added that for much of that period he and Moray had not been speaking to each other. Through writing this stinging indictment of the 'courtiers' and their failure to heed the admonitions of God's messengers, the 'venom of desperation' within Knox might have been dispersed. Since the political path taken by Moray and Lethington had failed, he could imply that all political compromise was inherently disastrous. In the longer term, this planted the seed of the enduring Presbyterian myth that the Scottish nobility had betrayed the Scottish Reformation.

Adding this extra section of narrative Knox was proving to himself, as much as to his readers, that he had fulfilled his prophetic duty and had continued without ceasing to warn and admonish his fellow Scots for their 'inobedience'. His narrative slipped perilously close to a long-winded 'I told you so'. By stopping in 1564, the story closed with Knox still at the centre of political debate. However, it implied a justification for his subsequent withdrawal from politics. By cataloguing failure, the book was intended as a further lesson in the collective and individual duties of the people of God. The concept of discipline became an underlying theme, with the emphasis upon penitence and the need to express collective and individual repentance. Though this ran counter to the message of Books II and III, the implication within Book IV was that since political, diplomatic and military methods had failed, spiritual weapons should be employed. In a strong echo of the analysis given in the *Order of the General Fast*, Knox emphasized in his Preface to Book IV that the spiritual weapon of repentance was the appropriate response to the divine punishment raining down upon Scotland in 1565 and 1566. 'The plagues have been, and in some part are present, that were before threatened; the rest approach. And yet who from the heart cries, "I have offended; the Lord knows. In Thee only is the trust of the oppressed; for vain is the help of man." '[25] Emerging strongly again in Book IV, the lament – that the faithful were few and the hypocrites many – had recurred throughout Knox's ministry. It chimed with the assumption behind the doctrine of predestination that many were called but few chosen and with the Protestant belief that the true Church had existed for many centuries as a persecuted minority.

The other addition Knox made in 1566 was an introduction to Book I that paralleled Book IV's emphasis upon the faithful remnant surviving amid a sea of hypocrisy. During the writing process in Ayrshire, he discussed his work with his 'brethren', and they convinced him it was essential to supply an introductory narrative to carry the story up to 1558. Within Kyle there was a profound awareness of the continuing tradition of religious dissent, and these Protestants wanted the tale told of their ancestors' and their own parts when Protestantism had existed as an underground movement. They pressed Knox to add these stories and include the names in his *History* of those whom 'God had made instruments of his glory, by opposing themselves to manifest abuses, superstition and idolatry'. Dubious at first, Knox admitted that once he started collecting he found more people and material than he had expected. For him, these early Scottish Protestants had to be located within the 'terrible conflict that has been betwix the saints of God and these bloody wolves who claim to themselves the title of clergy, and to have authority over the souls of men'.[26] By adding the prequel to his original story, Knox once more altered the focus of the *History*. He shifted the chronological lens from its narrow focus upon the particular divine intervention in 1559–60 to the wide sweep encompassing the decades of Catholic dominance when the true Church had survived in Scotland as a persecuted minority. In Book I, documents were introduced as a means of authenticating the events he narrated from the fifteenth century onwards. A few paragraphs into the book's opening, he inserted the Articles from the Register of Glasgow relating to the heresy trial of the Lollards of Kyle. These were probably supplied by one of his hosts in the area, most likely Elizabeth

Campbell, a direct descendant of George Campbell of Cessnock who had stood trial in 1494.[27]

Such an approach bore similarities to that adopted by Knox's friend John Foxe for his popular 'book of martyrs' which had such an influence upon the way the English understood their Church and Reformation. In 1559, Knox had collected, listed and published the names of English martyrs, but had not continued his project because Foxe was busy working on his *Acts and Monuments*. When faced with incorporating the roll call of Scottish martyrs in Book I, he adopted a different strategy. Knowing that the Scottish tally would be meagre compared to the English or French martyrs, he abandoned any listing and noted in the Preface that his story was not necessarily comprehensive. He chose instead to weave the early Scottish Protestants into a tale of persecution where the central characters were anti-heroes, such as Cardinal Beaton, instead of heroic martyrs. The exception was his personal tribute to George Wishart. With considerable literary expertise and flair he transformed the full-scale attack upon the Scottish Catholic hierarchy in Book I into a dramatic story full of detail and humour. It is the most lively and readable part of the *History* and one reason the volume has continued to be reprinted.

In addition to using similar techniques to the martyrologists Foxe and Crespin, Knox drew upon the broader field of Protestant chroniclers such as John Sleiden. In 1567–8 he was still collecting material from other parts of Europe and listening to the German chronicler Aventinus being read to him.[28] He sought to place Scotland within the common Protestant historical tradition and demonstrate that the experience of these faithful Scots was the same as that of their co-religionists. In a deliberate echo of the Preface to the Geneva Bible, he wrote of 'the same cloud of ignorance that long hath darkened many realms under this accursed kingdom of that Roman Antichrist, hath also overcovered this poor realm; that idolatry hath been maintained, the blood of innocents hath been shed, and Christ Jesus his eternal truth hath been abhorred, detested and blasphemed'.[29] Despite having identified the papacy as Antichrist from his first sermon, Knox did not embark upon a chronological summary of the survival of the true Church throughout the ages. In order to establish the cruelty and tyranny of the Scottish Catholic hierarchy, he concentrated upon the relatively recent Scottish past. Even in the extended *History* of Books I–IV, his relatively brief time frame provided a complete contrast to the centuries covered by Foxe's *Acts and Monuments*. As a consequence, Scots had at their disposal a different understanding of their past and sense of their Protestant identity.[30]

Knox did not write any more of his *History*, although he continued to revise his text and gather evidence until at least 1571. A continuator, most probably

Knox's secretary Richard Bannatyne, did add a fifth book in which the narrative was carried down to 1567 and the deposition of Mary, Queen of Scots, marking the end of the rule of an idolatrous monarch. Like the previous additions, Book V altered the character of the *History* by emphasizing its nature as a chronicle of the times. After 1567, Knox had become reconciled with Moray and had no wish to undermine his Regency or besmirch his name, especially following the Regent's assassination three years later. Consequently, he did not want the *History* published because it contained his bitter Book IV attacking Moray, and a complete version of the *History* was not printed until 1644. Once Regent Moray and his successors ruled on behalf of the Protestant 'cradle king' James VI, the lessons concerning the duty of the people of God when ruled by a female Catholic monarch became semi-redundant. However, Knox's overarching interpretation was disseminated through his general legacy, and his *History* developed an enduring importance across the centuries because it was the story of the mighty deliverance of God and the bringing of the light of 'true religion' to Scotland.

ASSIST YOU FOR A SEASON

When Knox left Edinburgh in March 1566 in great haste, his pregnant wife and sons had remained in the city. Since Margaret was not in any direct danger she probably stayed in Edinburgh until the birth of her daughter, Martha, before joining her husband in Ayrshire. Thanks to the Goodman papers, it has been possible to discover details about the following fifteen months of Knox's life. The safe arrival of his wife, seeing his baby daughter and becoming immersed in his writing lightened Knox's despairing mood. Surrounded by family, friends and supporters during the autumn of 1566, he settled into a house in Ayr where he was acting as a temporary minister. On the removal day, he wrote to Goodman mentioning that he was concerned about the prosaic domestic problem of finding sufficient furniture and fittings for his new home. His father-in-law, Andrew Stewart, Lord Ochiltree, was in close attendance, and Knox had the firm support of James Dalrymple, who became Ayr's minister in 1568, as well as leading merchants such as Charles Campbell and the burgh's Treasurer, Archibald Fergusshill. Knox's two sons, Nathaniel and Eleazer, now nine and seven years old, had gone to stay with their grandmother, Elizabeth Bowes, in County Durham to continue their education in England.

A tug-of-war over where Knox should pursue his ministry was under way. Edinburgh wanted their former minister to return to his old charge while he was reluctant to return to the capital and had already made a promise to serve in Ayr. The issue was further complicated by a letter Knox received from

Drogheda in Ireland sent by his close friend Christopher Goodman. Having been forced to flee from Scotland, Goodman had since joined Sir Henry Sidney's household. He probably accompanied Sidney on his arrival in Ireland at the start of 1566 to begin a first term as Lord Deputy (see Plate 11). Goodman had become a prominent member of Sidney's evangelical programme which included Adam Loftus, Archbishop of Armagh, Dr Robert Weston, Chancellor at Dublin, and Hugh Brady, Bishop of Meath, all of whom became his friends.[31] By the summer of 1566 while Loftus was recruiting younger preachers at Cambridge, Goodman had persuaded the Lord Deputy to invite Knox to assist in the campaign to bring the Protestant message to Ulster.[32] When he received the letters from Goodman and Sidney around September, Knox was sorely tempted to take the chance to join his old ministerial partner. They would run a preaching campaign and 'perform the work of ane evangist'.[33] Knox was once again caught between different calls and different tasks, just as he had been during the Marian exile. He still felt his primary calling lay within Scotland, 'so long as any congregation within the sam will call me to the preaching of the ewangill', but at the same time he appeared to want a reason to leave the country. He suggested to Goodman that he could 'assist you for a ceassoun', provided the General Assembly gave their permission. Goodman was instructed to write to the next Assembly meeting at Christmas and Knox was confident 'your just petitioun should not be denyed'. He joked that the more likely source of opposition would come from the English bishops, who would not want the two friends reunited.[34]

For several years Knox had been in contact with Sir Henry Sidney and his brother-in-law, the Earl of Leicester. Sitting at his listening post in Ayr, one of the main ports for the Irish trade, he had access to plenty of information about the situation across the Irish Sea. He was already acquainted with Adam Loftus and had probably been in touch with him concerning the recent interventions of the Earl of Argyll in Ulster politics. In his letter to Goodman, Knox relayed the hot news from the Scottish court: Argyll's latest Ulster expedition had been postponed at the Queen's command. He had gathered further highly sensitive information that he dare not 'commit to paper and ink'.[35] Though previously a firm supporter of the policy of amity, Argyll had been badly disillusioned by the conspicuous lack of assistance from England for him and his allies during their 1565 rebellion. The Earl was no longer prepared to frame his own policy within Ulster to suit the Lord Deputy and the English administration, and a series of messages and letters, both genuine and counterfeit, had passed between Argyll and Loftus. Argyll's new Ulster policy was of great concern to Knox, who remained a staunch advocate of the Anglo-Scottish alliance as the key to the creation of a fully Protestant British Isles.

During Christmas 1566 Knox attended the General Assembly in Edinburgh, though illness prevented him being present at all the sessions. He was unable to obtain a completely satisfactory resolution to his personal dilemma of where he should minister. He had 'repugned' the Church of Edinburgh's assumption that he 'should be subiect to thame whensoever thei should requyr me' and demanded instead that the Assembly make a specific appointment or 'sett me at libertie'. A compromise was reached whereby Knox should continue to preach 'whare god shall offer occasion' until appointed to 'a certan station'.[36] This was the type of roving preaching mission that he relished. The possibility of a visit to Ireland had not featured at the Assembly because Knox's letter of 27 October had been badly delayed and Goodman had only received it at the end of January, long after the Assembly. The two friends faced a common sixteenth-century problem of establishing a reliable communications link and of finding 'assured' messengers. Knox had sent several letters to Goodman by different routes, including one via Berwick to Chester when he heard that Goodman would be visiting his hometown.

At this juncture the most important and reliable agent moving between Ireland and Scotland was John Douglas, who had been a Protestant preacher in the Earl of Argyll's household in the late 1550s. Having been injured during the siege of Leith in 1560, he had left the ministry and gone to Ireland where he worked as a secret agent for Sir Henry Sidney. Knox had known Douglas from those early years and was hoping to use him as a trusted courier to carry, in addition to the written communications, all the confidential oral messages he wanted to send to Goodman and Sidney. Not having a trusted bearer, Knox kept his written comments relatively oblique, at one point including a reminder for Sidney about previous warnings and prophecies that were now being fulfilled.

Overtaken by events in Scotland, nothing came of Knox's visit to Ireland. An Irish tour remains one of the intriguing 'what ifs' during his life. With the full backing of the Lord Deputy, the powerful preaching of Knox and Goodman with the rest of the evangelical team might have kick-started the spread of Protestantism within Ireland and thereby altered the subsequent course of British history. In spite of Sidney's strong backing, Goodman left Ireland for good in the spring of 1567, possibly influenced by his failure to bring Knox across the Irish Sea. The lack of his friend's help might have been the final straw to add to the disappointment of finding his work and promotion in Ireland continually blocked by Queen Elizabeth.

The news of the murder of Darnley on 9 February 1567 had again plunged Knox deep into gloom. When writing to Goodman ten days later, he had spoken of God putting an 'end to my trubles, which time I am assured approchis verrey ney'. He admitted to Goodman about recent events, 'I can not nor will not wryte, for greafe & shame do both forbid.' The latest crisis had convinced him 'I dare not cast off that burden that god hath laid upon me to preach to unthankfull (yea allace miserable) Scotland.' He felt compelled to continue his vocation within his native country, even if all he could do was proclaim his message 'within my awen walles' and use his pen to reach beyond them.[37] Writing to his closest friend, he did manage to end his letter on a lighter note. In the previous letter he had teased Goodman about not forgetting the Scots language, and to keep him up to the mark he inserted the Scottish proverb, 'fayr hectes will only mack fooles fain', indicating that fools can be won over by fair words.[38] In his February letter he jokingly complained about 'my Meg' doting so much upon their baby Martha 'that all service is gone'. Margaret was sufficiently friendly with Goodman to name him individually in her prayers, and Knox's remark reads like an in-joke between the three of them. Since Alice, Goodman's wife, had made her displeasure abundantly clear when he gave up his post in Sidney's household, there might have been some teasing from Goodman in his letter about how extremely dutiful and full of service the young Margaret was to her husband.[39]

Invitations had been flying around the three kingdoms to Knox and his Marian exile colleagues offering the chance to move and preach elsewhere. Knox's old friend from Frankfurt and Geneva days, William Whittingham, had become Dean of Durham Cathedral and was personally embroiled in the vestments controversy. Summoned to London in the autumn of 1566, Whittingham 'had a great deale of trouble' and assumed he would be 'extremely dealt with' to ensure his conformity. As he informed Goodman, he was expecting a letter from Knox to be waiting for him on his return to Durham. One possible way of escaping the pressure to conform was to accept the invitation he had already received from the Earl of Moray to come to Scotland with the promise that some funds would be available for him. Whittingham did not accept the offer because he had finally decided to conform and wear the vestments. He had been persuaded by the arguments from most European Reformers in favour of remaining within the ministry and continuing to preach, even at the cost of wearing the offensive surplice and other items of clerical garb.[40] His conformity led to a sharp exchange with Goodman, who was strongly opposed to vestments, though as yet he had not personally faced the full enforcement campaign.[41] In his turn, Goodman was being pressed to return to St Andrews, where his previous position would again be made available.[42] In the spring of 1567 and while still in Ireland, he had received a range of offers.[43]

These separate invitations to the three individuals possibly indicate that there was a concerted effort to reunite Knox, Goodman and Whittingham in one or other of the three kingdoms. Each location offered its own possibilities and problems, but none of the opportunities could be taken because the situations within all three kingdoms changed during 1566–7. Goodman and Whittingham would have encountered difficulties obtaining licences to leave the Tudor state, and for the remainder of his life a vindictive Queen Elizabeth ensured that Goodman was not permitted so much as a temporary preaching tour to see his Scottish friends.[44] Reconstituting the successful Genevan team ministry held great appeal for Knox. When that failed to materialize, his planned visit to England in 1567 at least offered an opportunity to renew his friendship with members of that Genevan congregation. For the sake of all his English acquaintances as much as his own protection, it was important that he remained entirely out of Queen Elizabeth's sight. Consequently, he kept such a low profile during his English trip that his movements remain shrouded in mystery.

While invitations were criss-crossing the three kingdoms, Knox's friends from the Geneva days had been thinking about him. They had devised a scheme to make a presentation to their former minister, and both Whittingham and Goodman were aware of the plan to present Knox with a special copy of a Bible.[45] Knox's friends had chosen for the gift a handsome folio edition of the Great, or Matthews, Bible that they had had printed in Rouen in 1566 with one volume set aside for presentation. The French printer had no previous experience of biblical printing or English-language work and he probably ran off a special edition with Knox in mind.[46] The volume would have been sent to England under the licence held by John Bodley for the importation of English Bibles from the Continent. Having been an elder for the Genevan exile congregation, Bodley remained in touch with its former ministers and other members of the congregation. He was wealthy enough to resource such a project and could liaise with Richard Cawarden, another London merchant working in Customs, who organized the actual printing in Rouen.[47] The lavishing of such care and expense upon a present for Knox indicated the deep affection in which he was held by his friends and the long-lasting links he had forged among the London merchant community during the reign of King Edward VI.

MEN'S TRADITIONS BEARING THE NAME OF THE CHURCH

Knox had not always been diligent about his personal correspondence with English friends. In particular, when he became depressed and 'oppressed with melancholie' he found it hardest of all to write to them. In one case he apologized for not writing for seven years, though his 'brother', possibly Anthony Gilby in Leicestershire, had continued to send 'commendations and letters, diverse tokens of your unfained friendship'.[48] Knox had written to John Foxe around 1566 about the *Acts and Monuments* and had kept himself thoroughly informed about English matters.[49] The Scot also heard news of the trouble, particularly in London, caused by the vestments row. Probably at his instigation, the Scottish General Assembly in December 1566 had given Knox the task of writing and carrying the Assembly's letter asking the English bishops to be lenient with their ministerial colleagues and respect their conscientious objections to the ecclesiastical garments. The Assembly had also provided Knox with a letter of commendation to accompany his licence from the Scottish government to depart the realm to visit his children and mother-in-law in England. Given Queen Elizabeth's attitude, Knox probably did not obtain an official English licence to enter the realm. With his contacts on the Border there might have been a tacit understanding that if he remained out of sight and only visited his family, he could slip across unrecorded, as many migrant Scots did in the sixteenth century.[50]

Elizabeth Bowes and the boys would have been his first port of call on his trip south and it was probably the final time Knox saw them. He had made the decision that his boys should stay in England and remain as part of the Bowes family. At this point he might still have hoped he could come quietly to England to retire. A year later he was seeking to ensure the smooth acquisition of his sons' status as denizens, giving them official permission to reside in England. Nathaniel and Eleazer continued their English education and in 1572 went up to St John's College, Cambridge, eventually entering clerical careers within the Church of England. Within their mother's country, they had followed in their father's footsteps.[51] Following his visit to Elizabeth Bowes, probably at the family home at Barnard Castle, Knox possibly went to Durham city to see William Whittingham.

Knox did travel to Chester and stayed at Aldford, just outside the city, where Goodman was serving the parish. While there, the friends discussed the vestments controversy. Knox had accepted the view, possibly reinforced by Whittingham, that conformity was the lesser evil because it was better to remain in the Church and be able to continue preaching. Having probably indicated his support for Whittingham's choice, Knox tried to convince Goodman of the seriousness of the Church's loss if 'we shold have lost youe & your comfortable doctrine in Christ'. When they were talking about the issue while walking in Goodman's garden, his friend's impassioned plea persuaded Knox that to wear vestments was to forsake God. Goodman confessed that he 'durst not so to do, lest god wold forsake' him. Knox had been deeply moved by Goodman's declaration, feeling it strongly in the stomach – the seat of the emotions within sixteenth-century understanding. He later wrote to his friend, 'your wordes then presently so piersed my stomacke' that he admitted he had changed his mind on the entire issue. This marked one of the very rare occasions when Knox freely admitted to having his mind changed by discussion. From the time of their talk, he adopted Goodman's hard-line stance against vestments and any of 'men's traditions bearing the name of the church' and he subsequently urged Goodman to compose a pamphlet defending the anti-vestments case.[52]

From the north-west of England Knox travelled south to London and renewed his acquaintance with former Marian exiles. He also met for the first time members of the radical group who had been fighting against the wearing of vestments and were considering the major step of withdrawing from the Church of England. They regarded Knox and Goodman as heroes and believed that their Genevan congregation's *Forme of Prayers* was a far superior liturgy to the Book of Common Prayer. They employed Knox to ask Goodman, whom they knew only by reputation, to write a tract against 'Antichrists clothing' and refute the Roman Catholic polemic being published in Louvain.[53] These early separatists had gathered a congregation and saw themselves as direct descendants of the persecuted Protestants under Queen Mary who had covertly worshipped in London. By 1567 they were meeting secretly and following the *Forme of Prayers* in their worship in the Plumbers Hall, on the site now occupied by the railway station London Cannon Street. Their illegal gathering was discovered that June and many were arrested. With the Book of Common Prayer as the only legally permitted form of public worship, such meetings presented a direct challenge to the Elizabethan religious settlement. Knox's old antagonist from the Frankfurt Troubles, Bishop Grindal of London, examined the culprits and sent the ringleaders to prison. Later in the year a number of the separatists travelled north to Scotland because they wanted to witness in action a fully Reformed Church. Knox welcomed them, discussing ecclesiastical matters and the current dangers facing England and Scotland. When visiting Dunbar on Good Friday, Evans, one of the radical group, had his high expectations of Scottish perfection dashed when he thought he witnessed the Catholic practice of creeping to the cross on Good Friday, barelegged and barefoot. Bishop Grindal had a wry chuckle in his letter to Cecil about this great disappointment: 'If it be so, the church of Scotland will not be pure enough for our men.'[54]

Shortly after the separatists' return, in May 1568 one of them wrote to Knox thanking the Scot for his generosity, but making it clear how upset the group had been because he had not provided his full backing for their separation from the Church of England. Without being aware of its contents, the writer had carried back to London Knox's letter to the separatist congregation.

He explained that he would have debated the issue face to face with Knox if he had only realized that the Scot was advising against withdrawing from their parishes and separating from the established Church. With clear echoes of arguments Knox had frequently employed against past opponents, the separatist challenged in turn each of the preacher's biblical examples.[55] Knox's views and style appeared to be well known among the separatist group, and the writings of William White, a London baker and amateur theologian, contained many Knoxian-style phrases and sentiments, such as 'forked, flattering clawbacks'.[56]

In his original letter, Knox had urged the importance of preserving unity even when it involved compromises with those who held different views. Despite his past track record, he probably missed the irony of his stout defence of uniformity. The following year he expressed a worried warning to John Wood that this English separation or schism 'no doubt is a forerunner of greater desolation, unless there be speedie repentance'.[57] Having spent the past eight years trying to make a comprehensive national Kirk work, he had become more sensitive to the dangers of disunity and warmed a little to the positive virtues of conformity. The English separatist's letter demonstrated the opening of a generation gap between those who had lived through the reigns of Edward and Mary and those emerging to lead the radical groups within the Elizabethan Church. Despite his refusal to support the extreme solution of separatism, Knox, the Scottish Kirk and its *Book of Common Order* (as the *Forme of Prayers* was known in Scotland) continued to provide an inspiring ideal for the 'hotter sort' of English Protestants. Whether he would have cared to acknowledge this sincerest form of flattery, Elizabethan dissenters were imitating him, and Knox was already playing his future role as a 'father' of English Dissent.

DISPERSED LITTLE FLOCK

Following the visit to England and renewed contacts with friends from his former Genevan congregation, Knox thought seriously once again about serving that congregation in a form of retirement. His colleague John Willock had gone back to England and was enjoying semi-retirement in the congenial community that surrounded the godly Earl of Huntingdon and included the former Genevan exiles Anthony Gilby and Thomas Wood. An eloquent letter from the General Assembly in 1567 had not persuaded Willock to return to heavy ministerial duties in Scotland. Willock's example might have encouraged Knox in his dream of leaving the burden of his second Edinburgh ministry behind and returning to those among whom he had lived with a quiet conscience and contented heart. When struggling to come to terms with the knowledge that

Goodman was never going to rejoin him in Scotland, Knox explained his plan in 1568 to John Wood, Moray's secretary. He spoke with deep affection for his old congregation, 'God comfort that dispersed little flock . . . amongst whom I would be content to end my dayes . . . I would even as gladlie return to them, if they stood in need of my labours, as ever I was glad to be delivered from the rage of mine enemies.' He confided in a sad aside, 'I can give you no reason that I should so desire, other than that my heart so thristeth.'[58]

In the spring of 1567, Knox might have been tempted to stay somewhere quietly out of sight in England. His vocation dictated that he honour his promise and return to Scotland for the General Assembly of June 1567 and resume his ministry to his native land. Though he must have heard some news in London about the tumultuous final months of Mary, Queen of Scots' personal reign, he did not hurry back to Scotland to take an active role in the Queen's deposition. That tardiness demonstrated how far he had withdrawn from Scottish political life. For his mental wellbeing as well as his physical safety, Knox had been forced to leave Edinburgh in March 1566. He had already abandoned direct political action and turned to the spiritual weapons of fasting and repentance to fight the latest battle against Antichrist. As had happened at Mary Tudor's accession in 1553, he found it difficult to decide what he should do. His depression increased as he witnessed Mary, Queen of Scots' victory over the rebel lords and her triumphant celebration at Prince James' Roman Catholic baptism. Everything at the start of 1566 indicated that a major shift in royal religious policy was about to happen. Sending him helter-skelter into internal exile, the panic in the capital following Riccio's murder helped Knox by making his decision for him. Once safely in Ayrshire and busy with the *History*, he recovered his balance and reassessed his position.

Though he felt a general responsibility to continue to preach in 'unthankfull' Scotland, he had been discharged from St Giles' and could contemplate other possibilities outside the realm. He was strongly tempted to join Goodman in Ireland for an evangelical mission and, if the arrangements had been made, he would probably have crossed the Irish Sea. Though the plans to reunite the Genevan triumvirate of Whittingham, Goodman and Knox had failed, Knox had made an extended visit to England in 1567. As well as being a Scot, he never ceased to regard himself as an adoptive Englishman. With his intelligence network he was always well informed and became involved in the debates over vestments, conformity and separatism that were dividing the Church of England. He was very far from being forgotten by his London friends and other members of his Genevan congregation who had organized the presentation Bible for him. Chance survivals have revealed these glimpses of English and British connections and they serve as a reminder of how significant such links were to Knox's outlook and his life. In 1566–7, he might easily have left Scotland and, like Willock and Goodman, never returned.

Knox's *History* was the greatest achievement of this period. Its exclusive focus upon the experience of the Scottish Protestants helped reinforce the later impression that from 1559 Knox had become immersed in Scottish affairs and nothing else. This analysis has hidden the possibility that this work was him 'preaching by pen' when he assumed that his national, prophetic role in Edinburgh had finished. The *History* contains some of the best of his writing, with humour and wit helping to drive home his message. The long-lasting belief that the Scots were a people of God rested upon his portrayal of Scotland's 'exodus' and of the covenant made with God and then broken. His *History* pioneered the tradition of Presbyterian histories that have, until recent times, dominated the interpretation of Scotland's past. Knox and those later histories offered a distinctive vision of a Protestant Scotland that has helped mould Scottish identity down to the present.

CHAPTER SEVENTEEN

This most miraculous victory and overthrow

Knox returned to a Scotland turned upside down. During his second ministry at St Giles' he no longer had to battle against the presence of a Catholic queen in the capital because Mary had been replaced by her son, the 'cradle king' James VI. Knox had interpreted Mary's deposition and the Protestant Regency of the Earl of Moray as an example of God's deliverance and care for his people. In a deeply divided Scotland the preacher was a strong supporter of the King's Party and became increasingly suspicious and antagonistic towards the Queen's Party. In Europe the outbreak of the Dutch Revolt had brought a large Spanish army into the Low Countries, and its presence increased Knox's fears about the long-term survival of Protestantism. After Mary, Queen of Scots' escape, her defeat at the battle of Langside and flight into England in 1568, those fears were heightened as he saw the contagion of 'that wicked woman' spread to the southern kingdom. Despite having a 'godly magistrate' in Regent Moray to assist the Scottish Kirk, he did not greet this as a fresh and hopeful start. He remained weary and pessimistic and full of gloomy prophecies. At the start of 1570 one prediction was fulfilled when Moray was assassinated. Like the Old Testament prophet Jeremiah, Knox felt he was foretelling and then witnessing his country and his own life falling apart.

In June 1567, after 'this most miraculous victory and overthrow' Edinburgh had become a much safer place for Knox, and he could return to the capital without fearing what the Queen might do.[1] Mary was in prison in Lochleven Castle and her husband, the Earl of Bothwell, was on the run, narrowly escaping capture in the Orkneys. The Scottish ruling elite was split down the middle over what should happen next, while Queen Elizabeth and the other monarchs of Europe observed events in Scotland with a horrified fascination. Within Edinburgh feelings were running high against Mary, and the Queen had been heckled and abused when she rode into the city as a prisoner after the battle of Carberry on 15 June. It was possibly the confirmation of the Queen's capture and imprisonment that brought Knox back across the English Border.

In this febrile atmosphere the General Assembly, for which Knox had promised to return, convened on 25 June. It sat for several days conducting routine business though there was no mention of Knox's ambivalent ministerial position. Due to the unstable political situation, the Assembly was poorly attended and it was decided to reconvene the following month with as full a complement of commissioners as possible. Knox signed the letter of 26 June and its language and content incorporated some typical Knoxian concerns, including his permanent worry about a Europe-wide Catholic conspiracy, backed by a further citation of the fictitious Tridentine decree to destroy all Protestants. Alongside the concern for the 'flock of Jesus Christ' was the hope that Mary's fall offered a great opportunity to build 'this ruinous house of God within this realm'. Acutely aware of the deep divisions running through the political nation, the letter made a direct appeal to individual Protestant nobles to ensure that 'a sure union and conjunction may be had among all the members for the liberty of God's Kirk, whereby we may be able to withstand the rage and violence of the aforesaid enemies'.[2]

In the period before the next session of the Assembly, Knox returned to Ayrshire where his wife and daughter had probably remained throughout his trip to England.[3] The staunchly Protestant lairds from that shire were mobilized and came in force to 'assist' at the July Assembly and the Convention of Estates. Knox was back in Edinburgh on 17 July, and by then had decided he would accept a second call from the Church in Edinburgh and re-enter his ministry in the capital. During the fifteen months he had been away, John Craig had carried the ministerial burden on his own. Placed in an awkward situation by Bothwell's insistence upon a Protestant wedding, Craig had been brave and forthright over his opposition to the Queen's third marriage. He had agreed to publish the banns only in a legal sense while at the same time explaining in his sermon why the marriage was not legitimate.[4] Craig's calming presence would have helped persuade Knox to accept Edinburgh's second call. He was able to supply information and interpretation concerning the tangled political events of the previous few months that had lost the Queen her throne. Craig would have provided Knox with details of the allegations that Mary had been implicated in Darnley's murder and had committed adultery with Bothwell, the prime suspect for the murder. Three years earlier when Craig had supported Knox during the General Assembly debate with Maitland, he had highlighted the contractual nature of monarchy, putting forward the view that rulers could be deposed when they broke the promises in their coronation oaths. Working together again as close colleagues, Knox and Craig were able to review all the arguments for Mary's deposition. By July 1567, they had gathered a comprehensive array of reasons drawn from the Bible, histories and chronicles, Scots law and constitutional practices and the coronation oath. These were rehearsed for Sir Nicholas Throckmorton, the special Ambassador sent from England.[5]

FOOLISH PITY

Knox was strongly predisposed to accept that the Queen was guilty of all the accusations levelled against her. His central contention in the *First Blast* had been that female rule was, by its very existence, against the natural order and therefore 'monstrous': a reigning queen was bound to be a disaster waiting to happen. Knox believed that this general proposition about female rule had been vindicated by Mary's personal reign and that the hand of God had been clearly displayed in the Queen's downfall. He rejoiced that divine intervention had happened before the horrors of Catholic persecution reached Scotland, and celebrated another of God's deliverances. He never wavered in his total condemnation of Mary, Queen of Scots, and as time progressed he became yet more vitriolic in his outbursts against 'that wicked woman'.[6] In the summer of 1567, he gloried in the realization that the Almighty had struck this Catholic Queen Mary from her throne and urged the Scottish nobility to complete the process by executing the Queen of Scots for her crimes.

He chose to preach from the history books of the Old Testament, using 2 Kings and 2 Chronicles, covering the same period within the kingdoms of Israel and Judah. He had been drawn to the story of Ahab and Jezebel many times in the past. However, on this occasion he dwelt upon the fulfilment of the prophecy that Ahab's House should not keep the throne because the king had permitted the idolatry of Jezebel. For many years Knox had called the Scottish Queen a Jezebel and thought that she was destined to share that queen's fate. Instead of a defenestration, in 1567 Knox was calling for a judicial sentence, because he believed that the blood of those who had been unjustly slain cried out for vengeance. With full Old Testament vigour he asserted that only blood would cleanse the land and restore the covenant. In 2 Kings 9:33, where Jehu commanded the eunuchs to cast Jezebel down from the window to her death, the Geneva Bible's side note to that verse commented, 'This he did by the motion of the Spirit of God, y[a]t her blood shulde be shed, that had shed the blood of innocents, to be a spectacle and example of Gods judgements to all tyrants.'[7] When he became an adult ruler, King James took exception to this particular interpretation, especially the mention of the Holy Spirit prompting Jehu's action.

During the previous months, the Confederate Lords who had joined together to oppose the Queen had employed to the full the imagery and rhetoric of vengeance and justice. On their battle ensign at Carberry field where they confronted the Queen's forces, the Lords displayed a picture of Darnley's half-naked corpse lying under a tree with the young Prince James kneeling and praying, 'Judge and revenge my caus O Lord' – the first line of the metrical Psalm 43. Carrying the banner on the march back to Edinburgh with Mary as their prisoner, the troops probably sang Psalm 43. They placed the banner outside the Provost's House, where Mary was lodged overnight, and, as soon as she noticed it the following morning, the Queen closed her window.[8] This call for justice and punishment was an attractively simple slogan for the Confederate Lords. As it fitted so well into his theory of punishment and covenant responsibilities, Knox exploited that theme as much as he could. The English Ambassador noted with alarm that Knox was threatening in his sermons 'the greate plage of God to thys wholle countrey and nation yf she be spared from her condigne ponyshment'.[9]

The preacher was afraid of the 'foolishe pitie' that prevented the Protestant nobles implementing in full the divine command to punish with death those who had committed murder and adultery. This was their duty as 'lesser magistrates' and Knox castigated any failure to enforce God's law as a serious breach of the covenant and disobedience to divine commands. A couple of years later, he summed up the great mistake he was convinced had been made in the summer of 1567: 'For foolishe Scotland wold not obey the mouth of God, when he had delivered that vile adulteresse, and cruell murtherer of her owne husbande, in their owne hands, to have suffered, as her iniquitie deserved; and therefore now sob they for the foolish pitie.'[10] In 1570 after Moray's assassination, Knox identified this 'foolish pity' as the only mistake the Good Regent had made, and that misjudgement had brought the divine punishment of his death upon the entire realm.[11] The phrase 'foolish pity' was taken from the Geneva Bible where it described good King Asa's failure to execute Maacah, his idolatrous mother, whom he had deposed. She had brought idolatry to the country and, as the side note to 2 Chronicles 15:16 explained, Asa 'shewed y[a]t he lacked zeale: for she oght to haue dyed bothe by the couenant, and by the Lawe of God; but he gaue place to foolish pitie'. Many years later, the deeply offended King James VI identified this as the 'bitter note' that had prompted him to commission a new translation of the Bible, now known as the King James or Authorized Version, and command that it contained no such notes or interpretations.[12]

Knox and his hearers believed that the almost bewildering succession of kings and queens recorded in Kings and Chronicles was directly relevant to what was happening in Scotland. The story of the falling from, and return to, the covenant with God within the kingdoms of Israel and Judah was a model for the Scottish Kirk and the realm. As the Geneva Bible explained, the book of 2 Kings contained 'notable examples of Gods favour towardes those rulers and people which obey his Prophetes and imbrace his worde: and contrary wise of his plagues towardes those commune weales which neglect his ministers and do not obey his commandements'.[13] During the revolutionary crisis of 1567, Knox chose the story of the downfall of the House of Ahab as the model for what should be done by the Confederate Lords. He stuck to biblical material to hammer home his fundamental point: when punishing the guilty there should be no half-measures, no lack of zeal and, certainly, no foolish pity. He did not need to provide more elaborate justifications because George Buchanan was constructing his sophisticated constitutional rationale underpinning the deposition of Mary, Queen of Scots.[14]

Lord give thy judgements to the King

At the coronation of King James in the Stirling parish church of Holy Rude on 29 July 1567, Knox returned to the royal line of Judah to provide the text for his sermon. He preached about the crowning of the young King Joash after the successful coup against Queen Athaliah organized by Jehoida and the other priests in the Temple. In his *First Blast* Knox had related in detail the story of how Athaliah,

> by murdering her son's children, had obtained the empire over the land and had most unhappily reigned in Judah six years, Jehoida the high priest called together the captains and chief rulers of the people, and showing to them the king's son Joash did bind them by an oath to depose that wicked woman and to promote the king to his royal seat, which they faithfully did, killing at his commandment not only that cruel and mischievous woman, but also the people did destroy the temple of Baal, break his altars and images, and kill Mattan, Baal's high priest, before his altars.[15]

Following the successful seizure of power, Jehoida had renewed the covenants between God, the people and the King and also between the King and the people. Knox's sermon was delivered before the crowning itself and probably commented on the new location within the ceremony of the coronation oath, taken by the Earl of Morton on James' behalf. By having the oath before the crowning, the emphasis was placed upon the contractual nature of the bond between King and people. This interpretation had been drawn in the General

Assembly's Articles written a few days earlier and it was central to Buchanan's constitutional justifications for Mary's deposition and his view of the nature of monarchy in Scotland.[16] In the Joash story the renewal of the covenants led to the destruction of Baal's temple, and Knox probably drew the parallel with the Earl of Glencairn's removal from the Chapel Royal at Holyrood of all signs of Catholic worship. Commenting upon the people's rejoicing at the crowning of Joash and the peace following Athaliah's death, the Geneva Bible had added, 'For where a tyrant and an idolater reigneth, there can be no quietnes: for ye plagues of God are ever among such people.'[17]

In Knox's view peace and quietness in Scotland would follow provided there were no half-measures. Though James had been crowned, Mary remained in prison. The preacher was convinced it was essential to rid the realm of 'the spirit of Jezebel and Athaliah' that he had first detected in Queen Mary Tudor and then found in Mary, Queen of Scots. In his *First Blast* he had suggested that 'Jezebel and Athaliah, before their miserable end, were convicted in their cankered consciences to acknowledge that the murder which they had committed and the empire which the one had six years usurped were repugnant to justice.'[18] The Scottish Queen, whose personal reign had coincidentally lasted six years, should have the opportunity to repent before she met her 'miserable end'. In a later letter, Knox remarked upon the complete absence of signs of repentance in Mary, Queen of Scots.[19]

Following Knox's sermon, Adam Bothwell, Bishop of Orkney, and two superintendents, John Spottiswood and John Erskine of Dun, conducted the crowning of the boy king. Despite Knox's disapproval, James was also anointed as a king because the Confederate Lords wanted to retain as much as possible of the traditional coronation ceremony to enhance its shaky legitimacy.[20] Though he had only preached the coronation sermon, Knox's role in the establishment of James' reign, alongside that of George Buchanan and Regent Moray, slipped into legend. In his debate with the adult King James in 1592, Andrew Melville reminded him that 'These men set the crown on his head.' It was an interpretation the monarch sharply challenged.[21]

A few weeks after the coronation, the new regime gained greater credibility when the Earl of Moray returned from his conveniently timed visit to France and accepted the Regency for the young King James. Repeating the oath from the coronation service, he was inaugurated at the market cross in Edinburgh on 24 August. In a very Protestant addition, Moray himself sang or recited the 'royal psalm'. The new Regent took Psalm 72 from the Psalm Book and, possibly singing the musical setting he had earlier commissioned from David Peebles, began with the first verse:

Lord give thy judgements to the King, therin instruct him wel,
And with his sone that princely thing, Lord, let thy justice dwel.
That he may governe uprightly and rule thy folk aright:
And so defend through equitie, the poor that have no might.[22]

Moray employed these themes in the letters he sent to nobles who were continuing to support Queen Mary. In addition to upholding justice and defending the weak, the new Regent stressed his duty to sustain and protect the Protestant Kirk and sought the aid of his fellow peers 'in planting of the treu religion, Justice, and polycye within this meserable cuntrye'.[23]

The General Assembly and Knox believed that at last Scotland possessed a 'godly magistrate'.[24] Recognizing the workings of divine providence in the elevation of Moray to the Regency, Knox became a wholehearted supporter and completed the personal reconciliation begun in 1565. However, he was not willing to concede that he had been wrong to criticize the Earl for his initial policy of conciliation towards the Queen, especially of allowing her to retain her private Mass. With the Regent struggling to establish his authority, Knox was careful not to damage Moray's reputation. In the autumn of 1567 he was still revising his *History*, but by the start of the next year had decided it should not be published during his lifetime because Book IV contained the swingeing attack upon that policy and upon Moray. He did not tone down Book IV, instead leaving it intact for posterity to make its own judgements.[25]

The Regent's first Parliament confirmed Knox's confidence that Moray's regime was prepared to give its full support to the Reformed Kirk. With the General Assembly meeting alongside Parliament in the capital's Tolbooth, for the first time full consultation and co-operation were possible between the civil and ecclesiastical bodies. The Assembly appointed a committee of seven ministers, led by those based in Edinburgh, assisted by two advocates, to deal with 'such affairs as pertain to the Kirk and the jurisdiction thereof'.[26] The 1567 Parliament re-enacted the 1560 religious legislation, thereby removing the legal doubts about the validity of the Reformation Parliament and its laws. While stoutly defending the 1560 laws, Knox had also wanted a completely secure legal foundation for the Kirk and he could applaud the action taken on the Kirk's financial position. It confirmed that the entire revenue from the Thirds' tax would be devoted to ministerial support and that the General Assembly instead of the Crown would appoint Collectors of the Thirds. In Parliament Mary, Queen of Scots, was directly accused of involvement in her husband's murder and an act was proposed declaring that female rule was no longer approved in the Scottish kingdom. These were substantial concessions to the hard-line stance championed by Knox and would have given him considerable encouragement.

There is a glimpse of a more positive view of the Kirk and its post-1560 achievements in the *Letter to Tyrie*. Though begun in the more optimistic climate of 1567–8, it was eventually published in 1572, by which time it appeared out of step with Knox's more pessimistic outlook. The tract had been occasioned by the attempt of the Roman Catholic James Tyrie to persuade his brother to return to the true faith. Knox took up the challenge of refuting Tyrie's arguments concerning the nature of the true Church and how it might be recognized. In many respects this final publication travelled full circle back to assertions made in Knox's first sermon about the Roman Catholic Church as a false Church and the papacy as Antichrist. Given the dark and depressed analysis Knox often produced about the religious state of the kingdom, it was noticeable that he chose to portray in bright colours the thriving Reformed Kirk that existed in Scotland. When he started his reply to Tyrie he was happy to boast, 'The Realme of Scotland (all praise to God) hes refused the Pape, that Romane Antichrist; and not only be preaching, bot also be the publict lawes, hes dampned his tyrannicall lawes, his odious superstitiounis, and usurped jurisdiction.'[27] Knox confidently declared that the Kirk of God was visible in Scotland 'and as beutifull in all her proper ornamentes this day' as the churches had been in apostolic times.[28] On doctrinal matters he made the bold and implausible claim that within Scotland 'all the preacheoures within our kirkis uniformely aggre in doctrine and judgement', though he did concede there were differences among the varied branches of Protestantism.[29] When facing outwards against the Roman Catholic enemy, he presented the classic united front. It was one of the few occasions during this final phase of his life when Knox gave optimism its head and recognized the achievement since 1560 of establishing a functioning Reformed Kirk within Scotland. It marks a sharp contrast with the fears he expressed in his sermons and correspondence that the Kirk was not secure politically and financially, and that the people of Scotland were not living up to their covenant promise to obey the laws of God.

From September 1567, Knox had also been checking further evidence concerning the perils of female rule, possibly in connection with that December legislation. Since Aylmer's rebuttal of Knox's *First Blast*, there had been persistent rumours that further refutations were being prepared. At the same time, Knox was revising his *History* and examining equivalent chronicles and histories, including his friend Foxe's *Acts and Monuments*. Knox's young nephew Paul, the son of his elder brother William, was acting as an assistant to his uncle, reading to him and noting Knox's comments on the books they read as well as making a fair copy of sections of the *History*. As carefully noted in the surviving copy of Aventinus' *Annalium Boiorum libri septem*, Paul read this work by Johannes Thurmayr to his uncle between September 1567 and January

1568.[30] Knox's friend George Hay, minister of Rathven, had given him these Bavarian chronicles. Written in the opening decades of the century, the work had not been published in Ingolstadt until 1554 because it contained material critical of the papacy and the Catholic Church. Knox was interested in those sections and he also noted with considerable interest the historical tales concerning women. He paid particular attention to the story of Brunhylda, executed for her nephew's murder by being tied to the tails of wild horses. Although remarking that it was a cruel punishment, he deemed it just, having Paul write 'iustum supplicium' in the margin. He was quick to pick up similarities with his own time and twice drew specific attention to parallels between the stories in the *Annals* and life under the rule of miserable Mary – 'sub infelix Maria' – in the marginal note.[31]

LET HER LIFE SPEAK

In May 1568 when she escaped from her confinement in Lochleven Castle, all Knox's fears about Mary, Queen of Scots, appeared vindicated. Within a couple of weeks, a large fighting force had rallied to her side and Regent Moray's position looked extremely precarious. Against the odds, the Regent's forces marshalled by William Kirkcaldy of Grange won the battle of Langside, but the kingdom had been split apart by the Queen's escape. Mary fled from the battlefield and from the prospect of recapture and in her panic crossed the Solway Firth into England hoping for support from her sister queen, Elizabeth. With Mary out of the country and outside the reach of the Regent's justice, Knox was fearful she would infect Scotland's Protestant neighbour. Shortly after the battle of Langside, Knox had drawn his thoughts together into a 'letter'. It was circulated among his supporters in the summer of 1568 while he was conducting a visitation within the south-west. He enclosed a copy of the letter in the package he sent to Goodman on 3 November 1568, explaining that it had caused an uproar among former friends who

> ar becumed my enemies & repute me more then mortall enemy to thame, & all because I will not justify tham in thare devillishe interprise. The hole crimes that I have committed against such as unto whom somtymes I have been comfortable, & now are so far offended at me that thei cannot conclud whether deaht or banishement shall be greatest torment for me.

Knox explained that his 'crimes' were

> conteined in this other letter which at the request of some brethren I drew up immediately after the field of Longsyd & caused it to be published in some

parts of the west countrey, becaus I was then appointed commissioner there. This letter offended more then the knowen enemies, as the most part of things that come throught [*sic*] my hands do. And therefor I send it unto you that after advissement ye may as opportunitie shall serve signifye unto me my errors & offences.[32]

Unfortunately, Goodman's papers do not contain Knox's tract and no other copy has yet been identified.

Support for its existence and possible content can be found in an unlikely source: a caricature of Knox written in the following year. Its author was Thomas Maitland, the younger brother of William Maitland of Lethington. He put into the mouth of his Knox character a reference to a new book: 'I have written in lyk manner, and hes it reddie for the printing, a bouke, whairin I prove by sufficient reasones, that all kingis, princis, and rewleris, goes not be successione: and that birth hes no power to promote, nor bastardy to seclude men from government.'[33] The final phrase had a specific slant to cover Moray's situation as the illegitimate son of King James V and therefore his exclusion from inheriting the Scottish crown. However, the remaining propositions bear a close resemblance to Knox's notes for his proposed *Second Blast* printed in 1558.[34] Maitland's tract was deliberately defamatory, but it suggests it was common knowledge Knox had written another tract.

Any material Knox had gathered or written against the Queen at this time would have been sucked into the process now known as 'the first trial of Mary, Queen of Scots'. The arrival of the Scottish Queen created a serious problem for the Elizabethan regime because it brought on to English soil this possible claimant or heir to the throne of England. In a clever plan devised by William Cecil, Elizabeth's Secretary, the English Queen declared that she was unable to receive or support her cousin until Mary's good name had been vindicated. This paved the way for an English judicial hearing held at York and Westminster lasting from October to December 1568. Although Mary did not attend in person, Regent Moray brought a strong legal team from Scotland to present a 'prosecution case' against Mary, including the famous Casket Letters, love letters allegedly written by the Queen to Bothwell and 'proving' her guilt. The Scottish team included many of Knox's friends and colleagues, most notably George Buchanan, but also Henry Balnaves of Halhill, his friend from his galley days, and James McGill of Nether Rankeillour, with whom Knox had often worked. If Knox's material found its way into the team's notes, it would have done so anonymously given that his *First Blast* and his views had infuriated Queen Elizabeth.

Already more than convinced of Mary's guilt, Knox realized that the 'trial' was an elaborate device for the Elizabethan regime to gain a stronger bargaining position. Like the rest of Scotland, he could only watch and wait for news of what was happening in England. With his excellent communications network, he was better informed than most of his countrymen and was receiving regular letters from John Wood, Moray's secretary, who was privy to the behind-the-scenes negotiations as well as the public proceedings. Wood was the probable source for Knox's extensive and early knowledge of plans for a match between the Duke of Norfolk and Mary. The Duke had mentioned the possibility to Regent Moray during the autumn of 1568, and Wood had been sent to Cecil to persuade him of its merits. It was one of a number of schemes being floated in England that might allow Mary to be restored to her throne under very strict conditions, and such proposals gave considerable encouragement to the Queen's Party in Scotland. Conversely, the idea horrified Knox and plunged him into despondency. When writing to Goodman in May 1569, he protested that if he were even slightly acquainted with the Duke he would have written directly to warn him 'that as assuredlie as god lyveht he & his assistants shall perishe'. To his friend he poured out the fear and frustration Mary provoked: 'yf ever there was more wickednes in one woman then has burst furht hyr (besides that which yet lurks) . . . let hyr lief speak'.[35]

The Norfolk marriage proposal ceased to be a viable political option after it became embroiled in the English crisis of the Northern Rebellion that rocked the Tudor state through the winter of 1569-70. Queen Elizabeth was furious when the proposal became public knowledge that November because Norfolk's sister and brother-in-law, the Countess and Earl of Westmoreland, were leaders of the rebellion. Shortly afterwards Knox wrote a brief and direct appeal to Cecil urging him to deal with the cause of the problems – Mary herself. 'Yf ye strike not att the roote, the branches that appear to be brocken will budd againe (and that mor quicklye then men can beleve) with greater forse then we wolde wyshe.' In the event, the person who was struck down was the Duke. He was beheaded for treason when the marriage proposal to Mary became entangled in the Ridolfi Plot that had planned in 1571 to depose Elizabeth and place Mary on the English throne.[36]

Knox assumed everyone would perceive that his analysis of Mary had been proved correct and then been confirmed by the battle of Langside and he could not understand why his warnings continued to be ignored. Though wanting to withdraw completely from political involvement, he found he could not do so. He would not relinquish his intelligence network and his interest in politics nor forgo his prophetic messages for national life. Yet he still exclaimed to John Wood, 'I live as a man alreadie deid from all affairs civil' and 'this miserable life is bitter unto me'.[37] Whatever he might protest, his opponents were convinced he still wielded considerable political influence.[38] During the summer of 1569, Regent Moray and William Maitland had fallen out, and Lethington's considerable political talents henceforth served the Queen's Party. Knox had always been deeply suspicious of the former Secretary and could not accept his different values and priorities. The Regent proceeded to charge Maitland with complicity in Darnley's murder, though, when the Queen's Party rallied to his support on his 'day of law' on 21 November, the trial was prorogued. During that autumn Lethington's brother Thomas had written a brilliant propaganda piece attacking the Regent and caricaturing Moray's six closest friends and advisers, including Knox. Maitland employed the literary conceit of a narration allegedly made by a 'hidden observer'. In this case an anonymous member of the court was supposed to have fallen asleep in a bed within a curtained recess of a chamber when the Regent and his friends had entered that chamber and discussed confidential plans. The letter relayed what the informant supposedly overheard and saw, as he peeped through the curtain, during this 'conference'. Each of the six advisers gave his opinion on how the Regent should keep and increase his power, going so far as to suggest that Moray should take the throne and suppress all opposition to his rule.[39]

As in the best caricatures, every person was carefully portrayed, with individual styles and well-known mannerisms to the fore. Although exaggerated or taken to extremes for effect, these were easily recognizable to contemporaries and the description of Knox in particular provided some fascinating details of how he behaved when speaking. Patrick, sixth Lord Lindsay, was the first character among the Regent's advisers to give his opinion in this 'pretended conference'. He was portrayed as the straight-talking, no-nonsense, rude military man who wanted to dispose of all the regime's enemies in a direct fashion. As the leading commoner and voice of the Kirk, Knox was the second character to advise the Regent. Maitland's readers would have laughed at the description of Knox casting his eyes heavenwards, as if he were starting his prayer before the sermon. This was followed by a very long dramatic pause, as if the preacher were in silent prayer. Then Knox's powerful and commanding voice with its harsh, broken tone was heard. The opening sentences given to the Knox character were remarkably similar to phrases in his reported speech and writings and they had probably been pieced together from Knox's utterances during the services in St Giles' that Thomas Maitland attended. They began:

> I praise my God grittumlie [greatly] that hes hard my prayer, which often tymes I powreth furth befoir the throne of his Majestie, in angwuse of my hart, and that hes made his evangell to be preached with so notabill a succes,

undir so waike instrumentis; which, indeid, could never bene done, except your grace had bene constitute a member over his churche, especiallie endewit with sic ane singular and ardent affectione to obey the will of God and voice of his ministeris.[40]

Knox's character then proclaimed his great loyalty to the Regent, whom he esteemed above any other man on earth, and asserted that if Moray fell, the Kirk would soon be lost since the preservation of the Kirk and the Regent were so closely entwined.

The argument placed in Knox's mouth became increasingly extreme. Moray should continue to rule and not be restricted to the length of James' minority. There followed the wish that 'Machiavelli's disciples', the name used to describe Lethington and his associates, 'war out of the way, gif it wer possibill'.[41] Probably raising another smile among readers as being true to life, the Knox character was then given a classic, 'I told you so' passage: none of the current troubles would have happened if only the Regent and Confederate Lords had followed Knox's advice at the Queen's fall. Knox's genuine phrase, 'that wicked woman', describing Mary, Queen of Scots, slipped easily into this caricature, as did the sentiments about forthcoming divine judgement. The climax of the advice from the Knox character was that the need 'to establishe true religione' justified changing the Scottish law of succession. It was argued that there was no guarantee the young James would make a suitable monarch, and it was more likely he would inherit the 'lychtness' of Darnley and the 'inquitie' of Mary. It was therefore better to retain 'the gravitie of ane aiged reler, to the intemperancie of ane unbridled childe'.[42]

Knox's character mentioned that his completed book, on the new rules of succession and the election of rulers, was waiting to be printed and an act of the General Assembly would endorse it and conduct a supportive, preaching campaign. A double-pronged enforcement was suggested: 'This beand solempnedlie done, the buik of God opened and laid befoir the nobilitie, who will say the contrare, except he that will nocht feir the wechtie hand of the magistrat stryking with the sword, and the censure of the churche, rejecting him as the scabbit scheip from the rest of the floke, be excommunicatioune?'[43] It would also be effective in blocking any claims from the Hamiltons or the Lennox Stewarts, if the young King died. In return, the Regent would be expected to punish without pity those who displeased the Church and ensure that ministers were adequately rewarded. After the Knox character had agreed to circulate his advice in sermons, the 'pretended conference' gave the opinions of Sir John Wishart of Pittarrow, James McGill of Nether Rankeillour and James Halyburton, Tutor of Pitcur and formerly Provost of Dundee, though the Regent's secretary, John Wood, was not given his own speech. The different characters were so well drawn that in his *Memorials* Richard Bannatyne, Knox's secretary, had to concede that the writer 'laboures wonderfullie to counterfoute the countenance, the knawledge and the affectiounes of sic as ar brought in to give counsall to the Regent'.[44] These wickedly observed portraits were convincing enough to lend verisimilitude to the accusation that Moray was aiming for the throne.

Maitland's tract was widely circulated in manuscript, with one copy finding its way down to London. Another came in a circuitous route into Knox's hands, via one of his closest female supporters, Alice Sandilands, Lady Ormiston, whom he had known since the 1540s. She had received it from her friend and another Knox supporter David Forrester, 'the General'. She brought the copy straight to Knox because Forrester had believed it was true – an interesting comment on the pamphlet's plausibility. Knox chose the pulpit to refute the pamphlet's contents 'that the thingis be thame affirmed, and be utheris believed, ar als fals as God is true'.[45] He also foretold that its author would die young in a foreign land without a friend to hold up his head. When Thomas Maitland did die on his way to Rome, this was remembered and noted as a prophecy that had been fulfilled. However Knox might thunder in the pulpit, the brilliance of Maitland's characterization damaged the King's Party, though its message was later interpreted as a form of justification for Moray's murder.

THY IMAGE, LORD, DID SO CLEARLY SHINE IN THAT PERSONAGE

Knox's understanding of his vocation as a preacher and a prophet gave him no choice but to continue to preach sermons in which he 'applied' biblical texts to the pressing issues of the day. These admonitions frequently included forecasts of the consequences of political actions and policies, and as the years went by this ability to foretell future events became increasingly important to Knox and to his supporters. It was treated as a God-given verification of his prophetic role. As he preached at St Giles' from 'the chief chair within the realme', Knox's words reverberated around the capital and the court. In his letter to Wood of September 1568, he recalled a sermon preached on John 13 in which he had attacked the Hamiltons. Having found it almost impossible to treat this mighty kin group as trustworthy, in this instance he had gone so far as to compare their behaviour to that of Christ's betrayer. He predicted they would leave the Protestant cause and 'sall depart and follow Judas, how soon the expectatioun of gaine and worldlie promotioun faileth them'. He knew that the Duke and the Queen's Party were negotiating with France and was sure they were linked to 'the malice of the house of Guise'. He was afraid it would be impossible, without English help, for the King's Party to resist troops from

Catholic Europe. It was natural for Knox to set Scotland's struggle within its international context. This enabled him, via Wood, to impress upon his English allies that this threat was part of a papal-driven Catholic conspiracy against Protestantism throughout Britain.

Knox also harboured the deeper and darker fear that the Hamiltons were aiming for the Scottish crown. Possessing the strongest claim to be next in line to the Scottish throne, at the proclamation of King James the Duke had appended a special declaration safeguarding his rights. Knox worried about Hamilton strategies to clear their way to the throne, 'be treasoun or other meanes they cutt off the Regent, and then cutt the throat of the innocent King'.[46] Such concerns were not entirely the product of his fevered imagination. He mentioned to Wood the plot against Moray's life that had already been uncovered, probably a reference to the conviction of William Stewart for necromancy directed against the Regent. When Moray returned to Scotland in February 1569, Stewart was executed in St Andrews.[47] Stewart would have been well known to Knox because he had been a staunch Protestant whose sonnet praising the Psalm Book had been included in the book's first edition. The alarming discovery that one of the 'brethren' had turned against Moray and undertaken such terrible deeds increased Knox's sense of embattlement, verging on paranoia.

The inconclusive ending of Mary's first trial and the Regent's return to Scotland generated a flurry of propaganda activity from both sides. The Queen's and King's Men threw public accusations and counter-accusations against each other concerning the murder of Darnley. Knox was aware that many Scottish nobles were trying to keep secret their own activities during the final months of Mary's personal reign. He had earlier commented to Goodman that there was a strong vested interest in things remaining murky, 'lest that yf the ayre was calm & clear thare faces shuld be sein to be blotted with blood, which misty & troubled dark wedther hydes for a seasson, but god will revealle in tyme opportune'.[48] Throughout 1569 the Regent had sought a settlement with the different components among the Queen's Party, and a few green shoots of hope that reconciliation might be possible appeared towards the end of the year. By Christmas the Earl of Mar had brought together his two friends and kinsmen Argyll and Moray. Throughout the political conflict, Argyll had remained firm in his Protestant convictions and he was happy to work once more with Knox in trying to unite the Protestant nobility in a religious band against the common enemy of Catholicism. At the start of 1570, Gavin Hamilton, Abbot of Kilwinning, approached Knox to intercede with the Regent on behalf of the Duke and his Hamilton kindred. The preacher was extremely wary about any involvement with the Hamiltons and refused to work alongside John, Archbishop of

St Andrews, as long as the Archbishop was an 'enemie to Christ Jesus'. Provided the Hamiltons submitted to the King's authority and were willing to serve the Regent, Knox was prepared to make representations on their behalf. He had heard rumours of a possible plot against Moray and warned Kilwinning before God that, if there were any attempt upon the Regent, 'I discharge my self to you and thame for ever. For I am als assuired as that I am that my God liveth, gif ye be not quyet, the distructioun of that hous approaches.'[49]

Shortly after his meeting with Gavin Hamilton, Knox's worst fears were realized when Regent Moray was shot as he rode through the High Street in Linlithgow and died of his wounds several hours later. Knox had received sufficient intelligence about the plot to send a warning via Annas, Countess of Moray, that she must insist her husband avoid Linlithgow. Planned by Archbishop John Hamilton, the murder was performed by James Hamilton of Bothwellhaugh, a trained hitman, and some of their kindred celebrated openly when they heard the news of Moray's death. Most Scots on both sides of the political divide were shocked by the cold-blooded assassination. Protestants were grief-stricken and, as one commentator reported, Moray's death 'was the cause of a great dollour of all thame of Chrystis religioun'.[50] When Gavin Hamilton tried to recommence negotiations after the Regent's murder, Knox refused even to speak to him and, in a vivid and damning insult, likened his protestations of innocence to Caiaphas' face and answers.[51] Knox found it impossible to forgive or forget the assassination and a deep and vindictive hatred replaced his existing distrust of all those who bore the Hamilton name.

The knowledge that Moray's death might have been prevented probably increased the devastating impact of the tragedy. Knox was at such a low ebb in the weeks following the assassination that he made a form of will, recorded by Bannatyne in his *Memorials*. Knox gave the final commendation of his soul to God and prayed for the 'small flock within this realm'.[52] In his extreme 'dolour' on the Sunday following the murder, he poured out his anger and grief in a great prayer of lamentation and vengeance. Using Christ-like language to describe the Regent, he noted that the Devil and his accomplices beset Moray, because 'thy image, Lord, did so clearlie shyne in that personage'. God 'hast permitted him to fall, to our great griefe, in the hands of cruell and traterous murtherers' as a punishment for Scotland's lack of obedience. Consequently, the realm was 'now left as a flock without a pastor in civill policie, and as a shippe without a rudder in the midst of the storm'. The Regent's sole mistake had been to spare the life of Mary, Queen of Scots, and this 'foolish pity' was doubly compounded across the mainland of Britain because 'Scotland hath spared, and England hath maintained, the lyfe of that most wicked woman'. The punishment of Moray's murderers was a national duty because 'the shedding of innocent bloode ... defileth the whole land where it is shed and not punished'.[53]

On 14 February, Knox poured more of his grief into his sermon during the Regent's burial service. With full honours and no expense spared, Moray's body was brought from Holyrood to lie in state in the Tolbooth. The procession was led by Moray's friend and military commander William Kirkcaldy of Grange, dressed in full mourning and carrying a heraldic banner displaying the red lion of the royal Stewarts. Following him was the Moray's Master of Household carrying the Regent's personal arms. The coffin was finally placed before the pulpit and Knox 'maid ane lamentable sermond tuitching the said murther'.[54] Reducing to tears the three thousand-strong congregation, Knox preached on the text 'Blessed are they that die in the Lord'.[55] Robert Sempill, whose ballad 'Regentis Tragedie'was written a few days later, heard the powerful sermon and ensured that Knox's themes received an even wider circulation.[56] The Regent was laid to rest in the south aisle of St Giles' in the side chapel previously dedicated to St Anthony, despite the *First Book of Discipline*'s stricture against burial inside a church. The tomb, with a dignified bronze plaque, was commissioned and overseen by Annas, Moray's widow, who was delivered of their third daughter the following month. George Buchanan, who reportedly had not smiled for weeks after the assassination, composed the Latin epitaph and later through his major political writings immortalized the Regent as the model of a just ruler. Moray's political achievements were also celebrated in a Latin poem written by the lawyer and poet Thomas Craig.[57]

By hailing Moray immediately as the Protestant equivalent of a saint, though not quite a Protestant martyr, Knox set the legend of the Good Regent rolling. His ministerial colleagues in England, as well as Scotland, joined the eulogies. Knox received letters written by Goodman, Willock and Laurence Humphrey, a friend from the Marian exile. Praising the man he had known so well in St Andrews, Goodman expressed sentiments that were even more ornate than Knox's: 'The floure of Scotland, the crowne of nobilitie, the pillar of peace, the patrone of godlie governement, and signe of Godis favour, hes taken his leave, and gone (I doubt not) to our mercifull God, whom he served.' In these ministerial laments, the punishment of Moray's murderers formed an equally important strand. Both Willock and Goodman selected the Old Testament example of the extermination of the Benjaminites to encourage the full pursuit of the Hamiltons without mercy. Echoing Knox, Goodman had thundered prophetic maledictions: 'Woe to that unnaturall monster, enemie to God and his countrey, and fullie possessit with Sathan, that hes beine the instrument' of the 'foul devilish murther ... Lat yit the devysaris of the murther take heid, for God sieth thame, and his servantis smellis thame furth!'[58] Vengeance was equally prominent in the popular ballads written about Moray's murder, with one employing as a refrain the first line of Psalm 43, 'Judge and revenge my cause O Lord.' The repeated use of this 'blood-feud psalm' was an indication of a process of conflation encouraged by Knox. In his mind and in the polemical literature of the King's Party, the murders of Darnley and Moray were being run together. While the Hamiltons remained the central villains, this device allowed the inclusion of Mary, Queen of Scots, who became the murderous schemer in the background. The Queen and the entire Queen's Party could be vilified as a single unit.

The hope Knox had kept alive during Moray's regency disappeared with Moray's assassination and he found the Regent's death one of the hardest events he had ever borne. Personal loss was compounded by political chaos as Scottish politics tottered on the brink of disintegration with both King's and Queen's Men fracturing into separate factions. It took six months for a second Regent to be appointed; finally the King's grandfather, the Earl of Lennox, returned from England and took up the regency. Feeling increasingly bitter and isolated, Knox was unsure whom he could trust, even among the King's Party. For him, the Queen's Men were a motley association of 'papists', 'atheists' and, worst of all, Protestant turncoats. In his accustomed manner, he viewed the civil strife as another black and white division with anyone not 'for us', the small flock of his zealous Protestant supporters, lumped together in the 'against' camp. He reacted by withdrawing once more from political life, declaring that he had made his final farewell to the world. When refusing to assist his friend and Moray's half-brother William Douglas of Lochleven, he wrote, 'I remitt to God, to whose counsall I committ yow in that and all other cases worldly, for I have tacken my gude nycht of it.'[59]

Given Knox's past prophecies, the overthrow of Mary, Queen of Scots, should have marked the arrival of the Scots in the Promised Land where they could live under the covenant. Significantly, at King James' coronation he had not preached on the end of Scotland's 'exodus', choosing instead the overthrow of Athaliah and the struggles of the Judean monarchy. It encompassed a rejoicing at the 'miraculous victory' while conveying muted hope for the future. Knox knew that the Queen had fallen not because of her Catholicism but as a consequence of her conduct of affairs. He wanted the emphasis to be on her idolatry and guilt as a murderer and adulterer, and so he had proclaimed the need to overcome 'foolish pity' and proceed with due punishment. Once more he believed that his prophetic warnings were ignored and he was fearful of the consequences. The repeated failure to persuade his hearers to adhere to his admonitory messages drove him to seek to withdraw from political life. However, he felt compelled to continue as God's watchman and, because he could not relinquish this prophetic role, he was sucked back into political life as a strong partisan of Regent Moray. This encouraged a form of bunker mentality and magnified his suspicions of anyone not within that charmed circle of the 'brethren'. Moray's assassination horrified him, and the cry for vengeance became the main outlet for his desperate depression. It turned into vitriolic hatred of the Hamiltons, and increased his fears about the machinations of that 'wicked woman'. Although deprived of Goodman's company, he could at least write to his friend. These letters revealed the depth of his fears, his intense weariness and his longing for death's release.

CHAPTER EIGHTEEN

Weary of the world

The year of Moray's assassination marked a switch in Knox's physical health and his mental outlook. For years he had been talking about his weariness and death as bringing a release from his 'battle'. Following his mild stroke in the autumn of 1570, he assumed that he was living on borrowed time and acted as if he were. With his body and voice becoming weaker, his tongue and temper became sharper and he lashed out at all those he identified as enemies, making little distinction between political and religious opponents. During this phase of the Marian civil wars, Edinburgh witnessed bitter fighting and the core of the King's Party and Regent's government relocated to Leith. Knox also remained deeply concerned about the situation in Europe and the threat from Roman Catholic rulers. The Pope's excommunication of Queen Elizabeth of England in 1570 became linked to plots surrounding Mary, Queen of Scots, in her English prison, and this situation filled Knox with great fear. News from the French religious wars, culminating in the profound shock he felt over the massacre of Protestants in August 1572, confirmed his conviction of a grand Catholic plan to exterminate all Protestants. His second ministry at St Giles' ended when he was forced to leave Edinburgh and he went into semi-retirement in St Andrews, not expecting to return. Apart from a weekly effort to preach, his world shrank to his household, though he never lost interest in external affairs. That household was a busy place run by his wife Margaret, who had three young daughters in her care as well as her husband. Her friend from Ayrshire, Richard Bannatyne, Knox's secretary and companion, was able to keep his master functioning during the final years and proved a most able assistant.

SERVANT TO THE MAN OF GOD, JOHN KNOX

Richard Bannatyne was proud to sign himself as 'servant to the man of God' and took immense care of 'my master' during the closing years of Knox's life.[1] Without Bannatyne's constant presence and assistance in all aspects of his life, Knox would have been more restricted and less comfortable and would probably have died sooner than he did. Bannatyne came from a merchant family in Ayr, where his mother was still living in 1572 and where his brother James was a burgess. In the first General Assembly he had been recognized in the Kyle listing as suitably qualified to serve as a Reader in the new Kirk.[2] Christopher Goodman, who was minister of Ayr in 1559–60, possibly recommended the young man to the 1560 Assembly, and the two of them remained friends and in contact in later years. When Knox was based in Ayr in 1566, Bannatyne probably joined the household as his secretary. Being Ayrshire bred and part of the tight-knit circle of Protestant supporters in that shire, Margaret, Knox's wife, had probably known Richard since childhood. Less like a minister's wife and his secretary and more like adult offspring looking after an elderly parent, as he grew weaker they shared Knox's care. At the end of his own life, Bannatyne was friends with Elizabeth, Knox's youngest daughter, whom he would have known as a baby and young child. By then she was married to John Welsh, minister at Irvine, one of the friends mentioned in Bannatyne's will.[3]

As Knox's health deteriorated, Bannatyne played an increasingly important role in running his master's affairs. Since his days in the galleys, Knox had suffered from a range of chronic ailments, including bad headaches, fevers and the 'gravel' or digestive difficulties such as kidney stones. Such health problems were not unusual in the sixteenth century and there was little that contemporary medicine could do to help sufferers. Though he could be temporarily incapacitated, Knox remained extremely active during his ministerial career. As he entered his fifties, which contemporaries would have regarded as the beginning of old age, he was probably worn out by the workload, and his frequent use of the word 'weary' in his correspondence indicated his sense of exhaustion as well as his pessimistic outlook.

In October 1570 Knox had suffered a mild stroke probably caused by cerebral thrombosis, which left him like 'ane deid man'. Initially, the stroke disrupted his speech and it left him permanently weakened down his left side.[4] Although he made a good recovery, he walked thereafter slowly and with difficulty, needing a stick in his right hand and requiring Bannatyne's assistance. It was Knox's continuing weakness more than his years that made him feel like an old man with little time before death. By the final year of his life, he had to be virtually carried along with Bannatyne's arm under his left oxter (or armpit) and another man on the right side and then lifted into the pulpit in order to preach. By the time he returned to Edinburgh in the autumn of 1572, Knox could no longer project his voice properly when preaching and delivered his sermons in the small Tolbooth part of St Giles'.

Throughout his ministry, Knox had occasionally been afflicted by attacks of pain that made it difficult for him to write. This problem worsened with age and illness, and in 1571 he complained he was unable to write more than two lines with his own hand.[5] Bannatyne, with some assistance from Knox's young nephew Paul, acted as an amanuensis, enabling the preacher to continue to function and maintain his note-taking, writing and considerable correspondence. Bannatyne was an enthusiastic participant in Knox's *History*, helping with the editing and writing of a fair copy of the manuscript.[6] He was probably the continuator who wrote Book V of the *History* carrying the story from 1564 until 1567. In his own *Memorials*, covering the following years 1568–72, Bannatyne embraced Knox's technique of combining a narration of events with the insertion of contemporary documents. When in 1572 Knox had grown 'so feabled & weak that he may not write', Richard was concerned that work on preparing a version of the *History* for publication would cease and 'he sall leave that work as a thing manked & sall never answer to the expectation that men hes of it'. After his own urgings proved insufficient, Bannatyne wrote to Goodman in July 1572 asking Knox's closest friend to send a letter encouraging 'your broder my Master' to 'put an end of that he hes alreadie done & to desyre some other to put ther hand to the pen that thir dayes & the doinges therof perish not in oblivion'.[7] As a result, Knox probably handed over the completion of the project to his secretary. After his death, Bannatyne successfully petitioned the General Assembly for a pension to enable him to sort Knox's papers into a proper order.[8] Long-term exposure to the preacher's way of thinking rubbed off on Bannatyne, and he became a fervent and wholehearted supporter of Knox and defender of his reputation. During the last two years of Knox's life, Richard at times literally became his master's voice, attending the General Assembly in person to present Knox's case in the most forthright terms.[9]

Working at his master's side, Bannatyne heard and noted down many of Knox's sayings, leaving portions of his 'table talk' embedded within the *Memorials*. Bannatyne was particularly alert for any remarks in which Knox foresaw the future and, when the prediction proved accurate, added to his narrative that later corroboration. He was acutely conscious of his duty to furnish proof of Knox's status as a prophet. Knoxian phrases such as 'tyme will try, bot the singis [signs] are evill' were left like signposts within the *Memorials*, reminding the reader to check what had in fact happened. More explicit comments, probably from Knox's own mouth, were also included, such as the identity of the Darnley murderers, 'whom God will disclose . . . whairof we ceise to speike, abying farder knowledge of the end'.[10] As further support for Knox's prophetic calling, Bannatyne included a number of his rhetorical appeals to God or to man's judgement. Many of these implored the Almighty to inter-vene to thwart evil schemes, such as Lethington's plans: 'Confound him, Lord and his malitious mynd!'[11] The most chilling exclamation was that the entire Queen's Party should be put to death, when in 1571 Knox added the wish 'And sa fair all the cumpany!', to the description of the hanging of every member of the troop of Queen's Men who had surrendered Brechin cathedral tower – an episode that had shocked even hardened military men.[12] Biblical allusions were often included, such as the comparison Knox made between Isaiah's prophecy about the broken reed of Egypt and expecting, though not receiving, help from England.[13] Knox favoured proverbs or similes to add colour to his points, and Bannatyne noted several, such as 'Clene as gold befoir men; but alace! sic shiftis will nocht serve quhen God arises to judge with equitie.'[14]

As he listened to Knox, Bannatyne remembered best the pithy, devastating asides or characterizations summing up a person or situation. Occasionally, he directly credited his master in the *Memorials*, including reported speech or inserting a brief extract from a document, such as Knox's 'protest' against the proclamation warning the King's Men to depart from Edinburgh. More often, the reference was oblique or Knox's views were inserted under an umbrella category – the opinions of 'all godly minds'.[15] In most instances, the vividness of the language and the uncompromising opinions it expressed signalled that they came from Knox's mouth. In a rare complimentary comment, Knox declared James Campbell of Ardkinglas to be 'ane hieland man of the fynest sort'.[16] However, the overwhelming majority of such remarks were critical and were provoked by the mention of a person he deemed untrustworthy or an enemy. When Scottish Catholics were featured, he was dismissive, and frequently highly offensive. He described the Earl of Atholl as an 'idolater and dependar upon witches' and an 'obstinate dolt and witles man'. Atholl was associated with Lord Home, 'a gredie godles man', and both were totally under the control of the arch-villain Lethington, for 'they can do no moir than the wheillis can do without the extrie [axle]'.[17] Following the collapse of the Northern Rebellion in England, its noble leaders fled into Scotland. The Earl of Northumberland was handed over to Regent Moray, who imprisoned him, and Bannatyne recorded that the Countess took ship for the Continent with her fellow Catholic Lord Seton. Knox's aside combined insult with innuendo: 'a meit matche, a Scottis cukcald and ane Inglis messmonger! Wha knaweth her better judge quhat I spair to speike!'[18] As so often Knox suggested he knew more than he would say and in this case implied that others could testify that the Catholic Countess had dubious sexual morals thus making her a fit companion for Seton who allegedly had been cuckolded by his wife. After the fall of Dumbarton Castle, its Keeper attracted one of Knox's vivid descriptions: 'goat of the gilteane [gilded] horne, Lord Fleming, who knew not one but the king of France'.[19] Knox reserved his harshest language for former allies and Protestants who had joined the Queen's Party. He was relentless in his denigration of the Hamiltons, Lethington and William Kirkcaldy of Grange, but his venom extended to all whom he designated traitors. He believed that the hapless James Stewart, Commendator Abbot of St Colm's Inch, had betrayed his namesake, the Regent, and spoke of 'that fals and feble traitore, St Colme ... [who] is the shame of all Stewartis, and unworthie to be rekned amongis men, for that dowbill treasone that he committed against that puire man, the Regent James Stewart'.[20]

The tradition of 'flyting', or trading poetic insults, had already become well established in Scottish writing, and during the sixteenth century it was not uncommon for all levels of society to employ forthright and offensive insults that frequently included sexual allusions. However, defamation was also treated as an extremely serious matter, normally punished by civil courts and Kirk sessions. While Bannatyne was noting Knox's comments made in private that did not mean they were kept secret. Many appear to have circulated orally at the time and in the long run some passed into the Presbyterian historical tradition via David Calderwood the early seventeenth-century chronicler of the Kirk who had direct access to those stories and to Knox's papers.[21] The kind of insults that came so freely to Knox's lips defamed individuals and impugned their honour. In the pulpit, they often came wrapped in a see-through layer of biblical characterization. During his final years Knox became more specific and direct in his condemnations, especially concerning those who supported the Queen's cause. A number of his ministerial successors, such as John Davidson, inherited this direct and personal form of sermon rebuke.

Throughout his ministry, Knox had been in trouble for overstepping the invisible line between necessary admonitions and gratuitous offence. On a number of occasions his English colleagues judged he had gone too far and had become too personal. In 1554, his written comments on the Emperor Charles V had caused his eviction from Frankfurt. Over time the preacher had become hypersensitive to criticism of his sermons and treated it as an attempt to muzzle him or the Holy Spirit speaking through him. He was quick to generalize such criticism into a perceived attack upon ministerial freedom, especially the liberty of all preachers to admonish sin without fear or favour. Acutely conscious of his prophetic calling, Knox believed that he had been granted the power to recognize the pattern of future events and could not resist reminding the General Assembly in 1571 that God had heard him and acted upon his just prayers.[22] In that year there was another example of his extreme sensitivity, verging on paranoia, when he solemnly refuted an old joke.[23] He felt it necessary to rebut the humorous comment that he was a member of God's Privy Council. Probably first coined by his friend Randolph, the English Ambassador, the joke had been circulating for years. It was recycled in 1569 by Thomas Maitland, and was also linked to Knox's dispute with Kirkcaldy of Grange. During these final years Knox assumed that when he was preaching he was six feet above contradiction, and carried that pulpit immunity with him when delivering pronouncements elsewhere.

KIRK OF JESUS CHRIST, EVER FIGHTING UNDER THE CROSS

Knox developed a greater partisanship as he was forced to withdraw from direct involvement in civil affairs. Indiscriminately running together political and religious opponents, he found it harder to believe that those who supported the cause of Mary, Queen of Scots, could remain true and sincere Protestants. They had not only made the wrong political choice, they had also blindly committed a sin for which they should repent. That suggested to him that they must always have been hypocrites and diseased members of the body of Christ. When addressing his 'brethren of the church of Edinburgh' after he had been forced to leave them in 1571, he insisted they must separate from those who had 'joyned handes with impietie'. He said of those who had now defected, 'when they were with us, they were but corrupted humoures within the body, which behoved to be expelled further'. These medical terms were routinely used about excommunication, and showed that even at this early point ecclesiastical discipline was being contemplated against Queen's Men in Edinburgh. Though Knox conceded that repentance might forestall God's judgements, the sting was in the tail: 'which to wishe is godlie, but to beleve is foolishe presumption'.[24] The lines between different types of opponents had disappeared for Knox and all were to be punished as sinners.

When describing the 'Kirke of Jesus Christ', the language of warfare and persecution came unbidden to Knox's mind, and as a reflex action he added the phrase 'ever fightand under the crosse' when sending a brief note to his fellow minister James Lawson.[25] During these final years Knox spoke of his death as the end of his battle because he assumed every Christian's life involved an endless striving. He also conflated the spiritual struggle with his personal confrontations against opponents. Within his black and white world, those who did not wholeheartedly support his understanding of the 'guid cause' were automatically placed in the enemy camp. From his very first sermon, he had spoken of the division between the forces of Christ and Antichrist and had consistently refused to recognize any middle ground.

Held in an uneasy tension, Knox's writings had presented two images of the Church: the people of God and the persecuted flock. From the Old Testament prophets he had appropriated the language of the people of God returning to their covenant obligations by abandoning political alliances with idolatrous or ungodly nations. One of his favourite similes was of shaking hands, the outward and recognizable gesture of alliance, bonding and reconciliation in Scottish society. He was fond of referring to Jeremiah's warnings about Judah's attempt to attain protection by negotiating with the superpowers of Egypt and Babylon. The biblical parallel became a reference point among Knox's supporters and in July 1570 was employed in a suitably indignant and Knoxian intonation by Patrick Murray of Tibbermuir to his kinswoman Katherine Ruthven, Lady Glenorchy, who supported the Queen's Party: 'Bot allace, I fear ye have schakyn handis with Egypt and I never luikit for your punyschment utorly quhill now. And that I se you enterit in leig and covenant with the Babilonians in ather of your handis.' Murray had imbibed additional Knoxian attitudes because he added, 'Bot becaus ye ar ane waik veschell and ane woman God strenthen yow in your afflictiounis as he did to trew Juda.' He apologized for being quite so forthright because he was deeply upset to hear 'of your gryt defeccion from God'. However, this had not prevented him offering Lady Glenorchy his service, even to the death, in all her disputes that were 'nocht agans God nor his glore the commonewelth of this pure countrey'.[26] Though he had absorbed so much of Knox's rhetoric and his uncompromising support of the King's Party, Murray of Tibbermuir continued to be loyal to the obligations of kinship and his duty of service to his 'Lady', Katherine Ruthven, and her husband, his 'Lord', Colin Campbell of Glenorchy. It produced the curious mix of Old Testament history and imagery with the language of bonding that fed into Scottish covenant thought.

Knox's categorization of the civil wars in Scotland as a religious conflict between the faithful and unfaithful did not take root because it did not match the experience of most Scots. The exception was Edinburgh, where the protracted siege bitterly divided the capital's Protestants. As the Queen's Men were fond of pointing out, many ministers of the Kirk supported them, though the General Assembly usually came out firmly on the King's side. One divisive issue was praying for the 'magistrate', either Queen Mary or King James, and this was linked to praying for Mary's repentance. By refusing to concede the likelihood of the Queen's repentance, Knox appeared to undermine the Kirk's pastoral teaching. A month after Knox's forced departure from Edinburgh, the Queen's Man, Alexander Gordon, Bishop of Galloway, was preaching in the pulpit of St Giles'. He openly admitted that Mary was an adulteress, while insisting she was still Queen of Scots; prayers should continue to be made for her and her repentance. He employed the example of the Old Testament King David who had committed adultery with Bathsheba and had her husband murdered. The composer of the Psalms had traditionally been employed as the archetype of the penitent sinner, proving that even after such terrible crimes true repentance would bring reconciliation with God.

Several months before Gordon's sermon, the Queen's repentance had featured in anonymous bills attacking Knox that were posted around the burgh and delivered to the General Assembly meeting. After annotating these attacks with indignant marginalia, Knox penned extensive written replies. Protesting that he had not said it was impossible for Mary to repent, he maintained that pride and repentance could not coexist in the same heart. He did not pray for Mary because 'soveran to me sho is not'.[27] The *Diurnal*, an anonymous journal of events written in Edinburgh between 1557 and 1575, recorded an even stronger formulation and popular disapproval of it: 'sho wes never, nor sall never be his soverane, and thairfoir he was nocht addeitit to pray for hir, nor wald nocht pray for hir; quhairat the maist pairt of the pepill grudgit'.[28] Bannatyne, attending the Assembly in person, demanded a full declaration of support for his master and was furious when the Assembly declined to provide a ringing endorsement. When fellow clergy urged him to tone down his admonitions, Knox produced the defiant reply, 'The Kirk may forbid me preiching, but to stop my toung being in the pulpet it may not; and thairfoir, either lat me be discharget, or else lat you and the adversaires both looke for ane ansuer.'[29]

Knox's assessment of Mary's repentance had been outlined in his letter to Goodman in 1569: 'Yf repentance be pretended, I demand the signes therof. Yf thei alledge, god searches the heart, I confess, but to that I add, that where god touches the heart with unfeaned reapentance [*sic*] it shewes the self visibly to men, principally when the crimes ar so notorious.'[30] The signs of repentance were a reference to the disciplinary process of the Reformed Kirk, the successor and continuator of the former sacrament of penance. Knox had been the main author of the *Order of Excommunication*, in preparation since 1563 and finally published in 1569. As well as providing the order for excommunication, he had inserted explanations and categorizations of sin. He distinguished between ordinary sins and those 'notorious' sins that caused 'slander' to the Kirk and commonwealth. Mary's crimes were firmly in the latter category and justified a higher level of proof of repentance. Whatever his arguments, Knox believed that the Catholic Queen of Scots was a contemporary Athaliah or Jezebel. He was convinced that everything he had said since Mary's return to Scotland had been proved correct and found incomprehensible the failure of others to appreciate this plain fact. When dealing with other individuals he stressed traditional Church teaching that repentance was efficacious, even in life's final moments. Confession and penitence might still save the soul as the body faced death at an execution, and Bannatyne recorded the notorious case of John Kello, the minister at Spott near Dunbar, who had concealed his premeditated murder of his wife, for which crime he was executed on 4 October 1570. Knox may have encouraged the printer Robert Lekprevik to publish Kello's detailed confession of his crime and his 'earnest repentance' as an excellent moral lesson.[31]

The example is terrible

Repentance and the exercise of the Kirk's discipline also featured in Knox's confrontations with two of the chief supporters of the Queen who were members of the Reformed Kirk, William Kirkcaldy of Grange and William Maitland of Lethington. Grange had been a Protestant from the 1540s and after the fall of St Andrews Castle had been taken with Knox into captivity in France. He had an exemplary record fighting for the Lords of the Congregation and was the chief architect of Regent Moray's victory at Langside. Having been such an old and close friend, Knox was cast down and extremely angry when Grange changed his allegiance. For some time Knox had suspected that Grange, who was Captain of Edinburgh Castle, was being persuaded from afar by Lethington to join the Queen's Party. His thunderous outburst, during his sermon on the morning of 24 December 1570, was provoked by an incident that had nothing directly to do with high politics. In Dunfermline John, Grange's nephew, was beaten and his face slashed in continuance of a long-running feud provoked by the murder of Grange's grandfather. When one of the attackers returned to Edinburgh, Grange sent soldiers to avenge John's dishonourable beating. In the fracas the man was killed and one soldier was caught and imprisoned in the Tolbooth jail on a murder charge. With military precision, Grange rescued his soldier from jail, doing very little damage but putting Edinburgh in 'grit feire'. As well as showing deliberate defiance of the legal authority of the Burgh Council and the Regent, Knox regarded the rescue as proof positive of Grange's switch of political allegiance.

In the pulpit Knox pronounced upon this incident within a blood feud in the strongest terms declaring, 'he never sawe so slanderous, so malepairte, so fearfull, and so tyrannous a fact'. Since the perpetrator was a well-known Protestant, this brought great 'slander' to the Kirk, and Knox lamented, 'to sie starris fall from heavin, and a man of knowledge to commit so manifest treasone, what godlie hart can not lament, trimble, and feare? God be mercifull, for the example is terrible.' With a strong echo of Christ's words that a good or bad tree would be known by its fruits, he added that the congregation 'wald have luiked for uther fruits of that man then now buddeth furth'.[32] On hearing that Knox had called him a 'throat-cutter' and 'murderer', Grange was furious and sent an angry note to John Craig, delivered as he was taking the afternoon service, and a formal complaint was later sent to Edinburgh's Kirk session. In it Grange explained to the session the circumstances of the original feud and complained that he had been slandered by name in Knox's sermon. He further charged the minister with departing from the Kirk's normal disciplinary process because 'the rewle of Christiane charitie' had been broken, there having been no attempt beforehand at private admonition. He asserted that the minister had exceeded the bounds of his calling and was motivated by a 'private grudge' instead of following the 'custome of ane cairfull pastore'. Knox had offended, 'being bot fleshe and blood, and cled with manlie passiones' and should face discipline, like any other member of the congregation.[33] Given Knox's great emphasis upon upholding discipline, this was a well-aimed and serious indictment.

Knox's health was poor and he only ventured out each Sunday to preach, and because he had not attended the session meeting he was sent Grange's complaint. Although promising to reply in writing for the next session meeting, he also entered the special plea that 'seing he was ane preicher' he would defend 'his awin innocencie' in his next sermon. The following Sunday he explained that he had identified the deeds of killing, murder and 'violating the house of justice to be treasone', rather than the person. He repeated that witnessing one who had been reputed godly 'so far cariet away, that both God and man are nocht only forget, but also publictlie dispyset, is both dolorous and feirfull to be remembered'. Loath to forgo hyperbole, Knox added that it 'is the maist terrible example that ever I sawe in Scotland'. In his written reply to the session, as well as denying once more using the personalized terms reported to Grange, Knox went on the offensive. He seemed to contradict himself by declaring that Grange was indeed a murderer, in the sense that he had hatred in his heart against the victim, and his guilt before God was the same as if he had done the deed. He vigorously denied the charge about breaking the Kirk's disciplinary process, citing the concept he had developed in the *Order of Excommunication* of a 'notorious offence'. He insisted that the consequent 'scandal' demanded an immediate public admonition rather than a private approach. Failure to admonish would, he asserted, be the real dereliction of his ministerial duty. Accepting Knox's distinction between criticism of the deeds and of the person, Grange withdrew his complaint. Having battled his way up the High Street leaning heavily on his stick to attend that session in person,

Knox did not leap at the chance to be fully reconciled with his old friend. He generalized the complaint into a threat to all preachers in the discharge of their office and demanded that action be taken about the slander caused by Grange's offence to God, to the magistrates, to the Kirk and to him. To resolve the matter the Superintendent, John Spottiswood, went to the castle and was convinced of Grange's repentance and willingness to satisfy the Church.[34]

With the process finished in the session and the affair apparently ended, a rumour circulated around Edinburgh that Knox had apologized. Infuriated, Knox preached a sermon on the nature of true repentance. The Captain had come out of Edinburgh Castle to meet his dear friend Annas, Countess of Moray, who was visiting Edinburgh, and together they attended St Giles'. Grange correctly assumed that he was the main target of Knox's exposition of the story of Naboth's vineyard, his murder and Elijah's admonition of King Ahab. He and his retinue listened to Knox revisiting the topic of the penitent sinner and describing his opposite, a proud condemner of admonitions. The angry words Grange subsequently spoke put the Edinburgh rumour-mill into overdrive with gossip circulating that he had actually threatened Knox's life.

In his detailed retelling of the dispute in his *Memorials*, Bannatyne made an inaccurate, and possibly deliberately misleading, link between those threats and a letter sent to Grange from the brethren in the west. The letter was dated 3 January 1571 and mentioned a meeting in Ayr the previous day. Consequently, it had nothing to do with Grange's reactions after Knox's sermons in the middle of January. With or without her husband's permission, Knox's wife Margaret probably sent messages to her family and friends in Ayrshire immediately after Grange's initial complaint of 28 December. She had been made painfully aware of the local dangers to her husband and family because the previous year her brother, the Master of Ochiltree, had been shot through a window of his Edinburgh lodgings. The news in Ayrshire of a possible threat to Knox provoked the immediate response of a warning letter to Grange protesting that 'the death and lyfe of that our said brother [Knox] is to us so pretious and deir, as is our owin lyves and deathis'. The message was simple: if Knox came to harm, Grange would be at feud with the thirteen nobles who signed the letter, including Margaret's father, Lord Ochiltree.

There was an irony that the language of feud and noble honour was employed to defend Knox when the dispute with Grange had originated following a blood-feud incident. These Ayrshire nobles did accept, in a way Knox never managed, that it was possible for sincere Protestants to be political opponents and differ 'in matteris of civile regiment'. What they could not understand was how Grange, who had always been not 'a simple professore only' but a 'chiefe defender' of Protestantism, could threaten the man who was essential to 'the prosperitie and incres of Godis Kirke and religione'.[35] This was an appeal for solidarity within a common Protestant kindred rather than kindreds formed by blood or alliance, but it rested upon the same assumptions about loyalty to that group. Throughout his ministerial career, Knox had transposed the rich Scottish understandings about kinship and applied them to his Protestant 'brothers and sisters', the small groups of zealots with whom he was most comfortable. This had worked well, and within the Scottish Kirk in particular the familiarity of the language and conceptual world of bonding and kinship helped covenant thinking send down deep roots that allowed the flowering of a distinctive Scottish covenanting tradition and identity.

Although Grange had gone through the normal channels of Kirk discipline, at the first sign of trouble Knox's national prophetic status had been exploited to give him special immunity. The following year, when Lethington chose to complain to the Edinburgh session about Knox's defamations, he addressed the central issue of the preacher's privileged status. Objecting to Knox publicly calling him an atheist and an enemy of religion, he warned the session not to receive 'every word proceeding from his [Knox's] mouth as oracles; and knaw that he is bot a man subject to vanitie; and that mony tymes dois utter his owin passiones and uther menis inordinat affectiones, in place of trew doctrine'. Maitland of Lethington could quote his Bible with the best and as a parting shot inserted a quotation from Knox's favourite Apostle, 1 John 4:1: 'believe not every spirit, but try the spreits, whither thai ar of God or not'.[36] Despite, or even because of, the complaints, Knox remained confident in his prophetic vocation and drew encouragement from being in the minority, even a minority of one. He cited the prophet Elijah to prove that one man could be right when the multitude was wrong, explaining that this 'one man opponed himself to the King, to his Counsall, to his Prophets, Preastes, and people and in plane words accused them all'.[37] The lone voice and the small remnant provided powerful images of the faithful flock to which Knox constantly returned.

THY POOR FLOCK CHIEFLY WITHIN THIS CITY

During his second ministry at St Giles' and as a consequence of his weariness with the world, Knox was more willing to disregard personal danger. At times he appeared to offer God the chance to grant him a glorious death. In 1568 when Edinburgh was being ravaged by the plague and many left the capital, he stayed with his congregation, possibly with thoughts of Wishart's earlier ministry to the plague victims in Dundee. He explained to Goodman that, as long as ten people remained, he would be there in the burgh preaching to them.[38] Three years later, requesting that God give him strength to continue to fight his battle, he was also 'trusting end of travellis'. In 1571, fully expecting that his death would end his second ministry at St Giles', Knox believed he would be killed by one of the groups of Hamiltons roaming the streets. Willing 'my bluid sall wattir the doctrine taucht be me', he added that his demise would be welcome, for 'in death I doubt not to overcome death, and get entrance in eternall lyfe, be Jesus Chryst, in whose handis I commend my spreit'.[39] Though careful not to voice the wish, Knox might have been grateful to the Hamiltons for handing him the martyr's crown he had avoided earlier in life. On 20 April 1571, with 'the strongest throatcutteris of the Hammiltounes' boldly walking through the burgh, Knox had prayed for his congregation: 'be mercieful to thy puire flocke ... chieflie within this cities'. Casting them as players on the great stage of God's providence, he wanted the current events to be written into the drama of the persecuted Church through the ages, 'that the posterities to come may praise thy holie name, for thy great graces plentifully powred fourth upoun this unthankfull generatione!'[40]

The influx of the Hamilton kindred and their allies into Edinburgh was the result of the daring, and successful, attack by the King's Men upon Dumbarton Castle. The fall of this great fortress, controlling the River Clyde and access to the western Lowlands, was an extremely serious strategic loss for the Queen's Party. Archbishop John Hamilton was captured in the castle, to the particular delight of his sworn enemy, Regent Lennox. The Archbishop was bundled off to Stirling, tried and hanged, before there was time for a rescue or negotiations to secure his release. Combining anti-Catholic with anti-Hamilton sentiments, the former primate of Scotland was sent to the gibbet in his full episcopal vestments and with a placard bearing a verse in Latin: 'Forever flourish, happy tree, and always bear lush foliage, that you may again produce such fruit for us.'[41]

Given his relentless campaign against the Hamiltons, especially following Moray's assassination, Knox would have welcomed the fall of one of his old enemies. It was surprising Bannatyne did not specifically record Knox's approval or select the Archbishop's fate as another example of the accuracy of the preacher's predictions. However, when the Hamiltons arrived in Edinburgh, there was no doubt Knox was a prime target for revenge after his years of vilifying the kindred. While the leaders of the Queen's Party realized that making him a martyr would be disastrous, such considerations weighed less with the Hamilton kindred for whom this was, first and foremost, a feud. Aware of the imminent threat to their minister's life, members of the Edinburgh congregation mounted a guard on Knox's house at night. The concern for his safety crossed the political divide, and Protestants among the Queen's Men were as involved as the King's supporters. A flurry of messages and letters flowed back and forth trying to sort out adequate protection. Having declared unequivocally for the Queen, Kirkcaldy of Grange offered a company of soldiers, under the staunchly Protestant Captain Melville, to serve as Knox's guards. When this offer was refused, Melville wrote to Robert Fairlie of Braid, one of Knox's closest friends, urging him to persuade the minister to leave the capital. The major obstacle to these plans was Knox himself. He refused to accept the sincerity or trustworthiness of any Queen's Men, even 'auld' Protestants such as Captain Melville. Using the well-known Aesop's fable, he made the joke that such a guard was the equivalent to asking a wolf to look after the sheep.[42]

As Fairlie had predicted, his friend would not relinquish his vocation. The previous March Knox had been stung by the accusation that he would flee rather than be disciplined by the General Assembly and had indignantly replied that he had never left one of his flocks without their permission and direction. It took John Craig and other members of the Edinburgh Kirk session to find a way out of the impasse. They told Knox that by staying in the burgh he was needlessly putting his supporters in danger because they would be defending him with their lives. Craig effectively ordered Knox to leave, and discharged him from his second ministry at St Giles'. Craig's insistence might have opened the breach that later developed between the two men over how best to deal with the Queen's Party. Once more denied a martyr's end, Knox departed from Edinburgh on 5 May 1571, 'sore against his will', as he constantly reminded everyone.[43]

Since the threat was directed at him alone, Margaret and their three daughters remained in Edinburgh while Bannatyne got Knox on to a boat in Leith. He sailed to Abbotshall, near Kirkcaldy, and spent time there recovering from the journey. A couple of months later and travelling in slow stages, he reached St Andrews, completing the circle of his ministerial life and assuming that it would be his final resting place. By July he had settled into the 'new lodgings' within the Priory of St Andrews, part of the same complex as the house occupied by his old friend John Winram, the Superintendent of Fife, who still held his office of Subprior.

KNOX'S BIRD

Over the following fifteen months Knox's life settled into a new routine, one that reflected his increasing frailty. His family later joined him in St Andrews, and others arrived on visits. The ministers from Leith, John Durie and David Lindsay, came across the Forth to talk to him. As Melville recalled, after the service Lindsay did a quick change and seized his opportunity for some field shooting: 'For the gown was na sooner af, and the Byble out of hand fra the kirk, when on ged the corslet, and fangit was the hagbot [snatching up the arquebus or gun], and to the fields!'[44] Knox, mindful of his former congregation, sent a letter of consolation back to them. As he had so many times in the past, he wrote from exile, urging his persecuted flock to bear the afflictions they faced. With Bannatyne sometimes acting as a courier, he kept up a correspondence with the King's Party now based in Leith and they sent items he was constantly requesting.[45]

During the spring of 1572 Knox felt his health deteriorating and decided to complete his will and testament on 13 May. Appended to the normal disposition of his worldly goods, he added a written spiritual legacy, 'ane testimony of my mynd', addressed alike to 'the Papistis, and to the unthankfull warld' and his 'belovit in the Lord Jesus'.[46] It was a robust defence of his ministry and a repetition of the main prophetic themes of repentance and punishment. Probably because his secretary and printer were nagging him, Knox got to the press his *Letter to Tyrie*.[47] Having been forced to move his printing press from the capital, Robert Lekprevik produced the tract in St Andrews during July 1572. Following her recent death, Knox felt able to include one of Elizabeth Bowes' letters in this publication, using it as proof against his enemies that he had a pastoral, not sexual, relationship with his mother-in-law. In the preface to the *Letter to Tyrie* he wrote a farewell to his English and Scottish flocks: 'I hartly salute and take my good-night of all the faithfull in bothe the Realmes; earnestly desyring the assistance of their prayers, that without any notable sclander to the Evangell of Jesus Christ I may end my battell: for as the worlde is wearie of me, so am I of it.'[48] Around the same time, he wrote his valedictory letters to Goodman, Wishart of Pitarrow and probably other close friends.[49]

At his own insistence, Knox continued to preach and directed his energy towards that weekly task, often spending the rest of the time in his bed.[50] With his health severely restricting his other activities, he became less willing to relinquish the pulpit because he felt it was the only place in which his prophetic voice could ring out. During the remainder of 1571 he preached on a Sunday in the parish church of Holy Trinity. The general decree, made at this time by the Superintendent and session of St Andrews concerning the times and lengths of sermons, might have been a tactful way of reminding him that his sermons should not run far past the hour.[51] The young student James Melville was awestruck by the arrival in St Andrews 'of that maist notable profet and apostle of our nation'. This fifteen-year old attended Knox's sermons and tried to take notes on the exposition he gave upon Daniel 1–9. 'I haid my pen and my litle book, and tuk away sic things as I could comprehend. In the opening upe of the text he was moderat the space of an halff houre; bot when he enterit to application, he maid me sa to grew [shudder] and tremble, that I could nocht hald a pen to wryt.'[52] Melville's vivid description in his diary detailed how as his sermon progressed Knox became more animated and ended thumping the pulpit hard enough to break it and becoming so demonstrative he would almost fly out of it. Having had to be lifted into the pulpit at the start, he would lean heavily upon it, 'bot or he haid done with his sermont, he was sa active and vigorus that he was lyk to ding that pulpit in blads, and fly out of it!'[53]

Given his sense of calling to be a prophet and preacher, Knox could not forsake the pulpit, nor could he keep out of controversy. Along with John Winram, he became embroiled in the dispute over the appointment as Archbishop of St Andrews of John Douglas, the Principal of St Mary's College. These three Johns, all past members of the six who composed the *First Book of Discipline*, argued about recent developments in ecclesiastical organization. Unlike what had happened with Grange, differing views did not cause Knox to sever his long-standing relationship with Douglas. The three clerics continued to be able to work together and, at the inauguration of Douglas as Archbishop, Knox preached the sermon and Winram conducted the service.[54] When he had the strength, Knox would traverse the short distance from his lodgings to St Leonard's College to sit in a chair in the Yards giving his blessing and talking to the students, exhorting them 'to knaw God and his wark in our countrey, and stand be the guid cause'. He probably told them the stories of his first disputation in those Yards where he defended Protestant doctrine in 1547. After supper James Wilkie, the college's Master, and his staff frequently came next door to visit Knox and one of the young instructors or regents, John Davidson, became very friendly with his hero. The aged preacher regaled the young man with stories from his life that Davidson later inserted into his poem in praise of Knox. He also absorbed many of Knox's stringent views upon the political conflict. In July 1571 he celebrated the marriage of his fellow regent John Colville by writing a play reflecting what Knox had been saying. Though an unlikely subject for a wedding day, much to Knox's enjoyment the St Leonard's students performed the drama, which included scenes of the future siege and fall of Edinburgh Castle and the hanging in effigy of its Captain.

Unfortunately, Knox brought with him to St Andrews the hatreds and bitterness raging in Edinburgh during the siege. Existing tensions and disputes that had previously remained below the surface within the burgh and the university surfaced as a result of his presence. His definition of what supporting the 'guid cause' entailed had been zealously adopted by the St Leonard's students – though, as Melville noted, 'the uther twa Collages nocht sa'. Under the leadership of John Rutherford, St Salvator's was hostile and, despite having a broadly sympathetic Rector in John Douglas, St Mary's College had three teachers who were Hamiltons, and who 'hated Mr Knox and the guid cause'. These political animosities exacerbated traditional rivalries between the three university colleges.[55]

In his sermons Knox continued to castigate the Hamiltons, and predictably various members of that kindred took offence. Robert Hamilton, the minister in Holy Trinity, had to listen to Knox decrying all Hamiltons from his own pulpit. In the application section of his sermons, Robert had adopted the opposite approach to Knox. With the onset of the civil wars, he had abandoned his former hard-hitting political comments, concentrating instead upon general lessons that might apply to all sides. Following the assassination of Moray, who had been Commendator of St Andrews Priory, feelings had been running high and there had been complaints that Hamilton had not condemned the murderers with sufficient vigour. The St Leonard's students continued to nurse a grievance against the burgh's minister, even though the St Andrews Kirk session had given him their testimonial. Knox's unvarnished views on the Hamilton kindred brought things back to the boil.[56]

Robert remained outwardly polite and friendly towards the aged preacher, though in private he gave vent to some of his annoyance. He suggested that Knox was condemning one political murder even though he had been privy to a plot to assassinate Darnley in Perth that had also involved the Earl of Moray. Hamilton had probably heard some details about plans hatched in June 1565 at Lochleven, the home of William Douglas, Moray's half-brother. In order to prevent his marriage with Mary, Queen of Scots, it was hoped to kidnap Darnley when he was on his way to Perth. Though the possibility of killing Darnley might also have been discussed, the plan was to dump him over the border into England. With his fine intelligence network, Knox probably knew something of what was being considered, though he had distanced himself from those who later rebelled against the Queen and her new husband.[57] In November 1571, James Hamilton, from St Mary's College, was present when his kinsman Robert made the remarks about Knox's double standard over political murders. James unwisely repeated them to Richard Bannatyne, who went straight to his master, told the tale and delivered an angry letter from Knox to Robert Hamilton. Robert denied or explained away his remarks, protesting that there had been no need for Knox to put pen to paper since if asked he would have come to speak to him. The unfortunate James found himself in extremely bad odour with Robert and the rest of his kinsmen and he was taunted at St Mary's by the nickname 'Knox's bird' and forced to leave the college.[58]

Another teacher at St Mary's, Archibald Hamilton, also became entangled in controversy with Knox. Having enthusiastically embraced Protestantism, in 1560 he was recognized as fit for ministry, though did not serve in a parish. By the time Knox arrived in St Andrews, Archibald had returned to his college and was teaching rhetoric. Once the pulpit tirades against the Hamiltons began, Archibald absented himself from those services. As well as setting a bad example to his students, non-attendance at church was a disciplinary offence for which Archibald could be summoned before the Kirk session. His absenteeism continued for some time before any action was taken. The affair became part of the wider rivalries and recriminations between the three colleges in the university. John Winram, the Superintendent of Fife, and John Douglas, the newly installed Archbishop of St Andrews, summoned Archibald to appear, possibly as a result of a complaint from Knox or one of his supporters. As a courtesy to Knox's frailty a tribunal drawn from senior clergy in Kirk and university met in the inner chamber of Knox's lodgings on 18 July 1572. These experienced clerics probably intended to end the matter and effect a form of reconciliation. However, neither of the chief protagonists wanted to tread that peaceful path or be subject to the jurisdiction of this 'private assembly', as Knox termed it.[59]

The dispute had moved beyond the partisan nature of Knox's sermons and his attacks upon the Hamiltons and on to the fundamental issue of discipline and the relationship of preaching to academic theology. Archibald Hamilton was objecting to Knox, or any other minister, being exempt 'fra ordore and godly discipline'. He believed that, when challenged, the doctrine expounded in a preacher's sermon should be defended in formal disputation to prove it agreed with the Word of God – by implication something Knox had refused to do. Archibald asserted that European Reformed kirks used universities to retain doctrinal purity and act as guardians against heresy or schism. For his part, Knox was extremely concerned about the extension of academic jurisdiction or university control over the pulpit or the congregation.[60] He feared the spectre of heresy-hunting schoolmen rising up once again to oppress the Kirk, as they had done to the true Church during the Middle Ages. The following month he wrote a Cassandra-type warning to the General Assembly: 'Above all things, preserve the Kirk from the bondage of the Universities . . . subject never the pulpit to their Judgment, neither yet exempt them from your Jurisdiction.'[61] Knox's departure from St Andrews saved the tribunal from trying to reconcile these two obdurate antagonists. A few months later, Archibald Hamilton was elected as an elder on the St Andrews Kirk session, perhaps indicating support for him.[62] Ironically, it was Archibald's reading of Knox's *Letter to Tyrie* that helped change his mind and his confessional allegiance. Knox's statements about the nature of the Church served to increase Hamilton's doubts and led in the long run to his conversion to Roman Catholicism. Subsequently, he entered the polemical battle against the 'Calvinian sect' in Scotland and directly attacked Knox's memory. For Knox's supporters, Archibald became known simply as 'the apostate' and his actions confirmed them in the opinion that their hero had been right from the start.

As noted, during the final years of his life, Knox's sphere of activity shrank to his household and the pulpit, though his spoken and written words continued to travel far beyond these confines. Margaret and Bannatyne protected him as best they could within the household, and a circle of loyal spiritual sisters and brothers gave him support. They accorded him the special status of a national prophet whose views must not be criticized. Those who challenged him became enemies, and with a touch of paranoia Knox saw enemies wherever he looked. As his quarrelsomeness increased, his sense of proportion diminished and he lost his former ability to laugh at himself. Much of this pessimistic outlook can be attributed to his stroke, the bouts of depression and the general decline in his physical health. For several years after Moray's assassination, Scottish politics was highly unstable and, in the Edinburgh siege in particular, the civil war intensified and generated a deep bitterness. His continued interest in British and European affairs brought Knox further causes for alarm and despondency and provided him with additional proof of the grand Catholic conspiracy to exterminate all Protestants. It was meagre consolation to know that his dire prophecies were being fulfilled. Like an Old Testament prophet, he believed he was standing alone and, weary of the world, his thoughts frequently turned to the end of his battle in death.

CHAPTER NINETEEN

Haste, lest you come too late

During the final year of Knox's life the shocking news of the massacres of the Huguenots in France during the late summer brought Protestant fears for their existence to fever pitch. Even though she was a prisoner in England, Knox remained afraid of Mary, Queen of Scots, and of the plots that gathered about her and he also remained concerned about her links with King Philip II of Spain and the Duke of Alba, Philip's general in the Low Countries. In Scotland the civil wars were slowly drawing to a ragged close as Regent Mar struggled to reconcile the two parties. He was least successful in Edinburgh, where the castle under Grange's captaincy held out to the bitter end in 1573 and the burgh continued to face recriminations and disciplinary proceedings for several years. Knox's own intransigence while alive and that of his supporters after his death did little to heal these wounds. With all aware that he was returning to the capital to die, Knox accepted a third and final call back to St Giles'. He lived long enough to induct his ministerial successor and during his last illness he was finally able to lay down the burden of his calling and prepare for a peaceful end. With his heightened appreciation of the dramatic, he took care over his performance of the 'good death' and consciously provided a legacy for his loyal supporters.

Under the peace-loving Regent Mar a truce was agreed between the warring factions in July 1572. In a triumphant procession the King's Men, who had been forced to decamp to Leith, marched back into Edinburgh. Ready for peace and war, they were headed by the Canongate and Leith ministers John Brand, wearing his gown and with a Bible under the arm, and John Durie, armoured in a corslet and with a gun over his shoulder. The hard core of the King's Party had watched from Leith as their Edinburgh houses had been torn down and property confiscated during the siege. This had aroused a lasting bitterness and a desire to force repentance through the disciplinary process of

Edinburgh's Kirk session. Hard-liners in the congregation had fallen out with their minister, John Craig, because they felt he had taken too soft a line while the Queen's Men were in military control of the burgh. Bannatyne recorded Knox's uncharacteristically mild verdict upon Craig. It began with a proverb, asserting that Knox's fellow minister had 'swayed over meikle [much] to the swerd-hand. I will say no moir of that man; but I pray God continow with him his Holy Spreit, and that he be not drawin asyde be Lethingtoun.'[1]

With the General Assembly's assent, Craig had transferred to Montrose, and Spottiswood as Superintendent and a committee set about calling another minister to Edinburgh. The two Edinburgh commissioners sent to the General Assembly in Perth in July 1572 travelled back via St Andrews carrying a letter for Knox. It contained a touching appeal, from 'your brethern and childrene in God', to Knox to return to Edinburgh, 'that ones againe your voice mycht be hard amonges us, and that thing reformed whilk sumtymes be you, under God, amonges us was planted'. Comparing the link between a minister and his congregation to a marriage, they sought Knox's return, 'we being so joyned together in love be God'. Knowing that Knox was weak, they protested that they did not want to damage his health, though they begged him to make the journey, providing he was fit enough to travel.[2] He was Edinburgh's celebrity preacher and by implication they wanted him among them when he died. After a discussion, Knox, Spottiswood and the Edinburgh commissioners agreed that James Lawson at Aberdeen University should be called to St Giles' Kirk. Bowing to the letter's emotional pressure, Knox then accepted his third call to minister in the capital. He attached a firm condition to his return, reflecting Craig's difficulties during the siege and his own recent clashes in St Andrews. He insisted that 'he suld not be desyred or preissed in ony sort to temper his toung, or ceise to speake against the treassonabill dealingis of the Castell of Edinburgh; whois treassonabill and tyrannous doingis he wald cry out against, sa long as he wer able to speike'. Knox was assured that his tongue would not be bridled and that he should freely 'speike his conscience' as he had before.[3] Once more the prophet would be honoured in his own burgh.

His name shall remain in execration

On 17 August, Knox left St Andrews on his last journey. He travelled to the southern Fife coast and across the Forth to Leith. After recovering his strength he made the final stage into Edinburgh and received an especial welcome from 'those that wer banishit, as he was'.[4] He and the family were settled into new lodgings, the building (John Knox's House) that had belonged to the gold-smith James Mossman, who was currently taking refuge in the castle. On

Sunday, 31 August, when he preached once more in St Giles', Knox's voice was so weak he could scarcely be heard. As a result, subsequent sermons were given in a much smaller room used for worship known as the Tolbooth Church that lay above the area used until 1564 for the Tolbooth. For this final set of sermons to a comparatively small group, Knox chose to expound the history of the Passion and had reached the death of Christ before illness stopped him preaching. Henry Killigrew, the English Ambassador, heard Knox at the end of October and noted that the old fire still burned in the sermon's content, though the voice was weak.[5]

While the company to whom he spoke were much reduced, in his outlook Knox remained a member of the great body of international Calvinism. The terrible news of the massacre of the Huguenots on St Bartholomew's Eve had hit him hard. As Thomas Smeton later recalled, the news had 'sunk deeply into the breast of every good man, and in an especial manner grieved and agitated Knox'.[6] Cast into a great gloom, Knox grieved for his many friends among the French Protestant community. The event confirmed the grand Catholic conspiracy to exterminate Protestants which he had been warning about since 1565 and which placed the entire European Protestant movement in imminent danger of destruction. While he hoped that the Scottish Kirk would be spared such divine punishment, his thoughts dwelt upon the wider battle being waged between Christ and Antichrist. Though certain of the ultimate victory of Christ's forces, he had little confidence that the work of reformation in Scotland or Europe would survive.

Characteristically, his mind turned to vengeance and he pronounced a solemn curse upon King Charles IX and the French royal dynasty: 'God's vengeance sall never depart from him nor his hous, but that his name sall remaine in execratioun to the posterities to come; and that none sall come of his loynes, that sall injoye the kingdome in peace and quietnesse.'[7] To demonstrate solidarity with their French brethren, defiance of the Roman Catholics and their own need for penitence and amendment, the emergency General Assembly in October declared a national fast for 23 November and urged the signing of a new religious bond. The strict enforcement of punishment was a typically Knoxian response to the perceived Catholic threat, and Knox and his allies began the process of ecclesiastical discipline against those burgesses who had assisted the Queen's Men during the siege, including those whose sin was simply to remain inside the burgh after June 1571.[8] Knox did not live to see the string of penitents make their satisfaction to the Kirk and was spared the embarrassment of the revelation that his friend and final dinner guest Archibald Stewart had been lending money to the Queen's Men in the castle. In line with Knox's habit of conflating religious and political enemies this unprecedented use of ecclesiastical discipline against political opponents was only to be found in Edinburgh.[9]

By giving him a specific goal, the weekly sermon kept Knox going. Knowing that time was running out and wanting to hand over personally to his successor, on 7 September he sent the plea to James Lawson: 'Haist, leist ye come to[o] laite.' In Aberdeen Lawson packed speedily, travelled in haste and was not too late to 'conferre together of heavinlie thingis' with Knox.[10] He gave his trial sermon to the congregation on Friday, 19 September, and Knox preached in the new minister on 9 November. That sermon explained a minister's duties, using the image of the spiritual marriage between the 'minister and the folke' to which Knox had responded when answering his third call to St Giles'. Knox's valediction to his congregation followed, 'calling God to witness that he had walked in a good conscience amongst them, not seeking to please men, nor serving either his own or other men's affections, but in all sincerity and truth preached the gospel of Christ'. Having urged them to continue to stand fast in their faith, he called down blessings upon the new minister and his congregation and finally 'gave them his last farewell'. Marking the significance of the occasion, many of the congregation escorted him down the High Street and stayed with him at his lodgings saying their goodbyes.[11] The physical effort of that emotionally charged day took its toll. The following Tuesday, Knox was assailed by a serious coughing fit, bringing up a great deal of phlegm. He had to take to his bed and was not able to leave his house again.

An end of your battle

Knox had been mentally preparing for his death for years. As a young man saying his rosary, he had asked the Blessed Virgin Mary for her help at 'the hour of my death'. As an old man he was granted what he had prayed he would receive – warning of the approach of that dangerous hour. Though in 1572 he no longer believed in the intercessory power of the Mother of God, he was as concerned as a medieval Christian to make a 'good death'. He felt a duty to set an example for his congregation by demonstrating how a Protestant died in the certain knowledge of his faith in Christ. In preparation for this time he had discussed arrangements with Bannatyne, and they had produced the formula that Richard employed to permit Knox at the moment he was leaving this world to signal he was holding fast to that faith. Bannatyne would ask, 'Now, Sir, the tyme that ye have long callit God for, to wit, ane end of your battell is cum! And seing all naturall power now failes, remember upon these comfortable promises, which often tymes ye have schawin to us of our Saviour Jesus Christ! And that we may understand and know that ye heir us, make us some sign.'[12]

Though Knox had often said he was 'wearie of the world' and hoped God would soon end his battle, he did not reject earthly assistance. After his coughing fit, Dr Preston was summoned, though there was little a sixteenth-century doctor could do to alleviate the bronchial pneumonia. By Thursday, 13 November, Knox was too weak to manage his daily readings, so Margaret and Bannatyne took it in turns to read to him. The following morning he was discovered struggling to rise because he thought it was Sunday and he had to preach. He had been composing a final sermon on the resurrection of Christ. Knox insisted on keeping the next day's long-standing arrangement to entertain his friends, his fellow minister John Durie and the Edinburgh merchant Archibald Stewart. Not aware how sick he was, they arrived about noon and Knox dressed and came to sit and eat at the table with them. He was in good form, sending for a new hogshead of wine for the meal and encouraging Stewart to drink his fill, remarking humorously that the burgess should drink up because his host would not be around to finish the wine. As his pneumonia worsened, breathing and speaking became harder for Knox. Thinking the General Fast had started, he refused to take food on Sunday until his friend Fairlie of Braid demonstrated that he had been mistaken about the date by eating his own dinner in front of the preacher and encouraging him to take some refreshment.

Dying in the sixteenth century was a public occasion and bedchambers automatically filled with family, friends and neighbours. The relatively sudden death of Regent Mar a few weeks earlier, without due provision for a successor, was a reminder of the need to order one's affairs, whether they involved the charge of a realm or a congregation. Mindful of his final duty as a minister, Knox had summoned the entire Edinburgh Kirk session and they came on Monday, 17 November, to hear his last words for his flock. Following a justification of his prophetic vocation, preaching and teaching, he insisted that his harsh words against individuals had not been personal – merely an attempt to 'beat down vice'. He charged the elders and deacons to remain constant in their faith and never join with wickedness, explicitly citing the castle in Edinburgh. The effort to deliver this oration made Knox's breathing much worse. It also brought those holding Edinburgh Castle to the front of his mind and he sent one last plea to Kirkcaldy of Grange, with whom he 'had been so familiar'.[13] David Lindsay and James Lawson were despatched to the castle where Grange was reported to have wavered, but there was to be no deathbed reconciliation. When the castle finally fell in 1573 and Grange was 'hung on a gallows in the face of the sun', Knox's supporters seized upon the details to provide ghoulish proof of the fulfilment of another of Knox's prophecies.[14]

Provision for his wife and family was naturally on Knox's mind and, probably assuming that they would return to Ayrshire, he asked his staunchest supporter and long-standing friends Robert and Elizabeth Campbell of Kinzeancleuch to take care of Margaret and his young daughters, Martha, Margaret and Elizabeth. He had already arranged for his sons to continue their education at St John's College, Cambridge, and they entered the college a few days after his death. Knox was intent upon making his personal farewells and last messages, such as talking to John Johnson or thanking Fairlie of Braid, though he knew the debt could not be repaid to his friend.[15] A procession of noble visitors arrived to make their peace with Knox or take a private farewell. Robert, Lord Boyd, craved Knox's pardon because he had previously supported the Queen's cause. The Earl of Morton later recalled his final parting when Knox had asked him to his face whether he had been involved in Darnley's murder. In front of the assembled company one lady launched into a paean of praise of the minister after she had said her farewell. This so irritated Knox that he told her to be quiet, stop the flattery and recall the time she had been told by another woman she was talking about things she did not understand. Though struggling to speak, his tongue had not lost its sharpness. The preacher remained in charge and in control of his own dying, deciding when it was time to order his coffin.[16]

Through his final week Knox had been comforted by the readings he had requested. His ministerial colleagues read the Psalm Book's 'Prayer for the Sick', which Knox had often read to his own parishioners when they were dying. Calvin's French commentary on Ephesians had probably been the book on which he was working before his illness. He enjoyed listening to it being read and appreciated how Calvin helped him understand the biblical text much better. The series of passages Knox had requested to be read to him from the Bible all carried a strong Christological message: Isaiah's description of the suffering servant, the meaning of Christ's resurrection in 1 Corinthians 15 and the beloved 'first anchor' of John 17. As well as leaning on his old friends, the Psalms, Knox turned to the basic texts of the Lord's Prayer and the Creed. On Monday, 24 November, he seemed a little brighter and managed to dress and spend about half an hour sitting on a chair. Having heard some of his favourite biblical passages, he remarked, 'Is not that a comfortable chapter?' and, with his accustomed preacher's gesture, ticked off on his fingers the three points – body, soul and spirit – as he commended them to God. Around 5 p.m., he called for Margaret to read again his 'first anchor'. Thinking he was still sleeping, his family and friends conducted their usual evening prayers after 10 p.m. When asked by Dr Preston if he had heard the psalm-singing and prayers, Knox replied, 'I wald to God that ye and all men hard thame as I have hard thame; and I praise God of that heavenlie sound.' At about 11 p.m., Robert Campbell, sitting on a stool by the bed, heard Knox give a long sigh and sob and say, 'Now it is done.' When asked by Bannatyne to give the signal to show that he remembered Christ's promises, Knox raised his hand for the last time and 'sleipit away without ony pain'.[17] Knox's battle had ended.

JOHN KNOX, OF BLESSED MEMORY

Knox died peacefully in his bed – an achievement that confounded the taunts his enemies had flung at him during his life.[18] Two days later at his funeral, the Earl of Morton emphasized the point: 'Here lyeth a man who in his life never feared the face of man; who hath beene often threatned with dagge [pistol] and dagger, but yet hath ended his dayes in peace and honour. For he had God's providence watching over him in a speciall maner, when his verie life was sought.'[19] As Morton was skilled at intimidating people, his tribute to Knox's fearlessness carried considerable weight. Years later the former Regent at his execution acknowledged Knox's prophetic powers and the accuracy of his foresight. The minister of St Giles' was buried with no specific marker alongside his parishioners and probably his first wife, though tradition retained a memory of the place within the churchyard, lying now under the car park outside the Court of Session. Many nobles were in Edinburgh to confirm the Earl of Morton as the new Regent and they added to the substantial funeral procession. It being a Wednesday there was the usual weekday sermon – though, as was stipulated in the *Book of Common Order*, no special funeral service.

Acknowledging the Kirk's debt to one of its renowned leaders, Knox's wife Margaret and his three young daughters were remembered and received a special extra payment from the resources assigned to the ministry to help them in the year after his death.[20] Many years later Margaret remarried, becoming the wife of Sir Andrew Ker of Faudonside. All of Knox's children served the Church in their adult years. His first son Nathaniel became a Fellow of St John's College, Cambridge, though he died at an early age in 1580. Eleazer, the second son, was ordained into the Church of England and served in the parish of Clacton Magna, also dying young, and being buried in the chapel of St John's in 1591. Knox's three daughters married Scottish ministers. The eldest, Martha, married James Fleming, while Margaret married Zachary Pont, Robert Pont's son, and probably a friend since their Edinburgh childhood. Elizabeth's husband John Welsh was acutely conscious of being Knox's son-in-law and regarded his own preaching and prophecy as being in a direct line of prophetic succession from Knox.[21] Elizabeth inherited her father's sharp tongue and in 1622 spoke with King James VI to ask him to lift her husband's banishment. Having found who her father was, the King exclaimed, 'Knox and

Welsh, the devil never made such a match as that,' to which he received the instant reply, 'It's right like, sir, for we never speired [asked] his advice.' On discovering that Knox's surviving children were all daughters, James remarked, 'God be thanked. For an they had been three lads, I had never bruiked [enjoyed] my three kingdoms in peace.' In a dramatic gesture reminiscent of her father, Elizabeth lifted her apron and holding it towards the King said that, if the condition of her husband's liberty was submission to the bishops, 'Please your majesty, I'd rather kep [receive] his head there.'[22]

Knox's secretary Richard Bannatyne was actively involved in preserving Knox's legacy and did his best to organize his master's papers.[23] Along with James Lawson who had sat for many of the last hours by Knox's bedside, Bannatyne constructed a careful account of those final days to prove that his master died a 'good death' in exemplary fashion. These two accounts were the first salvoes in the polemical battle over Knox's posthumous reputation that started before his body was cold.[24] Although his ministerial successor James Lawson was already in place, this did not prevent Edinburgh's Burgh Council seeking to bring Christopher Goodman back to Scotland to replace his close friend. The idea might have originated with Knox since Bannatyne had urged it upon Goodman in his letter in July 1572. In their letter to Goodman, the Provost and bailies of Edinburgh demonstrated how conscious they were of the importance of continuing in the spirit of Knox's ministry. God sent 'his faithfull servande our minister Jhone Knox, deliverit ws fra thraldome, alsweill of bodie as conscience, swa that on oure part (except we be altogidder unthankfull) it becumis ws swa to walk before him, yat his name in us may be glorifiet, and speciallie to be cairfull that his wourde anis here plantit decay not'.[25] As with all other attempts to return, Goodman's moves were blocked by the lack of permission from the English government, as a result of Queen Elizabeth's undying anger towards him. Writing to the English ambassador Sir Henry Killigrew Goodman penned his brief moving tribute to his friend: 'John Knox of blessed memory.'[26]

In his own lifetime, Knox had become a symbol of the triumph of Protestantism that, for the Ayrshire brethren at least, placed him within a special and almost untouchable category. In their warning letter to Grange, the nobles had characterized Knox as 'the first planter, and also the chief waterer of his Kirk amonges us'.[27] Knox had an eye to his posthumous reputation and possessed a sharply defined self-image he wanted to transmit to posterity. Towards the end of his life he exclaimed, 'what I have bene to my countrie, albeit this unthankful aige will not knowe, yet the aiges to come wilbe compelled to beir witnes to the treuth'.[28] If some of his secret dealings to which he alluded have still not come to light, he did write his 'testimony of the mind' as part of his Testament and in it distilled his life into a single over-arching purpose. His was the voice preaching 'the sermon of truth', a message divided between admonition and comfort. In one of those vivid juxtapositions in which he delighted, he described the raising up of those troubled by the knowledge of sin and the beating down of the pride of the arrogant. Two audiences were exposed to that message, the faithful who listened and the papists and unthankful who did not. In a self-justificatory tone, he boasted that he had 'nevir excedit the boundis of Godis Scripturis' and boldly proclaimed that from his first call God had 'sent me, conductit me, and prosperet the work in my hand aganis Sathan'.

Looking back across his life, he saw God's chosen prophet, but the puzzle for Knox was why so many had refused to 'admit me for ane admoniser'. In his Testament he left them to God and, aware that he would shortly be standing before that 'Just Judge', he was confident he could 'gif compt befoir His Majestie of the stewartschip He committed unto me'.[29] It was a brilliant presentation, and Knox was one of the few commoners during the early modern period successfully to define their legacy. He has been remembered primarily as an 'admonisher', whether as a champion of Protestant belief and morality or as a ranting, sectarian killjoy. As the different perspectives and generations have come and gone, the labels 'good' or 'bad' have been variously used to describe Knox's undoubted ability to 'rebuke magnificently'.[30]

No speculative Theologian

The statues of Calvin and Beza, the two major Reformed theologians, stand on the Reformation Wall in Geneva. They are flanked by the statues of William Farel, the first of the city's Reformers and of Knox, whose theological ideas were hammered out in their preaching rather than formulated on paper. Knox was in awe of Calvin's theological expertise and had a great respect for Beza and knew he did not belong in their theological league. Believing that he stood firmly within the Reformed theological family, he would have been proud of the place his statue was given. He had first been introduced to the Swiss Reformed approach when he had encountered his 'Master', George Wishart, with his pronounced Zwinglian emphases. His association with John a Lasco in London strengthened Knox's radical and Reformed stance and in 1554 he had instinctively turned for advice to Bullinger in Zurich and Calvin in Geneva. The Troubles at Frankfurt further clarified his views on worship, and the time he spent in Geneva cemented his alignment with Calvin's doctrinal stance. However, within the arena of political theology, he was not afraid to disagree with Calvin. Knox's handling of the subject of female rule demonstrated a characteristic tendency within his thought. Starting from a conventional premise he carried his position to the extreme limits of the argument and then beyond. Though he did not develop an original doctrinal position, he did produce a distinctive blend of Reformed ideas.

At the very beginning of his ministerial career, Knox wanted his congregation to understand that he was not a speculative theologian and, significantly, he chose instead to appeal as a brother to their shared experience of affliction.[31] His theology was driven by his heart and soul and rooted in his own experience. Most of its emphases reflected the doctrines that mattered most to him in his spiritual life. Even when writing, he spoke his theology to an audience. Most of his theological statements were made in response to the particular situations and problems he encountered during his ministry: they were never intended to be systematic or even consistent. In his one attempt to deal with a particular doctrine, predestination, and present a considered theological justification, he was still constrained by its context as a reply to a specific Anabaptist. To doubt that the elect were predestined for salvation threatened essential aspects of Knox's faith and, in particular, undermined one of his own theological and spiritual anchors. Though passionate in its defence of Calvin's exposition, this book was one of his least convincing performances and demonstrated that he was not comfortable writing within this genre.

Slightly self-consciously, when he published his 1565 sermon Knox noted that he was not in the business of writing theological books or biblical commentaries for the edification of future generations, despite over twenty years of biblical study. His job was to preach for the present situation and warn about the future.[32] He delivered his theology through the interpretation and 'application' of the Word in his role as a prophet, preacher and pastor. This did not prevent him being a firm advocate of theological study as a permanent activity for a preacher. He set time aside every day and week for his 'reading' and criticized fellow ministers for not being sufficiently diligent in this respect.[33] He was totally committed to measuring all things by the Word, and he expected his listeners and readers to follow the wealth of Scriptural allusion he employed. An intense biblicism saturated his writings and encouraged his habit of producing composite biblical texts. Convinced he understood the sense of Scripture, Knox often ignored a humanist precision over linguistic meaning or variants within the text and happily ranged between different biblical translations or supplied his own. For him, theology was never confined to an intellectual activity. It was experienced within the believer's life, understood with the assistance of the Holy Spirit and nourished through prayer. Like faith, with which it was intimately connected, belief had to be lived. Beliefs automatically produced deeds and, turning to one of his favourite biblical images, Knox stressed that every tree produced good or bad fruit: deeds spoke louder than words. This emphasis upon deeds underscored his belief that admonition was central to the task of the prophet and preacher because divine justice and retribution played an essential part in the life of the people of God and its individual members. If Knox seemed to stand permanently in the shadow of the wrath of God, he did so because divine justice played a key role in the process of salvation. He believed that the light of the mercy of God and the salvation brought by Christ would not shine brightly unless the shadow and darkness of punishment from God also existed. He knew he must preach divine grace as well as wrath to realms and individuals alike. When his sermons concentrated upon warnings at the expense of comfort, he felt most strongly his kinship with the Old Testament prophets.

Knox often seized upon one doctrinal feature and placed it at the core of his argument to the exclusion of all other aspects. This habit tended to upset the careful balances created within Reformed doctrine. Knox placed great weight upon the attribute of immutability in the doctrine of God. Knowing that God was the same yesterday, today and for ever played a vital role in his own spiritual life. In his pastoral counselling, he employed his personal appreciation of the rock-solid security of an unchanging God to offer assurance for others with troubled consciences. The same doctrine played a critical part in many of his expositions. His phrase 'the same God' appeared as part of clinching arguments for the purification of worship, against female rule and in relation to the responsibilities of the covenant relationship. Knox's prophetic role was predicated upon the assumption that God's justice did not alter and that what had been demanded of Old Testament Israel was still required from the new people of God, the Church. The unchanging nature of God also underpinned the extensive and comprehensive parallels he drew between the Old Testament and his own times. As he constantly reminded his audience, the experiences of the kingdoms of Israel and Judah were part of their history and those providential lessons had a pressing relevance for their lives. In the sweep of many of his arguments, Knox appeared to collapse the differences between the old and new dispensations of the Old and New Testaments. Richard Bertie, a fellow Marian exile, put his finger upon this weakness, accusing Knox of seeking to reintroduce the entire Mosaic law code, as if Christ had not fulfilled the law.[34]

In Knox's pastoral writings and the confessional and liturgical documents he helped produce there was a much stronger emphasis upon the person of Christ, and the believer's union with Christ. This shone through the discussion of the Lord's Supper that provoked some of Knox's most tender and moving language. In more controversial terms, he insisted upon the practice of sitting to receive the communion bread and wine. Despite criticism, he clung to a simple, visible parallel – being seated at the Lord's Supper recreated what he understood had happened at the Last Supper. The Scottish Kirk adopted sitting at communion and within a couple of generations the practice had become a defining element within the country's Reformed tradition that seventeenth-century Scots were prepared to fight and die to defend. More generally, the regulative principle, Knox's rigorist positive and negative formulation of what constituted true worship, entered Scottish Reformed tradition accompanied by his virulent attacks upon the Roman Catholic Mass. They forged theological badges of identity for Scottish Protestantism, for the English Puritan tradition and, in the following century, for Irish Presbyterianism.

Knox's doctrine of the Church contained the most noticeable, unreconciled tension in his theology. He presented two models of the Church: the people of God and the small, persecuted flock. In his final published tract, the *Letter to Tyrie*, he came closest to bringing the two concepts into step. However, from that first perception of being a brother 'in affliction' talking to his St Andrews congregation, he experienced the strong, emotional need to identify the true Church as the suffering, faithful few. Although strongly committed to the concept of a national Church encompassing an entire political community, he constantly reverted to the language of the persecuted minority. This chimed with his own experience, especially of the various 'exiles' he had endured during his life, and with his strong sense of spiritual belonging when in the company of the 'brethren'. The assumption that struggle and persecution were the norm for the life of the Church and of the individual Christian coloured the language and outlook of the Scottish Reformed Kirk. Alongside the set of texts produced in Geneva, the Kirk absorbed into its own identity Knox's own deep awareness of exile and persecution.

Knox did justice to his vision of Scotland as the people of God in his *History* rather than his theological writings. He chronicled the providential story of Scotland's deliverance from Roman Catholicism and the kingdom's entry into a covenant with God. Less autobiographical than sometimes assumed, it was a self-conscious creation that conveyed his interpretation of the 'Reformation of religion'. Thanks to the efforts of Richard Bannatyne and David Calderwood, its content and approach had an abiding influence upon Scottish historiography and helped establish the concept of the 'Scottish Reformation'. In the *History*, Knox's literary skills are seen to best advantage, with his humour, wit and rhetorical craft creating a compelling story. By contrast his polemical writings possess a strong flavour of the sermons in which some of them started life, and Knox was most comfortable when composing within this style.

Knox's book title, *The First Blast of the Trumpet against the Monstrous Regiment of Women*, has become almost as famous as its author. The tract's publication in 1558, and the reaction it received, blackened the entire example of Geneva in Queen Elizabeth's eyes as well as making a major difference to Knox's future career. It helped undermine the Anglo-Scottish strategy devised by the Genevan exiles, sending the Protestant Churches of the two countries on diverging paths that altered the history of the British Isles. In the *First Blast*, Knox was addressing the most pressing political problem faced by the English exiles: what to do about the persecutions of Queen Mary Tudor's Roman Catholic regime. While his attack on the principle of female rule had revolutionary implications, he did not offer a theory of resistance to rulers – that came later and only in complete form in 1564. Throughout his political career, there was a split between the rhetoric of biblical imperatives and a viable programme of direct action. With the 1559 Reformation crisis in Scotland following directly upon his 1558 tracts, later generations assumed a causal relationship. Knox was not a strategist of revolution, though he did play an invaluable and indispensable part in the Wars of the Congregation as a preacher and propagandist. Most noticeably during those wars, the power of his oratory with the sonorous rhythm of its biblically soaked language caught certain moments and changed them. As Martin Luther King was later to do with his famous 'I have a dream' speech, Knox had been able to make that indefinable difference that redirected the future flow of events.

Knox possessed a profoundly ambivalent attitude to political involvement and was fascinated and repelled in equal measure by politics. While fearing the contamination of involvement in the political game, he felt compelled by his prophetic vocation to admonish those who held political power. He remained a political animal to the end and never succeeded in withdrawing entirely from political involvement. Most of his major confrontations with enemies were found within the political, rather than the ecclesiastical, world. His main hate figures were the three queens named Mary, whose Catholicism was coupled with their female rule to produce a 'monster'. In his writings, Knox subsumed each woman within a single stereotype. In the tradition of medieval morality plays and possibly influenced directly by Sir David Lindsay's writings, he subconsciously transformed the individuals into a stock character – the personification of a Vice. Each woman was stripped of her individual attributes and made to conform to the behaviour of this stereotype. Knox drew the lineaments of this character from the lives of the wicked and idolatress queens of the Old Testament, Jezebel and Athaliah. In reducing Mary Tudor to a caricature of a persecuting monarch, he was in good company among the English Protestant exiles. It formed part of the exiles' increasingly desperate polemic in response to the executions in England and helped create the legend of 'Bloody Mary'.

Such a dehumanizing approach to an enemy made it easier for Knox to fix upon the generic category of Mary Tudor's gender that underlay his attack upon all female rule: one of the most serious errors of his career. His stereotype of Mary Tudor profoundly altered his view of Mary of Guise as he tried unsuccessfully to fit her behaviour into his pre-existing model. The stereotype was equally unsuitable for Mary, Queen of Scots. Even before she returned to Scotland, Knox was convinced she would behave 'in character', and no evidence to the contrary persuaded him otherwise. By concentrating upon the stereotype, he formed a disastrously inaccurate analysis of the politics of Mary's personal reign that helped split the Protestant party in Scotland. Convinced he was fighting the same enemy, he was obsessed with avoiding the same mistakes that had been made in England during the 1550s. With God mercifully offering a second chance, he was desperate to stop his own country following England down the path of apostasy.

In his final years Knox tried, and failed, to transform his arch-villain, William Maitland of Lethington, into another stock character. In a back-handed tribute to his influence, he blamed Lethington for everything, calling him 'the chiefe author of all the trubill done both in England and Scotland'.[35] Although an important Protestant ally, Lethington had never been Knox's friend. He was one of the ablest and most cultured men of his generation and was particularly witty and persuasive. With a hint of jealousy and allowing a tone of dismissal to enter his criticisms, Knox was extremely wary of this expert spin doctor. Lethington was not overawed by Knox's prophetic role and the preacher found himself the butt of some of Lethington's jokes and instant repartee. Happy enough to indulge his own barbed wit, he found how much it stung when he was on the receiving end. In the General Assembly debate on political obedience, Lethington's rapier thrusts made Knox's broadsword battering look ponderous as he struggled against his opponent's learning and rhetorical skills. Knox had long feared the influence of this master of the art of persuasion, and once he had joined the Queen's Party, Lethington became Knox's chief enemy within Scotland. Regarding him as the manipulative evil genius who had all the Queen's Men dancing to his tune, Knox was one of the first to adopt the nickname 'Michel Wylie' for Lethington.[36] He might have been the origin of this punning name because he was convinced the former Secretary had adopted Machiavelli's ideas, both the political duplicity and the Italian's 'atheism'. He had publicly named Lethington 'ane atheist and enemie to all religione' and when Psalms 9 and 10 were being read to Knox in his last illness, he had Lethington's attitude in mind for Psalm 10:4, 'the wicked is so proude that he seketh not for God: he thinketh alwaies, There is no God.'[37] Knox thought Lethington was precisely the type of godless man who presented

a rational explanation for historical events instead of acknowledging the providential hand of God at work.

MANFUL SOLDIER OF CHRIST

Knox was unwilling to accept as valid the cerebral, humanist brand of Protestant
belief that Lethington espoused since for him intellectual assent to doctrines
was never sufficient. His experience of God acting in the world and in the
heart was so strong, he assumed that true belief could not exist without it and
that the affections needed to be 'moved' to generate religious zeal. This reflected
the worst and best of Knox's theological understanding. On the one hand, he
was uncompromising and unbending in his condemnation of anything he felt
strayed from the core of Reformed beliefs. On the other hand, he was a
passionate champion of those beliefs and they flowed directly from his experience and his heart. This strong strand of affective piety expressed in public and
private worship was reflected in the 'heart work' that developed in post-
Reformation Scotland and continued within Presbyterian devotion.

At the core of his own beliefs were those 'secure anchors', especially the
sense of union with Christ, expressed in the high-priestly prayer of John 17.
Knox was also anchored during his life by the kinship, friendship and love he
received from others that sustained him through his deepest crises. Having
been raised within the world of Scottish kinship and bonding, he viewed his
relationships through those lenses. He gave, and expected to receive, the same
strong loyalty from his friends and religious brethren that would be given by
blood kin. If friends or allies failed to provide such loyalty, he experienced a
terrible sense of personal betrayal. In Wishart's footsteps, he extended that
concept of loyalty and obedience to Christ as his Captain in the battle with
Antichrist. After 1560 he railed against the disloyalty and disobedience of the
Scots to their bond or covenant with God; they had broken their faith in both
senses. He often employed the language of soldiers and male camaraderie
to describe the closeness of their bond and the struggles they faced, though
many of his most loyal and devoted spiritual kindred were women. His 'sisters',
like Anne Locke, provided the spiritual comfort and material support that
sustained him, and he relied heavily upon the love of his wives, Marjorie and
Margaret, and his family.

The lack of surviving evidence is most acute when trying to reconstruct
these relationships within Knox's intimate family circle. This biography has
employed newly discovered material to reveal fresh aspects of his life and character. As far as possible, it has followed him through his life re-evaluating what
happened to him. Such an approach has underlined the truism that, if the

clock had stopped or Knox had died at an earlier date, his career and character would be assessed in a very different way. If he had not recovered from the illness on the French galley as it lay off St Andrews, he would have rated a short entry on the list of early Scottish Protestants or even disappeared from historical sight altogether. If, when he sailed from Dieppe in 1559, his ship had foundered, his career would form part of the radical wing of English Protestantism and would merit a footnote in French Huguenot history. Some type of ecclesiastical reform would probably have still happened in Scotland, though it might have followed a less confrontational route. A Knox-style opponent might have needed to be invented for incorporation into the romantic myth of Mary, Queen of Scots. If they had not drawn sustenance from the narrative of the Scots as God's people in Knox's *History*, Scottish history and identity would have developed a different flavour. However, Knox survived and lived until 1572. When he died in the closing stages of a Scottish civil war and with 'that wicked woman' still alive in an English prison, there was good reason to be afraid for Protestantism. Knox worried it would not survive in Scotland or in Europe and had no way of knowing that a lasting regal union between his beloved countries of Scotland and England was merely a generation away. He based his hopes for the future upon the faith that, when things looked to be at their worst, divine deliverance was at hand.

Knox cultivated the image of the lone watchman on guard, and in his darker moments he complained that he was the only one left standing against the enemy. Like Elijah, he sometimes needed reminding that he had many others at his side, still fighting the good fight. In fact he thrived best when working as part of a team or in the midst of his brethren and sisters. Most of the positive and long-lasting legacies that now carry his name were the result of these collaborative projects. They produced the *Book of Common Order*, the metrical psalter, the Geneva Bible, the *Confession of Faith* and the *First Book of Discipline*. Together these volumes have defined the post-Reformation Church of Scotland and influenced the Reformed tradition within the British Isles and across the world.

Knox strode on to the stage of his own *History* carrying a great two-handed sword. He subsequently swapped his weapon for the sword of the Spirit, the metaphor from Ephesians to describe the Word of God and its proclamation. During his ministerial career, he swung this spiritual claymore to devastating effect, sure that he was fighting among the soldiers of Christ against the forces of Antichrist. As the years went by, he found it harder and harder to distinguish between enemies and opponents. Speaking about the exile congregation he shared with Knox, Goodman had described the group as 'manfull souldiers of Christ' who had mustered 'where his [Christ's] banner is displayed, and his standarde sett uppe: where the assemble of your brethern is, and his worde openly preached, and sacramentes faithfully ministered'.[38]

Soldiering among this particular assembly of brethren was the pivot around which Knox's life turned. Up to that point, his career as a preacher, prophet and pastor had been practised largely within an English ecclesiastical context, leading to the establishment of that model congregation in Geneva and to his own 1558 tracts. After he left Geneva in 1559, he spent most of the remainder of his life within Scotland. He carried to his native land the positive achievements of the example of Geneva – ecclesiastical practice as well as the community of texts. He also carried with him the stereotypes and assumptions developed in response to Protestant suffering and persecution. Once in Scotland, his vision of the struggle for reformation as part of the great battle with Antichrist aided the success of the Lords of the Congregation. Following 1560, he was dominated by his fear of a repetition of English apostasy. The problem was not his English accent, mocked by Ninian Winzet, but his English experience. Knox's contribution to the establishment of the new Scottish Kirk was restricted because he could never see beyond the Old Testament model of disobedience to God's covenant that he had grasped in the 1550s.

Knox's multifaceted personality cannot be contained within the labels too easily attached to him. Today he is usually identified as a Scottish Reformer; the opponent of Mary, Queen of Scots, and disparager of women; the anti-Catholic Presbyterian hero or villain according to perspective; the personification of the Calvinist dourness and puritanism that have blighted Scottish identity. In the caricature version, he has become the ranting Scotsman with the long beard and preaching gown. Though the biography started with a happy man, much of the new evidence from the Goodman letters demonstrates how much Knox struggled with his negative thoughts. He has been given plenty of opportunity to speak in his own words and to be seen in a number of surprising roles in this biography. The Geneva pivot of his life underlines that Knox was a proud member of the international Protestant community and that its battle dominated his outlook. He was an Englishman by adoption, a warm friend of France, Geneva and the European Reformed network and a potential missionary to Ireland. However, his passion and his fighting spirit never let the reader forget he was born, bred and remained a Scot; he was Tinoterius, the man from the banks of the River Tyne in Haddington.

Notes

CHAPTER 1 RARE AND WONDERFUL GIFTS

1. *Livre des Anglois*, p. 73, printed in Charles Martin, *Les Protestants anglais réfugiés à Genève au temps du Calvin* (Librairie A. Jullien, Geneva, 1915), pp. 331–8, at p. 336.
2. *The Works of John Knox*, ed. D. Laing, 6 vols (Bannatyne Club, Edinburgh, 1846–64), vol. IV, p. 187.
3. Ibid., p. 191. In the exposition of Ephesians 1:5 in his tract on predestination, Knox inserted 'in children' into his explanation of adoption into Christ: God 'hathe predestinat us that he should adoptat us in children by Jesus Christe': David Wright, 'John Knox's Bible', in *The Bible as Book: The Reformation* (Oak Knoll Press, British Library, London, 2000), p. 55.
4. For a full discussion of the find, see Jane E. A. Dawson and Lionel K. Glassey, 'Some Unpublished Letters from John Knox to Christopher Goodman', *Scottish Historical Review*, 84 (2005), pp. 166–201.
5. From the end of the nineteenth century, the identification of Tinoterius as Knox had been made, though it was assumed to be a mistranscription for 'Sinclerius': e.g. P. Hume Brown, *John Knox: A Biography*, 2 vols (Adam and Charles Black, London, 1895), vol. I, pp. 175–6 and n. 3. Its significance and proper dating became much clearer when placed within the new Goodman material; see below, Chapter 7.
6. Wright, 'John Knox's Bible', pp. 51–63. I am most grateful to my late colleague, Professor David Wright and to Anne-Marie, his wife, for giving me his research notes on the Melbourne volume. See below, Chapter 16.
7. The report on the painting explained, 'Conservators cleaning the portrait have established that the work is probably the only known authentic painting of Knox, and not merely a copy of an earlier print as was previously thought ... Until now, the only known authentic Knox portrait has been a small oval woodcut, published by Theodore Beza in Geneva in 1580. It was copied from a picture painted in Edinburgh the previous year by King James VI's artist, Adrian Vanson. It had always been thought that the University's portrait was based on the woodcut, but the restoration suggests that the picture could instead be a contemporary copy of Vanson's portrait. While restoring the portrait, conservator Clare Meredith discovered that the painting had, in fact, been later restored to look like the woodcut. The most significant differences between the cleaned painting and the woodcut are in the area of Knox's hands and the book he holds. With Vanson's portrait now unaccounted for, the restored portrait appears to the only authentic known painting of Knox.' Object Lessons exhibition at Talbot Rice Gallery, University of Edinburgh. Image on http://images.is.ed.ac.uk/luna/servlet/allCollections (accessed 28 October 2013).
8. Knox's assertion of 'plain speaking' to Mary, Queen of Scots, *John Knox's History of the Reformation in Scotland*, ed. W. C. Dickinson, 2 vols (Nelson, Edinburgh, 1949), vol. II, p. 83; his 'simplicity', Knox's Epistle to Berwick and Newcastle, 1558, *Works*, vol. V, pp. 480–1.
9. The Knox–Bowes correspondence and its dating, A. Daniel Frankforter, 'Elizabeth Bowes and John Knox: A Woman in Reformation Theology', *Church History*, 56 (1987), pp. 333–47;

Knox–Locke correspondence, Susan M. Felch (ed.), *The Collected Works of Anne Vaughan Locke*, Medieval and Renaissance Texts and Studies (MRTS), 185 (Arizona Center for Medieval and Renaissance Studies,Tempe, AZ, 1999); Susan M. Felch, '"Deir Sister": The Letters of John Knox to Anne Vaughan Lok', *Renaissance and Reformation*, 19 (1995), pp. 47–65; Knox–Goodman correspondence, Dawson and Glassey, 'Some Unpublished Letters'.

10. John Field to Anne Locke, 1 January 1583: Knox, *Works*, vol. VI, p. 91.

11. Knox, *History*, and Roger A. Mason (ed.), *Knox on Rebellion* (Cambridge University Press, Cambridge, 1994).

12. Dictionary of the Scots Language [incorporating the *Dictionary of the Older Scottish Tongue*] http://www.dsl.ac.uk/.

CHAPTER 2 TINOTERIUS: THE MAN FROM THE BANKS OF THE TYNE

1. Knox to Goodman, 27 October 1566, Dawson and Glassey, 'Some Unpublished Letters', p. 185.

2. For the early sixteenth-century Church in Scotland, see Jane E. A. Dawson, *Scotland Re-formed 1488–1587* (Edinburgh University Press, Edinburgh, 2007), Part II, and for the effect of Luther's revolt, Diarmaid MacCulloch, *Reformation: Europe's House Divided 1490–1700* (Allen Lane, London, 2003), Part I.

3. There are two statements about Knox's age at his death in November 1572, both made within a decade of the death and both from good sources, though neither particularly close to Knox. The first was Sir Peter Young's description written on 13 November 1579 to Theodore Beza which noted that Knox had died in his fifty-ninth year. The second account was from Beza himself in his *Icones*. He had known Knox well from the 1550s and had written that the Scot was fifty-seven when he died. Jasper Ridley provides a detailed discussion of the evidence: Jasper Ridley, *John Knox* (Clarendon Press, Oxford, 1968), pp. 531–4.

4. For a detailed examination of baptism and kinship, W. Coster, *Baptism and Spiritual Kinship in Early Modern England* (Ashgate, Aldershot, 2002), Part 1.

5. Knox, *History*, vol. I, p. 90.

6. Jane E. A. Dawson, '"There is Nothing like a Good Gossip": Godparenting, Baptism and Alliance in Early Modern Scotland', in M. Mackay and C. Kay (eds), *Perspectives on the Older Scottish Tongue* (Edinburgh University Press, Edinburgh, 2005), pp. 38–47.

7. Letter from Tinoterius to Calvin and the Genevan pastors newly confirmed as from John Knox, see *Ioannis Calvini Opera quae supersunt omnia*, ed. G. Baum, E. Cunitz and E. Reuss, 59 vols (1863–1900), vol. 15, pp. 370–2, and see below, Chapter 7.

8. Blaeu's atlas can be viewed on the National Library of Scotland site, http://maps.nls.uk/atlas/blaeu/, accessed 6 November 2013.

9. Knox, *History*, vol. I, p. 113.

10. Ibid., vol. II, p. 38.

11. Knox to Elizabeth Bowes, *c.*December 1552, Knox, *Works*, vol. III, p. 356.

12. Knox to Elizabeth Bowes, June–July 1553, Knox, *Works*, vol. III, p. 379.

13. Knox, *History*, vol. I, p. 11.

14. Richard Fawcett, *The Architectural History of Scotland: Scottish Architecture from the Accession of the Stewarts to the Reformation 1371–1560* (Edinburgh University Press, Edinburgh, 1994), pp. 194–7.

15. In the Protestant versions of the Psalms the numbering changes at Psalm 9. Psalm 10 was turned into a separate psalm whereas in the Vulgate version it had formed the second section of Psalm 9. On his deathbed Knox spoke of Psalm 9 when he meant a verse that belonged to the Protestant Psalm 10: Knox, *Works*, vol. VI, p. 638, and see below, Chapter 19. For Knox's use of the 'oral bible', see Wright, 'John Knox's Bible', p. 58.

16. Knox to Elizabeth Bowes, 23 June 1553, Knox, *Works*, vol. III, p. 339.

17. Knox, *History*, vol. I, p. 113.

18. Wright, 'John Knox's Bible', p. 53.

19. From *The Dialogue of the Twa Wyfeis*, cited in Mark Loughlin, 'The Dialogue of the Twa Wyfeis: Maitland, Machiavelli and the Propaganda of the Scottish Civil War', in A. A. MacDonald, Michael Lynch and I. B. Cowan (eds), *The Renaissance in Scotland: Studies in Literature, Religion, History and Culture* (Brill, Leiden, 1994), p. 226.

20. Knox, *History*, vol. I, p. 15. For a discussion of this phase of Knox's life and its subsequent influence, J. H. Burns, 'Knox: Scholastic and Canonistic Echoes', in Roger A. Mason (ed.), *John Knox and the British Reformations* (Ashgate, Aldershot, 1998), pp. 117–29.

21. Wright, 'John Knox's Bible', p. 58.

22. Little details in the *History* demonstrated this awareness, e.g. Wishart's preaching in Dundee: Knox, *History*, vol. I, p. 62.

23. Ibid., pp. 24–5.

24. Kenneth D. Farrow, *John Knox: Reformation Rhetoric and the Traditions of Scots Prose 1490–1570* (Peter Lang, Bern, 2004), pp. 70–4.

25. N. Winzet, *Certane Tractatis*, in *Works*, ed. J. Hewison, 2 vols (Scottish Text Society, first series, 15 and 22, Edinburgh, 1888 and 1890), vol. I, pp. 18 and 21.

26. Ridley, *Knox*, p. 17.

27. Knox, *Works*, vol. VI, p. 229.

28. From Sir Peter Young's description, Knox, *History*, vol. I, p. lxxxvii.

29. Knox, *Works*, vol. VI, pp. xxi–xxii and engraving. Documents in David Laing, 'A Supplementary Notice by Mr Laing' to John Richardson, 'On the Present State of the Question, "Where was John Knox born?"', *Proceedings of the Society of Antiquaries of Scotland*, III (Edinburgh, 1858), pp. 57–63; W. Fraser, *Memorials of the Earls of Haddington* (Constable, Edinburgh, 1889), pp. xl–xliii and plate. For general background on notaries, John Durkan, 'The Early Scottish Notary', in I. B. Cowan and Duncan Shaw (eds), *Renaissance and Reformation in Scotland* (Scottish Academic Press, Edinburgh, 1983), pp. 22–40.

30. Used in the opening to his 1558 tract *Appellation*; see below, Chapter 10.

CHAPTER 3 MY FIRST ANCHOR

1. Background in Dawson, *Scotland Re-formed*, chapter 7; Marcus Merriman, *The Rough Wooings: Mary, Queen of Scots 1542–1551* (Tuckwell Press, East Linton, 2000).

2. Laing, 'A Supplementary Notice by Mr Laing', *Proceedings of the Society of Antiquaries of Scotland*, III (Edinburgh, 1858), pp. 57–63.

3. David Calderwood, *History of the Church of Scotland*, ed. T. Thomson, 8 vols (Wodrow Society, Edinburgh, 1842–9), vol. I, pp. 155–6.

4. Knox, *History*, vol. I, p. 42.

5. Ibid., pp. 48–9.

6. Ibid., pp. 43–5.

7. Knox to Elizabeth Bowes, 20 July 1554, Knox, *Works*, vol. III, p. 346.

8. Wright, 'John Knox's Bible', pp. 59–60. I am grateful to the late Professor Wright for his many insights on Knox and for sharing the fruits of his research on the Melbourne Bible.

9. Knox, *Works*, vol. VI, p. 643.

10. Ibid.; see below, Chapter 19.

11. *The Geneva Bible*, facsimile of the 1560 edn with an introduction by Lloyd E. Berry (University of Wisconsin Press, Madison, WI, 1969), f. 51v.

12. Knox, *Works*, vol. V, pp. 51–2.

13. John 17:20, 21, 23, *Geneva Bible*, 1560 edn, f. 52r.

14. Note for John 17:6 that included cross-references to the well-known proof texts for predestination, Romans 8:39 and Ephesians 1:4, *Geneva Bible*, 1560 edn, f. 51v.

15. Note for John 17:24, *Geneva Bible*, 1560 edn, f. 52r.

16. Note for John 17:26, *Geneva Bible*, 1560 edn, f. 52r.

17. Knox, *Works*, vol. VI, p. 297.

18. Knox, *History*, vol. I, pp. 332–4; J. McEwen, *The Faith of John Knox* (Lutterworth, London, 1961), pp. 106–8.

19. John 10, especially verses 3–5.

20. Knox, *History*, vol. I, p. 67.

21. For a discussion of the evangelical movements, M. Dotterweich, 'The Emergence of Evangelical Theology in Scotland to 1550' (University of Edinburgh PhD thesis, 2002), and A. Ryrie, *The Origins of the Scottish Reformation* (Manchester University Press, Manchester, 2006), chapter 4.

22. Winzet, *Certane Tractatis*, vol. I, pp. 18–20.

23. Knox, *History*, vol. I, p. 67.

24. *First Helvetic Confession* in *Miscellany of the Wodrow Society*, ed. David Laing (Wodrow Society, Edinburgh, 1844), vol. I, pp. 1–23; Article 19, p. 17; and see below, Chapter 18.

25. Knox, *History*, vol. II, p. 12.

26. Ibid., vol. I, p. 60.

27. Ibid., pp. 67–8; cf. Knox, *Works*, vol. VI, p. 619.

28. Knox, *History*, vol. I, p. 69.

29. Ibid., p. 74.

30. Knox to John Foxe, 18 May 1558, Knox, *Works*, vol. V, p. 5.

31. *First Helvetic Confession*, Article 12, p. 15; Article 19, p. 18.

32. Knox to Elizabeth Bowes, December 1552, Knox, *Works*, vol. IV, pp. 367, 369.

33. Knox, *History*, vol. I, p. 68.

34. Ibid., p. 113.

35. Ibid., p. 64.

36. Martin Holt Dotterweich, 'Wishart, George (*c.*1513?–1546)', *Oxford Dictionary of National Biography*, Oxford University Press, 2004 (http://www.oxforddnb.com/view/article/29793, accessed 25 November 2013).

37. Farrow, *John Knox*, p. 91.

38. Jane E. A. Dawson, 'Patterns of Worship in Reformation Scotland', in Duncan B. Forrester and Douglas C. Gay (eds), *Worship and Liturgy in Context: Studies of Theology and Practice* (SCM Press, London, 2009), pp. 136–51.

CHAPTER 4 CALLED BY MY GOD

1. Knox, *Works*, vol. VI, p. 229.

2. Knox to Elizabeth Bowes, December 1552, ibid., vol. IV, p. 368.

3. Knox, *History*, vol. I, p. 71.

4. Farrow, *John Knox*, pp. 270–2.

5. Margaret H. B. Sanderson, *Cardinal of Scotland: David Beaton c.1494–1546* (John Donald, Edinburgh, 2001 edn), chapter 13.

6. Ridley, *Knox*, p. 50.

7. Knox, *History*, vol. I, p. 82.

8. Ibid.

9. Ibid., p. 83.

10. Knox, *Works*, vol. IV, p. 467.

11. Ibid., vol. VI, p. 230.

12. Ibid., vol. III, p. 389.

13. Knox, *History*, vol. I, p. 83.

14. Ibid., p. 84.

15. See the note in the *Geneva Bible*, 1560 edn, f. 54r on John 21:17.

16. *Geneva Bible*, 1560 edn, f. 54r, running heading for John 21.

17. Knox to Elizabeth Bowes, end 1553, Knox, *Works*, vol. III, pp. 387–8.

18. John 21:15, *Geneva Bible*, 1560 edn, f. 54r.

19. Knox to Goodman, 18 February 1567, Dawson and Glassey, 'Some Unpublished Letters', p. 190.

20. E.g. Knox, *Works*, vol. III, pp. 40–1. This is a conflation of John 10:27 and John 5. See Wright, 'John Knox's Bible', p. 52.

21. Note at John 10:3, *Geneva Bible*, 1560 edn, f. 48r.

22. Knox to Elizabeth Bowes, end 1553, Knox, *Works*, vol. III, p. 389.

23. Knox, *History*, vol. II, pp. 276–7.

24. Knox to Elizabeth Bowes, 1552, Knox, *Works*, vol. III, p. 352.

25. Knox, *History*, vol. I, p. 90; Pierre Janton, *John Knox (ca. 1513–1572): L'homme et l'oeuvre* (Didier, Paris, 1967), p. 68.

26. Knox, *Works*, vol. VI, p. 590, and see below, Chapter 16.

27. W. Rankin, *The Parish Church of Holy Trinity, St Andrews, Pre-Reformation* (Oliver & Boyd, Edinburgh, 1955), pp. 49–99.

28. Knox, *History*, vol. I, p. 84.

29. Ibid., p. 86.

30. Ibid.

31. Ibid., p. 109.

32. Knox to Elizabeth Bowes, end 1553, Knox, *Works*, vol. III, pp. 387–91.

33. Knox's term 'express' attached to the 'Word of God' meant both explicit and specific: Wright, 'John Knox's Bible', p. 51.

34. Knox, *History*, vol. I, p. 91.

35. Ibid., p. 93.

36. Ibid., pp. 94–6.

37. Ibid., p. 97.

38. John Davidson, *Ane Brief Commendatioun of Uprichtnes*, printed in *Three Scottish Reformers: Alexander Cunningham, fifth earl of Glencairn, Henry Balnavis of Halhill and John Davidson of Prestonpans with their poetical remains*, ed. Rev. Charles Rogers (English Reprint Society, London, 1874), pp. 80–99, at p. 97.

1. E.g. Knox to Elizabeth Bowes, 22 December 1551 and early 1552, Knox, *Works*, vol. III, pp. 351 and 355; Janton, *John Knox*, pp. 98–100.

2. Jane E. A. Dawson, 'The Two John Knoxes: England, Scotland and the 1558 Tracts', *Journal of Ecclesiastical History*, 42 (1991), pp. 555–76.

3. Knox, *Works*, vol. III, p. 133.

4. For Edwardian Protestantism, see Diarmaid MacCulloch, *Tudor Church Militant: Edward VI and the Protestant Reformation* (Allen Lane, The Penguin Press, London, 1999), and for the continuing importance of the Edwardian mindset, Stephen Alford, *Kingship and Politics in the Reign of Edward VI* (Cambridge University Press, Cambridge, 2002), chapter 6.

5. Knox, *History*, vol. I, p. 97; Knox, *Works*, vol. III, p. 8; Ridley, *Knox*, chapter 5.

6. Details of galley life, W. Stanford Reid, *Trumpeter of God: A Biography of John Knox* (Charles Scribner's Sons, New York, 1974), pp. 56–7.

7. E.g. Knox, *Works*, vol. III, p. 387; vol. IV, p. 104. Letter to Berwick, 1552, Peter Lorimer, *John Knox and the Church of England* (Henry S. King, London, 1875), p. 260.

8. E.g. *Declaration of Prayer*, Knox, *Works*, vol. III, pp. 90–1.

9. Anon. (John Aylmer), *An Harborowe for faithfull and trewe subjectes* ('Strasbourg', London, 1559), sig. P2; Ridley, *Knox*, p. 68.

10. Knox, *History*, vol. I, p. 108.

11. Davidson, *Uprichtnes*, p. 87.

12. Knox, *History*, vol. I, p. 104.

13. Ibid., p. 109.

14. Ibid., p. 93.

15. *An Epistle to the Congregation of the Castle of St Andrews* and *A briefe Sommarie of the Work by Balnaves on Justification*, Knox, *Works*, vol. III, pp. 5–28.

16. Lorimer, *Knox*, chapter 1; Ridley, *Knox*, chapter 6. For the wars of the Rough Wooings, see Merriman, *Rough Wooings*, *passim*, and his comment on how they 'made' Knox, p. 350.

17. Knox, *History*, vol. II, pp. 15–16.

18. Letter to Berwick, 1552, Lorimer, *Knox*, p. 264; *Epistle to the Inhabitants of Newcastle and Berwick*, 1558, Knox, *Works*, vol. V, pp. 480–1.

19. Lorimer, *Knox*, pp. 259–61, 264–5.

20. Knox, *Works*, vol. III, p. 355.

21. Northumberland to Cecil, 28 October 1552, Lorimer, *Knox*, pp. 149–52; full text in Patrick Fraser Tytler, *England under the Reigns of Edward VI and Mary*, 2 vols (Samuel Bentley, London, 1839), vol. II, pp. 142–3.

22. 'The Practice of the Lord's Supper in Berwick', Lorimer, *Knox*, pp. 290–7. In his 1558 Letter, Knox explicitly said the Berwick and Newcastle congregations had followed the practice 'as Christ Jesus dyd institute' rather than 'as the King's procedinges dyd alowe': Knox, *Works*, vol. V, p. 480.

23. *A Vindication of the Doctrine that the Sacrifice of Mass is Idolatry*, Knox, *Works*, vol. III, pp. 33–70.

24. Knox, *Works*, vol. III, p. 247.

25. Tunstal's *De veritate corporis et sanguinis domini nostri Jesu Christi in eucharistia*, see D. G. Newcombe, 'Tunstal, Cuthbert (1474–1559)', *Oxford Dictionary of National Biography*, Oxford University Press, 2004; online edn, September 2013 (www.oxforddnb.com/view/article/27817, accessed 25 November 2013).

26. Knox's stipend as royal chaplain, Reid, *Trumpeter of God*, p. 83.

27. Northumberland to Cecil, 28 October 1552, Tytler, *Edward VI and Mary*, p. 142.

28. Knox, *Works*, vol. III, p. 361, and note Ridley, *Knox*, p. 541.

29. Knox, *History*, vol. II, p. 78; Ridley, *Knox*, p. 115.

30. Knox, *Works*, vol. III, pp. 277–8, 297, 357; Lorimer, *Knox*, chapter 5; Reid, *Trumpeter of God*, p. 94.

31. Christine M. Newman, 'The Reformation and Elizabeth Bowes: A Study of a Sixteenth-Century Northern Gentlewoman', in W. J. Sheils and Diana Wood (eds), *Women and the Church*, Studies in Church History 27 (Blackwell, Oxford, 1990), pp. 325–33.

32. Knox to Marjorie Bowes, December 1552, Knox, *Works*, vol. III, p. 395.

33. Ibid., pp. 394–5.

34. Knox–Bowes correspondence and its dating, Frankforter, 'Elizabeth Bowes and John Knox', pp. 333–47; Farrow, *John Knox*, chapter 3.

35. Knox, *Works*, vol. III, pp. 119–56.

36. E.g. Knox to Elizabeth Bowes, 22 December 1551, early 1552, Knox, *Works*, vol. III, pp. 351, 352–3. Elizabeth Bowes was possibly meant in the Letter to Berwick, 1552: Lorimer, *Knox*, p. 260.

37. Knox to Elizabeth Bowes, December 1553, Knox, *Works*, vol. III, pp. 390–1.

38. Knox, *Works*, vol. VI, p. 513.

39. Ibid., p. 516.

40. Ibid., p. 514.

41. In his *Disputation*, Nicol Burne accused Knox of incest and adultery because he slept with both mother and daughter: *Catholic Tractates of the Sixteenth Century 1573–1600*, ed. Thomas G. Law (Scottish Text Society, o.s., 45, Edinburgh, 1901), pp. 143–4; Patrick Collinson, 'John Knox, the Church of England and the Women of England', in Mason (ed.), *John Knox and the British Reformations*, pp. 74–96.

42. Knox, *Works*, vol. III, p. 350.

43. Collinson, 'John Knox, the Church of England and the Women of England', p. 78, quoting Marjorie Bowen.

44. MacCulloch, *Reformation*, pp. 640, 655–6.

45. See 'daughter Bowes', Knox to Elizabeth Bowes, 22 December 1551, Knox, *Works*, vol. III, p. 354; Anne Bowes had married her cousin Robert Bowes, Elizabeth's son: C. A. McGladdery, 'Bowes, Robert (*d.* 1597)', *Oxford Dictionary of National Biography*, Oxford University Press, 2004 (www.oxforddnb.com/view/article/3059, accessed 25 November 2013).

46. Patrick Collinson, 'Not Sexual in the Ordinary Sense: Women, Men and Religious Transactions', in his *Elizabethan Essays* (Hambledon Press, London, 1994), pp. 119–50.

47. Knox, *Works*, vol. III, p. 317.

Chapter 6 Why held we back the salt?

1. Elbert Hubbard coined the phrase the 'university of hard knocks' in 1902 about his own education in an article in *Cosmopolitan*, 33 (November 1901–April 1902), p. 317.

2. Knox, *Works*, vol. III, p. 270.

3. Knox, *History*, vol. II, p. 48.

4. Knox, *Works*, vol. III, pp. 268–9.

5. Diarmaid MacCulloch, *Thomas Cranmer* (Yale University Press, New Haven, CT, 1996), p. 525.

6. Lorimer, *Knox*, pp. 103–5, quotation at p. 104.

7. It was No. 38 on the extended list and became No. 35 in the final list, Forty-Two Articles, MacCulloch, *Cranmer*, p. 527.

8. Lorimer, *Knox*, pp. 267–74.

9. MacCulloch, *Cranmer*, p. 529.

10. Knox, *Works*, vol. VI, p. xxx and facsimile; Alford, *Kingship and Politics in the Reign of Edward VI*, p. 176.

11. MacCulloch, *Cranmer*, p. 528.

12. Letter to Berwick, 1552, Lorimer, *Knox*, pp. 251–65.

13. Calderwood, *History*, vol. I, p. 280.

14. Lorimer, *Knox*, p. 175.

15. MacCulloch, *Cranmer*, p. 524.

16. Plans for Durham: Patrick Collinson, *Archbishop Grindal 1519–1583: The Struggle for a Reformed Church* (Jonathan Cape, London, 1979), pp. 60–4; D. Loades, *John Dudley, Duke of Northumberland 1504–1553* (Oxford University Press, Oxford, 1996), p. 199.

17. Northumberland to Cecil, 28 October 1552, Tytler, *Edward VI and Mary*, p. 142.

18. Northumberland to Cecil, 7 December 1552, Tytler, *Edward VI and Mary*, p. 148.

19. 9 December 1552, *Acts of the Privy Council of England* ed. J R Dasent *et al.* (46 vols, HMSO, London, 1890-1964), vol. IV, 1552–4, p. 658, and series of letters Knox wrote from Newcastle at end of 1552 and start of 1553, *Works*, vol. III, pp. 355–8, 360–2, 365–9, 382–5, 394–5.

20. Knox, *Works*, vol. III, p. 122.

21. Collinson, *Grindal*, p. 64.

22. Knox, *Works*, vol. III, pp. 175–8.

23. N. Ridley, *Piteous Lamentation* (1556), in *The Works of Bishop Ridley*, ed. H. Christmas (Parker Society, Cambridge, 1841), p. 59.

24. Knox, *Works*, vol. III, pp. 280–3; biblical references are to 2 Kings 18:18–19:2; Isaiah 22:15–19, 36–7.

25. In 1558 Anthony Gilby recalled a letter Northumberland had written to Harley, in his *Admonition to England and Scotland*, Knox, *Works*, vol. IV, p. 566.

26. The Saying of John late Duke of Northumberland upon the Scaffold, British Library, Cotton MS Titus B. ii, fols 144v–145r.

27. Wright, 'John Knox's Bible', pp. 59–60; William B. Robison, 'Cawarden, Sir Thomas (c.1514–1559)', *Oxford Dictionary of National Biography*, Oxford University Press, 2004; online edn, January 2008 (www.oxforddnb.com/view/article/37270, accessed 25 November 2013).

28. Knox, *Works*, vol. V, pp. 21–468; Anthony Penny, *Freewill or Predestination: The Battle over Saving Grace in mid-Tudor England* (Boydell, Woodbridge, 1990), chapter 7.

29. Knox, *Works*, vol. III, pp. 307–8.

30. Knox to Elizabeth Bowes, June–July 1553, Knox, *Works*, vol. III, p. 372.

31. J. Wright, 'Marian Exiles and the Legitimacy of Flight from Persecution', *Journal of Ecclesiastical History*, 52 (2001), pp. 220–43.

32. Knox to Elizabeth Bowes, end 1553, Knox, *Works*, vol. III, p. 370.

33. Ibid., pp. 378–9.

34. Knox to Elizabeth Bowes, October–November 1553, Knox, *Works*, vol. III, p. 370.

35. Dawson and Glassey, 'Some Unpublished Letters', pp. 192–3; for Knox's relationship with Goodman, see below, Chapter 9.

36. *Letters of Jean Calvin*, ed. J. Bonnet, trans. D. Constable, 4 vols (Constable, Edinburgh, 1855–7), vol. III, CCCXLV, pp. 28–9.

37. Knox, *Works*, vol. III, pp. 221–6.

38. Ibid., p. 223.

39. Ibid., p. 294; Knox to Elizabeth Bowes, 20 July 1554, ibid., p. 345.

40. Knox, *Works*, vol. III, pp. 277, 280.

41. Ibid., p. 328; Knox to Elizabeth Bowes, 20 July 1554, ibid., p. 343.

42. Knox, *Works*, vol. III, p. 257, indirect quotations from Isaiah 9:12, 14, 21; main text Matthew 14:22–33.

43. Knox, *Works*, vol. III, p. 329.

44. Ibid., pp. 295–6.

45. Ibid., p. 309.

46. The phrase 'listening post' was coined by Gordon Rupp in his 'The Europe of John Knox', in Duncan Shaw (ed.), *John Knox: A Quatercentenary Reappraisal* (Saint Andrew Press, Edinburgh, 1975), p. 4.

47. Duncan Shaw, *Renaissance and Zwinglian Influences in Sixteenth-Century Scotland* (Edina Press, Edinburgh, 2012), pp. 105–8.

48. Knox to Elizabeth Bowes, 20 July 1554, Knox, *Works*, vol. III, pp. 347–8.

49. Grindal hoped to study Hebrew with Tremellius: Grindal to Cox, 6 November 1554, Denbighshire Record Office, Plas Power MSS, DD/PP/839, pp. 37–9.

50. Letter from Jean de St André to William Whittingham, 15 December 1554, DD/PP/839, pp. 43–4.

51. Ninian Winzet's jibe about Knox's 'southeron' and forgetting 'our auld plane Scottis', discussed in Jeremy Smith, *Older Scots: A Linguistic Reader* (Scottish Text Society, fifth series, 9, Edinburgh, 2012), p. 9.

CHAPTER 7 A FARRAGO OF CEREMONIES

1. Knox, *History*, vol. I, p. 110. For the context of this part of Knox's life, Euan Cameron, 'Frankfurt and Geneva: The European Context of John Knox's Reformation', in Mason (ed.), *Knox and the British Reformations*, pp. 51–73. The standard source for the Troubles at Frankfurt was published anonymously in 1574, *A Brieff discours off the troubles begonne at Franckford*, ed. J. Petheram (London, 1845). It has now been supplemented by extensive new material found in Goodman's papers, DD/PP/839: see Jane E. A. Dawson, *Letters from Exile: New Documents on the Marian Exile 1553–9*, www.marianexile.div.ed.ac.uk.

2. Grindal to Cox, 6 November 1554, DD/PP/839, p. 38.

3. Foxe to Peter Martyr, 12 October 1554, cited in J. F. Mozley, *John Foxe and his Book* (SPCK, London, 1940), p. 43; Whitehead had arrived on 24 October, *A Brieff discours off the troubles*, p. xvii.

4. Scory to Frankfurt congregation, 3 September 1554, DD/PP/839, pp. 31–2.

5. This chapter follows the new chronology of the Frankfurt Troubles based on evidence from Goodman's papers, Timothy Duguid, 'The "Troubles at Frankfurt": A New Chronology', *Reformation and Renaissance Review*, 12 (2013), pp. 243–68, and Dawson, *Letters from Exile*.

6. Wood to Whittingham, 15 February 1574, Patrick Collinson, 'Letters of Thomas Wood, Puritan', *Godly People* (Hambledon Press, London, 1983), p. 89.

7. In the previously unknown letter, Knox to Williams, Wood, Gilby and Mr 'Eelk', 1 May 1555, DD/PP/839, pp. 45–7. Mr 'Eelk' was probably Thomas Huyck.

8. Tinoterius to Genevan Company of Pastors, 4 January 1555, *Ioannis Calvini Opera quae supersunt omnia*, ed. G. Baum, E. Cunitz and E. Reuss, 59 vols (Schwetschke, Brunswick, 1863–1900) (hereafter *CO*), vol. 15, pp. 370–2. Translation into English by Dr Jamie Reid-Baxter.

9. Calvin to Frankfurt congregation, the date is 18 January 1555 in *CO*, vol. 15, No. 2091, p. 394, though 20 January in *A Brieff discours off the troubles*, pp. xxxv–xxxvi.

10. The letter by Bale to Ashley and Memo, end December 1554, start January 1555, Inner Temple Petyt MS 538/47, ff. 380 and 473. Discussed in L. P. Fairfield, *John Bale: Mythmaker of the English Reformation* (Purdue University Press, W. Lafayette, IN, 1976), pp. 102–3; Patrick Collinson, *The Elizabeth Puritan Movement* (Jonathan Cape, London, 1967), p. 33, but the Goodman papers allow these manuscripts to be redated and placed in their proper context; see Dawson, *Letters from Exile*.

11. Causing the eighteenth-century editor, John Strype, in his *Ecclesiastical Memorials* (3 vols in 6 (Oxford, 1822)) to remove that section from his transcription: see Dawson, *Letters from Exile*.

12. Foxe to Lever, 18 June 1555, cited in Mozley, *John Foxe*, p. 47; Knox to Foxe, 18 May 1558, *Works*, vol. V, pp. 5–6.

13. Goodman to Peter Martyr, *c.*25 March 1555, DD/PP/839, pp. 50–2.

14. Fox to Peter Martyr, *c.*February 1555, cited in Mozley, *John Foxe*, pp. 46–7.

15. For a full discussion and reconstruction of the liturgy of the Frankfurt exiles, see *The Liturgy of the Frankfurt Exiles 1555*, ed. R. Leaver, Grove Liturgical Study No. 38 (Grove Books, Bramcote, 1984), and Bryan D. Spinks, *From the Lord, and 'The Best Reformed Church': A Study of the Eucharistic Liturgy in the English Puritan and Separatist Traditions 1550–1633* (Pickwick Publishing, Eugene, OR, 1985).

16. *A Brieff discours off the troubles*, p. xxxviii.

17. Knox's *Narrative* in Knox, *Works*, vol. IV, pp. 41–9.

18. Grindal to Cox, 6 November 1554, DD/PP/839, pp. 37–9.

19. *A Brieff discours off the troubles*, p. xxxviii.

20. Ibid., p. xlviii; Knox, *Works*, vol. IV, p. 42.

21. Whittingham to friend, 1555, *A Brieff discours off the troubles*, pp. xlvii–l.

22. Goodman to Peter Martyr, *c.*25 March 1555, DD/PP/839, p. 51.

23. Knox, *Works*, vol. IV, p. 46.

24. R. Targore, *Common Prayer: The Language of Public Devotion in Early Modern England* (University of Chicago Press, Chicago, 2001), p. 29.

25. Whitehead *et al.* to Calvin, 20 September 1555, *Original Letters Relative to the English Reformation*, ed. H. Robinson, 2 vols (Parker Society, Cambridge, 1846–7) (hereafter *OL*), vol. II, pp. 755–63, at p. 760.

26. Knox, *Works*, vol. IV, p. 46.

27. *A Brieff discours off the troubles*, p. xliiii.
28. The version in Goodman's papers added the date, 15 March 1555, and lists the names of those involved: Isaac, Sutton, Parry as complainers with the consent of Cox, Bale, Turner of Windsor, Jewel and Matchell, DD/PP/839, p. 45.
29. John Foxe, *The Unabridged Acts and Monuments Online*, 1583 edn (HRI Online Publications, Sheffield, 2011), p. 1875. Available from http//www.johnfoxe.org (accessed 2 February 2013).
30. Whitehead *et al.* to Calvin, 20 September 1555, *OL*, vol. II, pp. 761–2.
31. Chambers to Cox, 19 July 1555, DD/PP/839, pp. 52–3.
32. Ibid., p. 53.
33. *A Brieff discours off the troubles*, p. lxiii.
34. Goodman to Peter Martyr, around the end of March 1555, DD/PP/839, pp. 50–2, 56–8.
35. Goodman to Cox, 14 March 1557; Cox to Goodman, 15 April 1557, DD/PP/839, pp. 60–1, 61–2.
36. 28 and 31 March 1555: *A Brieff discours off the troubles*, pp. xlvi–xlvii; DD/PP/839, pp. 56–8.
37. *A Brieff discours off the troubles*, pp. liiii–lix.
38. Sulius [Sulzer] to Bullinger, 1 May 1555, cited in John Durkan, 'Heresy in Scotland, the Second Phase 1546–58', *Records of the Scottish Church History Society*, 24 (1992), p. 362.
39. Frankfurt congregation to Sulzer, 6 June 1555, DD/PP/839, p. 48, possibly carried by Goodman to Basle.
40. Knox to Williams, Wood, Gilby and Huyck, 1 May 1555, DD/PP/839, p. 47.

Chapter 8 Double cares

1. Knox to Anne Locke and Rose Hickman, 1556, Knox, *Works*, vol. IV, p. 219.
2. Knox, *Works*, vol. V, pp. 211–15. For the fight over Geneva, Bruce Gordon, *Calvin* (Yale University Press, New Haven, CT, 2009), pp. 211–16.
3. Knox to Elizabeth Bowes, 4 November 1555, Knox, *Works*, vol. IV, p. 217.
4. Knox, *History*, vol. I, p. 118. This may refer to the spiritual, rather than the agricultural, harvest.
5. Michael Lynch, *Edinburgh and the Reformation* (John Donald, Edinburgh, 1981), p. 279.
6. Goodman to a Lasco, 23 December 1555, DD/PP/839, p. 55.
7. Knox, *Works*, vol. IV, p. 217.
8. Robert M. Kingdon, *Adultery and Divorce in Calvin's Geneva* (Harvard University Press, Cambridge, MA, 1995).
9. Knox to Anne Locke, 9 December 1556, Knox, *Works*, vol. IV, pp. 239–41, at p. 240; and see n. 1 above.
10. Knox to Janet Adamson and Janet Henderson, Knox, *Works*, vol. IV, pp. 244–5.
11. Knox to Elizabeth Bowes, 4 November 1555, Knox, *Works*, vol. IV, p. 217.
12. Knox to Elizabeth Bowes, end 1555, Knox, *Works*, vol. IV, p. 218.
13. Knox to Janet Adamson and Janet Henderson, 1557, Knox, *Works*, vol. IV, p. 244.
14. Knox, *History*, vol. I, pp. 119–20.
15. Knox, *Works*, vol. IV, p. 240. This *Exposition upon Matthew IV, concerning the temptation of Christ in the wilderness* was subsequently published, ibid., pp. 91–114.
16. Knox, *History*, vol. I, p. 118.
17. Knox, *Works*, vol. IV, p. 240.
18. F. D. Bardgett, *Scotland Reformed: The Reformation in Angus and the Mearns* (John Donald, Edinburgh, 1989), chapter 3.
19. Knox, *History*, vol. I, p. 121.
20. For the part played by the future fifth Earl of Argyll, Jane E. A. Dawson, *The Politics of Religion in the Age of Mary, Queen of Scots: The Earl of Argyll and the Struggle for Britain and Ireland* (Cambridge University Press, Cambridge, 2002).
21. Ryrie, *Origins of the Scottish Reformation*, chapter 6.
22. Davidson, *Uprichtnes*, p. 98.
23. E.g. Knox wanted his 1557 Letter to the Brethren sent on to 'oure brethrene in Kyle', Knox, *Works*, vol. IV, p. 275.
24. Knox, *History*, vol. I, p. 121. Margaret H. B. Sanderson, *Ayrshire and the Reformation: People and Change 1490–1600* (Tuckwell Press, East Linton, 1997), chapter 4 on the Lollard legacy; chapter 6 on the 1550s.

25. No copy of the bond exists: Jane E. A. Dawson, 'Bonding, Religious Allegiance and Covenanting', in Steven Boardman and Julian Goodare (eds), *Kings, Lords and Men in Scotland and Britain: Essays in Honour of Jenny Wormald* (Edinburgh University Press, Edinburgh, 2014), pp. 155–72.

26. Knox, *Works*, vol. IV, p. 123.

27. Jenny Wormald, 'Bloodfeud, Kindred and Government in Early Modern Scotland', *Past & Present*, 87 (1980), pp. 54–97.

28. Knox, *Works*, vol. III, pp. 307–8; Dawson, *Scotland Re-formed*, pp. 13–15.

29. Knox, *History*, vol. I, p. 122.

30. Knox to Elizabeth Bowes, 4 November 1555, Knox, *Works*, vol. IV, p. 218.

31. Knox, *Works*, vol. IV, p. 75.

32. Ibid., pp. 77–8.

33. Ibid., pp. 82–3.

34. Ibid., p. 84.

35. Knox, *History*, vol. I, p. 123, and see below, Chapter 12.

36. *Livre des Anglois*, p. 2, in Martin, *Les Protestants anglais réfugiés à Genève*, p. 332.

37. *Forme of Prayers*, 1556 edn, printed in Knox, *Works*, vol. IV, pp. 149–214; W. D. Maxwell, *The Liturgical Portions of the Genevan Service Book* (Oliver & Boyd, London, 1931). Goodman to a Lasco, 23 December 1555, DD/PP/839, p. 55.

38. William Fuller referred to Goodman as the second preacher, *The Second Parte of a Register*, ed. A. Peel and C. H. Firth, 2 vols (Cambridge University Press, Cambridge, 1915), vol. II, p. 59.

39. Beza to Knox, 12 April 1572, Knox, *Works*, vol. VI, pp. 613, 615.

40. Goodman to a Lasco, 23 December 1555, DD/PP/839, p. 54.

41. Knox thanked Locke and Hickman for their 'speciall care over me, as the mother useth to be over hir naturall chyld': Knox to Anne Locke and Rose Hickman, 1556, Knox, *Works*, vol. IV, p. 220.

42. Knox to Anne Locke, 9 December 1556, Knox, *Works*, vol. IV, p. 239.

43. Knox to Scottish Lords, 27 October 1557, Knox, *History*, vol. I, p. 134.

44. Calvin to Knox, Calvin to Goodman, 23 April 1561, Knox, *Works*, vol. VI, pp. 124, 125.

45. Knox to John Foxe, 18 May 1558, Knox, *Works*, vol. V, p. 6 and facsimile of the letter.

46. Knox, *Works*, vol. IV, p. 239.

47. Knox to Anne Locke, 19 November 1556, Knox, *Works*, vol. IV, pp. 237–9.

48. *Livre des Anglois*, p. 49, in Martin, *Les Protestants anglais réfugiés à Genève*, p. 334.

49. *Second Parte of a Register*, vol. II, p. 60.

50. Knox, *History*, vol. I, p. 134.

51. The second section of *A Brieff discours off the troubles* dealt with the subsequent 'sturre and strife' of the Frankfurt congregation, p. lxii.

52. Knox, *Works*, vol. IV, p. 241.

53. The two sides of the letter were separated and later bound in different volumes, Bodleian Library MS Rawl D 857, f. 122r, and D 923, f. 189v.

54. Goodman to Cox, 14 March 1557, DD/PP/839, p. 61.

55. Cox to Goodman, 15 April 1557, DD/PP/839, p. 61.

56. Jewel to Goodman and Whittingham, 1 June 1557, *The Works of John Jewel, Bishop of Salisbury*, ed. J. Ayre, 4 vols (Parker Society, Cambridge, 1845–50), vol. IV, pp. 1192–3.

57. *A Brieff discours off the troubles*, p. clxxxvi.

58. Bale's comment cited in Thomas McCrie, *Life of John Knox* (Blackwood & Sons, Edinburgh, 1850 edn), p. 146 and note. The Genevan congregation's letter to other exile congregations, 15 December 1558: *A Brieff discours off the troubles*, pp. clxxxvi–clxxxvii.

59. Knox to Upcher, 1 August 1557, Knox, *Works*, vol. IV, pp. 241–4.

60. Penny, *Freewill or Predestination*: for King's Bench, see chapters 4–6; identification of Harte, chapter 7; Knox, *Works*, vol. V, p. 25.

61. *An Answer to a great nomber of blasphemous cavillations written by an Anabaptist, and adversarie to Gods eternal Predestination*, Knox, *Works*, vol. V, pp. 19–468.

62. Knox, *Works*, vol. IV, pp. 184–5.

63. *Second Parte of a Register*, pp. 57–8.

64. Horn and Chambers to Bullinger, 19 September 1556, *OL*, vol. I, pp. 132–3.

65. *Geneva Bible*, f. 30v at Exodus 14:10–11.

CHAPTER 9 PIERCED WITH ANGUISH AND SORROW

1. Knox to Goodman, late May or early June 1567, Dawson and Glassey, 'Some Unpublished Letters', p. 192; Jane E. A. Dawson, '"Satan's bludy clawses": How the Exile Congregation in Geneva Reacted to the Marian Persecution', working paper available on Edinburgh Research Explorer http://hdl.handle.net/1842/7629.
2. Knox to Goodman, July 1572, Knox, *Works*, vol. VI, p. 618.
3. The 'Erskine' signature belonged to Lord Erskine and not Erskine of Dun as had previously been supposed, e.g. Knox, *History*, vol. I, p. 132, n. 2, following Keith, *History*, vol. I, p. 153. The letter was written from Stirling where Erskine was hereditary keeper of the castle, and Lorne, Erskine and Lord James were cousins.
4. Knox, *History*, vol. I, p. 132; J. H. Burns, *The True Law of Kingship* (Clarendon Press, Oxford, 1996) notes the differences, pp. 140–1, n. 52.
5. Knox, *History*, vol. I, p. 133.
6. Ibid., p. 135; Mason, *Knox on Rebellion*, p. 137.
7. Knox to Scottish Lords, 27 October 1557, Knox, *History*, vol. I, pp. 133–6; Mason, *Knox on Rebellion*, p. 137.
8. John Spottiswood, *History*, vol. I, p. 185; for correct date see Knox, *History*, vol. I, p. 124.
9. Knox to Janet Henderson, 16 March 1557, Knox, *Works*, vol. IV, p. 247; dating 1557 not 1558, cf. Janton, *Knox*, pp. 124–5, n. 26.
10. Knox, *Works*, vol. IV, pp. 247–8.
11. Davidson, *Uprichtnes*, pp. 81, 87, 88. Reciting the prayers for the dead and naming a living person was the equivalent of putting a curse upon them.
12. The letter to Janet Adamson and Janet Henderson was written from Lyon in 1557: Knox, *Works*, vol. IV, pp. 244–5.
13. John Row, *The History of the Kirk of Scotland from the Year 1558 to August 1637*, ed. David Laing (Wodrow Society, Edinburgh, 1842), vol. I, pp. 9–10.
14. Knox, *History*, vol. I, p. 134.
15. Philip Benedict, *Christ's Churches Purely Reformed* (Yale University Press, New Haven, CT, 2002), chapter 4.
16. Reid, *Trumpeter of God*, p. 144.
17. Arran had been fighting for the French in the summer of 1557 and distinguished himself at the siege of St Quentin. He might have been the Scot named 'James' who was captured at the Rue St Jacques and finally released on 21 March 1558. If so, he was able to keep his identity hidden from the French authorities. Word would have travelled on the Scottish grapevine from Arran's company of men at arms, some of whom were Protestant, to Knox's merchant friends in Dieppe: John Durkan, 'James, Third Earl of Arran: The Hidden Years', *Scottish Historical Review*, 65 (1986), pp. 154–66.
18. Knox, *Works*, vol. IV, pp. 297–347; closing letter dated 7 December 1557, p. 347.
19. Knox, *History*, vol. I, pp. 133–4.
20. Ibid., p. 135.
21. Quentin Skinner, *The Foundations of Modern Political Thought*, 2 vols (Cambridge University Press, Cambridge, 1978), vol. II, chapter 7.
22. Lord Erskine, not Erskine of Dun: see Dawson, *Politics of Religion*, p. 24, see above, n. 3.
23. Knox, *History*, vol. I, pp. 136–7.
24. Knox to brethren in Scotland, 1 December 1557, Knox, *Works*, vol. IV, p. 267.
25. Knox to professors in Scotland, 17 December 1557, Knox, *Works*, vol. IV, p. 284.
26. Ibid., p. 285.
27. Knox to sisters in Edinburgh, 16 April 1558, Knox, *Works*, vol. IV, p. 250.
28. Ibid., p. 251.
29. Cecil to Sadler and Croft, 31 October 1559, *Calendar of State Papers, Foreign Series, Edward, Mary and Elizabeth*, ed. J. Stevenson *et al.*, 25 vols (HMSO, London, 1861–1950) (hereafter *CSP For.*), 1559-60 p. 73.
30. Knox to Goodman, July 1572, Knox, *Works*, vol. VI, p. 618; Goodman to Henry Killigrew, 6 March 1574, DD/PP/839, pp. 125–6.
31. Knox to John Wood, 14 February 1568, Knox, *Works*, vol. VI, p. 558.
32. Knox, *Works*, vol. VI, p. 618.
33. Knox to Goodman, 27 October 1566, Dawson and Glassey, 'Some Unpublished Letters', pp. 183–6.

34. Knox to Goodman, n.d., Dawson and Glassey, 'Some Unpublished Letters', p. 193.

35. Knox, *Works*, vol. VI, p. 27.

36. Knox to Goodman, 18 February 1567, Dawson and Glassey, 'Some Unpublished Letters', pp. 190–1.

37. Knox to 'a friend in England', 19 August 1569, Knox, *Works*, vol. VI, p. 566.

38. Knox to Goodman, 3 November 1568, Dawson and Glassey, 'Some Unpublished Letters', pp. 195–6.

39. Calvin to Goodman, 23 April 1561, Knox, *Works*, vol. VI, p. 125.

40. Jewel to Peter Martyr Vermigli, 28 April 1559, *Zurich Letters*, ed. H. Robinson, 2 vols (Parker Society, Cambridge, 1842–5) (hereafter *ZL*), vol. I, p. 21.

41. Knox to Goodman, 3 November 1568, Dawson and Glassey, 'Some Unpublished Letters', pp. 195–6.

42. Knox to Goodman, late May or early June 1567, Dawson and Glassey, 'Some Unpublished Letters', p. 193.

43. Knox to sisters in Edinburgh, 16 April 1558, Knox, *Works*, vol. IV, p. 251.

44. William Fuller did not like the content of the books by Knox and Goodman, *Second Parte of a Register*, p. 59.

45. For Knox's *Appellation* and its background, see Mason, *Knox on Rebellion*. Christopher Goodman, *How Superior Powers Oght to be Obeyd* (Jean Crespin, Geneva, 1558), see Jane E. A. Dawson, 'Trumpeting Resistance: Christopher Goodman and John Knox', in Mason (ed.), *Knox and the British Reformations*, pp. 130–53.

46. *Geneva Bible*, Acts 5:29; also Acts 4:19.

47. Knox to his sisters in Edinburgh, c.1556, Knox, *Works*, vol. IV, p. 232.

48. Dawson, 'Trumpeting Resistance', pp. 146–7.

49. Knox, *Works*, vol. IV, p. 429; Mason, *Knox on Rebellion*, p. 47.

50. Knox to his sisters in Edinburgh, c.1556, Knox, *Works*, vol. IV, p. 227.

51. Calvin did write about women's dress: W. Bouwsma, *John Calvin: A Sixteenth-Century Portrait* (Oxford University Press, Oxford, 1988), p. 53.

52. Deuteronomy 22:5.

53. Knox to his sisters in Edinburgh, c.1556, Knox, *Works*, vol. IV, p. 226.

54. Richard Bertie, 'These answers ... against the book of John Knox, 1558', British Library (hereafter BL) Add. MS 48043, ff. 1–9, and see below, Chapter 11.

55. Knox to his sisters in Edinburgh, c.1556, Knox, *Works*, vol. IV, p. 228.

56. Calvin to Cecil, 28 January 1559, *ZL*, vol. II, pp. 34–6.

57. A draft of Robert Beaumont's library list, Bodleian Library Rawl MS D 923, f. 189r. It was used as paper on which to draft the letter from the Genevan congregation to the Frankfurt congregation.

58. The *Second Blast* was printed at the end of *Appellation*: Mason, *Knox on Rebellion*, pp. 138–9.

59. Aylmer, *Harborowe*, sig. Bv.

60. Burns, *The True Law of Kingship*, p. 145, n. 61; Laing's assertion on timing, Knox, *Works*, vol. IV, p. 352.

61. Knox to Cecil, 10 April 1559, Knox, *Works*, vol. VI, p. 18.

62. Farrow, *John Knox*, p. 103.

63. Such a statement was a *definitio* in rhetoric: Farrow, *John Knox*, p. 103; Knox, *Works*, vol. IV, p. 373.

64. Numbers 27.

65. Farrow, *John Knox*, p. 104; Knox, *Works*, vol. IV, p. 400; Mason, *Knox on Rebellion*, p. 31.

66. Knox, *Works*, vol. IV, p. 413; Mason, *Knox on Rebellion*, pp. 41–2.

67. Knox, *Works*, vol. IV, p. 414; Mason, *Knox on Rebellion*, p. 42.

68. Knox, *Works*, vol. IV, p. 416; Mason, *Knox on Rebellion*, p. 44.

69. Charlotte Panofré, 'Radical Geneva? The Publication of Knox's *First Blast of the Trumpet* and Goodman's *How Superior Powers ought to be obeyed* in Context', *Historical Research*, 87 (2014), pp. 1–19. By the spring of 1559 Aylmer had already possessed a copy for a year.

70. Knox to Anne Locke, 6 April 1559, Knox, *Works*, vol. VI, p. 14.

71. Mason, *Knox on Rebellion*, pp. 128–9.

72. Ibid., p. 104.

CHAPTER 10 QUIETNESS OF CONSCIENCE AND CONTENTMENT OF HEART

1. *A Meditation of a Penitent Sinner*, on Psalm 51, probably composed by Anne Locke in Geneva, was printed at the back of her translation of *Sermons of John Calvin upon the songe that Ezechias made* (John Day, London, 1560 [STC 4450]). Modern edition in Felch, *The Collected Works of Anne Vaughan Locke*, pp. 62–71; J. Ottenhoff, 'Anne Locke', *Reading Early Modern Women: An Anthology of Texts in Manuscript and Print 1550–1700* (Routledge, New York, 2003), pp. 364–6. Text on *Renascence Editions*: .http://darkwing.uoregon.edu/~rbear/ren.htm.

2. For the use of the image of rebuilding the Temple in the Old Testament Book of Haggai, Karl Gunther, 'Rebuilding the Temple: James Pilkington, Aggeus and early Elizabethan Puritanism', *Journal of Ecclesiastical History*, 60 (2009), pp. 689–707.

3. For a brief description of his exile and time in Geneva, *The Autobiography of Sir Thomas Bodley*, ed. William Clennell (Bodleian Library, Oxford, 2006), pp. 37–8; Thomas Bodley's copy of Calvin's Genesis sermons: Bodleian Library MS Bodl 740.

4. D. DeVries, 'Calvin's Preaching', in *The Cambridge Companion to John Calvin*, ed. D. K. McKim (Cambridge University Press, Cambridge, 2004), p. 111.

5. Felch, '"Deir sister"', pp. 47–68.

6. 'Maister Gudman sumtyme minister of Sactandrous gave this letter to Andro Kempe maister of the sang scule to set it in four pairtes. It is verray hard till it be thryse or four tymis weill and rycht sung', Wode Altus Partbook, BL Add MS 33, 933 ff. 52v–53; see also Wode Treble, Tenor and Bass (2) Partbooks, Edinburgh University Library Laing MS III 483.1–3; Dk 5.15. All the Partbooks can be viewed on Digital Image Archive of Medieval Music: www.diamm.ac.uk/.

7. Clare Costley King'oo, *Miserere Mei: The Penitential Psalms in Late Medieval and Early Modern England* (University of Notre Dame Press, Notre Dame, IN, 2012).

8. Argument for Psalm 51 in *Geneva Bible*, f. 245v.

9. Cf. Knox in his Letter to the inhabitants of Newcastle and Berwick, 1558, Knox, *Works*, vol. V, p. 482.

10. Locke's Preface Sonnet 5, lines 13–14; Meditation Sonnet 13, line 7 Renascence Edition pp. 4, 9 http://scholarsbank.uoregon.edu/xmlui/bitstream/handle/1794/753/meditation.pdf?sequence=1.

11. Knox to Upcher, 1 August 1557, Knox, *Works*, vol. IV, pp. 241–4, and see above, Chapter 8; Locke, Meditation Sonnet 14, lines 13–14.

12. Knox to Cecil, 10 April 1559, Knox, *Works*, vol. VI, p. 18.

13. Knox to John Wood, 14 February 1568, Knox, *Works*, vol. VI, p. 559.

14. Martin, *Les Protestants anglais réfugiés à Genève*, p. 44.

15. Jane E. A. Dawson, 'Goodman, Christopher (1521/2–1603)', *Oxford Dictionary of National Biography*, Oxford University Press, 2004; online edn, January 2008 (www.oxforddnb.com/view/article/10975, accessed 25 November 2013).

16. Beth Quitslund, *The Reformation in Rhyme: Sternhold, Hopkins and the English Metrical Psalter 1547–1603* (Ashgate, Aldershot, 2008), p. 176.

17. Whittingham's 1557 New Testament, cited in ibid., pp. 177–8.

18. Martin, *Les Protestants anglais réfugiés à Genève*, p. 239.

19. David Daniell, *The Bible in English* (Yale University Press, New Haven, CT, 2003), chapters 16 and 17.

20. See above, Chapters 7 and 8.

21. Goodman's sermon at the opening of the church, 1 November 1555, DD/PP/839, pp. 17–21.

22. Knox to Anne Locke, 9 December 1556, Knox, *Works*, vol. IV, p. 240.

23. Thomas Hancock, 'Autobiography', in *Narratives of the Reformation*, ed. J. G. Nichols (Camden Society, London, 1859), p. 84.

24. William Cole to Goodman, 13 April 1556, DD/PP/839, pp. 59–60.

25. Jane E. A. Dawson, 'John Knox, Christopher Goodman and the "Example of Geneva"' in *The Reception of Continental Reformation in Britain*, ed. Polly Ha and Patrick Collinson, *Proceedings of the British Academy*, 164 (Oxford University Press, Oxford, 2010), pp. 107–35.

26. Martin, *Les Protestants anglais réfugiés à Genève*, p. 241; Cole sent the 'Truthful tidings' to Bale about Scottish events: Michael Lynch, 'John Knox, Minister of Edinburgh and Commissioner of the Kirk', in Mason (ed.), *Knox and the British Reformations*, pp. 242–67, at pp. 242–3, and see below, Chapter 11.

27. Daniell, *The Bible in English*, p. 278.
28. Martin, *Les Protestants anglais réfugiés à Genève*, p. 70.
29. For a full discussion of the different editions, see Timothy Duguid, 'Sing a New Song: English and Scottish Metrical Psalmody from 1549–1640', 2 vols (University of Edinburgh PhD thesis, 2011).
30. Preface to 1556 edn *Forme of Prayers*, Knox, *Works*, vol. IV, pp. 165–7.
31. Knox, *Works*, vol. IV, pp. 573–5.
32. Mason, *Knox on Rebellion*, p. 27.
33. Ibid., p. 111.
34. Ibid., p. 66.
35. Ibid., p. 65; Burns, *The True Law of Kingship*, p. 149.
36. Mason, *Knox on Rebellion*, pp. 56–7.
37. Ibid., p. 71.
38. Such 'private law' arguments had formed part of Lutheran resistance theories and were adopted by Goodman: Jane E. A. Dawson, 'Resistance and Revolution in Sixteenth-Century Thought: The Case of Christopher Goodman', in J. Van Den Berg and P. Hoftijzer (eds), *The Church, Change and Revolution* (Brill, Leiden, 1991), pp. 69–79.
39. Mason, *Knox on Rebellion*, p. 77; cf. Knox's 17 December letter, Knox, *Works*, vol. IV, p. 285.
40. For a comparison of the views of Goodman and Knox, see Dawson, 'Trumpeting Resistance'.
41. Mason, *Knox on Rebellion*, p. 102
42. Ibid., p. 97.
43. Although Knox only directly mentioned the book in 1564, he probably encountered it in exile: Skinner, *Foundations of Modern Political Thought*, vol. II, pp. 207–10.
44. Knox, *History*, vol. II, pp. 246–56.
45. Mason, *Knox on Rebellion*, p. 110.
46. Ibid., p. 114.
47. Ibid., p. 127; Farrow, *John Knox*, p. 110.
48. Mason, *Knox on Rebellion*, p. 118, side note.
49. Ibid., pp. 118 and 119.
50. Ibid., p. 124.
51. Ibid., p. 123.
52. Ibid., p. 126.
53. Anthony Gilby, *An Admonition to England and Scotland to Call Them to Repentance*, Knox, *Works*, vol. IV, p. 554.
54. Mason, *Knox on Rebellion*, p. 26.
55. For the unionist rhetoric of the Rough Wooings, Roger A. Mason, 'The Scottish Reformation and the Origins of Anglo-British Imperialism', in his *Kingship and the Commonweal: Political Thought in Renaissance and Reformation Scotland* (Tuckwell Press, East Linton, 1998), pp. 242–69.
56. Knox, *Works*, vol. IV, p. 553.
57. Gilby mentioned the text within his tract and Knox placed it prominently at the end of his *Second Blast* which followed Gilby's tract in the printed edition: Knox, *Works*, vol. IV, pp. 540 and 561.
58. Knox, *Works*, vol. IV, p. 571.
59. Ibid., vol. V, p. 478.
60. Ibid., p. 480.
61. Ibid., p. 481.
62. Ibid., p. 482.
63. Ibid., p. 485.
64. Ibid., p. 488.
65. Ibid., p. 490; Farrow, *John Knox*, p. 111.
66. Knox, *Works*, vol. V, p. 494.

CHAPTER 11 ENGLAND, IN REFUSING ME, REFUSED A FRIEND

1. Calvin to Earl of Arran, 1 August 1558, Bonnet, *Letters of Jean Calvin*, vol. III, p. 455.
2. The tract is discussed in Lynch, 'Minister of Edinburgh', pp. 242–3. I am grateful to Theo van Heijnsbergen for supplying me with a translation of this tract and information about it.
3. *A Brieff discours off the troubles*, p. clxxxvi.

4. Rowland Hall printed it in Geneva, 10 February 1559: Martin, *Les Protestants anglais réfugiés à Genève*, p. 309.
5. *Second Parte of a Register*, p. 58.
6. *A Brieff discours off the troubles*, p. cxcii; *Livre des Anglois*, p. 50, in Martin, *Les Protestants anglais réfugiés à Genève*, p. 335.
7. *Second Parte of a Register*, p. 58.
8. *A Brieff discours off the troubles*, pp. clxxxvi–clxxxviii.
9. Ibid., pp. clxxxviii–cxci.
10. Martin, *Les Protestants anglais réfugiés à Genève*, p. 258.
11. Knox, *Works*, vol. V, p. 513. The reference was to the opening of the fifth seal in Revelation 6:9.
12. Knox, *Works*, vol. V, pp. 515–22.
13. Reid, *Trumpeter of God*, p. 153.
14. Ridley, *Knox*, p. 309; Janton, *John Knox*, p. 147.
15. Reid, *Trumpeter of God*, p. 153.
16. Knox, *Works*, vol. VI, p. 11.
17. Sandys to Bullinger, 20–21 December 1558, *ZL*, vol. I, p. 5.
18. Randolph to Throckmorton, 6 December 1558, *CSP For.*, 1558–9, p. 22.
19. Calvin to Cecil, after 29 January 1559, *ZL*, vol. II, p. 34.
20. Martin, *Les Protestants anglais réfugiés à Genève*, p. 142.
21. Brett Usher, 'Aylmer, John (1520/21–1594)', *Oxford Dictionary of National Biography*, Oxford University Press, 2004; online edn January 2008 (www.oxforddnb.com/view/article/935, accessed 25 November 2013).
22. In 1571 Cox discussed Knox's work with Bishop John Leslie, 21 August 1571: Leslie's Diary, *Bannatyne Miscellany Vol. III*, ed. David Laing (Bannatyne Club, Edinburgh, 1855), p. 143.
23. Parker to Nicholas Bacon, 1 March 1559, *Correspondence of Matthew Parker*, ed. J. Bruce and T. T. Perowne (Parker Society, Cambridge, 1852), p. 61.
24. For the use of the terms precisian and Genevan, Dawson, 'John Knox, Christopher Goodman and the "Example of Geneva"', pp. 132-3.
25. Dawson, 'John Knox, Christopher Goodman and the "Example of Geneva"', pp. 108–9.
26. Anthony Ashe to Reformed Church in Emden, 28 April 1559, printed in Andrew Pettegree, *Marian Protestantism: Six Studies* (Ashgate, Aldershot, 1996), p. 197.
27. *Second Parte of a Register*, pp. 59–60.
28. Knox to Cecil, 10–22 April 1559, Knox, *Works*, vol. V, p. 18.
29. Knox to Anne Locke, 6 April 1559, Knox, *Works*, vol. VI, p. 14.
30. Knox to Anne Locke, 4 February 1560, Knox, *Works*, vol. VI, p. 109.
31. Beza to Bullinger, 3 September 1566, *ZL*, vol. II, p. 131.
32. Knox to Cecil, 10–22 April 1559, Knox, *Works*, vol. VI, p. 18.
33. Ibid., p. 20.
34. Knox to Cecil, 19 July 1559, Knox, *Works*, vol. VI, p. 47.
35. Knox to Cecil, 10–22 April 1559, Knox, *Works*, vol. VI, p. 20.
36. Ibid., p. 18.
37. Randolph to Cecil, 22 January 1563, Knox, *Works*, vol. VI, p. 532.
38. Aylmer, *Harborowe*, sig. Br.
39. Knox to Foxe, 18 May 1558, Knox, *Works*, vol. V, p. 5.
40. Knox to Queen Elizabeth, 6 August 1561, Knox, *Works*, vol. VI, pp. 126–7.
41. Knox to Cecil, 10–22 April 1559, Knox, *Works*, vol. VI, p. 18.
42. Ibid., p. 19.
43. Cecil to Knox, 28 July 1559, Knox, *Works*, vol. VI, p. 55.
44. Knox to Queen Elizabeth, 20 July 1559, Knox, *Works*, vol. VI, pp. 47–51; BL Add MS 32,091, ff. 167–9; also copy in Harleian MS 7004, f. 1. Knox enclosed his letter to the Queen in one to Cecil with the permission, 'Read and present it if ye think meat.': Knox to Cecil, 19 July 1559, Knox, *Works*, vol. VI, p. 47. The suggestion that these comments were Elizabeth's own annotations is made by A. N. McLaren, *Political Culture in the Reign of Elizabeth I: Queen and Commonwealth 1558–1585* (Cambridge University Press, Cambridge, 1999), p. 12, n. 1 and pp. 57–8.
45. BL Add MS 32,091, f. 167v. This might have been an echo of Aylmer's sentence 'no fyre brandes of sedicion be cast into the houses of mens hartes, to impayre thobedience of good subiectes': Aylmer, *Harborowe*, sig. Br. For the debate, see Amanda Shephard, *Gender*

and *Authority in Sixteenth-Century England: The Knox Debate* (Keele University Press, Keele, 1994).

46. BL Add MS 32,091, f. 168r.
47. Aylmer, *Harborowe*, sig. Cv.
48. Ibid., sig. C2r.
49. Ibid., sig. B2v.
50. Ibid., sig. F1v.
51. 'For nether the begerlines of the land, wilbe able to fede the fine mouthed French men, nor the nature of the Scotts can long suffer their yoke, and so wyll they together by the eares': ibid., sig. Q3r.
52. Ibid., sig. P4v.
53. 'The scripture medleth with no civill policie further then to teach obedience. And therfor what so ever is brought out of the scripture concerning any kynd of regiment is wothout the booke, pulled into the game place by the eares to wrastle whether it will or no': ibid., sig. Gv.
54. For Bertie's tract, see Chapter 10.
55. Bertie, 'These answers . . .', f. 3r.
56. Ibid., f. 6r.
57. Strype, *Ecclesiastical Memorials*, vol. 3(ii), p. 542.
58. Patrick Collinson's seminal study, *The Elizabethan Puritan Movement*; P. Kaufman, 'The Protestant Opposition to Elizabethan Religious Reform', in *A Companion to Tudor Britain* (Blackwell, Oxford, 2004), pp. 271–88.
59. Dawson, 'John Knox, Christopher Goodman and the "Example of Geneva"', p. 110.
60. Knox's phrase to describe the Marian persecution: Knox to Goodman, late May or early June 1567, Dawson and Glassey, 'Some Unpublished Letters', p. 192; Dawson, '"Satan's bludy clawses"', http://hdl.handle.net/1842/7629.
61. Knox, *Works*, vol. V, pp. 523–36. Knox's list of martyrs was superseded by Foxe's monumental work.
62. Ibid., p. 535.
63. E.g. Rupp's phrase in 'The Europe of John Knox', p. 4.
64. Knox to Cecil, 10–22 April 1559, Knox, *Works*, vol. VI, p. 17.

Chapter 12 Restorer of the Gospel among the Scots

1. Dawson, *Scotland Re-formed*, Part III.
2. Knox to Anne Locke, 3 May 1559, Knox, *Works*, vol. VI, p. 21.
3. 'Historie of the Estate of Scotland', ed. David Laing, *Wodrow Miscellany* (Wodrow Society, Edinburgh, 1844), vol. I, pp. 56–7.
4. Knox, *History*, vol. I, p. 159.
5. Mary Verschuur, *Politics or Religion?: The Reformation in Perth 1540–1570* (Dunedin Academic Press, Edinburgh, 2006), pp. 92–109.
6. Knox, *History*, vol. I, p. 163.
7. Verschuur, *Politics or Religion?*, p. 98.
8. Cited in ibid., p. 100.
9. Knox to Anne Locke, 23 June 1559, Knox, *Works*, vol. VI, p. 23.
10. Knox, *History*, vol. I, pp. 162–3.
11. Lord Herries, *Historie of the Reigne of Marie Queen of Scots*, ed. R. Pitcairn (Abbotsford Club 6, Edinburgh, 1836), p. 38.
12. Dawson, *Politics of Religion*, pp. 90–4.
13. Knox, *History*, vol. I, p. 181; Janet P. Foggie, *Renaissance Religion in Urban Scotland: The Dominican Order 1450–1560* (Brill, Leiden, 2003), pp. 51–2.
14. The Perth cleansing had happened on 11 May and the start of the preaching of Protestant doctrine in Holy Trinity was later said to be Whitsunday, 14 May: *Register of the Ministers, Elders and Deacons of the Christian Congregation of Saint Andrews 1559–1600*, ed. David Hay Fleming, 2 vols (Scottish History Society, Edinburgh, 1889–90) (hereafter *RStAKS*), vol. I, p. 11.
15. Herries, *Historie*, p. 38.
16. For a discussion of the chronology of the fate of the friaries, see Foggie, *Renaissance Religion in Urban Scotland*, pp. 51–2.
17. Knox, *History*, vol. I, pp. 183–4.
18. Annotation by Thomas Wode in his Tenor Part Book, EUL Laing MS III 483.2, p. 137.

19. Sermon at Stirling on 8 November 1559, Knox, *History*, vol. I, pp. 269–70; vol. II, p. 80.
20. Knox to Anne Locke, 18 November 1559, Knox, *Works*, vol. VI, p. 101.
21. Ibid., p. 100.
22. Randolph to Cecil, 7 September 1561, *Calendar of State Papers relating to Scotland and Mary, Queen of Scots 1547–1603*, ed. J. Bain *et al.*, 13 vols (HMSO, London, 1898–1969), vol. I, no. 1017.
23. Knox, *History*, vol. I, p. 201.
24. Ibid., pp. 192, n. 2; pp. 229–30, n. 2.
25. *Geneva Bible*, 'To the Reader', p. iiii.
26. Knox to Railton, 23 October 1559, Knox, *Works*, vol. VI, p. 87. The reference was to Matthew 6:22 and had been used by Knox and Gilby in their 1558 writings: see above, Chapter 10.
27. Knox to Cecil, 28 June and 19 July 1559, Knox, *Works*, vol. VI, pp. 31–2, 45–7.
28. Knox to Cecil, 18 November 1559, Knox, *Works*, vol. VI, p. 99.
29. For example, Knox, *Works*, vol. III, p. 206; Knox, *History*, vol. I, p. 373.
30. Knox to Cecil, 15 August 1559, Knox, *Works*, vol. VI, p. 68.
31. Cecil to Knox, 28 July 1559, Knox, *Works*, vol. VI, p. 56.
32. Jane E. A. Dawson, 'William Cecil and the British Dimension in Early Elizabethan Foreign Policy', *History*, 74 (1989), pp. 196–216.
33. Cecil to Sadler and Croft, 31 October 1559, *CSP For.*, 1559–60, p. 73.
34. Knox to Railton, 23 October 1559, Knox, *Works*, vol. VI, p. 88.
35. Knox to Anne Locke, 31 December 1559, Knox, *Works*, vol. VI, p. 104.
36. PS in letter Croft to Cecil, 29 August 1559, Knox, *Works*, vol. VI, p. 77.
37. Stephen Alford, *The Watchers: A Secret History of the Reign of Elizabeth I* (Allen Lane, London, 2012).
38. Croft to Knox, 27 October and Knox to Croft, 29 October 1559, Knox, *Works*, vol. VI, pp. 91–2, 94.
39. Knox to Croft, 25 October and Croft to Knox, 27 October 1559, Knox, *Works*, vol. VI, pp. 89–91, 91–2.
40. Knox to Railton, 23 October 1559, Knox, *Works*, vol. VI, p. 86.
41. Knox to Anne Locke, 18 November 1559, Knox, *Works*, vol. VI, p. 101.
42. Knox to Railton, 23 October 1559, 29 January 1560, Knox, *Works*, vol. VI, pp. 88 and 107.
43. Knox to Croft, 29 October 1559, Knox, *Works*, vol. VI, p. 94.
44. Dawson, *Politics of Religion*, pp. 98–9.
45. Knox, *History*, vol. I, p. 103.
46. Herries, *Historie*, p. 46.
47. Durkan, 'James, Third Earl of Arran', pp. 154–66.
48. Knox to Railton, 29 January 1560, Knox, *Works*, vol. VI, p. 105.
49. 6 February 1560, Knox, *History*, vol. I, pp. 299–300.
50. See below, Chapter 18.
51. Knox to Croft, 29 October 1559, Knox, *Works*, vol. VI, p. 93.
52. Knox, *History*, vol. I, pp. 278–9.
53. Knox to Railton, 29 January 1560, Knox, *Works*, vol. VI, p. 105.
54. Knox to Anne Locke, 4 February 1560, Knox, *Works*, vol. VI, p. 108.
55. William Douglas of Lochleven, cited in Margaret H. B. Sanderson, *Mary Stewart's People: Life in Mary Stewart's Scotland* (Mercat Press, Edinburgh, 1987), p. 57.
56. 'Historie of the Estate of Scotland', p. 78; *RStAKS*, vol. I, p. 12n.; recantation, February 1560, *RStAKS*, vol. I, pp. 11–13.
57. Knox, *History*, vol. I, p. 317.
58. Ibid., p. 322.
59. Ibid., pp. 322 and 329.
60. As a modern editor of Knox's *History* has remarked, 'Yet here is something more than the wrath of God; there is a narrow hate that diminishes the stature of the man and that chills us as we read': Knox, *History*, vol. I, p. lxxiiii.
61. Ibid., p. 333.

CHAPTER 13 CHURCHING IT LIKE A SCYTHIAN

1. Jewel to Martyr, 1 August 1559, *ZL*, vol. I, pp. 39–40.
2. Parker to Cecil, 6 November 1559, Parker, *Correspondence*, p. 105.

3. Knox, *History*, vol. I, p. 162 and n. 5.

4. Ibid., p. 191. There was evidence for the woman's views: see Margaret H. B. Sanderson, *A Kindly Place?: Living in Sixteenth-Century Scotland* (Tuckwell Press, East Linton, 2002), p. 19.

5. *The First Book of Discipline*, ed. James K. Cameron (Saint Andrew Press, Edinburgh, 1972), pp. 94–5.

6. Knox to Cecil, 28 June 1559, Knox, *Works*, vol. VI, p. 32.

7. For the agreement at the Abbey of Coupar Angus, see Dawson, *Politics of Religion*, pp. 90–1.

8. Knox, *History*, vol. I, pp. lxxiv, 26, 31.

9. Ibid., pp. 242–3.

10. J. Spottiswood, *The History of the Church of Scotland*, ed. M. Napier and M. Russell, 3 vols (Bannatyne Club, Edinburgh, 1850), vol. I, p. 372; Archbishop of St Andrews to Archbishop of Glasgow, 18 August 1560, Robert Keith, *History of the Affairs of Church and State in Scotland, from the Beginning of the Reformation to the Year 1568*, ed. J. P. Lawson and C. P. Lyon, 3 vols (Spottiswoode Society, Edinburgh, 1844–50), vol. III, p. 6.

11. Knox, *History*, vol. I, p. 79.

12. *RStAKS*, vol. I, pp. 16–18; Foggie, *Renaissance Religion in Urban Scotland*, pp. 279–84.

13. *RStAKS*, vol. I, p. 86.

14. Gordon Donaldson, *Reformed by Bishops* (Edina Press, Edinburgh, 1987), p. 3; Knox, *History*, vol. II, pp. 72–3.

15. Dawson, 'Goodman, Christopher (1521/2–1603)'.

16. *RStAKS*, vol. I, p. 198.

17. The first dated entry was 27 October 1559, ibid., p. 5.

18. For a full description of the changes in consistorial jurisdiction, see the Introduction to *The Consistorial Decisions of the Commissaries of Edinburgh 1564 to 1576/7*, ed. T. M. Green (The Stair Society, Edinburgh, 2014).

19. For the best recent description of the Reformation crisis and its long-term effects upon St Andrews, see E. Rhodes, 'The Reformation in the Burgh of St Andrews: Property, Piety and Power' (University of St Andrews PhD thesis, 2013), Part 2.

20. 'Historie of the Estate of Scotland', vol. I, p. 63; Knox, *History*, vol. I, p. 334, n. 1.

21. Knox to Elizabeth Bowes, 4 November 1555, Knox, *Works*, vol. IV, p. 218, and see above.

22. Knox, *History*, vol. I, p. 211.

23. Nicol Burnet in *Satirical Poems of the Time of the Reformation*, ed. J. Cranstoun, 2 vols (Scottish Text Society, Edinburgh, 1891–3), vol. I, p. 331, line 124.

24. *Extracts from the Records of the Burgh of Edinburgh*, ed. J. Marwick and M. Wood, 6 vols (Scottish Burgh Records Society, Edinburgh, 1869–92, 1927) (hereafter *Records of the Burgh of Edinburgh*), *1557–71*, p. 75.

25. Spottiswood, *History*, vol. I, p. 372.

26. Gunther, 'Rebuilding the Temple', and see above, Chapter 10.

27. Though the reference to the rebuilding of the Temple in the *Geneva Bible* (p. ii) was primarily to Ezra and Esdras rather than Haggai, the imagery and message were the same.

28. Knox, *History*, vol. I, p. 335.

29. Haggai 1:4 note c in *Geneva Bible*, f. 379v.

30. Knox, *History*, vol. I, p. 335.

31. Ibid., pp. 335–8.

32. Ibid., p. 338. W. I. P. Hazlett, 'The Scots Confession 1560: Context, Complexion and Critique', *Archiv für Reformationsgeschichte*, 78 (1987), pp. 287–320.

33. For example, Article 18, *The Scots Confession of Faith 1560*, ed. G. D. Henderson and J. Bulloch (Saint Andrew Press, Edinburgh, 1960), p. 44.

34. Article 24, *Scots Confession of Faith*, pp. 51–2.

35. Randolph to Cecil, 19 August 1560, Knox, *Works*, vol. VI, p. 117.

36. Knox, *History*, vol. II, p. 81; P. McNeill, ' "Our religion, established neither by law or parliament": Was the Reformation Legislation of 1560 Valid?', *Records of the Scottish Church History Society*, 35 (2005), pp. 68–89.

37. Randolph to William Cecil, 25 August 1560, Knox, *Works*, vol. IV, p. 119.

38. *The First Book of Discipline*, p. 165.

39. Knox, *Works*, vol. VI, pp. lvi–lvii.

40. 'comforting him (for he was in no small heaviness by reason of the late death of his dear bedfellow, Marjory Bowes)': Knox, *History*, vol. I, p. 351.

41. Randolph to Cecil, 4 August 1562, Knox, *Works*, vol. VI, p. 141.
42. Knox to Anne Locke, 6 October 1561, Knox, *Works*, vol. VI, pp. 129–30.
43. Knox, *History*, vol. I, pp. 346–7.
44. Ibid., pp. 349, 351.
45. Ibid., pp. 347–9.
46. *The Acts and Proceedings of the General Assemblies of the Church of Scotland 1560 to 1618*, ed. Duncan Shaw, 3 vols (Scottish Record Society, Edinburgh, 2004), vol. I, p. 5.
47. Knox, *History*, vol. I, p. 374; vol. II, pp. 280–325.
48. Ibid., vol. I, pp. 344–5.
49. Ibid., vol. II, p. 77.
50. Ibid., vol. I, p. 344.

CHAPTER 14 SORROW, DOLOUR, DARKNESS AND ALL IMPIETY

1. Knox, *History*, vol. II, p. 9.
2. Ibid., p. 7.
3. Randolph to Throckmorton, 26 August 1561, Knox, *Works*, vol. VI, p. 129.
4. For the uncomplimentary comment by the French poet Brantôme, see Knox, *Works*, vol. II, p. 270, n. 2.
5. Knox, *History*, vol. II, pp. 8–9.
6. Proclamation, 25 August 1561, *Register of the Privy Council of Scotland*, ed. J. Burton *et al.*, 14 vols (HMSO, Edinburgh, 1877–90), vol. I, pp. 266–7.
7. Knox, *History*, vol. II, pp. 9–11.
8. Ibid., p. 12.
9. Ibid., p. 13.
10. Ibid.
11. Knox to Cecil, 7 October 1561, Knox, *Works*, vol. VI, pp. 131–2.
12. Lynch, 'Minister of Edinburgh', pp. 236, 249–50.
13. For Knox's accounts of his encounters with the Queen, see Knox, *History*, vol. II, pp. 13–20, 43–6, 71–4, 81–4. Also see Jenny Wormald, 'Godly Reformer, Godless Monarch: John Knox and Mary, Queen of Scots', in Mason (ed.), *John Knox and the British Reformations*, pp. 220–41.
14. Knox, *History*, vol. II, p. 17 and n. 1.
15. Ibid., pp. 19–20.
16. Knox to Cecil, 7 October 1561, Knox, *Works*, vol. VI, p. 132.
17. Randolph to Cecil, 16 December 1562, Knox, *Works*, vol. VI, p. 146.
18. Knox to Cecil, 7 October 1561, Knox, *Works*, vol. VI, p. 132.
19. Ibid., pp. 131–2.
20. Knox to Calvin, 24 October 1561, Knox, *Works*, vol. VI, p. 134.
21. Knox, *History*, vol. II, p. 133.
22. Knox to Anne Locke, 6 May 1562, Knox, *Works*, vol. VI, p. 140.
23. *Records of the Burgh of Edinburgh 1557–71*, p. 132.
24. Knox, *History*, vol. II, p. 41.
25. Ibid., pp. 37–42.
26. Ibid., p. 38.
27. G. H. Thoms, 'The Bells of St Giles', *Proceedings of the Society of Antiquaries of Scotland* (1884), p. 95. During this period bells were routinely rung to pacify or divert thunderstorms.
28. On Knox's task, Lynch, 'Minister of Edinburgh', pp. 242–67. On church bells after the Reformation, Margo Todd, *The Culture of Protestantism in Early Modern Scotland* (Yale University Press, New Haven, CT, 2002), p. 340.
29. Knox, *Works*, vol. VI, p. 559.
30. Lynch, *Edinburgh and the Reformation*, p. 222.
31. G. Donaldson, *Accounts of the Collectors of Thirds of Benefices 1561–1572* (Scottish History Society, third series, 42, Edinburgh, 1949); J. Kirk (ed.), *The Books of Assumption of the Thirds of Benefices* (British Academy, Oxford, 1995). Knox's 'judgement of the Thirds', Knox, *History*, vol. II, p. 29.
32. G. Donaldson, 'John Knox on Queen Mary's Payroll', in J. Kirk (ed.), *Scotland's History: Approaches and Reflections* (Scottish Academic Press, Edinburgh, 1995), pp. 63–4.
33. *Records of the Burgh of Edinburgh 1557–71*, p. 76.

34. Rosalind Marshall, *John Knox* (Birlinn, Edinburgh, 2000), p. 155; Ridley, *Knox*, p. 511 and n. 1.

35. *Records of the Burgh of Edinburgh 1557–71*, p. 131.

36. Knox, *Works*, vol. VI, pp. 391–428, 447–70.

37. Knox, *History*, vol. II, pp. 131–3.

38. Spottiswood, *History*, vol. III, p. 91.

39. Calderwood, *History*, vol. III, pp. 75–6.

40. See below, Chapter 19.

41. Winzet, *Certane Tractatis*, vol. I, p. 78; vol. II, pp. 34–5.

42. Wright, 'John Knox's Bible', pp. 58–9.

43. Lynch, *Edinburgh and the Reformation*, p. 97; for the general reception of changes to worship, Jane E. A. Dawson, 'Patterns of Worship in Reformation Scotland', in D. B. Forrester and D. C. Gay (eds), *Worship and Liturgy in Context: Studies of Theology and Practice* (SCM Press, London, 2009), pp. 136–51.

44. Dundas said Knox was 'with ane commoun hure apprehendit and tane furth of ane killogie', *Records of the Burgh of Edinburgh 1557–71*, pp. 162, 164; Lynch, *Edinburgh and the Reformation*, pp. 33, 181, 194; Ridley, *Knox*, p. 417.

45. Knox, *History*, vol. II, p. 12.

46. Ibid., p. 55.

47. C. H. Kuipers, *Quintin Kennedy (1520–1564): Two Eucharistic Tracts* (Janssen, Nijmegen, 1964).

48. Kennedy's *Oration* in Knox, *Works*, vol. VI, p. 158; *Ane Compendious Ressonyng* in Kuipers, *Quintin Kennedy*, pp. 148–83.

49. Kuipers, *Quintin Kennedy*, p. 151.

50. For example, Dieric Bouts' painting (1464–7) of the meeting of Abraham and Melchizedek. M. Taylor, 'The Conflicting Doctrines of the Scottish Reformation', *Innes Review*, 10 (1959), pp. 97–125.

51. Kuipers, *Quintin Kennedy*, p. 41.

52. Knox, *History*, vol. II, p. 57.

53. Knox, *Works*, vol. VI, pp. 169–220.

54. There was a strong reference at the end of Knox's *Reasoning* (Knox, *Works*, vol. VI, p. 220) to Matthew 15:13, and the verse was found on the title page of Hay's *Confutation*, the anti-Catholic poem by Patrick Adamson and William Stewart's translation from the French *Ane breif Gathering of the Halie Signes* (Edinburgh. 1565). I am grateful to Stephen Holmes for drawing my attention to this cluster; see Stephen Holmes, 'Liturgical Interpretation and Church Reform in Renaissance Scotland' (University of Edinburgh PhD thesis, 2013), chapters 6 and 7.

55. Knox, *Works*, vol. VI, p. 529.

56. Knox, *History*, vol. II, p. 85.

57. Ibid., p. 36; Knox wrote to Kennedy from Ochiltree: Knox, *Works*, vol. VI, p. 182.

58. Knox, *Works*, vol. VI, p. 533.

59. Knox to Goodman, 18 February 1567, Dawson and Glassey, 'Some Unpublished Letters', p. 191.

60. *The buik of the kirk of the Canagait, 1564–7*, ed. A. B. Calderwood (Scottish Record Society, Edinburgh, 1961), p. 76.

61. John Mossman's Protocol Book has survived: Lynch, *Edinburgh and the Reformation*, pp. 351, 399.

CHAPTER 15 WHAT HAVE YOU TO DO WITH MY MARRIAGE?

1. Knox, *History*, vol. II, p. 47 and the side note, 'Sharp left preaching and took him to the law'; Margaret H. B. Sanderson, 'John Shairp: Advocate and Laird of Houston', in *Mary Stewart's People*, pp. 22–33.

2. Thanks to Litill's bequest of his library to 'Edinburgh & Kirk of God', copies of Beza's books remain within the Litill collection in Edinburgh University Library: C. P. Finlayson, *Clement Litill and his Library* (Edinburgh University Library, Edinburgh, 1980), Inventory No. 47, p. 32.

3. Knox to Mistress Guthrie, Janet Henderson, 16 March 1557, Knox, *Works*, vol. IV, pp. 246–8.

4. Biblical motto in Scots on outside of John Knox House, Edinburgh; see Donald Smith, *John Knox House: Gateway to Edinburgh's Old Town* (John Donald, Edinburgh, 1996), p. 16.

5. Theo van Heijnsbergen, 'The Interaction between Literature and History in Queen Mary's Edinburgh: The Bannatyne Manuscript and its Prosopographical Context', in A. A. MacDonald, Michael Lynch and I. B. Cowan (eds), *The Renaissance in Scotland: Studies in Literature, Religion, History and Culture* (Brill, Leiden, 1994), pp. 183–225.

6. For Mossman, see Bruce P. Lenman, 'Jacobean Goldsmith-Jewellers as Credit-Creators: The Cases of James Mossman, James Cockie and George Heriot', *Scottish Historical Review*, 74 (1995), pp. 159–77; for the context of James Mossman's fate, see G. R. Hewitt, 'Castilians in Edinburgh (*act.* 1570–1573)', *Oxford Dictionary of National Biography*, Oxford University Press, 2004 (www.oxforddnb.com/view/article/69952, accessed 25 November 2013).

7. Knox, *History*, vol. II, p. 134.

8. Ibid., p. 74.

9. For the Argylls' marital difficulties, see Jane E. A. Dawson, 'The Noble and the Bastard: The Earl of Argyll and the Law of Divorce in Reformation Scotland', in Julian Goodare and A. A. MacDonald (eds), *Sixteenth-Century Scotland: Essays in Honour of Michael Lynch* (Brill, Leiden, 2008), pp. 147–68.

10. Knox, *History*, vol. II, p. 85; interview with Mary, pp. 80–4.

11. Ibid., p. 80.

12. Ibid., p. 81.

13. Ibid., p. 83.

14. Knox, *Works*, vol. VI, p. 295.

15. Knox, *History*, vol. II, pp. 87–101.

16. Ibid., p. 109.

17. Ibid., p. 111.

18. Ibid., p. 122.

19. Ibid., p. 125.

20. Ibid., p. 117.

21. Knox to Lord Robert Dudley, 6 October 1563, Knox, *Works*, vol. VI, p. 530; printed and discussed in Smith, *Older Scots*, pp. 106–8.

22. Knox, *Works*, vol. VI, p. 541.

23. For the background to the Darnley marriage, see Dawson, *Politics of Religion*, chapter 4; S. Adams, 'The Release of Lord Darnley', in Michael Lynch (ed.), *Mary Stewart: Queen in Three Kingdoms* (Blackwell, Oxford, 1988), pp. 123–53.

24. Knox, *History*, vol. II, p. 142.

25. Lynch, *Edinburgh and the Reformation*, Appendix V: The Protestant Party 1560–1571, pp. 281–6.

26. Knox, *Works*, vol. VI, p. 273.

27. *A Diurnal of Remarkable Occurents . . . since the death of King James the fourth till the year 1575*, ed. T. Thomson (Bannatyne Club, Edinburgh, 1833), p. 81; Knox, *Works*, vol. VI, p. 224.

28. Knox, *History*, vol. II, p. 173.

29. Knox, *Works*, vol. VI, p. 273.

30. *Acts and Proceedings of the General Assemblies*, vol. I, p. 96.

31. Ibid., p. 99; W. I. P. Hazlett, 'Playing God's Card: Knox and Fasting', in Mason (ed.), *John Knox and the British Reformations*, pp. 176–98.

32. Knox, *Works*, vol. VI, p. 404.

33. Ibid., p. 408.

34. Ibid., p. 418.

35. Jane E. A. Dawson, 'Scotland and the Example of Geneva', *Theology in Scotland*, 16 (2009), pp. 55–73.

36. The General Fast started on 27 February and ran until 3 March: Hazlett, 'Playing God's Card', pp. 186–9.

37. Knox, *Works*, vol. VI, p. 413.

38. Ibid., p. 391. Joel 2:12 from *Geneva Bible*.

39. Knox, *Works*, vol. VI, p. 393.

40. Ibid., pp. 402–3; on the fictitious Tridentine decree, see Hazlett, 'Playing God's Card', p. 196.

41. Preface to Book V covering 1561–4, Knox, *History*, vol. II, pp. 3–4.

CHAPTER 16 UNTHANKFUL (YEA ALAS MISERABLE) SCOTLAND

1. Knox, *Works*, vol. VI, p. 399.
2. Ibid., p. 483.
3. Knox to 'a friend in England', 19 August 1569, Knox, *Works*, vol. VI, p. 566.
4. Knox's prayer, 12 March 1566, Knox, *Works*, vol. VI, p. 484.
5. Julian Goodare, 'Queen Mary's Catholic Interlude', in Lynch (ed.), *Mary Stewart*, pp. 154–70.
6. Knox, *History*, vol. I, p. 319.
7. Ibid., pp. 44, 112.
8. Ibid., vol. II, pp. 175, 177.
9. *Diurnal*, p. 94.
10. Knox to Goodman, 27 October 1566, Dawson and Glassey, 'Some Unpublished Letters', p. 183.
11. Knox, *History*, vol. II, p. 3.
12. Ibid., vol. I, p. 271.
13. Ibid., p. 146.
14. Bannatyne to Goodman, 17 July 1572, Dawson and Glassey, 'Some Unpublished Letters', p. 201; Knox, *History*, vol. I, p. 274.
15. Knox, *History*, vol. I, p. xci
16. Ibid., p. 6.
17. Ibid., p. 275.
18. Knox, *Works*, vol. VI, p. 401.
19. Knox, *History*, vol. II, pp. 4–5.
20. Ibid., p. 4.
21. Ibid., vol. I, p. 374.
22. Ibid., p. 347.
23. Ibid., vol. II, p. 4.
24. Ibid., vol. I, p. 5.
25. Ibid., vol. II, p. 6.
26. Ibid., vol. I, p. 6.
27. Ibid., pp. 8–9.
28. C. P. Finlayson, 'A Volume Associated with John Knox', *Scottish Historical Review*, 126 (1939), pp. 170–2, and see below, Chapter 17.
29. Knox, *History*, vol. I, p. 5.
30. Roger A. Mason, 'Useable Pasts: History and Identity in Reformation Scotland', in his *Kingship and the Commonweal*, pp. 165–86; A. H. Williamson, *Scottish National Consciousness in the Age of James VI* (John Donald, Edinburgh, 1979).
31. These Irish networks were revealed in Goodman's letters, DD/PP/839; see also Mark Hutchison, 'Reformed Protestantism and the Government of Ireland, *c*.1565 to 1580: The Lord Deputyships of Henry Sidney and Arthur Grey', *Sidney Journal*, 29 (2011), pp. 71–104.
32. Helga Robinson-Hammerstein, 'Loftus, Adam (1533/4–1605)', *Oxford Dictionary of National Biography*, Oxford University Press, 2004; online edn, January 2008 (www.oxforddnb.com/view/article/16934, accessed 27 November 2013).
33. Knox to Goodman, 27 October 1566, Dawson and Glassey, 'Some Unpublished Letters', p. 185.
34. Ibid., pp. 183–4.
35. Ibid., p. 184; also see Dawson, *Politics of Religion*, chapter 5.
36. Knox to Goodman, 18 February 1567, Dawson and Glassey, 'Some Unpublished Letters', p. 190.
37. Ibid., pp. 190–1.
38. Knox to Goodman, 27 October 1566, Dawson and Glassey, 'Some Unpublished Letters', pp. 184–5.
39. Goodman to Alice Goodman, 2 April 1567, DD/PP/839, pp. 104–5.
40. Whittingham to Goodman, 12 November 1566, DD/PP/839, p. 87.
41. Whittingham to Goodman, 13 January 1567, DD/PP/839, p. 94.
42. Knox to Goodman, 27 October 1566, Dawson and Glassey, 'Some Unpublished Letters', p. 185.
43. Henry Sidney to Goodman, 23 March 1567, DD/PP/839, p. 88.

44. For the details of Goodman's subsequent career and the blocked requests, see Dawson, 'Goodman, Christopher (1521/2–1603)'.
45. The opening sentences of Whittingham's letter to Goodman probably refer to the project: 12 November 1566, DD/PP/839, p. 87.
46. Based on information in Universal Short Title Catalogue, http://www.ustc.ac.uk/ (accessed 7 November 2013).
47. Based upon the late Professor David Wright's research notes on Knox's Bible; Charles G. D. Littleton, 'Bodley, John (c.1520–1591)', Oxford Dictionary of National Biography, Oxford University Press, 2004; online edn, January 2008 (www.oxforddnb.com/view/article/53707, accessed 27 November 2013).
48. Knox to friend in England, 19 August 1569, Knox, Works, vol. VI, p. 566.
49. Knox to Foxe, c.1566, BL Harley MS 416, f. 132.
50. David Ditchburn, Scotland and Europe: The Medieval Kingdom and its Contacts with Christendom 1214–1560 (Tuckwell Press, East Linton, 2001), chapter 5.
51. Knox to John Wood, 10 September 1568, Knox, Works, vol. VI, p. 560.
52. Knox to Goodman, late May or early June 1567, Dawson and Glassey, 'Some Unpublished Letters', pp. 193–5.
53. Ibid., p. 194.
54. Grindal, Remains, pp. 295–6.
55. 'A letter written to Mr Knoxe', c.May 1568, Lorimer, Knox, pp. 298–300; discussed pp. 229–40.
56. Seconde Part of a Register, pp. 65–6.
57. Knox to John Wood, 14 February 1568, Knox, Works, vol. VI, p. 559.
58. Ibid.

CHAPTER 17 THIS MOST MIRACULOUS VICTORY AND OVERTHROW

1. Knox, Works, vol. VI, p. 445.
2. Acts and Proceedings of the General Assemblies, vol. I, pp. 120–1.
3. Since Margaret Knox had not accompanied her husband to Aldford, Chester, or met Goodman's wife, it is most probable that she had remained in Scotland for Knox's trip to England.
4. Acts and Proceedings of the General Assemblies, vol. I, pp. 147–9.
5. Knox, Works, vol. VI, p. 553; Keith, History, vol. II, pp. 687–8.
6. 'Wicked woman' became Knox's normal description of Mary, for example Knox to Goodman, 20 May 1569, Dawson and Glassey, 'Some Unpublished Letters', p. 197.
7. Geneva Bible, 1560 edn, f. 169r.
8. Calderwood, History, vol. II, p. 365.
9. Throckmorton to Queen Elizabeth, 21 July 1567, Knox, Works, vol. VI, p. 554.
10. Knox to friend in England, 19 August 1569, Knox, Works, vol. VI, p. 566.
11. Prayer, 22 January 1570, Knox, Works, vol. VI, p. 569.
12. Dawson, 'John Knox, Christopher Goodman and the "Example of Geneva"', p. 117 and n. 42.
13. Argument before 2 Kings, Geneva Bible, 1560 edn, f. 164v.
14. Roger A. Mason and Martin S. Smith, A Dialogue on the Law of Kingship among the Scots: A Critical Edition and Translation of George Buchanan's De iure regni apud Scotos dialogus (Ashgate, Aldershot, 2004); Burns, The True Law of Kingship, chapter 6.
15. Mason, Knox on Rebellion, p. 44.
16. For an analysis of Buchanan's De iure regni see Mason and Smith, Buchanan's De iure regni, pp. xlv–lxxi.
17. 2 Chronicles 23:21 note, Geneva Bible, 1560 edn, f. 200r; cf. 'Which by her crueltie and persecution had vexed the whole land before': 2 Kings 11:20 note, Geneva Bible, 1560 edn, f. 170v.
18. Mason, Knox on Rebellion, pp. 32, 34.
19. Knox to Goodman, 20 May 1569, Dawson and Glassey, 'Some Unpublished Letters', p. 198.
20. Michael Lynch, 'Scotland's First Protestant Coronation', in L. A. J. R. Houwen (ed.), Literature and Religion in Late Medieval and Early Modern Scotland (Peeters, Leuven, 2012), pp. 177–207.
21. Calderwood, History, vol. V, p. 159.

22. Psalm 72, *(The Forme of Prayers ... with) The Whole Psalmes of David in English Metre* (Robert Lekprevik, Edinburgh, 1565) (hereafter *Psalm Book*, 1565 edn), pp. 201–5. David Peebles' setting was recorded in the Wode Partbooks, see above, Chapter 10. For Timothy Duguid's modern transcription of Peebles' Psalm 72, see Church Service Society, http://www.churchservicesociety.org/four-part-psalms (accessed 8 November 2013).

23. Moray to Herries, *c.*24 August 1567, cited by Stephen Alford, 'Knox, Cecil and the British Dimension', in Mason (ed.), *John Knox and the British Reformations*, p. 216.

24. General Assembly's letter to Willock, January 1568, Knox, *Works*, vol. VI, pp. 445–6.

25. Knox to Wood, 14 February 1568, Knox, *Works*, vol. VI, pp. 558–9.

26. *Acts and Proceedings of the General Assemblies*, vol. I, p. 145.

27. Knox, *Works*, vol. VI, p. 487.

28. Ibid., p. 494.

29. Ibid., p. 499.

30. Aventinus, *Annalium Boiorum libri septem* (Ingolstadt, 1554), copy donated in 1607 to Edinburgh University Library, Dd.1.32.

31. Finlayson, 'A Volume Associated with John Knox', pp. 170–2.

32. Knox to Goodman, 3 November 1568, Dawson and Glassey, 'Some Unpublished Letters', p. 196.

33. 'An Account of a Pretended Conference held by the Regent, earl of Murray, with the Lord Lindsay and others; January MDLXX', printed in *Bannatyne Miscellany*, vol. I, p. 42; and below n. 39.

34. Mason, *Knox on Rebellion*, pp. 128–9; see above, Chapter 10.

35. Knox to Goodman, 20 May 1569, Dawson and Glassey, 'Some Unpublished Letters', pp. 197–8. Using a Scottish form for 'eth' endings, Knox frequently transposed the 'h' and the 't': see Smith, *Older Scots*, pp. 106–8.

36. Knox to Cecil, 2 January 1570, Knox, *Works*, vol. VI, p. 568; Stephen Alford, *The Early Elizabethan Polity: William Cecil and the Succession Crisis 1558–1569* (Cambridge University Press, Cambridge, 1998), chapters 7–8.

37. Knox, *Works*, vol. VI, p. 561.

38. Thomas Archibald to Archbishop Beaton, October 1569, cited in Ridley, *Knox*, p. 482.

39. 'The copey of ane bill of adverteissment send be ane freind owt of court to ane kynisman of the earle of Argillis', dated 10 October 1569, in BL Cotton MS Calig. B IX, ff. 390r–394v; printed from another manuscript, dated January 1570 and with minor variations as 'An Account of a Pretended Conference' in *Bannatyne Miscellany*, vol. I, pp. 37–50; also see Richard Bannatyne, *Memorials of Transactions in Scotland 1569–1573*, ed. R. Pitcairn (Bannatyne Club, Edinburgh, 1836), pp. 5–13; Calderwood, *History*, vol. II, pp. 515–25; discussed in Dawson, *Politics of Religion*, pp. 178–9.

40. 'An Account of a Pretended Conference', *Bannatyne Miscellany*, vol. I, p. 40.

41. Ibid., p. 41.

42. Ibid., p. 42.

43. Ibid., p. 43.

44. Ibid., p. 34.

45. Ibid., p. 35.

46. Knox to Wood, 10 September 1568, Knox, *Works*, vol. VI, p. 561.

47. For the Geddy map of St Andrews, see National Library of Scotland Maps, http://maps.nls.uk/towns/detail.cfm?id=215 (accessed 8 November 2013). I am grateful to John di Folco for drawing my attention to the gibbet in the burgh's marketplace on the Geddy map.

48. Knox to Goodman, 20 May 1569, Dawson and Glassey, 'Some Unpublished Letters', p. 198.

49. Bannatyne, *Memorials*, p. 14.

50. *Diurnal*, p. 156.

51. Bannatyne, *Memorials*, p. 4.

52. Ibid., p. 16.

53. Prayer after Regent Moray's death, Knox, *Works*, vol. VI, pp. 569–70.

54. *Diurnal*, p. 158.

55. Randolph to Cecil, 22 February 1570, Knox, *Works*, vol. VI, p. 571; Calderwood, *History*, vol. II, p. 525.

56. *Satirical Poems*, vol. I, p. 103, l. 90.

57. Amy Blakeway, 'The Response to the Regent Moray's Assassination', *Scottish Historical Review*, 88 (2009), pp. 9–33.

58. Goodman to Knox on Regent Moray's death, c.February 1570, Knox, *Works*, vol. VI, p. 573.
59. Knox to Douglas of Lochleven, 31 March 1570, Knox, *Works*, vol. VI, p. 574.

CHAPTER 18 WEARY OF THE WORLD

1. Bannatyne to Goodman 17 July 1572, Dawson and Glassey, 'Some Unpublished Letters', p. 201.
2. *Acts and Proceedings of the General Assemblies*, vol. I, p. 3.
3. Bannatyne's Will, 27 August 1605, in Bannatyne, *Memorials*, pp. 363–6.
4. Knox, *Works*, vol. VI, p. lv; for medical analysis of Knox's stroke, John Wilkinson, *The Medical History of the Reformers: Luther, Calvin and Knox* (Handsel Press, Edinburgh, 2001), pp. 102–4.
5. Knox, *Works*, vol. VI, p. 602.
6. For a discussion of the manuscript of the *History*, see Introduction in Knox, *History*, vol. I, pp. xcii–xcv; Bannatyne was probably 'Hand C' among the eight scribes' hands found in the *History*, p. cvi, n. 6.
7. Bannatyne to Goodman, 17 July 1572, Dawson and Glassey, 'Some Unpublished Letters', p. 201.
8. *Acts and Proceedings of the General Assemblies*, vol. I, pp. 310–11.
9. Bannatyne, *Memorials*, p. 91.
10. Ibid., pp. 37, 108–9.
11. Ibid., p. 43.
12. Ibid., p. 51; for the Brechin steeple incident, see Dawson, *Politics of Religion*, p. 183.
13. 2 Kings 18:21; Isaiah 26:6; Bannatyne, *Memorials*, p. 53; and Bannatyne to Goodman, 17 July 1572, Dawson and Glassey, 'Some Unpublished Letters', p. 200.
14. Bannatyne, *Memorials*, p. 16.
15. Ibid., pp. 20–1, 91, 109.
16. Ibid., p. 18.
17. Ibid., pp. 15, 17.
18. Ibid., p. 52.
19. Ibid., p. 104.
20. Ibid., p. 51.
21. Probably thanks to Bannatyne, David Calderwood had access to some of Knox's and Bannatyne's papers: see A. R. Macdonald, 'David Calderwood: The Not So Hidden Years, 1590–1604', *Scottish Historical Review*, 74 (1995), pp. 69–74.
22. Knox, *Works*, vol. VI, p. 591.
23. Ibid., p. 592.
24. Knox to Brethren of the Church of Edinburgh, 17 July 1571, Knox, *Works*, vol. VI, p. 603.
25. Knox to Lawson, 7 September 1572, Knox, *Works*, vol. VI, p. 632.
26. Patrick Murray of Tibbermuir to Lady Glenorchy, 10 July 1570: *Clan Campbell Letters 1559–1583*, ed. Jane E. A. Dawson (Scottish History Society, fifth series, 10, Edinburgh, 1997), No. 113, p. 166. The biblical reference is to Jeremiah 43.
27. Knox, *Works*, vol. VI, p. 591.
28. *Diurnal*, p. 201.
29. Knox, *Works*, vol. VI, p. 590.
30. Knox to Goodman, 28 May 1569, Dawson and Glassey, 'Some Unpublished Letters', p. 198.
31. Bannatyne, *Memorials*, pp. 33–60.
32. Ibid.; the account of Knox's dispute with Grange taken from Bannatyne, *Memorials*, pp. 70–82.
33. Knox, *Works*, vol. VI, p. 579.
34. Ibid., p. 583.
35. Ibid., pp. 584–5.
36. Lethington to Edinburgh Kirk session, November 1572, Knox, *Works*, vol. VI, p. 635.
37. Knox, *Works*, vol. VI, p. 493.
38. Knox to Goodman, 3 November 1568, Dawson and Glassey, 'Some Unpublished Letters', p. 195.
39. Knox's Testament, Knox, *Works*, vol. VI, p. lvii.
40. Bannatyne, *Memorials*, p. 109.
41. Calderwood, *History*, vol. III, p. 59.
42. Bannatyne, *Memorials*, p. 111.
43. Knox, *Works*, vol. VI, p. 598.

44. James Melville, *The Autobiography and Diary of Mr James Melvill, Minister of Kilrenny in Fife and Professor of Theology at the University of St Andrews*, ed. R. Pitcairn (Wodrow Society, Edinburgh, 1842), p. 32.
45. Alexander Hay to Knox, 1 and 14 December 1571, Knox, *Works*, vol. VI, pp. 606–12.
46. Knox, *Works*, vol. VI, pp. liv–vi.
47. *Letter to Tyrie*, Knox, *Works*, vol. VI, pp. 479–520.
48. Preface to *Letter to Tyrie*, To the Faithfull Reader, 12 July 1572, Knox, *Works*, vol. VI, p. 514.
49. Knox to Wishart of Pittarrow, 19 July 1572; Knox to Goodman, July 1572, Knox, *Works*, vol. VI, pp. 616–19.
50. Knox to Wishart of Pittarrow, 19 July 1572, Knox, *Works*, vol. VI, p. 617.
51. *RStAKS*, vol. I, pp. 361–2.
52. Melville, *Diary*, p. 26.
53. Ibid., p. 33.
54. Ibid., p. 31.
55. Ibid., p. 26; for Knox's argument with John Rutherford, Provost of St Salvator's College, Knox, *Works*, vol. VI, pp. 625–7.
56. For the St Andrews disputes, Bannatyne, *Memorials*, pp. 255–63; testimonial for Robert Hamilton, *RStAKS*, vol. I, pp. 338–9; see Steven J. Reid, *Humanism and Calvinism: Andrew Melville and the Universities of Scotland 1560–1625* (Ashgate, Aldershot, 2011), pp. 42–5.
57. For Knox's dispute with Robert Hamilton, Knox, *Works*, vol. VI, pp. 627–30; Melville, *Diary*, p. 33; for the 1565 plot see, Dawson, *Politics of Religion*, p. 125.
58. Knox to Robert Hamilton, 15 November 1571, Knox, *Works*, vol. VI, pp. 629-30.
59. Knox, *Works*, vol. VI, p. 630.
60. For Knox's dispute with Archibald Hamilton, Knox, *Works*, vol. VI, pp. 630–1.
61. Knox to General Assembly, 5 August 1572, Knox, *Works*, vol. VI, p. 619.
62. *RStAKS*, vol. I, p. 368.

CHAPTER 19 HASTE, LEST YOU COME TOO LATE

1. Knox, *Works*, vol. VI, pp. 622–3; Bannatyne, *Memorials*, p. 247.
2. The Kirk and brethren of Edinburgh to Knox, 4 August 1572, Knox, *Works*, vol. VI, p. 623.
3. Knox, *Works*, vol. VI, p. 624.
4. Ibid., p. 631.
5. Spottiswood, *History*, vol. II, p. 180; Knox, *Works*, vol. VI, p. 632. Killigrew to Cecil and Leicester, 6 October 1572, Knox, *Works*, vol. VI, p. 633.
6. Smeton's account in Knox, *Works*, vol. VI, p. 652.
7. Calderwood, *History*, vol. III, p. 226.
8. Ibid., p. 225; Lynch, *Edinburgh and the Reformation*, p. 143.
9. Lynch, *Edinburgh and the Reformation*, p. 147; Michael F. Graham, *The Uses of Reform: 'Godly Discipline' and Popular Behaviour in Scotland and Beyond 1560–1610* (Brill, Leiden, 1996), pp. 105–10.
10. Knox, *Works*, vol. VI, p. 632.
11. Spottiswood, *History*, vol. II, p. 181.
12. Ibid., pp. 643–4. A fascinating modern medical analysis is provided by John Wilkinson, *Medical History*, pp. 85–117.
13. Knox, *Works*, vol. VI, p. 637.
14. Lawson's account of Knox's death, Knox, *Works*, vol. VI, p. 657; Melville, *Diary*, pp. 34–5; discussed in Harry Potter, *Edinburgh under Siege 1571–1573* (Tempus, Stroud, 2003), pp. 111–12, 146–7.
15. Knox, *Works*, vol. VI, pp. 641, 659.
16. Ibid., p. 641.
17. Ibid., p. 644.
18. Knox to Goodman, 3 November 1568, Dawson and Glassey, 'Some Unpublished Letters', p. 196.
19. Calderwood, *History*, vol. III, p. 242.
20. *Acts and Proceedings of the General Assemblies*, vol. I, pp. 309–10.
21. David G. Mullan, *Scottish Puritanism 1590–1638* (Oxford University Press, Oxford, 2000), pp. 21–2.
22. From an oral account gathered in the mid-seventeenth century, McCrie, *Knox*, p. 372.

23. *Acts and Proceedings of the General Assemblies*, vol. I, pp. 310–11.

24. For example, Bannatyne's *Memorials*, Davidson's poem, James Lawson's account, Knox, *Works*, vol. VI, pp. 649–60.

25. Bannatyne to Goodman, 17 July 1572, Dawson and Glassey, 'Some Unpublished Letters', pp. 199–201; Edinburgh Council to Goodman, 24 June 1573, DD/PP/839, p. 127.

26. Goodman to Killigrew, 6 March 1573, DD/PP/839, p. 126.

27. Knox, *Works*, vol. VI, p. 585.

28. Ibid., p. 596. In his last letter Knox reminded Goodman, July 1572, 'I ceassed not to fore-warne these publictlie, as Edinburgh can witness; and [secretlie as Mr Randolph, and other of that nation with whom I] secretlie conferred, can testifie'. The printed version in Knox, *Works*, vol. VI, p. 619 is missing the section in brackets: see Dawson and Glassey, 'Some Unpublished Letters', p. 178, n. 50.

29. Knox, *Works*, vol. VI, pp. lv–lvi.

30. Rupp, 'The Europe of John Knox', pp. 6–7.

31. Knox, *Works*, vol. III, p. 10.

32. See above, Chapter 14; Knox, *Works*, vol. VI, p. 229.

33. Knox, *Works*, vol. VI, p. 425.

34. See above, Chapter 11.

35. Knox, *Works*, vol. VI, p. 639.

36. See Loughlin, 'The Dialogue of the Twa Wyfeis', pp. 226–45; Mark Loughlin, 'Maitland, William, of Lethington (1525x30–1573)', *Oxford Dictionary of National Biography*, Oxford University Press, 2004; online edn, January 2008 (www.oxforddnb.com/view/article/17838, accessed 29 November 2013).

37. Knox, *Works*, vol. VI, pp. 635 and 638–9.

38. Goodman, *How Superior Powers*, pp. 226–7.

Further reading

The following items are a guide to further reading about Knox and are grouped under categories that broadly reflect the order of the chapters. They have been selected to offer useful suggestions with an awareness of availability and accessibility rather than any attempt at a comprehensive bibliography. After the first mention, details of books and articles are not subsequently repeated.

<small>Chapter 1 Rare and wonderful gifts: Sources and general works on Knox</small>

Editions of Knox's works

The main source is *The Works of John Knox*, ed. David Laing, 6 vols (Bannatyne Club, Edinburgh, 1846–64). A modernized edition of Knox's *History* was published as *John Knox's History of the Reformation in Scotland*, ed. W. C. Dickinson (Nelson, Edinburgh, 1949). Peter Lorimer, *John Knox and the Church of England* (Henry S. King, London, 1875) contains editions of the Epistle to the Congregation of Berwick 1552; Memo to Privy Council, 1552; Practice of Lord's Supper used in Berwick c.1550; Letter to Knox from London, 1566. Roger A. Mason (ed.), *John Knox on Rebellion* (Cambridge, Cambridge University Press, 1994) provides a modern edition of the 1558 tracts and Knox in Scotland 1557–64. Letters transcribed from the recently discovered Letter-book of Christopher Goodman can be found in Jane E. A. Dawson and Lionel K. Glassey, 'Some Unpublished Letters from John Knox to Christopher Goodman', *Scottish Historical Review*, 84 (2005), pp. 166–201. The dating and discussion of Knox's correspondence with Elizabeth Bowes and with Anne Locke can be followed in A. Daniel Frankforter, 'Elizabeth Bowes and John Knox: A Woman in Reformation Theology', *Church History*, 56 (1987), pp. 333–47, and Susan M. Felch (ed.), *The Collected Works of Anne Vaughan Locke*, MRTS, 185 (Arizona Center for Medieval and Renaissance Studies, Tempe, AZ, 1999). Details of the copy of Knox's Bible in Melbourne are given in David Wright, 'John Knox's Bible', in *The Bible as Book: The Reformation* (British Library, London, 2000), pp. 59–60. The *Livre des Anglois* (records of the English-speaking congregation in Geneva, 1555–60) was printed in Charles Martin, *Les Protestants anglais réfugiés à Genève au temps du Calvin* (Librairie A. Jullien, Geneva, 1915), pp. 331–8. At the back of Dickinson's edition of Knox's *History* there is an annotated bibliography of the sources and manuscripts for the *History*, and Knox's printed works are discussed in W. I. P. Hazlett, 'A Working Bibliography of Writings by John Knox', *Calviniana*, ed. Robert V. Schnucker, Sixteenth-Century Essays and Studies, 10 (Truman State University Press, Kirksville, MO, 1988), pp. 185–93. Henry R. Sefton, *John Knox* (Saint Andrew Press, Edinburgh, 1993) in The Devotional Library series offers an accessible and interesting collection of short extracts from Knox's writings.

General studies of Knox

The first 'modern' biography of Knox was Thomas McCrie, *Life of John Knox*, first published in Edinburgh in 1812 (Blackwood & Sons, Edinburgh, 1850 edn). A mine of information can be found in P. Hume Brown, *John Knox: A Biography*, 2 vols (Adam and Charles Black, London, 1895). During the twentieth century, the lively and perceptive study by Lord Eustace Percy, *John Knox*, first printed in 1937 and now reprinted (Lutterworth Press, Cambridge, 2013), continues to be an interesting read, and the essay collection produced for the quatercentenary, *John Knox: A Quatercentenary Reappraisal*, ed. Duncan Shaw (Saint Andrew Press, Edinburgh, 1975), still has some penetrating insights. Jasper Ridley, *John Knox* (Clarendon Press, Oxford, 1968) remains one of the most comprehensive biographies, while W. Stanford Reid, *Trumpeter of God: A Biography of John Knox* (Charles Scribner's Sons, New York, 1974) provides additional background, especially from the French sources. Rosalind Marshall's readable biography, *John Knox* (Birlinn, Edinburgh, 2000), gives a clear sense of the man and those around him. The most perceptive study of Knox has been written by Pierre Janton in his *John Knox (ca. 1513–1572): L'homme et l'oeuvre* (Didier, Paris, 1967), and his *John Knox (v.1513–1572): Réformateur écossais* (Cerf, Paris, 2013). Richard Kyle and Dale Johnson, *John Knox: An Introduction to his Life and Works* (Wipf & Stock, Eugene, OR, 2009) guide the reader through Knox's writings, and Kyle's collection of his extensive Knoxian studies in *God's Watchman* (Pickwick Publications, Eugene, OR, 2013) complements the *Introduction*. Kenneth D. Farrow's study, *John Knox: Reformation Rhetoric and the Traditions of Scots Prose 1490–1570* (Peter Lang, Bern, 2004), contains fresh insights into Knox's works. The Scots language of the period, and Knox's use of it, is discussed by Jeremy Smith, *Older Scots: A Linguistic Reader* (Scottish Text Society, fifth series, 9, Edinburgh, 2012). Many aspects of Knox's life were covered in the very fine collection of essays found in Roger A. Mason (ed.), *John Knox and the British Reformations* (Ashgate, Aldershot, 1998). Forming a starting point for this biography, a survey of Knox's life appeared in Jane E. A. Dawson, 'Knox, John (c.1514–1572)', *Oxford Dictionary of National Biography*, Oxford University Press, 2004; online edn, January 2008 (www.oxforddnb.com/view/article/15781, accessed 28 November 2013). The *Oxford Dictionary of National Biography* offers an extremely useful resource on the lives of many of Knox's contemporaries.

CHAPTER 2 TINTOTERIUS: THE MAN FROM THE BANKS OF THE TYNE

For the flow of Scottish history during Knox's entire life, see Jane E. A. Dawson, *Scotland Re-formed 1488–1587* (Edinburgh University Press, Edinburgh, 2007), and for the European and Reformation context, Diarmaid MacCulloch, *Reformation: Europe's House Divided 1490–1700* (Allen Lane, London, 2003). The best survey of how his educational training influenced Knox's life is J. H. Burns, 'Knox: Scholastic and Canonistic Echoes', in Mason (ed.), *John Knox and the British Reformations*, pp. 117–29. The different aspects and lacunae within Knox's theological education are revealed in David F. Wright, 'John Knox and the Early Church Fathers', in Mason (ed.), *John Knox and the British Reformations*, pp. 99–116. The debate about Knox's priesthood has been summarized in 'The Ordination of John Knox: A Symposium', *Innes Review*, 6 (1955), pp. 99–106, and John Durkan gives the context of a notary's life in 'The Early Scottish Notary', in I. B. Cowan and Duncan Shaw (eds), *Renaissance and Reformation in Scotland* (Scottish Academic Press, Edinburgh, 1983), pp. 22–40.

CHAPTER 3 MY FIRST ANCHOR

Alec Ryrie provides an overview of the early stages of Scottish Protestantism to 1560 in *Origins of the Scottish Reformation* (Manchester University Press, Manchester, 2006), and the links between Knox and the first Scottish Protestant martyr, Patrick Hamilton, are examined in Iain Torrance, 'Patrick Hamilton and John Knox: A Study in the Doctrine of Justification by Faith', *Archiv für Reformationsgeschichte*, 65 (1974), pp. 171–84. M. Dotterweich's entry on George Wishart in the *Oxford Dictionary of National Biography* gives a fine summary of the man, and some of Wishart's theological ideas are discussed in Duncan Shaw, *Renaissance and Zwinglian Influences in Sixteenth-Century Scotland* (Edina Press, Edinburgh, 2012). Margaret H. B. Sanderson, *Cardinal of Scotland: David Beaton c.1494–1546* (John Donald, Edinburgh, 2001 edn) has written an excellent biography of this complex man.

CHAPTER 4 CALLED BY MY GOD

The political and international context is brilliantly and comprehensively covered in Marcus Merriman, *The Rough Wooings: Mary, Queen of Scots 1542–1551* (Tuckwell Press, East Linton, 2000). Carol Edington, 'John Knox and the Castilians: A Crucible of Reforming Opinion', in Mason (ed.), *John Knox and the British Reformations*, pp. 29–50, discusses the context of Knox's experience in St Andrews Castle. Winram's career and his important role in 1547 are treated in Linda J. Dunbar, *Reforming the Scottish Church: John Winram (c.1492–1582) and the Example of Fife* (Ashgate, Aldershot, 2002). A balancing perspective is given in John Durkan, 'Scottish Reformers: The Less than Golden Legend', *Innes Review*, 45 (1994), pp. 1–28.

CHAPTER 5 THE REALM OF ENGLAND

Diarmaid MacCulloch, *Tudor Church Militant: Edward VI and the Protestant Reformation* (Allen Lane, The Penguin Press, London, 1999: published in North America as *The Boy King*), presents a stimulating survey of the Edwardian Church. Knox is placed within his Anglo-Scottish context in Clare Kellar, *Scotland, England and the Scottish Reformation 1534–1561* (Oxford University Press, Oxford, 2003). For discussions of Knox's relations with Marjory and Elizabeth Bowes, see Patrick Collinson, 'John Knox, the Church of England and the Women of England', in Mason (ed.), *John Knox and the British Reformations*, pp. 74–96, and Christine M. Newman, 'The Reformation and Elizabeth Bowes: A Study of a Sixteenth-Century Northern Gentlewoman', in W. J. Sheils and Diana Wood (eds), *Women and the Church*, Studies in Church History, 27 (Blackwell, Oxford, 1990), pp. 325–33.

CHAPTER 6 WHY HELD WE BACK THE SALT?

Catherine Davies analyses the themes of Edwardian Protestant propaganda in *A Religion of the Word: The Defence of the Reformation in the Reign of Edward VI* (Manchester University Press, Manchester, 2002). The definitive account of the making of the 1552 Book of Common Prayer, and so much more, can be found in Diarmaid MacCulloch's magisterial biography of *Thomas Cranmer* (Yale University Press, New Haven, CT, 1996). A useful collection, including essays on aspects of the Freewillers, printing and conventicles, all of which affected Knox, can be found in Peter Marshall and Alec Ryrie (eds), *The Beginnings of English Protestantism* (Cambridge University Press, Cambridge, 2002). The important relationship between Knox and Anne Locke is discussed in Susan M. Felch, '"Deir sister": The Letters of John Knox and Anne Vaughan Lok', *Renaissance and Reformation*, 19 (1995), pp. 47–68. Richard Greaves, *Theology and Revolution in the Scottish Reformation: Studies in the Thought of John Knox* (Christian University Press, Grand Rapids, MI, 1980) provides insights into Knox's writings, especially during the Marian exile. A recent evaluation of Knox's prophetic role has been made by Rudolph P. Almasy, 'John Knox and A Godly Letter: Fashioning and Refashioning the Exilic "I"', in C. Gribben and D. Mullan (eds), *Literature and the Scottish Reformation* (Ashgate, Farnham, Surrey, 2009), pp. 95–109.

CHAPTER 7 A FARRAGO OF CEREMONIES

Euan Cameron, 'Frankfurt and Geneva: The European Context of John Knox's Reformation', in Mason (ed.), *John Knox and the British Reformations*, pp. 51–73, provides an excellent overview. The standard source for the Troubles at Frankfurt was published anonymously in 1574, *A Brieff discours off the troubles begonne at Franckford*, the best edition provided by J. Petheram (London, 1845), though the text can also be found in Knox, *Works*, vol. IV. A new chronology for the Troubles at Frankfurt is presented by Timothy Duguid, 'The "Troubles at Frankfurt": A New Chronology', *Reformation and Renaissance Review*, 12 (2013), pp. 243–68, and in the new material from Jane E. A. Dawson, *Letters from Exile: New Documents on the Marian Exile, 1553–9*, www.marianexile.div.ed.ac.uk. For the background to the liturgical debates, see Bryan D. Spinks, *From the Lord and 'The Best Reformed Church': A Study of the Eucharistic Liturgy in the English Puritan and Separatist Traditions 1550–1633* (Pickwick Publishing, Eugene, OR, 1985).

Chapter 8 Double cares

The Genevan exiles can be followed in Dan G. Danner, *Pilgrimage to Puritanism: History and Theology of the Marian Exiles at Geneva 1555–1560* (Peter Lang, New York, 1999), and the English exile congregation is fully discussed in Martin, *Les Protestant anglais réfugiés à Genève au temps du Calvin*. A discussion of the text of the *Forme of Prayers* (later known as the *Book of Common Order*) can be found in W. D. Maxwell, *The Liturgical Portions of the Genevan Service Book* (Oliver & Boyd, London, 1931). On Calvin, see Bruce Gordon's excellent biography, *Calvin* (Yale University Press, New Haven, CT, 2009). The local contexts of Knox's visit to Scotland can be traced in Margaret H. B. Sanderson, *Ayrshire and the Reformation: People and Change 1490–1600* (Tuckwell Press, East Linton, 1997), and F. D. Bardgett, *Scotland Reformed: The Reformation in Angus and the Mearns* (John Donald, Edinburgh, 1989); and the Queen Regent's perspective is given in Pamela Ritchie, *Mary of Guise in Scotland 1546–1560* (Tuckwell, East Linton, 2002).

Chapter 9 Pierced with anguish and sorrow

Scottish noble support for the Protestant cause during for the rest of Knox's life can be traced in Jane E. A. Dawson, *The Politics of Religion in the Age of Mary, Queen of Scots: The Earl of Argyll and the Struggle for Britain and Ireland* (Cambridge University Press, Cambridge, 2002). For a comprehensive and readable survey of European Calvinism, see Philip Benedict, *Christ's Churches Purely Reformed* (Yale University Press, New Haven, CT, 2002). The best discussions of Knox's political ideas are J. H. Burns, *The True Law of Kingship* (Clarendon Press, Oxford, 1996); and Roger A. Mason, *Kingship and the Commonweal: Political Thought in Renaissance and Reformation Scotland* (Tuckwell Press, East Linton, 1998). For Goodman and Knox, see Jane E. A. Dawson, 'Trumpeting Resistance: Christopher Goodman and John Knox', in Mason (ed.), *Knox and British Reformations*, pp. 130–53; and her entry on Goodman in the *Oxford Dictionary of National Biography*.

Chapter 10 Quietness of conscience and contentment of heart

Locke's 'Have mercy God' is provided and discussed in Felch, *The Collected Works of Anne Vaughan Locke*, and background on the use of the penitential psalms can be found in Clare Costley King'oo, *Miserere Mei: The Penitential Psalms in Late Medieval and Early Modern England* (University of Notre Dame Press, Notre Dame, IN, 2012). An overview of the importance of the 'example of Geneva' can be found in Jane E. A. Dawson, 'John Knox, Christopher Goodman and the "Example of Geneva"', in Polly Ha and Patrick Collinson (eds), *The Reception of Continental Reformation in Britain*, Proceedings of the British Academy, 164 (Oxford University Press, Oxford, 2010), pp. 107–35. The Geneva Bible is discussed in detail in David Daniell, *The Bible in English* (Yale University Press, New Haven, CT, 2003), and see facsimile of 1560 edition with introduction by Lloyd E. Berry (University of Wisconsin Press, Madison, WI, 1969). For the Psalm Book, see Beth Quitslund, *The Reformation in Rhyme: Sternhold, Hopkins and the English Metrical Psalter 1547–1603* (Ashgate, Aldershot, 2008). For the Marian persecution, see Thomas S. Freeman and Thomas F. Mayer (eds), *Martyrs and Martyrdom in England c.1400–1700* (Boydell & Brewer, Woodbridge, 2007), and for a lively presentation of the perspective of the Marian regime, see Eamon Duffy, *The Fires of Faith: Catholic England under Mary Tudor* (Yale University Press, New Haven, CT, 2009).

Chapter 11 England, in refusing me, refused a friend

For Cecil's attitude to Knox, see Stephen Alford, 'Knox, Cecil and the British Dimension of the Scottish Reformation', in Mason (ed.), *John Knox and the British Reformations*, pp. 201–19. The best treatment of the links between the exiles and the later Puritans remains Patrick Collinson, *The Elizabethan Puritan Movement* (Jonathan Cape, London, 1967). The debate provoked by Knox's *First Blast* can be followed in Amanda Shephard, *Gender and Authority in Sixteenth-Century England: The Knox Debate* (Keele University Press, Keele, 1994), and A. N. McLaren, *Political Culture in the Reign of Elizabeth I: Queen and Commonwealth 1558–1585* (Cambridge University Press, Cambridge, 1999); and see the important point about women authors made by

Susan M. Felch, 'The Rhetoric of Biblical Authority: John Knox and the Question of Women Author(s)', *Sixteenth Century Journal*, 26 (1995), pp. 805–22.

Chapter 12 Restorer of the Gospel among the Scots

For the British context of the Scottish changes, see W. I. P. Hazlett, *The Reformation in Britain and Ireland: An Introduction* (T. & T. Clark, London, 2003). An analysis of the Lords of the Congregation can be found in G. Donaldson, *All the Queen's Men: Power and Politics in Mary Stewart's Scotland* (Batsford, London, 1983). The Perth crisis is explained in Mary M. Verschuur, *Politics or Religion?: The Reformation in Perth 1540–1570* (Dunedin Academic Press, Edinburgh, 2006).

Chapter 13 Churching it like a Scythian

Grindal's experience as a Marian exile and his views on Knox form part of the illuminating biography by Patrick Collinson, *Archbishop Grindal 1519–1583: The Struggle for a Reformed Church* (Jonathan Cape, London, 1979). For an assessment of the new Scottish Kirk and a comparison with the Protestant Churches in other parts of Britain and Ireland, see Felicity Heal, *Reformation in Britain and Ireland* (Oxford University Press, Oxford, 2003). The two major products of 1560 are discussed in W. I. P. Hazlett, 'The Scots Confession 1560: Context, Complexion and Critique', *Archiv für Reformationsgeschichte*, 78 (1987), pp. 287–320, and James K. Cameron's introduction to his edition of the *First Book of Discipline* (Saint Andrew Press, Edinburgh, 1972). The excellent, if slightly elderly, *Essays on the Scottish Reformation 1513–1625* edited by David McRoberts (Burns, Glasgow, 1962) contains correctives to the over-triumphalist Protestant view of the Reformation process. For the Scottish controversy following the *First Blast*, see Kenneth D. Farrow, 'Theological Controversy in the Wake of John Knox's *First Blast of the Trumpet*', in Gribben and Mullan (eds), *Literature and the Scottish Reformation*, pp. 111–26. The best explanation of the broader noble culture of lordship and feuds is Jenny Wormald, *Lords and Men in Scotland: Bonds of Manrent 1442–1603* (John Donald, Edinburgh, 1985), together with the essays in Steve Boardman and Julian Goodare (eds), *Kings, Lords and Men in Scotland and Britain: Essays in Honour of Jenny Wormald* (Edinburgh University Press, Edinburgh, 2014).

Chapter 14 Sorrow, dolour, darkness and all impiety

A lively and perceptive discussion of the encounters between Knox and Mary, Queen of Scots, can be found in Jenny Wormald, 'Godly Reformer, Godless Monarch: John Knox and Mary, Queen of Scots', in Mason (ed.), *John Knox and the British Reformations*, pp. 220–41, and her *Mary, Queen of Scots: A Study in Failure* (George Philip, London, 1988). The relationship is placed within the context of the other ruling queens in Robert M. Healey, 'Waiting for Deborah: John Knox and Four Ruling Queens', *Sixteenth Century Journal*, 25 (1994), pp. 371–86. For a fine discussion of Knox's views on resistance and royal supremacy, see Roger A. Mason, 'Knox, Resistance and the Royal Supremacy', in *John Knox and the British Reformations*, pp. 154–75. Essential reading on Knox in Edinburgh is Michael Lynch, 'John Knox: Minister of Edinburgh and Commissioner of the Kirk', in Mason (ed.), *Knox and the British Reformations*, pp. 242–67; and his *Edinburgh and the Reformation* (John Donald, Edinburgh, 1981). Michael F. Graham, 'Knox on Discipline: Conversionary Zeal or Rose-tinted Nostalgia?', in Mason (ed.), *John Knox and the British Reformations*, pp. 268–85 provides a discussion of the disciplinary record. An overview of Knox's ministry can be found in Richard Kyle, *The Ministry of John Knox: Pastor, Preacher and Prophet* (Edwin Mellon Press, Lewiston, NY, 2002). For Quintin Kennedy, see C. H. Kuipers (ed.), *Quintin Kennedy (1520–1564): Two Eucharistic Tracts* (Janssen, Nijmegen, 1964).

Chapter 15 What have you to do with my marriage?

An excellent study of the broader cultural changes that Protestantism brought to Scotland is Margo Todd, *The Culture of Protestantism in Early Modern Scotland* (Yale University Press, New

Haven, CT, 2002), and details on many of the key issues of the Reformation decades can be found in James Kirk, *Patterns of Reform: Continuity and Change in the Reformation Kirk* (T. & T. Clark, Edinburgh, 1989). A fascinating insight into the cultural life of Edinburgh's merchant elite can be found in Theo van Heijnsbergen, 'The Interaction between Literature and History in Queen Mary's Edinburgh: The Bannatyne Manuscript and its Prosopographical Context', in A. A. MacDonald, Michael Lynch and I. B. Cowan (eds), *The Renaissance in Scotland: Studies in Literature, Religion, History and Culture* (Brill, Leiden, 1994), pp. 183–225. The Argylls' divorce case can be followed in Jane E. A. Dawson, 'The Noble and the Bastard: The Earl of Argyll and the Law of Divorce in Reformation Scotland', in Julian Goodare and A. A. MacDonald (eds), *Sixteenth-Century Scotland: Essays in Honour of Michael Lynch* (Brill, Leiden, 2008), pp. 147–68. For the 1565 crisis, Julian Goodare provides a clear explanation of 'Queen Mary's Catholic Interlude', in Michael Lynch (ed.), *Mary Stewart: Queen in Three Kingdoms* (Blackwell, Oxford, 1988), pp. 154–70. An excellent discussion of the General Fast is found in W. I. P. Hazlett, 'Playing God's Card: Knox and Fasting, 1565–6', in Mason (ed.), *John Knox and the British Reformations*, pp. 176–98.

Chapter 16 Unthankful (yea alas miserable) Scotland

A recent survey of Knox's *History* can be found in Crawford Gribben, 'John Knox, Reformation History and National Self-Fashioning', *Reformation and Renaissance Review*, 8 (2006), pp. 48–66, and it is complemented by the description in Robert M. Healey, 'John Knox's "History": A "Compleat" Sermon on Christian Duty', *Church History*, 61 (1992), pp. 319–33. Knox's possible trip to Ireland is examined in the introduction to Dawson and Glassey, 'Some Unpublished Letters', and its context is explained fully in Mark Hutchison, 'Reformed Protestantism and the Government of Ireland, c.1565 to 1580: The Lord Deputyships of Henry Sidney and Arthur Grey', *Sidney Journal*, 29 (2011), pp. 71–104. The English vestments controversy is put into context by Peter Kaufman, 'The Protestant Opposition to Elizabethan Religious Reform', in *A Companion to Tudor Britain* (Blackwell, Oxford, 2004), pp. 271–88.

Chapter 17 This most miraculous victory and overthrow

On James VI's coronation, see Michael Lynch, 'Scotland's First Protestant Coronation', in L. Houwen (ed.), *Literature and Religion in Late Medieval and Early Modern Scotland* (Peeters, Louvain, 2012), pp. 177–207. For the regency and death of Regent Moray, see Maurice Lee, *James Stewart, Earl of Moray* (Columbia University Press, New York, 1971), and Amy Blakeway, 'The Response to the Regent Moray's Assassination', *Scottish Historical Review*, 88 (2009), pp. 9–33. Different aspects of the reign are covered in Julian Goodare and Michael Lynch (eds), *The Reign of James VI* (Tuckwell Press, East Linton, 2000 edn), and the Jacobean Kirk is examined in Alan R. MacDonald, *The Jacobean Kirk 1567–1625: Sovereignty, Polity and Liturgy* (Ashgate, Aldershot, 1998). Sir William Cecil's policy for coping with Mary, Queen of Scots, in England is examined by Stephen Alford, *The Early Elizabethan Polity: William Cecil and the Succession Crisis 1558–1569* (Cambridge University Press, Cambridge, 1998), and details of the trial are found in Gordon Donaldson, *The First Trial of Mary, Queen of Scots* (Batsford, London, 1969).

Chapter 18 Weary of the world

For the experience of Edinburgh during the civil wars, see Harry Potter, *Edinburgh under Siege 1571–1573* (Tempus, Stroud, 2003). For the propaganda aspects, see Mark Loughlin, 'The Dialogue of the Twa Wyfeis: Maitland, Machiavelli and the Propaganda of the Scottish Civil War', in MacDonald, Lynch and Cowan (eds), *The Renaissance in Scotland*, pp. 226–45. For the background in St Andrews and Fife, see John McCallum, *Reforming the Scottish Parish: The Reformation in Fife 1560–1640* (Ashgate, Farnham, 2010), and for the university during Knox's stay, see Steven J. Reid, *Humanism and Calvinism: Andrew Melville and the Universities of Scotland 1560–1625* (Ashgate, Aldershot, 2011).

CHAPTER 19 HASTE, LEST YOU COME TOO LATE

For Knox's illness and death, see John Wilkinson, *The Medical History of the Reformers: Luther, Calvin and Knox* (Hansel Press, Edinburgh, 2001). Mark Loughlin's entry on Maitland of Lethington in the *Oxford Dictionary of National Biography* provides a good, brief insight into this complex character. For a balanced discussion of the way Knox has been treated by historians over the centuries, see James Kirk, 'John Knox and the Historians', in Mason (ed.), *John Knox and the British Reformations*, pp. 7–26. Thomas F. Torrance discusses Knox as a theologian in *Scottish Theology: From John Knox to John McLeod Campbell* (T. & T. Clark, Edinburgh, 1996).

Index